this writer...

The History of the Simons,
An American Newspaper Family

by Dolph Simons Jr.
and Leeanne Seaver

THIS WRITER:
THE HISTORY OF THE SIMONS,
AN AMERICAN NEWSPAPER FAMILY

All net proceeds from book sales will benefit
the Kenneth Spencer Library at the University of Kansas.

ISBN 979-8-218-27459-7

© Dolph C. Simons Jr. 2023

Published by The Cedars Publishing
First Edition September 2023
Printed in the United States.

PHOTO CREDITS:
Simons family personal collection and archive
The Simons Collection at the Spencer Library
The University of Kansas
The World Company
The *Lawrence Journal-World*
Leeanne Seaver www.seavercreative.com
The Associated Press
The Kansas Historical Society

Cover and book design by 94 Design
Marthasville, Missouri
www.94design.com

Printed in the United States of America by
Walsworth, Marceline, Missouri

Library of Congress Cataloging
Simons, Dolph Jr. and Leeanne Seaver
    This Writer: the history of the Simons, an American newspaper family/Simons, Seaver. 1st edition

This book is dedicated to our ancestors
and our grandchildren... and their grandchildren.

Emily, Crosby, and Jane de Menocal
Briahn and Dan Simons Jr.
Kate, Elizabeth, Jennifer, and Whitney Simons

In 2023, this rock was retrieved
from what remains of the hewn limestone
foundation of Jennie Bessie Simons'
1878 homestead in Hodgeman County, Kansas.
It serves as a reminder of the
strong Simons family foundation
on which you stand.

Contents

Six Generations of Simons

Adolphus Simons
b. 1791 Enfield, Connecticut

Alfred Simons
b. 1809 New York

Adolphus Ezra Simons
b. 1835 New York

W.C. Simons
b. 1871 Owatonna, Minnesota

Dolph Simons Sr.
b. 1904 Lawrence, Kansas

Dolph Simons Jr.
b. 1930 Lawrence, Kansas

Preface

On August 20, 1635, the ship "Safety" sailed out of the Port of London and headed for the colonies in the New World. According to the ship's manifest, "William Symonds" of Buckinghamshire, England, was aboard. His grandson, also named William, would be the first American-born Simons at Salem, Massachusetts, in 1659. Young William's last name was recorded as "Simonds," the more common English spelling. This William Simonds became a landowner in Enfield, Connecticut. For all this family lore and much more, I have my grandfather, W.C. Simons, to thank. The exhaustive research documented in his booklet, *From the Landing of the Pilgrims*, has been a very valuable resource as we put this book together. And with that acknowledged, I'll skip ahead four generations later to Adolphus Simons, born in 1791 in Enfield, Connecticut. He was my third-great grandfather, and the first among us to be called "Dolph."

For me, it all began on March 11, 1930, when Dr. C.B. Johnson of nearby Eudora, Kansas, used forceps to pull me from my mother in the delivery room at Lawrence Memorial Hospital. I'm not sure of the time of day, nor do I know what my father may have been doing at the time, but I am certain he was not in the room, which seems to be the practice today.

My parents, Dolph Collins Simons and Ann Marie Nelson, were married in Auburn, Nebraska, two days after Valentine's Day in 1929. Dad was 26 and Mother was 24 years old when I entered the picture, their firstborn son. Now I am 93 years old, and don't have any idea how much longer I'll be living.

This prompts me to appreciate how well I have lived.

At the urging of my children, I've tried to put together some of my remembrances as accurately as possible, but realize I am likely to be fuzzy about some names, places, and dates. Some things are very clear. From the start, I want to say I have been extremely fortunate—my wife Pam says "blessed"—to have had so many wonderful experiences, all of which have combined to give me an exceedingly interesting, exciting life of opportunities.

I had the blessing of wonderful, supportive, encouraging parents and a great younger brother, John. I have had a fantastic wife and partner in Pam, with whom I have a beautiful family. And I have benefitted greatly from a head start in my career thanks to my grandfather, W.C. Simons, who launched a newspaper company in 1891, and my dad, Dolph Simons Sr., who edited and published the *Lawrence Journal-World* until I took over. They had so many stories… I have so many stories. So many of my friends have already passed, and who knows their stories? Once you're dead, it's all gone, so I guess I'd better do this.

I'll start by saying on the whole, I've had every possible break and I know it.

Dolph Simons Jr.

Introduction

Before 1800, there was virtually no press west of the original 13 states.[1] For the next 100 years, North American expansion could be mapped by frontier newspapers indicating where people were settling sustainably along the westward routes. These pioneer papers were usually short-lived and often printed under primitive conditions—even "out on the open prairie."[2] Yet, in spite of hardships like the printing press being "left on the Missouri river, by the failure of the last boat of the season to get up to Kansas,"[3] newspapers cropped up—and in Kansas, they had an agenda.

Beyond notions of "manifest destiny," control of the newly settled land for profit and political power was at stake, and the power to influence the growing pioneer-populace was wielded with newspapers. In the 1850s and early '60s, the question of slavery was undecided for Kansas territory—its pending statehood hinged on that pivotal issue. Newspapers were weaponized for the fight by both sides.

Consider the party of 30 from Boston who'd been tasked with spreading the pro-slavery gospel by their trip sponsors back east. They reached Kansas Territory in August 1854. Incredulously, while scouting the site that would become the town of Leavenworth, they found a printing press sitting in tall, untrampled weeds under an elm tree. With no owner or explanation, this incredible discovery was seen as the "special providence" of the divine. So in spite of fall coming on and the immediate need to undertake winter preparations coming with it, two of the party, William J. Osborn and William H. Adams, focused instead on producing a paper.

Without even taking the time to move the press from under the tree, Osborn and Adams published *The Kansas Weekly Herald* (a.k.a. *Leavenworth Herald*) within weeks, on September 15, 1854. It was the

Lawrence 1854-55, courtesy Kansas Historical Society

first newspaper west of the Mississippi, and its "Democratic and Proslavery sentiment"[4] tipped the scales accordingly—but not for long.

Thirty-four miles away "in the cluster of tents and rude cabins that then comprised Lawrence," those bent on "planting [anti-slavery values] in Kansas along with sawmills, hotels, and other business enterprises"[5] countered with several abolitionist newspapers. In October 1854, a correspondent in Lawrence wrote to the *New York Tribune*. "We have already three printing establishments, and early next week, three newspapers will be sent out to greet the country far and near."[6] They were the Kansas *Herald of Freedom*, the *Kansas Free State*, and the *Kansas Tribune*, all staunchly against slavery.

The press was on fire, figuratively speaking, and then literally. When a pro-slavery mob led by the local Douglas County Sheriff Samuel J. Jones attacked and ransacked Lawrence on May 21, 1856, the *Herald of Freedom* was destroyed. But by the following November, it was revived and back to its mission.[7]

Missouri Senator David Atchison proclaimed "Kansas must be secured for slavery by fair means or foul," and sent a thousand of his heavily-armed henchmen to Lawrence for the election.[8] And so it would go in "Bleeding Kansas" as each side fought—often violently— over the question of slavery. When Kansas was admitted to the union as a free state on January 21, 1861, the matter

> *... local newspapers "helped immeasurably to bind the far-flung population into a nation."*
>
> Frank L. Mott, *American Journalism: A History 1690-1960*

was officially decided, but things were hardly settled. How these issues were meted out across the state would be recorded in dramatic detail in its local newspapers.

While these historical events initially brought newspaper publishing to Kansas, "Many were pure political organs which lasted only a few weeks or months," W.C. Simons noted.[9] The papers with staying power were those with the most relevance to a community. Local papers were the mechanism through which individuals participated in a shared experience they themselves helped create. This had a remarkable effect. By chronicling the journey from settlers to a settlement, local papers "helped immeasurably to bind the far-flung population into a nation."[10]

By 1891, Lawrence was a bustling community with eight newspapers,[11] plus several more specifically serving the University of Kansas, which had been established in 1864. Into this crowded scene, 19-year-old Wilford Collins Simons entered on December 14. Simons would go on to establish The World Company in 1892. By 1914, W.C. had bought out his partners. Eventually, he consolidated more than 40 newspapers into the *Lawrence Journal-World*, including the 1854 flagship, the *Herald of Freedom*.[12]

W.C.'s son Dolph started as a carrier boy and learned every angle of the business from direct experience. Dolph Simons stepped into his father's shoes as editor and publisher in 1944. And his son, Dolph Jr., was "porching papers" from his bike by age eight, and learning the ropes just like his father had.

Dolph Simons Jr.'s name joined the masthead in 1957; he was publisher by 1962, and president of The World Company in 1969. His sons, Dolph III and Dan, worked with their father to bring the business into the digital era. Daughter Pam took a leadership role in expanding the family business into cable in Colorado. Daughter Linda worked for a New York City firm that did public opinion surveys. In 1995, she was instrumental in restarting the local newspaper in Bedford, New York, where she lived.

For more than 125 years, the Simons family would be integral to newspaper publishing and news dissemination in America's heartland and beyond. The Simons' information enterprise spanned the entire epoch of modern journalism from the frontier press into the Information Age.

As "this reporter" or "this writer," W.C. Simons, Dolph Sr., and Dolph Simons Jr. each witnessed and expressed views of some of the most important events of his time. *This Writer* chronicles that history and what it all meant to Dolph Simons Jr. from his long view of 90-plus years of lived experience. His perspective blends journalistic integrity with a powerful moral compass that has guided him, as former Kansas Senator Pat Roberts put it, as "the conscience of the community."[13]

CHAPTER 1

Momentous Times

Without fully comprehending the beginning
of a new era...we were fortunate in starting
at a momentous time.

W.C. Simons[1]

It was one of few times "this writer" was ever in the dark, figuratively speaking.

In a pitch-black tunnel off the central mineshaft 9,650 feet below the surface, he belly-crawled and skidded toward the stope where miners were engaged in the dangerous process of extracting gold ore from a deep-earth mine near Jabulani in South Africa. The rock grew hotter in proximity to the earth's core and from the machinery and explosions around him. At any moment, a pressure burst could obliterate him in an instant. Dolph Simons Jr. knew that, but he had to know firsthand what was going on down there, so down he went.

Frankly, Simons, who was researching for an article he'd write for the *Johannesburg Star*, wasn't much safer aboveground in 1958. His unvarnished reports on apartheid in South Africa had already marked him as a troublemaker at the paper. "I wasn't trying to preach. I was just trying to tell what was really going on," Dolph explained decades later. "Apparently, I caused some problems. I think that government damn near kicked me out of the country for that."

"I tell it like it I see it" would characterize Simons' life-long career in the newspaper business. He would go far and wide, not only as a journalist but as a director and officer of the Associated Press,

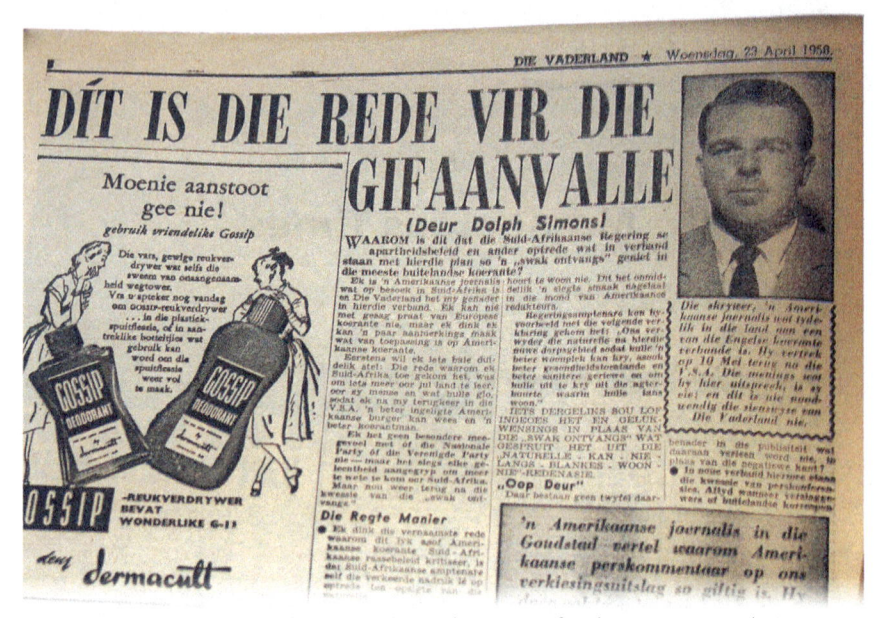

The headline translates to "This is the reason for the poison attacks" as reported by Dolph Simons Jr. in South Africa, April 23, 1958.

the American Newspaper Publishers Association, the Newspaper Advertising Bureau, the Gannett Foundation, the Freedom Forum, the Inland Daily Press Association, the American Society of Newspaper Editors, and as a Pulitzer Prize juror, among many other roles.

At age 93, Simons still sees clearly without reading glasses and blogs at the aptly-named LawrenceOpinions.com. Those who know him well or have, at some point, been in his crosshairs, don't find this surprising. Having walked the talk since his first steps growing up in a newspaper family, Dolph Simons Jr. was "born with ink in his veins," laughed Jill Chadwick, director of the Medical News Network that broadcasts out of the Dolph Simons Jr. Family Studio in Kansas City.

As a reporter and eventual editor, publisher, and president of The World Company his grandfather launched in 1891, Dolph Simons had big shoes to fill. From W.C. Simons' journalistic enterprise planted in the then-frontier town of Lawrence, Kansas, his father, Dolph Simons Sr., branched out and was a globe-circling reporter in the 1940s before the term "embedded" was coined. Dolph Jr. would earn his bars as a Marine Corps Public Information Officer at El Toro Air Base during the Korean War before working at *The Times* of London and *The Star* in Johannesburg, South Africa, as a civilian.

However far afield the Simons went, Kansas remained the center of their universe, and Lawrence was home. All tunnels, flight paths, trains, and roads led back to America's heartland.

Synergistically, the *Lawrence Journal-World* was influenced by the broadened perspectives of its publishers; the Simons were consistently invited to bring their thought leadership and solid midwestern values to the national fore of newspaper publishing.

It was a remarkable dynamic that an ambitious, young W.C. Simons had set in motion, even if he could not have imagined it growing up in a sod house on the plains of western Kansas.

Wilford Collins "W.C." Simons knew the newspaper business from pen to press to porch.

While a part-time student at Kansas Wesleyan University in 1888, he'd written news items for the *Salina Republican*. By 1890, he left Salina for a job at the *St. Joseph Herald* in Missouri. There, "the 'boys' in the mailing room of the old Herald were discussing the newspaper situation in general. 'Yessir—Lawrence, Kansas, looks like a good spot to start a newspaper,'" W.C. would recall for *Editor & Publisher* magazine in 1936.[2]

Seeking an opportunity to make his own mark, W.C. Simons headed to Kansas. The timing was good. *The Lawrence Record* was available without a down payment, so Simons, his brother Louie, and sister Julia's husband, John Brady, signed the lease. Brady had the most experience and took the lead.

A wary writer at the competing *Lawrence Journal* wished the new operators luck while noting there was "not much chance of success." Simons wasn't relying on luck. Recalling their endeavor decades later, W.C. wrote, "Young, vigorous, unafraid, we hardly looked the future in the face, but tackled the present with the best we had in us."[3]

Three optimistic entrepreneurs—my 19-year-old grandfather, W.C. Simons, his younger brother, Louis Adolphus Simons, 17, and his brother-in-law, J.L. Brady, 25—arrived in Lawrence after a hard, two-day journey by horse and buggy from St. Joseph, Missouri.

Lawrence was not a pretty sight. My grandfather described it many years later. "That December 14th day of 1891, it was raining, but instead of a town with wide-paved streets, brilliantly lighted and festooned with Christmas decorations, it was a sea of mud, wooden sidewalks, a faint and flickering single gas light at the central intersection, with burning gasoline or kerosene flares in front of a few enterprising stores." Today, the trip can be made in a little over an hour, but "it required two and a half days with a horse and phaeton, over almost impassible mud roads of that time."[4]

The young men had come to Lawrence with purpose—to enter the newspaper business. Competition was stiff—at least seven or eight papers were already covering the city with a population of less than 10,000, plus several at the university.

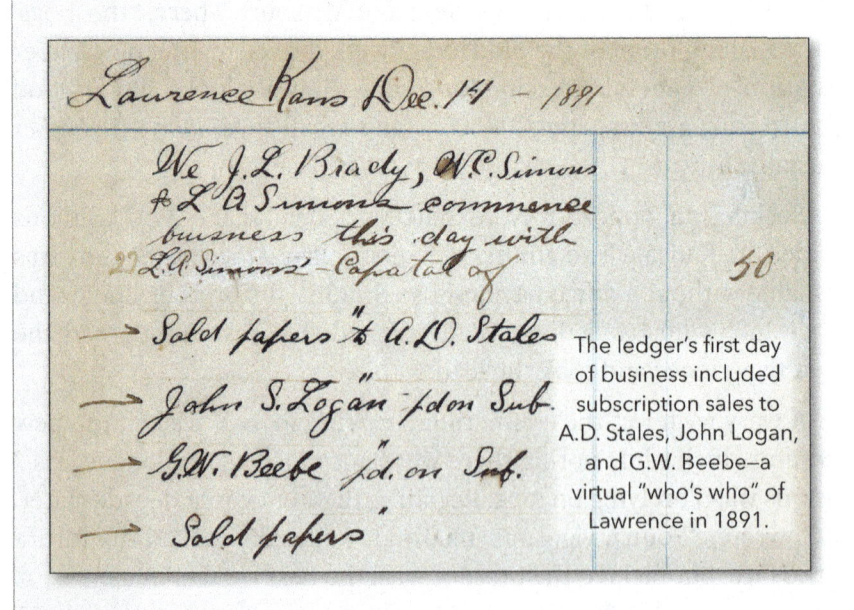

The ledger's first day of business included subscription sales to A.D. Stales, John Logan, and G.W. Beebe–a virtual "who's who" of Lawrence in 1891.

The three eager newspapermen leased *The Record* from its owner, Mr. Watkins, a successful Lawrence businessman.

The ledger sheet for the first day of business states: "Lawrence, Kansas, December 14, 1891   We J.L. Brady, W.C. Simons and L.A. Simons commence business this day with L.A. Simons' capital of $50.00."

Apparently, Watkins intended to maintain control over the policies and politics of the paper. No doubt, my grandfather and his partners had hoped to have more editorial independence, so after only three months, they decided not to renew their lease of *The Record*.

This untimely turn of events did not keep them from their goal. In fact, this lesson has been emphasized within our family time and time again: *No one can afford to be complacent as there is always someone who can come to town and beat you at your own game if you're not strong and alert.* Instead of throwing in the towel, Granddad and my great-uncles bought some rusty old discarded equipment and began independently publishing the *Lawrence World*, their own daily and weekly paper, on March 2, 1892.[5]

Over the next few years, other local papers were acquired by W.C.'s newly-minted publishing business, The World Company. It took over the *Daily Gazette* in 1895, via a partnership formed between W.C. and Brady, as L.A. Simons had been bought out.

Four years later, another consolidation took place when the *Weekly Jeffersonian* and *Weekly Gazette* were merged into the *Weekly Jeffersonian-Gazette* in 1899. Now there were just five papers being published in this riverfront town, not counting the university papers. The most prestigious among them was the *Daily Journal*.

The *Daily Journal* was owned by Colonel Oscar Learnard, a Civil War veteran of "considerable influence and considerable wealth" who used to drive a handsome team of horses around town. Learnard once owned the land that would become an "Indian school" and eventually Haskell Institute.[6] But his sons were "not shown to be particularly fitted to the newspaper business," so Learnard put the Journal up for sale. W.C. Simons bought it with a bank loan for $18,000 in early 1911, and the *Daily Journal* was added to The World Company assets.

Although the Journal had done more business than *The World*, it hadn't been as carefully managed. The World Company had to assume approximately $7,000 in debt on top of the $18,000 price to ink the deal—all paid for with borrowed money. One half of the notes were signed by The World Company, and the other half by the Journal.

The Journal was located in the Bowersock Opera House building at the corner of Seventh and Massachusetts, and *The World* was operating nearby at 722 Massachusetts Street. On February 17, 1911, a fire broke out, destroying the theater building including the newspaper offices and most of the equipment. Since there was common ownership, The World Company merged the Journal and *Lawrence World*. No time was lost… just two days after the fire, the first issue of the *Lawrence Journal-World* was published on February 19, 1911.

The advantages of a single owner-operator of the newspaper were coming clear by 1914. J.L. Brady had political aspirations and wasn't averse to using the paper to further his agenda. That didn't sit well with W.C., so he started looking around and found a newspaper for sale in Arkansas. Granddad told Brady he'd be willing to sell his stock in The World Company and move there himself, or buy Brady's stock if J.L. was inclined to pursue that opportunity. He was.

So W.C. bought back the 98.5% he'd issued to Brady in 1911. Those shares were valued at $27,000, but with the $10,000 note still owed by the *Journal-World*, Brady received a generously proportioned $22,500. Granddad borrowed the entire amount and the sale was finalized on December 19, 1914.[7]

The World Company's final purchases and consolidation came with the acquisition of the *Daily Gazette* and the *Weekly Jeffersonian-Gazette* for $15,750 in July 1921. And with that, the Journal-World now constituted what had once been more than 40 newspapers from over 100 that were reportedly published in Lawrence since the city was founded in 1854—starting with the original *Herald of Freedom*. The *Lawrence Journal-World* was now the only daily newspaper published in Lawrence.[8]

Granddad reached his goal while maintaining an uncompromised vision of what a newspaper should be—and what his role as editor and publisher required. He established the ethic and the ethos of The World Company that would guide four generations of this family in the information business.

Dolph Simons Jr.

Nascent as it was in the late 19th century, The World Company was creating something credible, viable, and necessary. While other pioneering papers went belly-up or were consumed by consolidation, the staying power of W.C. Simons' newspaper enterprise "symbolized the permanence of a community"[9] on the frontier.

Lawrence greatly needed that.

Having been established in 1854 "for strictly political reasons"[10] to secure Kansas as a free state, "Lawrence was the very center of the struggle," wrote W.C. Simons in an address to the Kansas Historical Society in 1924. "Lawrence was twice destroyed, once by Sheriff Jones under orders from the federal court, and later by Quantrill and his following of murderous cutthroats."[11]

These and other horrific events were front-page fodder back east. Horace Greeley popularized the term "Bleeding Kansas"[12] in his *New York Tribune* and the image of a lawless, wild, wild west became deeply embedded in the national psyche. Historian Carl Becker wrote, "Until 1895, the whole history of the state was a series of disasters, and always something new, extreme, bizarre, until the name of Kansas became a byword, a synonym for the impossible and ridiculous, inviting laughter, furnishing occasion for jest and hilarity."[13]

The University of Kansas opened its doors here just after the Civil War; women made up almost half of its first class. Haskell Indian

Louis (on left) and W.C. Simons freshly arrived in Lawrence in 1892.

Nations University, a college for Native Americans, opened here in
1884. After Mr. Simons's grandfather arrived in town more than a
century ago, he bought the local paper for $50.

Tim O'Brien, "The Newspaper of the Future."
The New York Times. June 26, 2005.

Lawrence was teeming with the "hair-triggered' vigilantism that characterized Kansas, according to Becker. When W.C. Simons arrived in 1891, there was still a "good size town row between North and South interests in the city." Everyone took sides—including the local papers. As such, Simons' lease on *The Lawrence Record* was short-lived because the owner, Jabez "J.B." Watkins, intended "to maintain intense interests in the policies of the paper."[14] Simons wasn't inclined to yield control, so three months into production, he opted out of the deal with Watkins.

It was a gutsy move grounded in principle, not profit. "Well, they certainly didn't have much to lose at that point—as far as profit was concerned," Dolph Simons Jr. wryly noted. "Knowing my grandfather, money wasn't his chief concern. Principles were his concern." Even in dire straits, W.C. Simons held himself to the highest standard.

And as it grew, The World Company's principled approach strengthened its stature in a town that sorely needed the exemplar. The newspaper wouldn't be compromised for a price or manipulated by power-brokers, and it survived. "Our competitors were backed by ample capital but perhaps they lacked the wider vision we possessed," W.C. theorized in a letter to former partner J.L. Brady many years later.[15]

Lawrence had in the *Journal-World*, "a champion of civility and social change," and in its editor and publisher, W.C. Simons, "an individualist and a community leader."[16]

"How little we knew, but we did our best," W.C. Simons wrote. "I think we really left a record of achievement in the old town that will compare favorably with anything the past had to offer. We made the business respectable and the time came when men who wanted to see us came to our office instead of telephoning us to come to theirs."[17]

As The World Company's prestige grew, so did the company's influence. Simons established, both financially and philosophically, a business his descendants would expand into a multimedia company with print, cable television, telephony, and internet.

The foundations of that enterprise were grounded in Kansas bedrock. "I'm sure my granddad would have been amazed by how his company grew," Dolph Simons Jr. reflected. "Considering there were times W.C. wasn't sure he'd survive his own childhood; I think he'd be stunned by what The World Company achieved."

In truth, surviving severe conditions on the Kansas frontier had everything to do with the man W.C. became, and the company he started. He learned to be "wiry, resourceful, and hard to kill,"[18] qualities he passed on to his intellectual son, his intrepid grandson, and his aspiring business, The World Company.

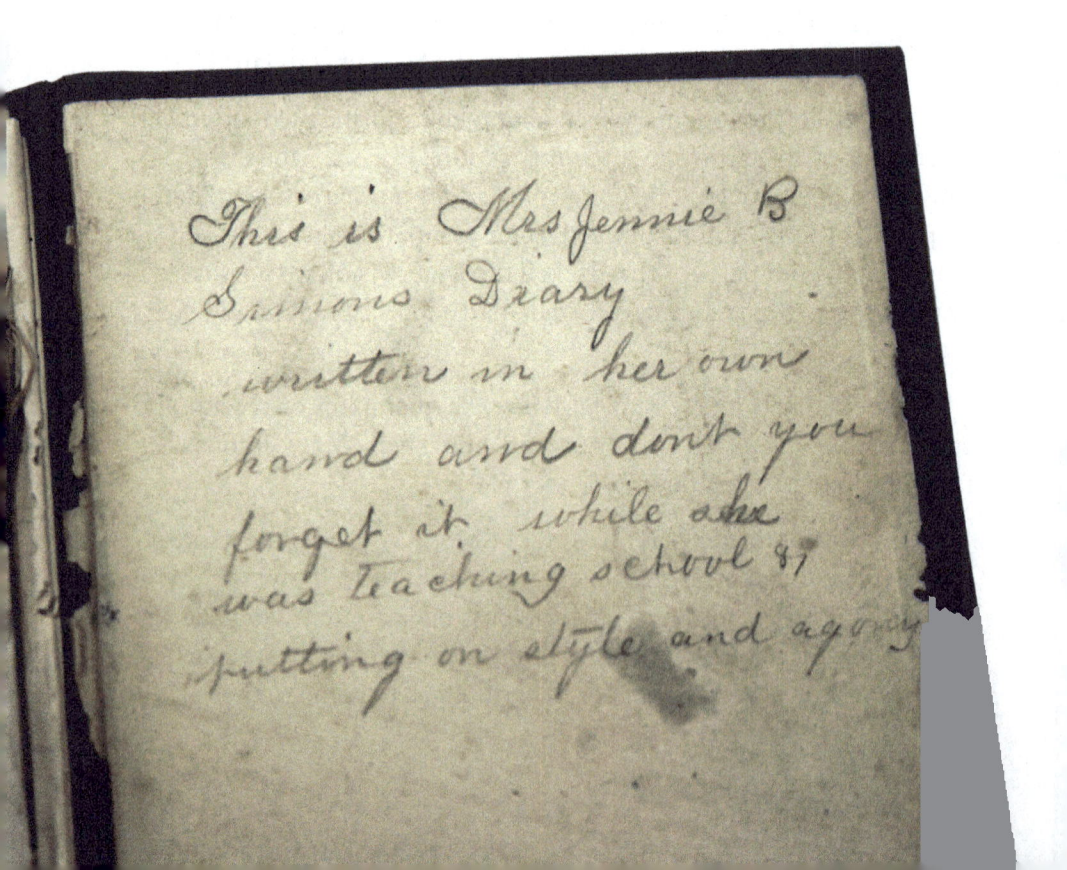

CHAPTER 2

Breaking Ground

"Two hundred miles to wood;
fifty miles to water; six inches to Hell.
God bless our home, this claim is not abandoned."

(tacked to the door of an empty sod house in western Kansas)

Excerpts as written from the diary of Jennie Bessie Simons.

July 3, 1880 **Hodgeman County, Kansas** *Today is the 14th anniversary of our marriage and Oh how I miss my darling husband but am anxious to live for my childrens sake and to comfort father who is so much comfort to me but hope I shall meet him in heaven and my dear mother. How different I am situated now from fourteen years ago Then we were gay and happy with sister Julia and family in Wilmington Ill now sister and brother both gone and I am here in the far west with father and five dear little ones suffering all the privations of a frontier life beside in a land that has been suffering a terrible drought for two years all asleep but me and I must go as I am very tired.*

November 30 sometimes get discouraged but God has said As thy day is so shall thy strength be we have been without flour for one week nearly we baked the last one week ago no meat and very little butter plenty of excellent sorghum syrup abut 6 gls of milk a day today we bought a sack of flour paid $1.40 for 50 lbs ½ gal kerosene paid .85 a gal. pretty cold today.

January 1881 We were out of flour and meal... I was tired and very much discouraged I cried and felt as if only trouble was before me a large family and very cold weather nothing to eat We went out we saw Mr. Whitman he was kind and told us to come to his place and get a load of brush I felt better hearted tonight My dear little Collie felt unwell with a pain in his stomach I hope he will be better in the morning for his mother thinks a great deal of her little man 9 years old who works hard every day like a little man Lord help us all

February 22   *Five years ago today I well remember my darling husband was alive. I hope I shall one day go to him when my life work is done.*

March 6   *It has snowed all day and tonight it is a wet rain All stayed at home we are almost out of cane stocks How are we to get a long in our destitution but—the Lord has had mercy upon us thus far and I don't think he will forsake us. The children take turns reading the Bible at prayer time which I think is very nice I hope God will take us through our trials and perplexities Our timber claims are to be seeded this month and I cannot see how we are going to accomplish all this without... God help... no I am thankful for all our blessings but we all feel sad*

April 6   *Our cow is gone I hope we shall find her.*

May 10   *Father and I went to see if we could get trusted a few dollars worth at Weares as we had only flour enough to last for supper but he said no He could not take care of anybody's family but his own we went to Mrs Armstrong four miles to borrow some money but no she had none on hand but she was ladylike and kind but oh how my heart ached I could not see why I lived.*

The call to "Go West, young man, and grow up with the country" came with a sense of destiny. But its buoyant promise of adventure, free land—maybe even gold—delivered instead a perilous journey with even greater hardships waiting for those who survived it. Many did not. How Jennie Gowdy Simons did—newly widowed with five little children—was nothing short of miraculous.

It was the dead of winter in Minnesota in 1878, hardly an ideal time to set off for Kansas Territory. But the land was free to those willing to live on it and "prove up" their claims for five continuous years. Jennie's two brothers and their families were going—her aging parents, too. If things went well, they'd be settled in time for spring planting. Having lost her husband Dolph just five months before, there was no reason to stay behind. So Jennie B. Simons packed her brood and went West.

The first leg of the trip was by train from Minnesota to Kansas. Jennie Simons paid most, if not all, the expenses for the group of 16,[5] possibly with the proceeds from the sale her property in Faribault. Her six-year-old son W.C. "Collie" Simons found the trip "a jovial, happy party for the youngsters, though Mamma and her parents must have been filled with anxious thoughts." In retrospect, it was probably a blessing they didn't know what lay ahead.

In fact, the journey was putting irretrievable distance between the comfortable life they had known and the "agony" that lay ahead. With every westward mile, plenitude and security were fading. But Jennie Bessie, who "had led a sheltered life,"[7] was about to discover her own resiliency and "a consciousness of what it meant to be a pioneer."[8]

She'd been born Betsy Jane Gowdy in Constantia, New York, in 1836. Notably, she descended from Reverend Nathaniel Collins and Alice Adams Collins, the great granddaughter of Governor William Bradford who arrived on the Mayflower to establish Plymouth Colony in 1620. The Gowdys were a family of some means and in good standing in their community.

> *The mysteries, the possibilities, the opportunities in this new land awakened vague yearnings. Confidence and courage were in the blood of the pioneer everywhere and at all times. He was to match himself against the forces of nature, and had no fears for the outcome. They were on their own, and they believed in themselves and in Providence and God.*
>
> W.C. Simons, *From the Landing of the Pilgrims*

Jennie's father, Collins Gowdy, was known for his strong moral convictions. At age 20, he vowed to abstain from alcohol, which he did for the rest of his life. Consistent with his principles, during the Civil War, he operated a temperance tavern that didn't serve spirits, among various other business pursuits including dairy farming. He was active in anti-slavery movements and an early member of the Free Soil party.[9]

Her mother, Betsy Ann (Nichols Cook) Gowdy, "was of English ancestry, and had beautiful auburn hair, and courage that never flinched or failed," according to Jennie Bessie's son, W.C. Simons. "Grandma, kindly and gentle to the family, was a whole army in herself. One day several men came on the place and started a disturbance with Grandfather and some of his boys. Grandma, overhearing the noise and not stopping to find out the occasion for the trouble, picked up a pitchfork and chased the trouble-makers off the place."[10]

Collins and Betsy Gowdy had 12 children, although only half of them survived to adulthood. According to their daughter, they were "a very kind mother and father"[11] who indulged her desire to change her name to Jennie Bessie—an homage to Jennie Lind, the popular Swedish songbird of the era. Herself "Blessed by nature with a sweet, pure soprano voice," according to her son Collie, Jennie Bessie was given "a fair education in music."[12]

By 1850, the Gowdys had moved to Waukegan, Illinois.[13] In her diary, Jennie Bessie also referenced living briefly with her mother in Saugatuck, Michigan, to run a "public house" of the temperance variety in 1851.[14] But by 1852, Collins and Betsy Gowdy were back in Waukegan where they remained for the next 25 years.

Jennie lived with them except when, as "Jane B. Goudy," she married Charles D. Johnson in Lake (County), Illinois, in 1857.[15] Almost nothing is known of this marriage except, according to her own notation on an application for increase in her Widow's Pension circa 1885, that it happened and ended in divorce in 1862. There were no children nor any family lore to shed light on this mysterious union. In W.C. Simons' record of this period, Jennie was teaching school and living with her parents. It was there that she met Dolph Simons, her brother William's friend who'd been invited to dinner one Sunday in 1860.

As the story goes, the invitation was actually at Dolph's behest because "Papa had seen the pretty little sister, Jennie Bessie, and had been much impressed. It was a case of mutual attraction. He was so gentle, tender, and thoughtful of her, though he was also a joker and a man's man," according to eldest daughter Julia, who wrote about her parents' meeting many years later.[16]

"Dolph" was Adolphus Ezra Simons. His parents, Alfred and Wealthy Ann (Mason) Simons, named their son after his paternal grandfather when he was born on February 7, 1835, in Ogden, New York. When Dolph was 15, his family moved to Lenawee, Michigan. By 1860, they were living in Grayslake, Illinois, where he enrolled at Dyrenforth Business College in nearby Waukegan. A gifted musician, Dolph was "strong, agile, and athletic... popular with both students and instructors." [17]

Dolph Simons was also an emerging leader in school politics at Dyrenforth, so his focus was necessarily on Abraham Lincoln's first call for 75,000 men on April 15, 1861. [18] He enlisted on August 1, 1861.

Simons and his close friend E.B. Payne organized the Dyrenforth students' response. Their volunteers would help comprise the 37th Illinois Volunteer Infantry that mustered into service on September 18, 1861. When Payne noted that Simons had assigned their allotment of officers and commands to everyone but himself, Dolph replied, "Ed, every war has to have some privates." At Payne's insistence, Dolph took the remaining post as the company's principal musician: the fife major.

As fife major, Simons' responsibilities included providing ceremonial and field music that regulated the daily activities of the troop from reveille to taps. He also had a tactical role in signaling the infantry to march, halt, charge, retreat, march at double-time, quick-time, wheel and fire. [19] This role engaged Major Simons directly in every battle. [20]

Among those battles were the Siege of Vicksburg, the Battle of Prairie Grove, and the particularly brutal Battle of Pea Ridge. [21] On May 15, 1866, "having been in the service of the United States four years and ten months, and having participated in eleven hard fought battles and sieges and innumerable skirmishes, and having marched a distance of 17,846 miles as follows: By steam 14,560 miles; on foot 3,286 miles, according to the tabulated statement kept by Henry Ketzel, veteran of Co. A," [22] the Illinois 37th Infantry was finally decommissioned. The corrosive physical aftermath of his duty would compromise Dolph's health for the rest of his life.

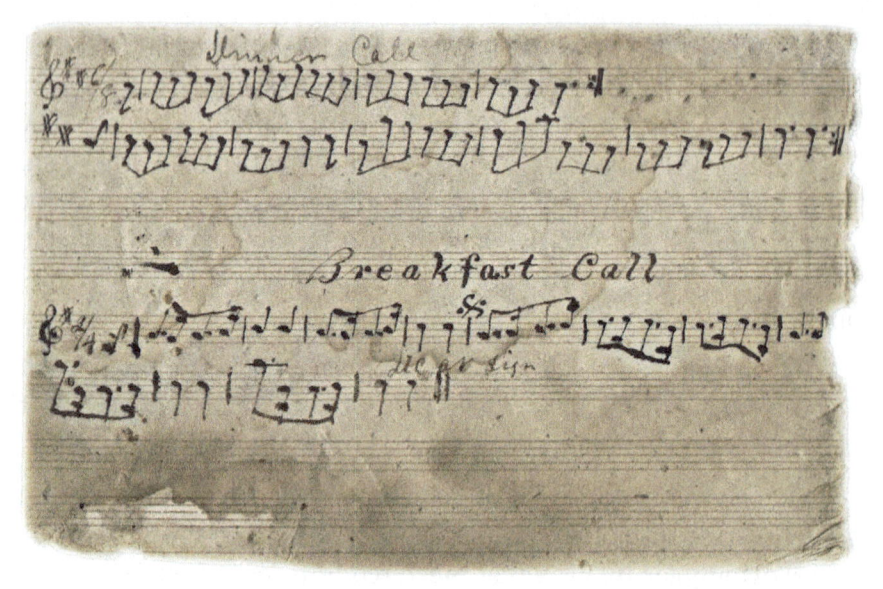

Major A.E. Simons wrote out the music to dinner and breakfast calls in 1861.

Dolph and Jennie stayed in touch as best they could during the war. "Papa spent every furlough he had visiting Mama," daughter Julia recalled. In 1862, Jennie Bessie enrolled at Hillsdale College in Michigan where her older brother William had studied before he transferred to Dyrenforth. She received a teaching certificate that would prove useful in supporting her young family in the years to come.

During the period his troop had been posted to Houston, Dolph had come to like the climate and prospects in Texas, so he sent an appealing letter to Jennie Bessie, hoping she'd join him there. They would be married upon her arrival, he proposed. But that idea was swiftly vetoed by her father and brothers, so Dolph returned to Illinois. Less than two months later on July 3, 1866, he married Jennie Bessie Gowdy at her parents' home in Waukegan.

Mama's trousseau was bought at Mandel Brothers in Chicago. She was married in golden brown silk, the skirt having fifteen breadths of silk in it, which would make it measure seven and one-half yards around the bottom if the silk were eighteen inches wide. Her waist was either eighteen or nineteen inches, and the fullness could not be gathered into so small a measurement, so it was held into a sort of little plaiting that made a little shelf at the waist. Her little bonnet was of cream color with rosebuds under the brim. She wore hoops, and had a long, spreading cloak that covered her.

Her going away dress was of ashes of roses alpaca, with silk facings and coat and little bonnet to match. Another of her dresses was an irregular plaid and stripes two shades of brown and some blue, with flowing sleeves all trimmed with blue silk fringe about two inches wide. All these flowing sleeves had little, lacy handmade undersleeves. Another dress was a changeable silk with a wide skirt and small, close-fitting bodice. A thin dress of sheer pink chambray,

Jennie Bessie Gowdy Simons, circa 1897

almost like handkerchief linen, was braided in a tiny little block pattern. The underwear was trimmed with narrow, handmade, lace-edged ruffles, and tiny, tiny hand tucks. Her gowns were buttoned from neck to hem with the smallest of pearl buttons, and the little ruffles going down all the way. Her little corset was hand-stitched, not over a foot or fourteen inches wide.

*Father was almost always a most immaculate dresser, and perfectly
groomed. Mother said he was the neatest, cleanest man in
the world, and even when he was doing "messy" work, he
looked as if he had just stepped out of a bandbox... [His]
wedding shirt ruffled, plaited, puffed and shirred, a work
of fine art.*

*[Papa's suit was made into a suit for six-year-old Collie.]
During the hard days in Hodgeman County, Kansas, Mama
cut up her beautiful and treasured gowns to make dresses
for her daughters.*

Julia Simons Brady Hoinville [23]

Following a wedding trip to Chicago, Dolph
and Jennie Simons set up housekeeping in
Waukegan where he built a "pretty house"
for them in time for the arrival of their first
child, Julia Mary, in March 1867. Another
daughter, Etoile Bessie, came on
April 27, 1869, the year they sold
the house and moved to Minnesota.
There, Dolph managed a hardware
store in Owatonna, and the couple
welcomed their first son, William
Collins, named from Jennie's
brother and promptly nicknamed
"Collie," on July 8, 1871.

The hardware store was doing
well and the owners offered Dolph a
share of the business, but his health
was failing. "Believing that the work
was too confining, and that he would
be better if out of doors, he declined
the offer, sold his house, and took
his family to a farm in Rich Valley,
Dakota County, Minnesota, in
1873." [24]

Two more children were born to Jennie and Dolph in Dakota County. In 1874, Louis Adolphus, nicknamed "Louie," arrived on Collie's birthday—July 8, followed by Jennie Grayce on February 22, 1876.

Adolphus Ezra on violin and his father,
Alfred Smith Simons on flute, circa 1876-77

Those who knew him spoke of my father as being one of the most perfect gentlemen they had ever known. He was an accomplished musician, played the violin well and also wind instruments. He had a fine tenor voice and had at times taught singing as an avocation. He was strong, agile, and athletic and was proficient as an amateur wrestler. He was five feet eleven inches tall, never weighed more than one hundred and eighty pounds, but was built like a wedge with broad shoulders, full chest, and small waist. Fifteen years after his death, I met a man who had served with him in the 37th Illinois Volunteers Infantry, and he said Papa could throw any man in the regiment.

W.C. Simons

Conditions were likely crowded with Jennie Bessie's brother Joseph and his family moving in with the Simons around 1875-76. That may or may not have been a factor in Dolph's decision to relocate. He found a buyer for the farm, "an Irishman who had two sons, one of ordinary size, and the other a fine-looking specimen six feet tall and weighing at least two hundred pounds," W.C. recounted. Tales celebrating mental and physical prowess were popular, and there were many in the Simons' lore, including this one. W.C. continued, "Papa knew of the Irish idea that the best man physically should dictate the deal, so when the father wanted to try his skill, Papa threw him. Then the smaller of the two sons wanted a try, and Papa threw him, and finally, also threw the pride of the family. After that, the deal went through easily just as Papa directed. That, undoubtedly, was the last time that he wrestled with anyone, and probably, also, the first time in several years."[25]

Dolph moved his family to a large white house on 15 acres he'd leased in Faribault, Minnesota. Grandfather Alfred Simons joined his son and Jennie there in 1877. It was a short-lived arrangement, literally. By October 29 of that year, Adolphus E. Simons finally succumbed to the detrimental effects of the Civil War, leaving a devastated widow with five young children.

In early 1878, Jennie Bessie cast her lot with her parents and brothers. It was Kansas or bust.

The Gowdy-Simons party arrived via train in Larned, about 60 miles from Dodge City, Kansas, that February, staying in a sandstone building known as "the Stone Block." The Gowdy brothers made their way out to locate their Hodgeman County claims and construct sod houses for shelter. After several weeks, the grandparents, women, and

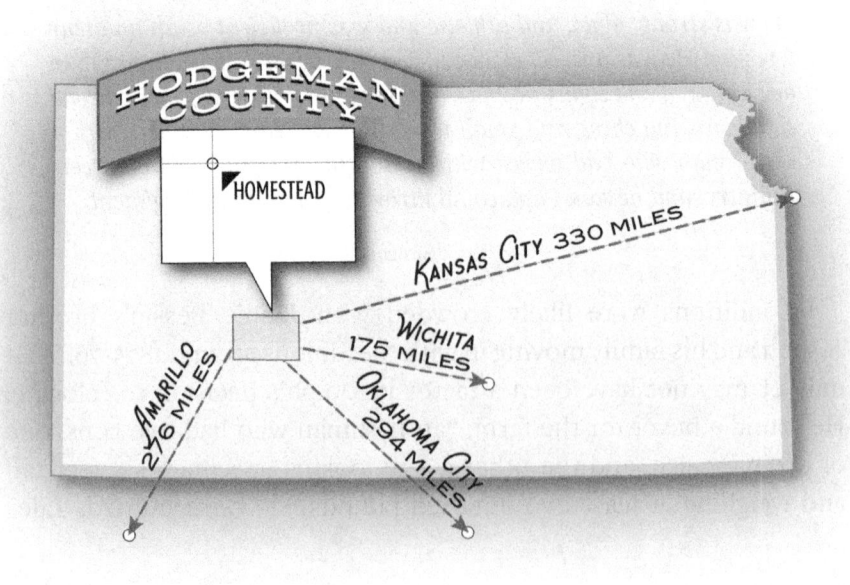

children made the 40-mile trek in a farm wagon to the next layover station at Duncan's Ranch. They were there ten more days until the uncles arrived to escort the party to their soddies.

> *Although the land was old as time and had been the habitat of buffalo and Indians for ages, yet to the white man it was as new as if it were a new creation fashioned for his benefit. Kansas can be most entrancing in the spring, when the buffalo grass is green and wild flowers are abundant. In that day, the winding creeks were heavily timbered and dark masses of verdure were almost constantly in view, though our road followed the early trails which avoided the deep ravines near running streams. There were no section lines, no graded roads, no bridges, and the trail extended in graceful curves as if there were no need for haste. There were no plowed fields, no dust, everywhere was a wealth of wild flowers.*
>
> W.C. Simons

"My uncles gave the best claims to their parents, took the next best themselves, and my mother was crowded pretty well back to the hills," W.C. reported.

W.C. was only six, but "little man Collie" Simons rose to the occasion as the man of the family—although he almost didn't. "Our sod house was unusual in that it had a board floor and a shingle roof. We had been living in it but a short time when there came a slow-falling rain lasting several days which thoroughly soaked the walls," he explained in his address to the Old Settlers Association of Lawrence, Kansas, in 1924. "When I awoke one morning, one whole side of the house had fallen out. I found myself looking out to the open prairie. Had it fallen in, the story might have been different."

Between Jennie Bessie's diaries and the recollections of W.C. and his sister, Julia, the "hard years" of homesteading were well chronicled. They managed to plow, harrow, and seed 50 acres in wheat during their first summer, but it was to no avail. A drought starved the land and family alike for their first two years on the claim.

Water was a constant concern—the overabundance of it, the lack of it, the quality of it, or the hazardous effects of it. At the Gowdy homestead, "Grandfather's well tasted strongly of minerals, and

Collins Gowdy, Julia Simons Brady with little Vera,
and Jennie Bessie Simons (seated), circa mid-1890s

perhaps it was the use of this water which caused Grandmother Gowdy to die of dysentery in August 1878," W.C. wrote, adding, "One of my cousins died soon afterwards and was buried beside her in a grave a few rods from Grandfather's house."[26]

> *Very few of the early settlers were able to make a living for themselves and families, and abandoned their claims, a term usually applied to the early homesteads and pre-emptions. At one time it was said that there was not an occupied house on the trail between our home and Dodge City, thirty-seven miles to the southwest. On the door of one soddy, the departed owners reportedly left his notice, "Two hundred miles to wood; fifty miles to water; six inches to Hell. God bless our home, this claim is not abandoned." And the signature.*

> W.C. Simons, *From the Landing of the Pilgrims*

There were few teachers and fewer places for children to attend school on the western Kansas frontier in the early 1880s. As such, "boarding around" was the common practice that brought the teacher to the students. Staying several weeks in one home and then onto the next for about $1.50 a week for room and board, Jennie Simons earned between $10 and $20 a month to help support her family—but she had to live away from them to do it. Circumstances being what they were, there was no alternative. The Widow Simons chronicled her situation in her 1881 diary.

> *May 13 started for home got to Marena found they wanted me to teach their school I stopped at Mr Hayes for dinner and commenced school in the afternoon with 8 pupils*

> *May 15 thought I would walk home but the river had raised in the draw and I came back*

> *Oct 21 Last Sunday Mr Waterman told me the district had objected to my having some of my children stay with me and go to school also he did not want little Grace here only on a visit I felt very sad and sorry for my children who expected to have an opportunity to come after Christmas for Mrs W spoke in the first place about my children coming here she is afraid there will be too many in the house I pay 1.50 a week and I think it is enough Mr Waterman has appeared very cold I don't know why I have tried to be kind and*

*make myself agreeable   ...but never mind it is better to suffer wrong
than do wrong*

Thanks to her Hillsdale preparation, Jennie Simons was given the first certificate issued in Hodgeman County to teach what was considered the hardest level—first grade. Eventually, daughter Julia, only 13, was approved to teach third graders, which didn't require a certificate. In this way, Julia could also earn an income while boarding with Jennie. Little Grayce, the youngest at age four, would come along with her mother and enroll as a student, or so Jennie hoped. Not all hosts were tolerant of the arrangement. Admittedly, it wasn't ideal for the Simons either. It left Etoile, age 11, with Collie, 9, and Louie, 6, to make-do on their own at the homestead. Then Etoile, too, went to work and boarded with another family for periods of time, leaving Collie in charge.

> *...our hens are all dying off 7 have died all ready we have no more
> corn to feed them they are lousy and have the collery...*
>
> ~ a letter from Etoile to her mother, Jennie Bessie and older sister Julia who
> were boarding elsewhere while teaching school, Nov. 30, 1881

Widowed as she was, Jennie Simons relied heavily, if reluctantly, on W.C., her "little man." Even though he was a young boy when they reached their claim in Hodgeman County, Collie dug wells, plowed, planted, managed the horses and livestock. He was, for all intents and purposes, the man of the family. He kept an eye on his siblings and tended the hearth when his mother boarded wherever she found work teaching.

"Altogether, I batched it for ten months, my first experience being the winter after I became eleven years old," W.C. wrote in 1924. "I was small but wiry and resourceful and hard to kill. For months, there was not a woman in the house with the exception of a few days visit from my eldest sister. It was a hard winter and my grandfather, Collins Gowdy, then 77 years old, could not be counted on for outside work. He kept the fire going, helped me wash the dishes, and did what he could, but it was up to me to attend to the stock, to make the bread, churn the butter, and do the work in general. I must have been a little runt at the time, for a year later, I only weighed eighty-two pounds."

As critical as the teaching income was, being away from her children was an untenable situation for Jennie Bessie. The dreams of farming had turned to dust in the most literal sense. So she changed course dramatically. W.C. recorded this astonishing development in an autobiographical sketch he drafted many years later. In 1887, "My mother bought for me a one-half interest in the weekly Gazette published for a short time at Houston, Kansas."[27]

There is no record of how the Widow Simons came to this decision, but it was likely influenced by John Leeford "J.L." Brady. Brady had been editor of the *Advance*, a small paper in Jetmore, the Hodgeman County seat. Jennie's oldest daughter Julia was teaching school and boarding with a local Jetmore family when she took an

After five years "proving up," Jennie B. Simons, widow of Adolphus E. Simons, filed her claim on 160 acres on January 20, 1883. It was acknowledged on June 13, 1901.

office position with the newspaper in 1886. She was 19 and J.L. was 20 when they were married in 1888.[28]

How Jennie Simons funded her investment also isn't clear. Her widow's pension was finally approved in 1888—a process that had been long-delayed because "the hospital record of her husband was lacking for many years and the regimental physician could not be found."[29] The additional income probably amounted to only $30 a year. Not much, but it helped, no doubt.

The most likely source of funding was a loan Jennie Simons borrowed against her land to secure the funds, or Brady got a loan to buy the land from her, netting Jennie some immediate cash. It would have been enough to invest in the *Houston Gazette* for Collie, although no record of that transaction or even a copy of the paper has been found.

Such a loan would also have been sufficient to move her family to Salina where Jennie Simons had also managed to purchase the *Salina Republican*. J.L. Brady was its new editor and W.C. Simons its fledgling reporter. The family's arrival made front-page news on Sunday, July 29, 1888: "Mrs. Jennie B. Simons and family arrived in the city Monday from Hodgeman County and will make this their future home."[30]

The Simons' abandoned farm sold at a public auction on December 27, 1893. J.L. and Julia Brady, Jennie Simons, and her father were all named in the proceedings.[31] They were hardly alone in this lamentable situation. As early as July 7, 1890, the Garnett, Kansas *Agitator* had reported "… a single law firm in Kansas has 1,800 mortgages to fore-close."[32]

W.C. would later write, "For the 1,120 acres which Mrs. Simons had secured through the toil of herself and her children, she received nothing. She had reared five healthy children, however, giving them a better education than that of most high school graduates, and best of all, she had inculcated a resoluteness of character and determined initiative which enabled them to make their own way and to give her the care and comfort in later years which a lifetime of unselfishness had merited for her."[33]

My great-grandmother's story is a book in itself. How she managed to keep her family going in the face of starvation and such hard times is difficult to imagine. She was a strong woman—not physically but in her character. Jennie Bessie was tiny, just over five feet tall. She never weighed more than 107 pounds in her life but "there was no burden she would not attempt to bear, no sacrifice she was unwilling to make for her children," according to my granddad, W.C. Simons.

She was called the "Widow Simons" even though she wasn't quite 40 when she moved to the plains with her children and her aging father. They struggled, nearly starved, yet her door was always open to anyone in need. There were many cowboys who stopped for a meal over the years. Not one of them used foul language or was less than chivalrous in her presence.

Jennie Bessie Simons was gentle and refined, and that brought out the kindness in those men.

Those were terribly hard times and most everyone who tried to make a go of it ended up leaving. Jennie Simons stayed on, working the land even after her mother died, and her brother and his family gave up and moved back east. She taught school which took her far away from her children for weeks or months at a time.

I remember the story of how she was teaching miles and miles away and one January evening as she walked home, her feet froze so badly they troubled her for the rest of the winter. There was another story about the terrible blizzards of 1886 when so many froze to death on those plains. Grandpa Gowdy, my grandfather "Collie," Louie, and Grace were alone at the homestead while the rest of the family was stuck in various places waiting for the weather to break. Anxious for her children, Jennie Bessie got Claude Hullett from Larned to bring her home in a wagon. The blizzard was so intense they couldn't see the road and didn't know where they were. Finally,

SHERIFF'S SALE.

First publication, Dec. 27th, 1893.

In the district court of the Sixteenth judicial district, sitting in and for the county of Hodgeman, in the state of Kansas.

Elizabeth Gill, Plaintiff.

Vs.

John L. Brady, Julia S. Brady, Jennie B. Simons, Mr. Simons her husband, William Gowdy and E. C. Gowdy, Defendants.

By virtue of an order of sale issued to me, out of said district court, in the above entitled action, I will, on Monday the 29th day of Jan. A. D. 1894, at 1 o'clock p. m. of said day, at the front door of the court house, in the city of Jetmore in the county of Hodgeman in the state of Kansas, offer at public sale and sell to the highest and best bidder, for cash in hand, all the following described real estate to-wit:

The Northeast quarter -N E ¼- of Section Thirty-four -34- in Township twenty-one -21- south of Range twenty-two -22- west of the 6th P. M.

Lying and situate in the County of Hodgeman in the State of Kansas.

Said property is levied on as the property of said defendants, and is directed by said Order of Sale to be sold, and will be sold without appraisment, to satisfy said Order of Sale.

1106   W. T. Welsh, Sheriff.

W. D. Miner Jr., Attorney.

The Simons land was sold on the auction block.

Hullett gave up the reins, wrapped Jennie Bessie in comforters from head to foot in the wagon bed, then loosed Bird, the horse, and gave one command: Go home. He kept calling out encouragement to Bird and at some time in the night, the horse just stopped. Claude looked out and realized they were at the Simons' doorstep. Bird had even crossed the frozen Pawnee River without a line of guidance.

Without a doubt, my great-grandmother's faith kept her going. She had a strong faith in God that sustained her.

Her children were all a great help. The oldest boy was my grandfather, W.C., a hard-worker who was smart as a whip. He'd be out at dawn and back after dark tending the stock and fields, so tired he'd nearly fall asleep standing up. Somehow, his mother also managed to educate him on top of all that.

Jennie Bessie taught all her children to read and write over a kerosene lamp after dinner at the end of the day. All of those Simons said they received a better education than most high school graduates thanks to their mother.

When Jennie Bessie finally moved her family to Salina in the spring of 1888, it was for the sole purpose of giving her children access to a better education. Each of them made good use of that opportunity and went on to great careers.

Julia Simons Brady Hoinville left her early teaching career to work for *The Advance*, a small newspaper in Jetmore, Kansas. She divorced J.L. Brady, and raised their daughter Vera. Eventually, she made her way to the big city of Chicago, married Charles Hoinville in 1909, and went on to organize and run the Welfare Department (the precursor to Human Resources) for Marshall Fields downtown.

Etoile Bessie Simons attended Kansas Wesleyan University at Salina, then the State University in Lawrence where she received both a baccalaureate and master's degree. She continued her studies at Woods Hole and Chicago University where she earned a Ph.D. Etoile taught for several years, then shifted focus to superintend the "Harvey Girls." These clean-cut, wholesome young women were employed by the Fred Harvey Company that provided food service on the trains taking passengers out west. Etoile was given her own car on the train where she lived while traveling the Santa Fe railroad back and forth in the execution of her duties. After she retired, Etoile remained in Chicago and dabbled in real estate towards the end of her life.

Wilford (Granddad changed his name from William in his early 20s) Collins Simons was schooled at home until age 12. His further education at Kansas Wesleyan University happened part-time and "after-hours" while working for the *Salina Republican* where he learned typesetting, copywriting, reporting, advertising sales, and other relevant skills on the job. He parlayed those skills into employment at the *St. Joseph Herald* in Missouri before settling in Lawrence, where he launched the *Lawrence Daily Journal-World* in the 1890s. Over his career, W.C. was so well respected that his obituary stated he was "a light for a generation walking along the pathway of ambition and enterprise."[34]

Louis Adolphus Simons attended the University of Kansas. His first professional foray was into newspaper publishing with W.C., his older brother. But Louie found his interests better suited to business. "He could buy a pencil for a penny and sell it for five cents," W.C. noted. So Louie became an agent with American Central Life Insurance Company of Kansas City.

Jennie Grayce Simons was educated at the University of Kansas, and taught school before marriage to Don A. Freeman.

Of the hardships they faced growing up on the frontier, Granddad wrote, "The privations were great, but to use the words of my sister Julia, 'Sorrow and unhappiness do not stay long with children who love their mother, as we did, and who were filled, as we were, with an overwhelming ambition. We lived so much in the future and could be so very happy together, when we divided fruit or candy, or anything special into eight parts, and then gave two parts to Grandpa.'

"We all grew to be physically strong and to have average common sense. We developed resourcefulness, initiative, courage, and the ability to carry on, together with kindly sympathy for those less fortunate. Mama lived to see her children able to care for themselves. She had fought a good fight and had kept the faith. I have no doubt of the crown of righteousness being hers. She earned it by both faith and works."

"The finest part of our story is that we all pulled through."

I marvel that they did, and feel a strong debt of gratitude to Jennie Bessie Simons for what she accomplished—not only for her children, but for the generations of us to come. She provided a model of resiliency and unconditional love. Her life set a standard—not only on a personal level but a professional one as well. I think every generation since has felt the desire to be worthy of what my great-grandmother made possible for this family.

Dolph Simons Jr.

W.C. Simons (left) and J.L. Brady (right) with
Lawrence Journal-World staff, circa 1913-'14

CHAPTER 3

Making News

If you've been given an opportunity
through the First Amendment for the free expression
of ideas, that comes with an obligation—and
a helluva lot of responsibilities.

Dolph Simons Jr.

For more than a century, the Simons family business was gathering and disseminating information, primarily through newspapers. In that process, the Simons would play a significant role in establishing the integrity of newspaper publishing itself—which took some time to evolve. There was the challenge of having the right skills, equipment, financing, etc. But the greater test was possessing the requisite fortitude and attitude that would define this quintessentially American industry.

To grasp its shaky start-up, consider the first reference to "certain articles" referencing freedom of speech and the press in a memo Thomas Jefferson sent to Congress three months after the Bill of Rights was ratified in 1791.

> *"I have the honor to send you herein enclosed, two copies duly authenticated, of an Act concerning certain fisheries of the United States, and for the regulation and government of the fisherman employed therein; also of an Act to establish the post office and post roads within the United States; also the ratification by three fourths of the Legislatures of the Several States, of certain articles in addition and amendment of the Constitution of the United States, proposed by Congress to the said Legislatures, and being with sentiments of the most perfect respect, your Excellency's &c."* [1]

According to University of Texas Law Professor David Anderson, "The original first amendment had to do with the method of electing Congressmen, and the second had to do with their compensation."[2] The states failed to ratify either of those, which brought the third proposed bill into the first position. In this way, without fanfare, pomp or circumstance, "Congress shall make no law abridging the freedom of speech or of the press" became the First Amendment.[3]

Incredulously, it was apparently not the Founding Fathers' intention to give freedom of speech and the press priority in the Bill of Rights, but providence seemed to have had a hand in this. The values expressed in the First Amendment embodied the enterprising spirit of being American. And, arguably, the most American of enterprises—particularly in the early days of this nation's emerging identity—was newspaper publishing. As Thomas Jefferson wrote in 1804, "Our first object should therefore be to leave open to him all the avenues to truth. The most effectual hitherto found is the freedom of the press."[4]

> *The values expressed in the First Amendment embodied the enterprising spirit of being American. And, arguably, the most American of enterprises—particularly in the early days of this nation's emerging identity—was newspaper publishing.*

Many early American presses deployed their newfound freedom in the partisan battle that's still recognizable today. The late 1700s was a no-holds barred news climate unfettered by decorum or journalistic standards. To wit, the New York editor of the federalist paper *American Minerva* (and future dictionary-publisher) Noah Webster was denounced as "a pusillanimous, half-begotten, self-dubbed patriot", "an incurable lunatic", and "a deceitful newsmonger ... Pedagogue and Quack", "traitor to the cause of Federalism", "a toad in the service of sans-culottism", "a prostitute wretch", "a great fool, and a barefaced liar", "a spiteful viper", and "a maniacal pedant" by his Jeffersonian Republican opponents.[5]

Indeed, it took some time to define and develop the ethical infrastructure of modern journalism.

According to Mitchell Stephens, author and New York University journalism professor, newspapers were more of a commodity than a public service in the 19th century.[6] The emphasis was on sales volume, not information-sharing as a public service.

We have to remember—those early colonists weren't bringing Americanized-thinking to the game. They had to shake off Mother England and learn how to use their freedom. It took a hundred years to think like an American.

Hell, we're still trying to figure that out.

Freedom of the press and freedom of speech have always been subject to that process. We came so close to not even having these most fundamental rights that define what it means to be an American. A lot of people disagree on what it looks like, but the First Amendment itself is what we must exercise to get the answers.

This is something we have to practice every day, and newspapers should be the shining example of that.

Dolph Simons Jr.

The notion of a balanced presentation of objective, fact-based reporting wasn't yet a part of the canon. In fact, James Gordon Bennett Sr., founder of the *New York Herald*, led the pack toward profit. He was the first to splash a sex-scandal (and the grisly murder of a prostitute) on the cover in 1836. His competitor, Henry J. Raymond, editor of *The New York Times*, acknowledged, "It would be worth my while, sir, to give a million dollars, if the Devil would come and tell me every evening, as he does Bennett, what the people of New York would like to read about next morning."[7]

Never a big proponent of "just the facts," Bennett predicted newspapers as "the circulators of intelligence merely" would go out of business with the advent of the telegraph in 1844.[8]

That's not what happened—not by a long shot. Newspapers were growing in circulation, expanding westward with the settlers, and their role in society was maturing.

Two primary purposes emerged: to inform and to advise.[9] Then, as now, the goal was aspirational but pragmatic because, as the American Press Association would eventually articulate it, "Democracy depends on citizens having reliable, accurate facts put in a meaningful context."[10]

Over time, newspapers increasingly owned their social responsibility. *New York Tribune* Editor Horace Greeley firmly believed, "We cannot afford to reject unexamined any idea which proposes to improve the moral, intellectual, or social condition of mankind."[11]

The duty to examine such ideas was taken up by editors themselves. According to an anthology of *Nineteenth Century Newspapers and Literature of Reform*, "The editorial voice of each newspaper grew more distinct and important, and the editorial page began to assume something of its modern form. The editorial signed with a pseudonym gradually died,"[12] and was replaced by opinion editorials signed by author-editors who wanted readers to know the issues and where the editor stood on them. In turn, their newspapers became more accountable for what they published. "These features grew in importance until they became the most vital part of the greater papers."[13]

The concept of freedom of speech and the press would be sorely tested by the developing nation. In that process, an expectation that newspapers would serve an unbiased, instructional role emerged in American culture. In the country's heartland, W.C. Simons did his part for the cause of a well-informed citizenry, but there was more going on here than answering who, what, when, where, how, and why. Simons and The World Company would help establish the imprimatur of professionalism in the newspaper industry nationwide.

W.C. Simons was "universally admired for his conduct and bearing."

Although the modern *Principles of Journalism* hadn't been codified yet, Simons held his newspaper to high standards—his own. His navigational "chart"[14] of values, drawn from hard work and "the early years of the struggle," was grounded in "the close relationship between the development of character and personal initiative applied to the famous and historic element of American freedom known as the 'right to work'."[15]

For Simons, that right wasn't an entitlement so much as opportunity... a duty even. That mindset made him not only a premier publisher and editor, but, as Burton Marvin, former dean of the University of Kansas William Allen White School of Journalism, wrote, "...more than a leader in Kansas business and community activities, he is a figure at the forefront in the respect of his neighbors and of all Kansans."[16]

W.C. Simons became "a man universally admired for his conduct and bearing."[17] He walked the talk... his reputation never tarnished. This imbued him with an almost ministerial authority. It informed his voice as editor and publisher, and set his newspaper apart from the sensationalized tabloids of the day.

Wrenching the industry from "salaciousness" was no easy feat. Simons' contemporary, Lorettus Metcalf, editor of the *Florida Daily Citizen*, wrote, "The evil grew until publishers all over the country began to think that perhaps at heart, the public might really prefer vulgarity."[18]

Quite the contrary, publisher W.C. Simons, and his editor/partner J.L. Brady, took the view that the public would benefit from some instruction on what it should prefer. From their first issues in the early 1890s, the *Lawrence Daily Journal* took a decidedly moral tone. One of Brady's first editorials in February 1892 noted "In Washington, a fallen woman died and no minister would preach a funeral sermon or would allow the polluted body to enter the church. For shame, for shame. Such Christianity would look as if Christ had come in vain."

There was also a regular feature titled "Things that Happen" that provided random advisory along the lines of "Some of the meanest people living often pretend to be your friend" and "The best medicine for some people who feel bad would be a little hard work."[19] A paternalistic resonance was not untypical of the era, but for Simons, it wasn't rhetorical. Providing guidance on acceptable conduct was a legitimate function of a local paper, in his view. Simons believed newspaper publishers in particular were subject to propriety at all times, and he didn't hesitate to call out his colleagues who couldn't pass muster.

In his December 30, 1931, letter to Chester Shore, editor of the *Augusta Gazette*, W.C. wrote "like a father would a son" to take his friend to task over the lack of consideration given Mrs. Chester Shore with regard to "suggestive matters." That Shore intended them (whatever they were) to be a humorous aspect of a Christmas letter was no excuse. An editor was "to think of suggestive matters as little as possible, to seldom receive them," admonished W.C., "and never print them."

Simons' approach wasn't academic, but reflective of his own innate sense of how things should be. In spite of the adversity and a lack of formal education in his youth, Collie Simons had two distinct advantages that helped forge his worldview: the abiding love of his mother, Jennie Bessie Simons, and his own inquisitive mind. Although he didn't go to school until he was 12 years old, Simons offered, "Even as a young boy I formed opinions."[20]

Collie Simons noticed things most youngsters didn't, like the variation in layers of sediment along the river banks—how that showed a kind of history of the place. He anticipated problems resulting from settlers hacking their claims into blocks of earth to build soddies, and opening acre after acre of virgin turf so it could be farmed. "It was my belief that the buffalo grass served as a cover for the soil and from it the rain ran off as from a tin roof. I believed that when the ground was put under general cultivation, the rains which fell would be absorbed, and the climate of western Kansas would undergo a change," W.C. wrote in his memoirs. With prescience, he continued, "This undoubtedly has proven true to a great extent, and the loss of the grass cover was held largely responsible for the 'Dust Bowl' period of the 1930s."[21]

Whatever W.C. Simons focused on or engaged in, it was with scrupulous attention and intention. His handshake was always the firmest; his clothing the best quality he could get; and he ate fried chicken with a knife and fork. "The story that gives an accurate picture of my great-grandfather," laughed Pam Simons, "is that he once went to the Mayo Clinic to determine if he had a skin condition. They told him no, you just take too many baths."

That story has become part of the family lore, to which Dolph Simons Jr. adds, "My granddad told me many times he could judge a man by his relationship with God; how he treated women; and if he availed himself of a bar of soap regularly. Granddad held some strong opinions, but by God, he'd earned the right to them. He was a man who'd faced some hard times. More than once, he had to pawn his gold watch to pay the bills and get the paper out on time."

Of those early years, W.C wrote, "I was 20, without capital... It was sink or swim, and sometimes it looked very much like swimming was a lost art."[22] At such times, Mary Gertrude "Gertie" Simons was an invaluable partner.

Gertrude and W.C. Simons, 1902

Gertrude Reineke of Kansas City met W.C. Simons when she was visiting her brother George, a merchant in Lawrence. In November of 1894, when he was 23 and she was 19, they married and settled into a white frame house at 919 Indiana Street in Lawrence.[23]

In 1898, I was just 27 years old, and Gertie 23. Blanche was three. Moneywise, we didn't have any, and working conditions were none too pleasant. We'd been housekeeping just a few years and found it very hard to raise the ten dollars a month we paid for house rent. It may have been about this time that Gertie helped out a bit by being the entire orchestra at the Bowersock for the big pay of $2.50 a night. We never made a wry mouth, we never said we were hard up, we never complained nor asked for help. And we enjoyed the few friends we had. I give Gertie great credit for making good friends—friends of good people—not because she honeyed about them, but because they could recognize real worth in her. Our social standing has largely come about through recognition of her worth.

[By 1908, we were] making a great show in doing a lot of job printing at insufficient prices... those were the days of starvation prices for subscriptions, advertising, and printing. We were working

W.C., baby Janet, Blanche, Gertie on piano, 1902

in one room, only 50 feet deep and had but one linotype. It was two years before the room was extended to the alley and a flatbed Duplex press installed. Big display advertisements were spread over the first page of the paper and the whole office force consisted of myself, a reporter, office girl, and circulation manager. What we owed, not great in amount, was nonetheless a heavy burden, and it was only by sheer grit and hanging on that we made this go.

W.C. Simons, Notes on his 67th birthday, July 1938.[24]

Those were lean years for the newly-established World Company, and Gertie leveraged her musical talent to support their budget by playing live piano accompaniment for the traveling shows and silent pictures showing at the old Bowersock Opera House in town, as well as for all the theater productions at nearby KU. With her contributions, W.C. and Gertie made ends meet. They would eventually have five children: Blanche, Janet, Dolph, Dorothea, and John Louis.

Family was a priority for W.C. Simons. This tenet was another tribute to his mother, Jennie Bessie Simons, whose influence he felt all his life.

Upon her death in 1921, W.C. wrote, "She was the kind of woman and the kind of a mother, who inspired mankind for all ages.[25] All that was good in her ancestry, which included Governor William Bradford of Plymouth Colony, seemed to come into full fruitage in her life. Small in stature and naturally timid, she became a giant in courage to face every difficulty for those she loved."

Why do I like being a Kansas editor?*

Between writing out a few checks, answering a long-distance call, and answering some late correspondence, W. C. Simons, editor of the **Lawrence Journal-World,** *answered a few questions which the reporter shot at him as to why he liked being an editor in this state.*

"It is a good thing to be an editor in any state, but in Kansas it is more than a good thing," the Lawrence editor said, "for to be an editor in Kansas means being associated with such personalities as William Allen White, Henry Allen, and Victor Murdock.

"These are the sort of men who are doing things in all of the work being done in their respective communities. The editors actually have a part in the very life of the place where they have their newspaper establishment."

Not only this but there is a chance to make considerable money in the newspaper field, Mr. Simons pointed out. Especially if the man chooses his field well, when he decides to start a paper, he said.

Then Mr. Simons grabbed his hat and coat, and said, as he hurried out of the office, that he must attend the night meeting of the Lawrence Rotary Club and he had promised to go to the first concert on the University concert course that night. It was only one of the many busy days which the Kansas newspaper editor has.

The editor of the Journal-World started this week by attending an active meeting of the Social Service League Monday night at the Chamber of Commerce, while on Monday morning he was busy helping to get the road petition signed up which will mean a concrete highway from Topeka to Lawrence.

Tuesday noon he was a guest at the meeting of the Chamber of Commerce. That night he was at the get-together meeting of towns-people and University student representatives. Wednesday was full as described, while Thursday meant a trip to Kansas City to meet Lord Northcliffe at a luncheon.

Today, as president of the Second Kansas Editorial Association, he was busy every instant looking after the visiting editors. Saturday will be a repetition, and then the Lawrence editor can rest until next week.

*Featured in University Daily Kansan. Friday, October 26, 1917

By 1914, the Journal-World was the dominant paper in Lawrence. By 1921, it was the only daily newspaper in town.[26] The industry noticed. So did the uncited author of this quote in the Kansas State Historical Society Annals of 1924, "Mr. Simons is one of the foremost editors in Kansas, the land of the best and most enterprising newspapers in America."[27]

W.C. Simons' "breadth of vision" was lauded in a 1925 trade magazine, the *National Printer Journalist*. Writer John L. Meyer noted the *Lawrence Daily Journal-World* "under its present management... [is] reportedly the only paper ever published in Lawrence to make money." Meyers praised the "all-around efficiency" of the operation that was "peculiar to itself in comparison with others I have studied."[28] He also heartily approved of the employee amenities that featured toilets conveniently located on each floor of the building. Also, "The men greatly enjoy the shower baths in the basement. They come to work dressed in good clothes, then change to their work garments. At the close of day, they take a shower, put on their street clothes and leave the shop looking as well as any other businessmen in the city."[29]

The article's emphasis on "the paper and its employees [taking] an active part in all civic affairs, giving time and money for the advancement and development of the community," may have given W.C. Simons the most satisfaction. He was proud of creating a work environment so congenial it produced numerous marriages and, subsequently, "enough handsome babies to form a good-sized baby show."[30] W.C. had a deep-seated sense of duty to be a model citizen and was unusually conscientious about his position of influence.

Among other self-imposed standards as a local publisher, Simons would decline to hold a political office or to withhold the unsavory facts of a news story, even if it cost him a friend. He did not shy away from controversial subjects. The "poor treatment of Negroes" and the practice of lynching—"the barbarism which it is"[31]—were common themes in his editorials.

A wide variety of subjects passed through his crosshairs. His December 6, 1938, editorial was fairly representative of the breadth. Among other topics, he addressed the definition of liberalism, New York City's new subway system, congressional over-spending, the recent FCC decision to not sue over Orson Welle's Halloween broadcast that had listeners believing Martians had invaded, and, last but not least, driving too fast under winter conditions.[32]

W.C. wore many hats. As owner, publisher, editor, writer, employer, salesman, financier, advertiser, adviser, and confidant, Simons performed his tasks with a sense of duty in the spirit of public service. From Lawrence's city planning to its board of health, chamber of commerce, hospital, Rotary Club (that he founded), and more, Simons chaired, directed, served, led, attended, and was active in many local community organizations and service clubs. For many years, he was moderator of the First Baptist Church of Lawrence; he was formerly director and twice president of the Kansas Baptist Convention, a member of the executive committee of the National Council of Northern Baptist Men, Kansas State Chair of the Baptist Laymen, and a member of the Commission of Kansas Baptist Institutions.[33]

Simons was also an honorary member of Sigma Delta Chi, a professional journalism fraternity, a 32nd degree Mason, Knight Commander Court of Honor, and a Shriner.[34] He served as president of the Kansas State Historical Society, a trustee of Ottawa University,[35] and vice president of the Kansas State Chamber of Commerce. In the newspaper industry, W.C. was a member of the Associated Press, the Kansas Press Association, the National Editorial Association, Employing Printers of America, and he represented small-town papers on the advisory board of the national Audit Bureau of Circulations.[36]

Although he might have resisted the description in deference to his mother's influence, W.C. was a self-made man. The curiosity so apparent in his childhood continued throughout a lifelong quest for learning. He sweated the details... how the window light in a room should be conducive to reading and how all lights must be turned off whenever leaving a room.

A voracious reader, he had a remarkable library at The Cedars, the stately old house where he and Gertie lived in Lawrence. It included everything from a hand-colored 1873 atlas of the 1855-established Douglas County, Kansas, to first editions of *Pilgrim's Progress* and Abbot's Civil War History published in 1864—its last chapter written in present tense. He also collected rare books like *Ramesey on Wormes*, a hand-pressed, leather-bound volume published in 1668. Its author, Sir William Ramesey, a "physic" (doctor) was attempting to provide a scientific explanation for the function of "wormes" around the same time the apple fell on Isaac Newton's head, i.e., before science had legs. Margin-notes jotted throughout suggest W.C.'s careful reading and rumination of what would have been heretical text in its day. Such intellectual pursuits were the regular topic at dinnertime or anytime.

In the first decades of the new century, Lawrence had streetcars, a hospital, and was teeming with the culture of a university town that bore no visible scars of its bloody past. The *Lawrence Journal-World* had much to do with its domestication. Whatever was happening was chronicled in paper—not just the facts that were known, but with the editorial wisdom of its principled publisher.

In this informative and stimulating environment, W.C. and Gertie's only surviving son, Dolph—named for his grandfather Adolphus Simons—grew into his own.

My grandfather, W.C. Simons, had a very manly physique. He was probably six feet tall, very physically fit. He had beautiful white hair... I never knew him without white hair. Granddad was an imposing individual in physical appearance but also in terms of what he stood for—and that was putting out the very best newspaper he could.

W.C. was all business. He expected people to perform, and believed your word was your bond. W.C. was stern but compassionate. He knew right from wrong, and as a publisher, that was the role he played in his town.

The job of a local paper—and its responsibility—is to provide the people with good, factual, honest presentation of the news. It must inform the public of what's going on in the community, and how bodies such as government and schools and the environment are doing. It must expose wrong-doings, as W.C. always said, without fear of making enemies. That means you have to have performed in a manner that has earned respect. You must act in a way that's honest and fair to deserve the trust of your readers.

My dad, Dolph Sr., approached things the same way when he took over as editor, and that carried over to me as well. It's very clear to me that W.C. set the standard. Even now, I can see how his policies and practice influenced my dad, me, and my children. The things he stood for are still important—not just for the newspaper, but for a newspaper family living in a community.

Growing up, I never wanted to do anything that would embarrass my family or the newspaper. Lawrence was the kind of town where everybody knew who your parents were, which was doubly true for a newspaper family. Both my parents and grandparents were very active in the community. I never felt like I had to follow suit because they expected me to, but because I could see how getting involved could make a difference. I could see from W.C. and my dad that it was possible to make a difference—and it was necessary. I saw the editorial role as helping rally people to a cause and action. It was editorial content, yes, but just as relevant as straight news.

Every person has the opportunity to help improve the community they're living in. It's our duty—and that's the point. It's our job to keep learning... don't be a sloth or a lard ass. Make a contribution to your community even if it's just for the satisfaction it gives you. A local newspaper is a critical means of connecting members of a community to the issues that need to be addressed.

Over my years as a member of this community, and as editor and publisher of the local newspaper, there have been many challenges. W.C. would be shocked and puzzled by things that are happening in the world today, I am sure of that. I'm also sure that what he and my dad stood for is still the foundation of a free press. It's not about filler or "making up" the news. It's about fulfilling the obligation of taking raw information and conveying it fairly and accurately. That's a huge responsibility... and a great privilege.

Dolph Simons Jr.

JOURN
LAWRENC

FRANCIS DILL · ROBERT BARNES · GEROLD BROWN · LAWRENCE LEIGH · HERBERT SMITH · HAROLD PETY

WILLIAM MCKOON · BILLY ROBINSON · JOE SUTTON · FRANK MELONE · WILMER BARNES · DUNN CONNER

ALLAN PHILLIPS · ANNA SCHUTZ · AMELIA ECK · SOPHIA AGLA · NINA NULE · C.R. BOLINGER

W.C. JENKINS SUPERINTENDENT · J.W. MURRAY · F.P. DIETRICH · EVAN EDWARDS · NACH OLIVER · KATHRINE WILSON

EARL A. FARRIS · GRACE FARRAS · MARGARET SAUNDERS · A.E. PEARSON · C.T. NEWBY · CARL RUMOLD

NELLIE YATES · WM. NEUSTIFTER · W.W. RICHARDSON · CHARLES TUTTLE · MYRTLE MUZZY · J.D. PARKISH

WORLD. KANSAS

PHOTO BY MOORE.

A.K. TRIVETT · WM. HINES · H.L. ZWI

CHAPTER 4

The Journalist

*I wanted to be a newspaper man
more than anything else.*

Dolph Simons Sr.

"This reporter" in Nuremberg, Germany, May 1947

Rudolph Hess, deputy to the Führer Adolph Hitler, "has a grey, pasty look and it is difficult for guards to get him outdoors for exercise, or to have him visit with other prisoners. He is the only Nazi among the seven sentenced to prison terms who has refused to see members of his family," this reporter wrote on May 27, 1947. "After spending

Simons (bottom row, second from right) at the Nuremberg Military Tribunal

He also saw the gas chambers at Dachau (holding his hat) in May 1947.

several minutes today at the door to his cell, I can understand why jurors and military men are undecided as to his sanity. At first, he was normal appearing except for a peculiar glassy stare, but when we walked way, he was most certainly acting the part of a crazy man."

"This reporter" was Dolph Simons Sr., in Nuremberg at the war crimes trials. "Witnesses are evasive with answers," he noted, "making it appear that in the remnants of the high command, it continues to be honorable to lie, and dishonorable to tell the truth."[1] about what Nazi Germany inflicted—27 million deaths in the Soviet Union alone.

At the invitation of U.S. Secretary of War Robert Patterson, Simons had joined a military tour of Germany and Austria in May and June 1947, documenting his impressions on the conditions facing American occupation forces. His stories went further to capture "the wreckage and ruin" of those countries and what remained for their citizens "who brought great suffering to all parts of the world"[2] and now had to recreate their lives.

As he wrote of the things he saw—the gas chambers at Dachau, the bombed-out cities, the near-starving families living underground and eking out an existence in the rubble above—Simons always looked for an angle connecting the story to readers back home in Kansas.

Simons (on left) standing where Hitler often orated on the Speer Balcony in Berlin.

On a visit to the former summer lodgings of Kaiser Wilhelm in Bad Homburg, Simons pointed out "the Headman here is Captain John O. Nottingham, a lifelong Lawrencian... who is doing a splendid job, has the respect of the people, and handles his duties with consideration and dispatch." Simons emphasized Nottingham had grown up outside Lawrence on "a farm where his mother and brother Everett continue to live." Furthermore, Nottingham's wife "was the former Edna Garber, KU Class of '32, who grew up five miles southwest of..." Then he provided specific directions conducive to a visit out to the Garbers for anyone who might want to drive out and inquire about Edna and John.

When fleshing out his story about a formal dinner he attended in Austria, Simons noted how Lieutenant General Geoffrey Keyes, commanding officer of American troops in Vienna, asked him, "Are those Indian tepees still located at the road intersection out north of town? It was a landmark Mrs. Keyes and I will long remember." That sidelight would have made the rounds at the faculty lounge, local diner, and beauty shop with the folks back home.

Simons' knack for bringing Lawrence into the narrative was his trademark. He wasn't being myopic, he was fulfilling the agenda ascribed by the title of his newspaper, the *Lawrence Journal-World*. News of the world had relevance to his hometown, and people from Lawrence had a part in making that news. As editor and publisher, Dolph Simons Sr. consistently drew those storylines together in the Journal-World. For many, if not all its readers, it was the most important news source they had.

In the 1940s, Americans were far more likely to get a local newspaper than have a television set in their home.[3] A good local paper put the issues into context for its readers, which wasn't easy to do when news traveled slowly and the issues were meted out thousands of miles away. Consider the liberation of the Auschwitz concentration camp on January 27, 1945. Only a few papers in the country reported it, including *The New York Times* which gave it just three sentences in its February 2 issue.[4] Clearly, it had taken some time for this momentous revelation to reach an American audience; its significance was barely skimmed by the United Press wire service.

In the aftermath of World War II, such "fragmentary reports" made it difficult to provide an accurate story. War correspondents weren't common yet, and it would take years to fully grasp all that had happened. To that end, in the spring of 1947, the U.S. War Department decided to make an official, month-long reconnaissance with a select group of twelve editors and publishers from across the country who would write their own firsthand accounts of what they saw. Joseph Ridder, president of Ridder Newspapers, was on that list; so was Larry Fanning of the *San Francisco Chronicle* and Ralph Coghlan, editor of the *St. Louis Post-Dispatch*. The names went on, comprising a veritable Who's Who of America's most influential newspapermen of the era. And Dolph Simons Sr., publisher of the *Lawrence Journal World* who'd been a trusted source for General Robert Patterson, was one of them.

In truth, the assignment was ideally suited to Simons who'd cut his teeth covering the shocking 1924 Leopold-Loeb trials in Chicago when he was only 21. What Simons brought to the table in 1947 was intellectual knowledge and experiential wisdom. He could turn raw facts into a story with meaning and application for its readers.

Dolph Simons Sr. was, in short, an extraordinary journalist.

His father, W.C. Simons, had observed—no doubt with great satisfaction—this proclivity in Dolph, noting, "From early childhood, he showed a marked interest in the newspaper business."

Dolph Collins Simons was born to Wilford Collins and Gertrude (Reineke) Simons in Lawrence on November 24, 1904. He was a precocious lad who "had some rather forceful ideas," according to his father. During one Sunday school when he was five, Dolph "burst out with a story that his father had a herd of five hundred wild horses," W.C. would recall in his personal memoirs. "When his teacher tried to impress them with the miracle crossing of the Red Sea, Dolph contended that it was only a common-place affair. 'Do you mean to tell me, Dolph,' said the teacher, 'that you could go down to the Kaw River and make the water stop flowing, so people could cross?' 'Yes,' said Dolph. 'And I'm going to do it sometime.'"[5]

In 1908, young Dolph between his Uncle Louie and father, W.C. Simons (right)

Dolph Simons, circa 1925

W.C.'s newspaper was getting a solid foothold in Lawrence, and young Dolph soon became a part of it.

"It began when I put on a bulky carrier bag, reaching almost to my ankles, which labeled me then and there as a member of the force," Dolph later wrote.[6] Next, he went onto the mailing department, and when he was 17, Dolph took over direction of national advertising for the *Lawrence Daily Journal-World*. He "strayed into other jobs a few times, but only as a visitor, soon to be back at the mailer's table, holding the lever on the flat bed, making stereotype casts, sweeping and baling, selling ads, covering a beat, and occasionally writing a special piece," Dolph would recall.

He was a dutiful, responsible, highly intelligent young man who loved the business he was born into, and took it and his future very seriously. But nothing of that was apparent to the woman who would factor significantly in that future, when she—Miss Ann Marie Nelson—saw Dolph Simons dancing onstage at the old Bowersock Opera House in Lawrence in 1926 or '27.

It was the Roaring Twenties and, outside his workaday world, Dolph reveled in its joie de vivre. By all accounts, he led a remarkably social life, as so many did at the dawn of the Jazz Age following WWI.

In his early teens, Dolph was already attending chaperoned dances sponsored by the "Four O'Clock Club" at the Eagles' Hall. Honey Warfield and his band were usually on hand with the music for guests who were listed by name in the society pages of *The Daily Gazette*, including Dolph Simons and his buddies, Bernard Gufler, a future U.S. Ambassador to Ceylon, among them.[7]

> *There were the two years I was a part-time farmer, milking cows, fighting flies, bottling milk, running a neighborhood route, cleaning the chicken house, raising stubborn pigs and operating a perverse coal-oil incubator. Then there was the bill-peddling in the lush era of circulars when the town had to be covered before the morning school bell rang. It nearly always seemed to be raining or snowing when the youthful crew was rounded up for the pre-dawn assault on front porches. The year at the grocery store, week-days weren't so bad, but Saturday's marathon duty lasted from 5:30 am until 11 at night with a few minutes off at noon and again in the evening for a chunk of*

lunch ham, a handful of crackers, and a bottle of milk. There was the year selling life insurance when too many personal friendships were put to an unfair test. Along the route came several more samplings of how other people work to make a living, but that's all they were— only samplings.

I wanted to be a newspaper man more than anything else.

Dolph Simons Sr. from "Talks" circa 1950

There's no record of whether W.C. and Gertie Simons approved of their son's extra-curricular activities, although others considered them scandalous. In his March 1, 1916, article in the Lawrence *Gazette*, Clair M. Patee, who owned the local theater and wrote for the "Moving Picture Section" of the paper, warned, "The Cats are dancing too close together, they should be at least a foot apart. Besides, lively actions indicate 'rag-time' music is being played, and that music will not be permitted in motion picture theaters."[8] Patee would be proven wrong on that count.

It was an exhilarating time to come of age.

After enrolling at KU in 1921, Dolph joined Phi Kappa Psi and began writing for the *Sour Owl*, a tongue-in-cheek student rag that took a humorous but edgy view of campus life. One of his closest friends was Charles Rogers from Olathe, but "Everybody called him Buddy... Buddy Rogers and Dad were fraternity brothers," Dolph Jr. noted. "Buddy was a musician and aspiring actor. He wanted to go to Hollywood, which he did." Rogers returned to Lawrence and paid Dolph a visit to have his old friend look over the contract Buddy had been offered. It must have been acceptable. Rogers made it big in movies, on Broadway, and with marriage to silent film star Mary Pickford.

Another of Dolph's KU friends with a stratospheric career was Julius Holmes of Pleasanton, Kansas. Holmes would go on to serve as brigadier general on General Dwight Eisenhower's staff, playing an integral role in planning the North Africa invasion during WWII. Holmes became minister to the American Embassy in London, the senior political adviser to the American delegation to the United

Nations, and special assistant to the secretary of state for the North Atlantic Treaty Organization (NATO).

Kansas was clearly fertile ground. For Simons, those college days were "a place of bliss for the scholar." In later years, he would admit to a "homesickness, if it can be called that" for a time when "the English department was confronted by nothing greater than the perplexing problem of whether to choose actors for the forthcoming Shakespearian play on the basis of grade marks or acting ability... when committees would require several meetings to determine if the May Day dance and pole-winding should be held in Fowler Grove or on McCook Field."[9]

Simons made the most of his higher education, culminating in his senior year with an internship for the Associated Press in Chicago that would widen his scope considerably.

As a 21-year-old AP intern learning the ropes in Chicago, Dolph honed his skills. When his boss gave him 20 minutes and no press pass to get through security and into the closed-courtroom of the Leopold-Loeb trial, Dolph wasn't even sure how to find the Criminal Court Building downtown. That was quickly solved, but the next part took some finagling. He managed it, thanks to a "determination [that] had won out over almost impossible barriers."[10]

> *"I can distinctly remember that eight different times I was taken down the stairs and ordered out of the building," Simons would later recall. "The ninth attempt was successful and I entered the courtroom just as Justice Caverly came from his private chamber and strode toward the chair behind the bench. I looked about the crowded room for a chair and finally sighted one far toward the front of the room. I knew that it must be reserved for one of the lawyers or court attendants, but decided to take a chance on getting it for myself. Assuming the air of a bravado reporter, I slowly walked forward and took the chair. After a deep sigh of relief, I looked about to get my bearings and found that I was seated next to Nathan Leopold. Next to him was Richard Loeb, his colleague in crime."*[11]

Simons held his position beside the psychotic killers and got the story. He bolted from his chair to make the filing deadline before the

Dolph at Miami Beach in 1928

judge officially closed the session, "which caused the gavel of Justice Caverly to sound heavily on the bench and nearly caused me to be brought under a charge of contempt of court," Simons later wrote. [12]

Leopold-Loeb was a trial by fire for the young journalist in 1924, and it emboldened him. He graduated a year early with a degree in Liberal Arts in 1925, and joined the Journal-World staff full-time early the next year.

For Miss Ann Marie Nelson, a future in Kansas began unfolding when she arrived in Lawrence in 1926. She'd spent two years at Lindenwood College for Women in St. Charles, Missouri, before transferring to the University of Kansas that year to complete her studies in music and education. A dark-haired beauty with luminous eyes, Marie (as she preferred to be called) pledged Kappa Kappa Gamma and spread her wings on Mt. Oread.

Life at KU was a contrast from her conservative, very-Swedish upbringing in rural Nebraska. Her parents, Oscar and Emily Nelson, owned a successful Farmall (the forerunner to International Harvester) farm implement dealership in Auburn, so she had enjoyed a life of some privilege. Marie was a gifted pianist, according to her eldest son, Dolph Jr., who remembered "the story of Mother playing piano in the main intersection of downtown Auburn when she was in high school. Apparently, this was broadcast live across the whole state from a radio station in Omaha. I don't know what they were celebrating, but it was a very big deal. My mother was also the only student in Auburn High School who received a green blanket with the school's initials on it—this was the equivalent of lettering in a sport. She won for debate. I think she was a state champion."

After the portentous stage-dance at the Bowersock, Dolph and Marie met and dating commenced. They made a handsome couple... stylish, socially graceful, and well-suited to each other. Still, "to this day, I find the stories hard to believe because this doesn't sound like my very proper mother," Dolph Jr. admits. "Apparently, she would climb out of her upper-story sorority house window to meet up with Dad after curfew. That might have contributed to her parents' concerns about Dad. I guess they thought he was some kind of 'dandy'."

Dolph and Marie tied the knot on February 16, 1929. "There was a joke in the family that Mom only married Dad to get out of teaching in a one-room schoolhouse," Dolph Jr. said. His brother John added, "Our parents were married

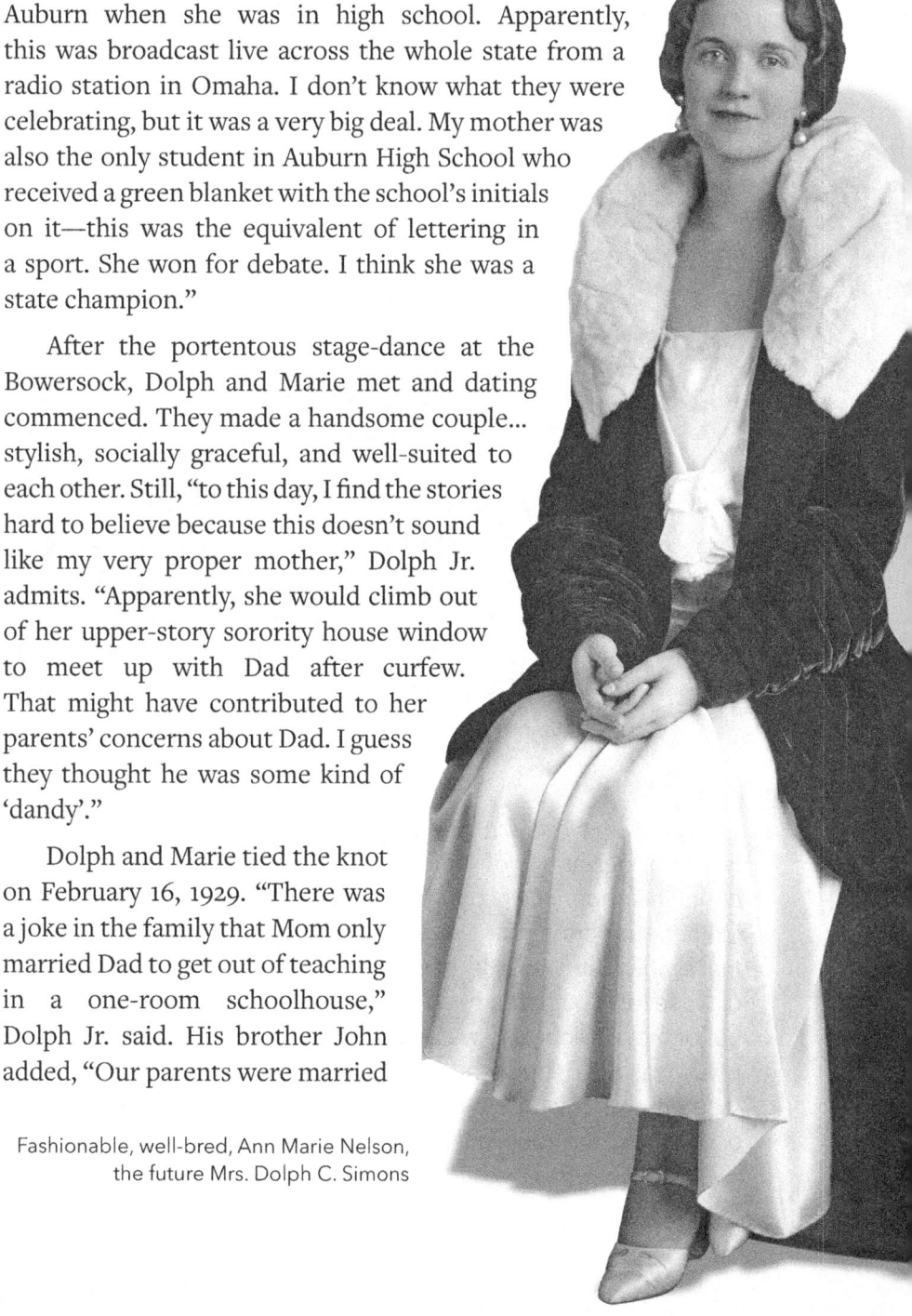

Fashionable, well-bred, Ann Marie Nelson, the future Mrs. Dolph C. Simons

for over 60 years, so it worked out... I guess they proved her parents wrong. They set up housekeeping in a small house on Massachusetts Street. It was furnished with what Dad made from various wood cartons or cases, or purchased with savings he'd put aside from the brief time he sold life insurance and the *Saturday Evening Post*. Eventually, they moved over to 1509 Massachusetts where we grew up. My brother and I had a very happy childhood."

Dolph Jr., Dolph Sr., John, and Marie at home, circa 1940

We always had dinner as a family. Mother and Dad would talk, and John and I would pick up on it sometimes. It was usually about the paper or whether Dad should get involved in politics. Mother supported him 100% with whatever he wanted to do, that's how she was. He had migraine headaches, Ménière's disease, and he had a heart defect of some kind that kept him out of the service. She wanted to take care of him. My mother Marie was the perfect partner for Dad. They'd get into a project together like saving the old Watkins Bank Building downtown or planning the renovation of the Journal-World plant. She'd be asked to take the lead on something because she'd get it done. Marie was the one who had us start a full-page in the paper to recognize the arts. We were the first paper around with a section devoted to the arts. Behind the scenes, Mother probably played more of a role than I realized at the paper.

Dolph Simons Jr.

From 1925 on, Dolph Simons Sr.'s name was on the masthead of the *Lawrence Journal-World* with his various titles including business manager, editor, publisher, president, owner, and chairman of the board. Photo-journalist wasn't one of them, but "Dad took the first locally-produced photo used in the Journal-World when he covered a terrible fire in an old folks' home where many residents were killed," son Dolph Jr. noted.

From the get-go, W.C. made no effort to shield his son from what the paper was up against. Straight out of college, Dolph was confronted with the Ku Klux Klan. The KKK was straining for a foothold in Kansas when it was denied a charter for the second time in 1925.[13] William Allen White, award-winning editor of the Emporia Gazette and leader of the Progressive Movement, was one of the KKK's greatest adversaries. Both W.C. and Dolph Sr. were close colleagues of White, and took the same position in the Journal-World, apparently with enough vitriol to incite the wrath of the "hooded order."

The KKK retaliated with a national advertisement inviting any takers to start a newspaper in Lawrence to beat the *Journal-World*. Dolph Jr. remembers his dad saying "the KKK had offered $100,000 to fund a competing paper, but no one took them up on it." Dolph Jr.'s son Dan Simons recalled the story, adding, "Imagine that, our paper was too 'liberal' for the KKK!"

In the face of many such controversies and challenges over the years, Simons' signature move was to turn the event into a bully pulpit for decency and democracy. His manner was self-assured, and his confident stance was grounded in ethics as personal as they were professional. In short, he was a paragon of principles in practice. A transcript of a 1943 KFKU live radio broadcast of a roundtable on censorship captures Simons' ideology:

> *"Some few years ago, I was asked to sign a petition to the postmaster general requesting withdrawal of mailing privileges to a newspaper supported by a communist organization. I did not sign because, although I thoroughly disapproved of the communist doctrine, I value highly the right of freedom of expression in this country. The right to tell the story of our national successes and our national disgraces has contributed to better government and a greater nation. While we may disagree with another point of view, we should respect the right of the other person to express his views as long as those views are not treasonous or blasphemous. I think the communist should have the right to speak his piece just the same as the Republican, the Democrat, the Odd Fellow, the Methodist, and the Rotarian, as long as he does not threaten or encourage violence or incite disorderly conduct."[14]*

Dolph took over as publisher of the *Lawrence Journal-World* in 1944. Eager to make his own mark, he explored diversification. He secured a radio franchise for The World Company, but in a classic Simons' turn at the fork of integrity versus enterprise, "Dad gave it up," Dolph Jr. said. "He just didn't feel it was right to corner the news market."

Simons gave careful consideration to each challenge he faced as editor and publisher of the local paper. From double-checking the print run to ensure good color reproduction of photographs to delivering an enthusiastic and affirming commencement address to the 1945 indigenous graduates of Haskell Institute, he approached every situation earnestly.

> *Then there is Haskell Institute, the largest Indian school in America, with a thousand young Indian students representing more than 70 tribes, all the way from the Seminoles of Florida to the Eskimos of Point Barrow. Haskell Institute, to the American Indian, is his "Yale, Harvard, and Princeton" all wrapped up into one.*

> *Before looking into the future, let us devote a few minutes to the heroic part American Indians have had in the present war to*

defend our great nation from an evil enemy—a few minutes to think
of your heritage from this great institution, Haskell Institute, and
the precious heritage you have received from your brave and loyal
Indian race.

The respect gained by Indian soldiers in peacetime was a
natural forerunner of what was to come in war. Even before the
Nazis declared war on the United States in December 1941, German
General Karl von Prutch solemnly told his goose-stepping soldiers:
"The most dangerous of the American soldiers is the Indian. He is
brave above all else. He knows far more about camouflage inherited
from his ancestors than any modern soldier who has had the benefit
of science and great laboratories. He is a dead shot who needs no
orders when he advances. He is an army within himself. He is the one
American soldier Germany must fear."

Dolph Simons Sr., excerpted from his commencement address
to graduates of Haskell Institute, May 23, 1945

Doing the right thing undergirded every decision, imbuing
Simons with an innately magisterial tone. He had a "final word" kind
of authority about him, and, like his father before him, put it to use.
When *Kansas City Star* Editor Cruise Palmer exhorted on acceptable
language standards in a family newspaper, Simons sent a reassuring
affirmation. "I appreciated your kind note," Palmer replied. "Yours
was among the more favorable letters I received."[15]

After returning from the military reconnaissance tour in 1947,
Dolph Simons Sr. published *"Austria and Germany in May-June,"* his
report of U.S.-occupied zones in post-WWII Europe. It was well-
received. The chief of the War Department's Public Information
Division, Major Walter R. King, wrote, "I received the copy of the
brochure of your articles resulting from your European trip and think
you have done a splendid job of presenting the facts, and in making
up an interesting booklet. As you know, I am the architect, historian,
keeper of the archives and just about everything else concerning these
trips, except the luggage carrier. I would appreciate having about 8
or 10 more copies of the booklet, if available, for official use. If you
can spare them, I can assure you they will be seen by more influential
brass in the army, civilian, and military."[16]

(WX10) WASHINGTON, FEB. 24—AFTER WORLD TOUR—DOLPH SIMONS (LEFT), PUBLISHER OF THE LAWRENCE (KAS.) JOURNAL WORLD, AND VICE ADM. ROBERT B. CARNEY, DEPUTY CHIEF OF NAVAL OPERATIONS, VIEW A GLOBE AT THE PENTAGON TODAY AFTER THEIR RETURN FROM A SIX-WEEK 'ROUND-THE-WORLD TRIP BY NAVY PLANE TO INSPECT NAVAL INSTALLATIONS. (AP WIREPHOTO) (RMB51715STF-JR) 1949

Simons had made a good impression—good enough to be invited back again in 1949. This time, the assignment was as an embedded "civilian observer" accompanying Admiral Louis Denfeld, chief of naval operations, and Vice Admiral Robert B. Carney on a Navy inspection flight around the world. They would visit 22 countries in six weeks.

Simons titled his account of this 35,000-mile tour *A Globe Circler's Diary*. In it, he went deep and wide. As historian-journalist and author Mitchell Stevens describes it, this kind of documentation goes "beyond merely noting who said what at some public event—mere 'stenographic' reporting."[17] Dolph's essays captured the unique times, places, and people with ambidextrous mastery—he could deliver both journalistic facts and a fascinating story. "Dad really was a damn fine writer," Dolph Jr. mused. "I think that 'Diary' shows how good he was... that he could be serious and entertaining."

A *Globe Circler's Diary* was a smart and engaging read. Consider Simons' evening in Paris on the 21st of January, 1949, when "this reporter" wrote, "Fiftyish Ely Culbertson, the bridge expert, and his charming new wife, introduced as 'Vassar '46,' were present at the embassy reception given by Ambassador and Mrs. Jefferson Caffery." The sentence was classy as the people it described.

When in Singapore on February 10, he described the weather "as the duplication of the damp underside of a setting hen." In each exotic locale, Dolph Simons' wit and skill reigned over the narrative. Notwithstanding the awkward lingo of the era ("Japs" and "Frenchies"), *A Globe Circler's Diary* remains an articulate and accurate report on the state of the world in 1949. It was a world still recovering from war, and he captured that in situ:

"Many burnt out buildings in London have not been repaired and stand empty with blackened windows. The bomb damage to London was slight compared to Berlin and other large German cities, but a first view to many Americans would be startling. In some sections, several city blocks were completely flattened."

Then he broadened the scope to take a longer look that showcased his literary chops...

- Gibraltar was carved with *"mountain roads which have hairpin turns far more hair-pinny than anything in Colorado. Two of the turns require three separate backaways before being able to proceed."*

- *"In the late twilight, glows of Bedouin campfires are seen sparingly—perhaps 50 miles apart. The comfort of a large airplane above these rough mountains seems so much more pleasant and cozy than any life imaginable down below in the dark crevices"* of eastern Arabia.

- Ceylon (now Sri Lanka) was full of stalls where *"Workmen sit on the floor using bare feet as a vise for the black wood, which is chiseled and chopped in to proper rough shape before the knife work begins and the polishing is complete. It is a wonder the human vises have any toes left after thousands of near-misses that come from the banging on a razor-sharp chisel."*

Throughout, Simons would routinely draw folks back home into the story. "Try to imagine between 5,000 and 10,000 wild elephants in the eastern fourth of Kansas, and in that number, numerous 'rogues,' or frustrated and unhappy bulls, are roaming the country looking for trouble."

His visit to the Sheikh of Bahrain produced this memorable description replete with a reference any KU insider would recognize:

> At a proper signal, the scarlet-robed servants appear with giant, long-snouted coffee pots (similar in general shape to a Jayhawk) and several small, handless cups about a third the size of the average custard cup. With at least a half dozen cups in one hand, and the big pot in the other, the pourer makes one grand whirling gesture as the coffee shoots through the air and reaches the cup without a drop missing the bullseye. It is called coffee but is unrecognizable as such to the visiting American because the strange ingredients include cardamom seed.
>
> In a matter of seconds, the attendants are back and unless the guest gives the cup a certain wiggling motion, he will have another service. To show disdain for something or other, any unconsumed coffee is tossed onto the beautiful rugs. A few minutes later, the same

act is repeated, except for a smaller pot, and tea scented with rose water. And while the taste of the rose-watered tea is still fresh, the big black fellows come back with the original coffee pot. To be sociable is to accept all three, as they are served.

The three warm liquids have the staying quality of fried mackerel.

Indeed, Kansans were still a primary audience for Simons' essays. Not only because he would publish 25 articles about his trip in the *Lawrence Journal-World* and further share them to other newspapers throughout the state, but again, he wanted to demonstrate how Kansas figured into the post-war recovery in significant ways. Rear Admiral John D. Murphy, director of war crimes trials for the U.S. Pacific Fleet, was a KU alum. U.S. Foreign Service Chief Chris Ravndal was a frequent visitor to Lawrence where his brother Olaf was married to a local girl. The mastermind behind the grain-farming experiment to bolster Turkey's economy was KSU graduate Charles Enlow. Simons was greeted by KU ROTC instructor Harry Meyers when he got off the plane in Karachi, except Harry was now Brigadier General Meyers, military attaché and interim head of the U.S. Embassy in Karachi. And Brigadier General Julius Holmes, a KU alum from Olathe, "is recognized by many observers as one of the ablest men in the foreign service," Simons recorded. "He is permanently the number two man in the London Embassy, which heads up our general European planning and is our most important foreign office."

Kansas, in turn, read and reviewed *The Globe Circler's Diary*. On June 8, 1950, the *Belleville Telescope* mentioned the Simons' book and emphasized his principal concern: "England is balancing its budget with our money and at the same time taking away some of our markets. I believe in charity and the golden rule and that some of the money the U.S. is pouring into other countries has been well spent, but I don't believe, however, in an international WPA supported by U.S. taxpayers. We are spending $15,000,000,000 on foreign aid and are going into debt $6,000,000,000 this year."[18]

After reading the book, William Lathrop of the Kansas City Bar Association wrote Simons, "I can understand well why Admiral

The Globe Circler's Diary gets a good review from the Topeka paper.

And Captain Zahid Kiraghi of Ankara, Turkey, liked its "precise realism." [20]

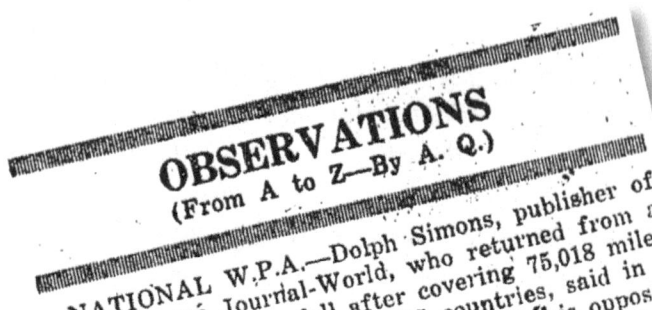

OBSERVATIONS
(From A to Z—By A. Q.)

NATIONAL W.P.A.—Dolph Simons, publisher of the Lawrence Journal-World, who returned from a tour of Europe last fall after covering 75,018 miles and making observations in 35 countries, said in a speech at Kansas City last week that he is opposed to financing countries all over the world while Uncle Sam is going into the "red" to the tune of $6,000,000,000 a year. "England is balancing its budget with our money and at the same time taking away some of our markets," said Simons. He further remarked: "I believe in charity and the golden rule and that some of the money the U.S. is pouring into other countries has been well spent," he added, "I don't believe, however, in an international WPA supported by U.S. taxpayers. We are spending $15,000,000,000 on foreign aid and are going into debt $6,000,000,000 this year."

Akarsuray Egitim
Ankara —Tu
14 – July – 19

Dear Mr. Simons,

I thank you very much for remembering me as to sent me a copy of your interesting "A Globe Circular's Diary".

I wish you were stay much longer my country. I believe a writer of your who can ballance every thing and idea with a realism, will always help us in every especially to make us known in U.S.

I still have not any chance to see your country, but I hope someday I will.

Thank you for the book Mr. Simons remaining.

Your's Faithf

Zahid Kira

Denfeld invited you to make the trip around the world, but the question that interests me is how he discovered you in the first place."[19]

An American ex-pat in Dhahran wrote this: "Your 'Globe Circler's Diary' has reached me, and I have gone through it from cover to cover," wrote J. MacPherson, vice president and resident administrative officer of the Arabian American Oil Company (ARAMCO) in Saudi Arabia. "These pages contain a good deal of keen observation tempered with 'horse sense,' humor and some pretty sound advice, which might well be taken. Your final article, 'One Man's Opinions,' I subscribe to 100%—indicating that apparently there are a few people who think alike, since my thoughts agree identically to yours."[21]

Both Simons' Austria-Germany journal in 1947 and *The Globe Circler's Diary* in 1949 found a following, particularly within the military realm. Those who read it wanted others to read it, too. Major J.D. Willoughby, deputy chief of public information in the War Department was one of many who requested copies: "Our Analysis Branch endeavors to compile files of overall and general press opinion clippings concerning the Army and its operations. Your clippings would be of great value in these files especially because of your first-hand opinions on location."[22]

> *Dolph Simons Sr.'s extensive reporting on post-WWII conditions compelled him to include this strong message in nearly every speech he gave for the rest of his life: "We must defend our freedoms. The United States must never lose a war... the results are terrible beyond imagination."*

Simons' instructional and illustrious approach resonated for readers far and wide, but there was one story from the Philippines that hit much closer to home and was never published.

No doubt Dolph did a double take when a letter in a Kansas Public Service Company envelope caught up with him "In care of Admiral Carney's Party arriving Manila on February 11." It was from Caryl Dodds Sr., a friend of W.C. who'd provided Dodds with a possible way to reach Simons while he was in the Philippines. Dodds was writing with "not even a request, but just an idea... only if you have time, only if it isn't too much trouble." Then he went on to explain that

"Jack," a Lawrence boy who'd been killed in action one month before WWII ended in 1945, had been buried in British New Guinea, but disinterred and relocated to a U.S. military cemetery near Manila. "No grave number was included in the report," Dodds continued. Still, the family would very much like to know where he was finally laid to rest. "Jack, you know, was known in the army as Corporal Caryl J. Dodds Jr., #17,135,685," revealed Dodds Sr. "I have felt that if we could have a report from someone who had seen this cemetery and knew the conditions, whether it really seemed permanent and well cared for... it would be a great satisfaction."

It was a daunting challenge, but Dolph's handwritten notes on Dodds' original letter are evidence of his response. He made inquiries and used his connections that eventually led three miles inland from Manila. There, the remains of more than 30,000 U.S. soldiers lost in the Pacific arena were, at the time of his writing, assembled for reinterment. "I saw the records with proof of identification. [Jack's] body is in a dark metal casket inside a large wooden container in the Army Mausoleum at Nichols Field about four miles from Navy Pier," Simons wrote to Dodds. Simons added that he was "most favorably impressed" with the setting and with the leadership of Captain H.B. McNemar, chief of the Public Records Section, whose postal address he provided so Dodds could follow up directly for further information. The only persons more relieved than Simons had to have been Jack's parents who could finally close that sad chapter about their son.

No one was surprised when Dolph Sr. was elected first vice president of the national Associated Press board in 1950. His editorials, articles, speeches, and talks could have been anthologized in a journalism textbook, but they were also indicative of his abiding interest in almost everything. Dolph Simons was erudite on a wide variety of topics. When taking on a subject, his approach was practically dissertational. Whether addressing Journal-World subscribers, journalism classes, a convocation, Chamber of Commerce, Rotary, or the "Saturday Night Club" in Lawrence, he was thorough and didactic.

A random curation of his voluminous output underscores this point.

On the Associated Press: On January 20, 1936, Dolph spoke to the Olathe Chamber of Commerce on the subject of the world's largest news gathering service, the Associated Press. He described its purpose, its membership corporate status, how the bureaus worked, and the gamut of its operations "like a huge octopus with scores of main tentacles and hundreds of lesser ones." It was a nuts-and-bolts guide focused on how the AP functioned.

(L – R) Dolph Sr. expounds as AP board colleagues Wes Gallagher, AP President and General Manager, Henry Bradley, St. Joseph, and Roy Roberts, *Kansas City Star* listen in, circa late 1950s.

More than 20 years later, Simons addressed the topic again with "The History of the AP."[23] A read of the two missives shows his variability as a journalist and his evolution as a writer who'd found his voice. Dolph explored the facts and features with finely-crafted copy points that landed on every major milestone of the AP's journey:

- AP Western Division Chief Paul *"Cowles also directed coverage of the San Francisco earthquake in 1906, an event which introduced the word 'FLASH' into AP procedure."*

- In the winter of 1938, the AP moved its headquarters into its 15-story building at Rockefeller Plaza. *"There, on September 3, 1939, the bells of the London cable printer sounded the flash signal. It reported that Prime Minister Neville Chamberlain had proclaimed Britain at war with Germany, which was already busy dismembering the Polish army."*

- *"Between hot spells, the Cold War presented its own peculiar challenges. In some Iron Curtain lands, it soon developed, objective reporting could readily be twisted into charges of 'espionage' and offense against the state."*

On Bee-Keeping: *"Then there was the honey career when I was president of the Douglas County Bee Keepers Association and envisioned someday being the Honey King of Kansas. That endeavor ended abruptly one day when the bees ganged up on me."* [24]

On Freedom of the Press: *"I know some of you bite your lip and turn red when you read editorials that are in full conflict with your own ideas on government and business, but the right of the editor to express his opinions and your right to send a letter to the editor are precious annoyances that go with the freedoms of democracy.*

Democracy can succeed only if the people are well-informed. It is the duty of American newspapermen to provide the public with an accurate, full and impartial news report, and to protect them from unscrupulous advertising. And the public also has the right to demand that editorial comment be confined to editorial columns, and not scattered about in news reports.

Go ahead and cuss the editor whenever you like, but lend your efforts always to keeping our newspapers free and uncontrolled. Otherwise, you some day may confine your reading to an American edition of Pravda." [25]

"The printed word is permanent; it can be studied over and over again. There is no better way to develop a well-informed body politic than through a comprehensive printed news report. This can only happen where newspapers have freedom to report both the good and the bad... only where people are protected from regimentation, repression, and abuse by a genuine and real Freedom of the Press." [26]

"The press needs much more than freedom. It needs a sense of dignity, responsibility, and a strong desire to serve the best interests of the public." [27]

On Lawrence: Although he was sometimes its critic, Simons was at all times a cheerleader for his hometown. Lawrence was *"a delightful place in which to live and work, primarily because the people who live here are a friendly, wholesome, and progressive lot,"* he pointed out to the local Chamber-of-Commerce on November 4, 1957. It was the occasion of the Hallmark Company moving to town, and Simons had a significant (if unofficial) role in facilitating this commercial coup. He was delighted to see Hallmark's *"cards with clever verse and the sparkling gift package that make millions of people feel better"* become an economic engine for the citizens of Lawrence who could now join the ranks of the company's *"happiness producers"* and *"have more fun out of life than people who manufacture straitjackets, caskets, or castor oil."*[28]

Simons wasn't just true to *his* school, he wanted everyone else to feel the same way about Lawrence. *"Did you realize that Lawrence is the best business town in the state of Kansas? We know it is a pleasant place in which to live and that our school advantages are far superior to any other community in the Midwest... We have every reason to have great pride in our community. We have the best people, the best schools, and we have the best business. I, for one, always welcome an opportunity to tell the stranger about my wonderful home city."*[29]

He felt he same way about Kansas: *"That's what we've been trying to tell the world for several years. There is no place on earth where there is as much 100 percent Americanism in this particular section of the Middle West. If we had the ability to write a song, it would be entitled, "God Bless the Men of Kansas." We don't think there is another state in the union that can produce the caliber of any comparable quantity. About 85% of our population are these types of men and others can't go far wrong under such broad-shouldered influence."*[30]

On Politics: Early on, Dolph seemed somewhat enamored of the political arena, and undeniably thrilled with what may have been his first speech-writing gig. *"While I do not want to appear as one of the candidate's chief advisors, yet I could not help but be pleased with the enthusiastic reception of the speech which the Governor told a large number of people was 'Dolph's speech',"* Simons wrote as ex officio speechwriter. Officially, he was a member of the press corps traveling on the campaign train with Kansas Governor Alf Landon, the Republican candidate for president in 1936.

This was his first such assignment, so Simons made note of what he was learning, like *"how a man well-schooled in dramatics should be a member of the committee of arrangements in every political campaign. The front rows of the platform should be filled with substantial looking people from all classes of business who not only make a good appearance but know how to cheer at the right times and conduct themselves properly throughout the meeting. Some sedate old fat committee member who waves a flag awkwardly doesn't help much at a time like this.*"[31]

In 1944, Dolph attended the Republican National Convention as a delegate from Kansas. But by 1952, the scene had lost its allure. He wrote, "*Because millions of Americans will see General Eisenhower on television today, the question of glamor is getting into politics. We hear that it takes a special kind of grooming to make a person look his best on TV. And some of Ike's supporters are wondering whether Ike's tortoise shell glasses will detract from his video appeal. It may come to be a matter of looks vs. brains—in which event we may hope that brains will not lose out completely. The country has use for more of them than have been exerted on its behalf in some areas of the government recently. Letting Hollywood have the glamor if we could capture the brains for government—that might be a good trade.*"[32]

When Philip Young, chief advisor to Dwight D. Eisenhower, asked Simons to weigh in on what the general should address in a speech announcing his candidacy for president in 1952, Dolph offered various ideas but emphasized his standard axiom, "*I would like to see him state emphatically that as yet there is no better rule to follow than the golden rule—wherein men will treat other men in a way they would like to be treated.*"[33]

As an imperious Republican and an astute observer of the body politic, eventually, it was Dolph's name that came up for office. Dolph Jr. recalled numerous encouraging nudges from various sources that his dad shrugged off. Supporters weren't easily dissuaded. During the 1954 Kansas gubernatorial race, the *Salina Business Journal* endorsed him. "Simons is an honest, capable business executive with an unblemished reputation and proved ability to win friends and influence people. He would make a cracking good governor." Richard Seaton, editor of the *Manhattan Mercury*, also supported Simons, "a name to be reckoned with," admittedly, "without knowing whether Simons entertains running for office or could be urged to."[34]

He would not. Dolph had already concluded that mingling politics with newspaper ownership was not consistent with his philosophy of a free press. When he attended the Republican National Convention in 1952, it was strictly as a member of the press corps. "Dad felt getting involved in politics would forever tarnish the impartiality of the paper and his role as editor," Dolph Jr. reflected. "There were numerous politicos including two U.S. senators encouraging him to throw his hat into that ring, but he wouldn't do it."

On Advice for College Graduates: *"Learn to like people and to enjoy visiting. Don't sit. Go places and do things. Go down into coal mines. Visit courtrooms. Learn how to draw a pear; maybe shoot a little pool. Travel. Follow the wheat harvest. Avoid the frills. In place of frills, use your time in broadening your knowledge in political science, literature, philosophy, history, and economics. Save some time for speech and languages. Get a look at skid row. Learn how to tie your own black tie. Take in the opera, after you've seen a good burlesque. Visit the hiring hall. Perhaps do a hitch in the Army or Marines, or see some new places in the Navy or Air Corps. Whatever you do, don't sit. And don't depend too much upon text books."* [35]

On Gambling and Lotteries: *"Wagering has been practiced since the activities of man were first recorded... If they must stake their money on an uncertain event, why not have a strict state regulation of their play? Regulation has dealt a severe blow to the criminal and the cheat who have always found gambling a lucrative field. The gambler will not be victimized. The loot of the crook would become state tax money. Why not try socialism on gambling?"* [36]

On Community Engagement: In 1925, Simons was quoted in the *National Printer Journalist*: *"The paper and its employees take an active part in all civic affairs, giving time and money for the advancement and development of the community."* [37] He delivered on that value in many ways.

When the war effort desperately needed scrap materials in 1942, Dolph made an all-out appeal. *"With alarming word from Washington that many steel mills will be forced to close down this fall unless more scrap metal is dug out of farm lots, garages, and basements, Kansas must join in and help meet the desperate need for the materials which provide weapons of war for the United States fighting forces.*"[38] And he led the statewide response committee for all Kansas newspapers.

It didn't take a war to prompt Simons to action. From starting up the local 4-H chapter to leading efforts to establish KU's Spencer Museum of Art, he was always looking for ways to support the community. The Lawrence Chamber of Commerce recognized his 50 years of service to that organization and the community with its Citizen of the Year award in 1985. John T. Stewart III, a former president of the KU Alumni Association and chairman of the KU Endowment Association, considered Simons a father figure. "Everything that was done—and was good—had his name etched on the project."

On Race Relations: *"Here again, the golden rule applies as well as any rule.... The attitude of men is far more important than any individual law which might be passed."*[39] And with that, Simons distilled the issue of race relations to its essence.

He would readily publish opposition to his views on the matter. One such diatribe by a "Mr. Kunz" who didn't want "coloreds" swimming the community pool drew a heated reply. "Let me draw his attention to the fact that the Negroes of Lawrence are being taxed for the airport which they do not use, also the 4-H Club grounds and building which they do not enjoy as no Negro child can join a 4-H Club in this area. Then, too, let me point out to him that the four new schools that have been built recently are out of bounds for Negro children and always will be since Negroes cannot buy property in that area. Qualified Negroes cannot get good jobs here nor can they find a decent place to live unless they buy. Hence, there are many Negro homeowners, therefore many Negro taxpayers. It seems to me that they are entitled to some of the benefits of the tax money spent."[40]

The author wasn't Simons, but Rose Spears, a Lawrencian whose castigation of Kunz was also published in the Journal-World "Letters to the Editor." From Simons' point of view, such exchanges should be encouraged and published so citizens had a forum in which to express opinions and influence the growth and development of their community.

Simons didn't hesitate to wield his own pen against discrimination. Dr. E.D.B. Charles, a British Medical Service physician who came to KU with the World Health Organization in 1956, was refused service at several restaurants in Lawrence *"because he is a Negro,"* wrote Simons in a scathing editorial that dared to point fingers. *"This is not an isolated incident. Various Negroes and students from India who are studying at the University have received similar treatment in Lawrence. It might be pointed out that Dr. Charles stayed at Manhattan, Kans., for several days prior to his arrival in Lawrence and had no similar unpleasant experiences there,"* he admonished.[41]

"My dad was so ahead of his time on civil rights," Dolph Jr. said. "If an African American was doing well in academics or sports or in the community in some way, he'd elevate that to give it better position in the paper. He'd go out of his way to find ways to shine some light on anyone who was disadvantaged."

On Money and the Federal Reserve: *"One of the troubles with money, of course, is that as individuals we never feel we have enough of it. But another trouble is that a country may sometimes have too much of it,"* Dolph Sr. wrote in the 1960s as chair of the Kansas City-based Federal Reserve Bank. In his inimitable style, Simons delivered a tome that covered everything from wampum to wildcat banking, greenbacks to silver and gold certificates. *"The United States now seems to have solved the technical currency problems which bedeviled our forebears,"* he concluded. *"But the basic task of maintaining the dollar's purchasing power is one that must be faced anew each year. To this end, the Federal Reserve System works to keep our modern money supply—coin, currency, and checkbook money—in reasonable balance with the economy's ability to produce, but that's another story."*[42]

On Education: *"The great value in formal education is not the actual knowledge that is brought to the student through classroom activities, but in the way it awakens our minds and causes us to seek out more information."*[43]

Simons held strong opinions about academics, particularly at KU, and was ever ready *"to offer suggestions for several basic changes in the operation of the University of Kansas wherein I believe the institution would more closely follow the intent of the state as a whole, and would better serve today's populace and all succeeding generations."*[44] He did not refrain from sharing his opinions, including that the Liberal Arts and Sciences' *"curriculum be completely revised with the elimination of useless, wasteful, and befogging courses, and the addition of new classes and courses of study more correctly geared to society's present-day needs."*[45]

On the whole, Dolph Sr. seemed to appreciate the school of hard knocks as much as an institution of higher learning, which he valued greatly.

On the University of Kansas: *"Anyone who has the privilege of living this long under the shadow of Mount Oread is a lucky person,"* Dolph said at a KU Commencement dinner in 1975.[46] He was 71 at the time, and had enjoyed that privilege his whole life. In official, unofficial, and practical ways, he'd been a student, guest lecturer, alumnus, alumni leader, endowment officer, benefactor, critic, recruiter, publicist, and advisor "with selfless concern for the well-being of the institution," according to former Chancellor Gene Budig. "The University of Kansas had no greater friend than Dolph Simons."

Perhaps one reason he remained a close confidante to each of seven successive chancellors was his ability to speak truth to their power. Simons never just ranted; he brought solutions to the problems. When the university lacked resources to support a world-class science and pharmacy program, Dolph Simons Sr. stepped up. He recruited Takeru Higuchi, "already the acknowledged international leader of his discipline" to the KU faculty in 1967. Simons went on to actively participate with Higuchi and others in the creation of INTERx, a Lawrence-based pharmaceutical research operation that was eventually sold to Merck & Company.[47]

Simons was a recipient of KU's highest honor, the Distinguished Service Citation, as well as its Ellsworth Award for Significant Service to the University. In 1996, KU dedicated the Dolph Simons Biosciences

A lot of networking was accomplished during a hunt. (left to right) Weaver's Department store owner Art Weaver, Rusty Casteel, a prominent St. Louis attorney, Dolph Sr., Dolph Jr., and John Simons shooting at John Olin's Nilo Farm in Missouri, home of "the best Labradors that ever flushed a pheasant or retrieved a duck."

Dolph Sr. and Marie Simons made a great team.

Research Laboratories on west campus in honor of the journalist who'd played such a significant role in the life of the university.

On Hunting and Fishing: *"I was on a 28-foot launch out in the Gulf Stream off the coast of Florida with Ray Holland, editor of Field and Stream magazine and Victor Murdock of Wichita. The big fellows were striking at our bait but I failed to land a fish before the big waves got the best of Mr. Murdock and we had to turn back for shore. Not a fish, and yet a wonderful day of fishing. It was the sport of it and the good company. I have often said that you can size up a man better in a few days of hunting and fishing than in years of ordinary association. It is a time for both work and philosophy, and if there are unpleasant traits, they will soon show up."*[48]

On Conservation: *"My dad was one of the first to try to make the Flint Hills into a large park. There's all this acreage that's never been turned and tilled... the grass grows high as a horse. Dad and Walt Menninger and a few others tried to put together a group to work to preserve this,"* Dolph Jr. noted.

On Women: Although he valued higher education for the "college girl," he was a traditionalist. Dolph believed a woman was *"almost certain to discover her most important task in life shall be as the housekeeper and family raiser."*[49] In a 1967 editorial, Simons vaguely inferred that the First Lady lacked sufficient ardor for that role. *"Mrs. Lyndon Johnson makes a couple small slips when discussing her new grandson, Patrick Lyndon. First, Lady Bird referred to the new baby as 'it,' and...Second, Mrs. Johnson said that while she relishes the role of grandmother, she isn't particularly enamored of the title as such."*[50]

Regarding his own wife, Dolph's avid approval was more than apparent. He listened to Marie's views and supported her interests. "They would get into projects together like saving the old Watkins Bank Building downtown," according to Dolph Jr. "Mother was smart. She'd be asked to lead something or take on a task in the community because everyone knew she'd get it done. When we built the new plant, Mother worked so hard to get the mortar a certain color, and the coursing of the brick a certain way. She brought style and class to whatever she put her mind to."

"Dad played more of a role in what she was doing," in reference to a speech Marie gave to a local group. "Certainly reads like something Dad had a hand in writing or editing... *'Who's going to take care of the cities? Who's taking care of the schools and hospitals? The paper, by one means or another, holds the unique position of reporting the news, but also at the same time providing a window or chalkboard of the community itself. So the residents of that city use the paper in order to have an idea of the city, their neighbors, the life of the community. Without that, we're all kind of drifting.'* There's a lot of Dad in what Mother wrote," Dolph acknowledged.

On Travel: "*From palaces to filthy grass huts, carriers to dinghies, high flying aircraft to submarines, unclad Parisians to robed Arabians, snowdrifts to scorched deserts, and London's Clydesdales to Karachi's camels, we looked until our eyes would no longer function. Sleep was unavoidable at certain intervals, but not much time was wasted at it. If more Americans would visit more foreign countries, they would have greater appreciation for the wonderful life we have in our own country. With all of our troubles, and all of our faults, we are so much happier, more comfortable, and better off in every way than any other nation on earth. May it always be so.*"[51]

On the Red Scare: "*We have been too soft in the treatment of Communists.*"[52]

"*Another interesting sight which could be seen on almost any street was a crowd of some 75 to 150 men gathered around two men in a political argument. Some Communists and Reds used this as a means to get a crowd for their regular lecture. Something which looked like simply an argument was a means to get a large crowd and then the Communist would start in with his harangue.*"[53]

"*A greater danger than Russia is the fact that there are 70,000 Communists in America working in a party that has designs to overthrow our government.*"[54]

On Life in America: "*Those dedicated to the proposition that most of what America [does] is wrong say that our society is hypocritical. They add that society proclaims to espouse a number of ideals in the Declaration of Independence and the Constitution, then does not measure up to them.*

...Bear in mind that the ideals of the Declaration of Independence and the Constitution are designed to create a state of perfection. Computers might be able to achieve such, but not humans, and humans still control the earth. ...our system has helped bring [perfection] nearer than it has been for any society—this dignity and equality in the matters of life, liberty, and the pursuit of happiness."[55]

"With all of our faults in the U.S., and with all our troubles, our life here in America is the happiest, most comfortable, and the most secure on earth. This is true largely because America was the first to provide education for the masses instead of only for the upper classes. Young men and women who have had the desire to learn, to invent, and to improve, have always had a classroom and a laboratory available. Millions of others who did not have a desire to learn have been inoculated with ambition simply through enforced school attendance in the early impressionable years.

From the classrooms and laboratories have come new skills and new methods of production, improved government, better health conditions, better housing, greater recreational facilities, and all things which have made it a privilege for you and me to live in this country."[56]

Above all things, let us not give way to our fears. Our ancestors saw dark days, even in America, but courage, self-confidence, and faith carried them through.[57]

You're among the lucky few if you can call your father your hero—I definitely fall into that category. I had so much respect for my dad and granddad alike. W.C. worked his ass off, then Dolph, my father, came up very smart and ambitious. He turned down jobs in Miami and elsewhere to stay at the Journal-World and work for his father. They had a strong relationship and respect for each other. I never saw them at odds, but apparently, Dad took Granddad's office key away at one point, which I'm sure is a good story even if we'll never know if it was true or why.

If Granddad and Dad did struggle over anything, they certainly never brought it home with them. W.C. and Dolph Sr.

were entirely professional but also patriarchs who put family before work. Somehow, they managed to do both well. It was amazing to me to witness how they did that. Dad rarely missed dinner with the family each night, and I heard that was true for W.C. as well. Those ethics and their engagement in community life outside the office had a huge influence on me, although I never felt I managed all that as well as they did.

As the third generation running our newspaper company, I could have had a tough time stepping into their shoes, but I didn't. W.C. and Dad were both very skilled publishers, editors, and writers who ran the business like a tight ship. Theirs was a hard act to follow. Looking back, I'll bet Dad had concerns about whether I could pull it off, but he set me up for success. That was a great gift to me, one I'm not sure I fully appreciated or recognized at the time. Other newspaper families have broken apart under the strain of working together or letting go when it was time for the son take over. It's a tricky thing—being part of that dynamic. I have been the son working my way up, knowing I'd have to prove myself, but also knowing I had my own way of doing things. I've also been the father watching my sons and daughters grow into the business and leave their mark.

Over the years whenever I was worried about something, I'd ask myself what would Dad do, or what would W.C. think about this? If I was writing something negative or critical, I'd think of my dad's advice to sleep on it and see if how I felt the next day. There have been a number of my letters never sent and editorials not published thanks to Dad's discretion.

My dad was the person I'd go to if I was having a crisis. Nowadays, I tend to talk to my grown kids to get their views of a topic, particularly if it's about something I want to write. I respect them... I sure hope my dad was able to say the same thing.

Dolph Simons Jr.

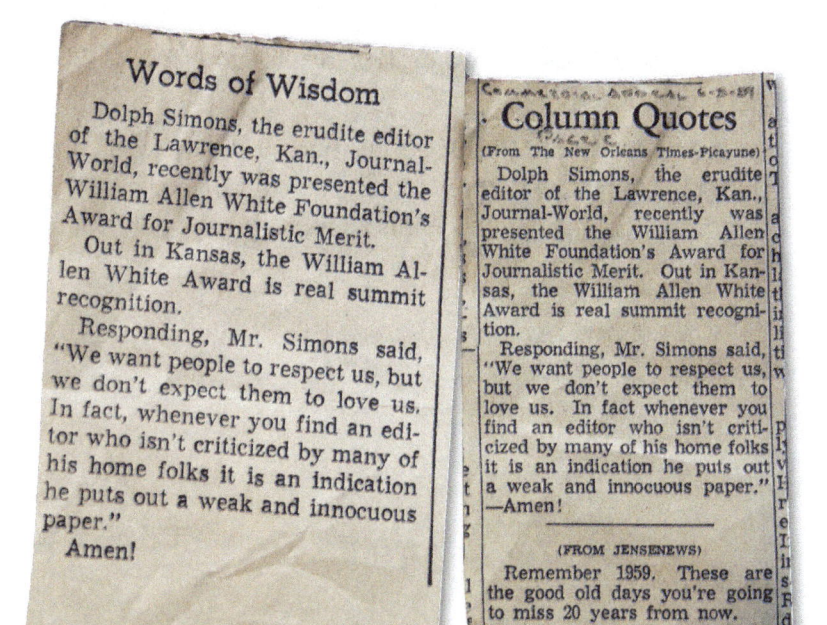

Words of Wisdom

Dolph Simons, the erudite editor of the Lawrence, Kan., Journal-World, recently was presented the William Allen White Foundation's Award for Journalistic Merit.

Out in Kansas, the William Allen White Award is real summit recognition.

Responding, Mr. Simons said, "We want people to respect us, but we don't expect them to love us. In fact, whenever you find an editor who isn't criticized by many of his home folks it is an indication he puts out a weak and innocuous paper."

Amen!

Column Quotes

(From The New Orleans Times-Picayune)

Dolph Simons, the erudite editor of the Lawrence, Kan., Journal-World, recently was presented the William Allen White Foundation's Award for Journalistic Merit. Out in Kansas, the William Allen White Award is real summit recognition.

Responding, Mr. Simons said, "We want people to respect us, but we don't expect them to love us. In fact whenever you find an editor who isn't criticized by many of his home folks it is an indication he puts out a weak and innocuous paper." —Amen!

(FROM JENSENEWS)

Remember 1959. These are the good old days you're going to miss 20 years from now.

After his retirement in 1978, Dolph Sr. remained engaged with ideas and input. His was a lifelong tenure during which some of the most dramatic events in the nation's history occurred—World War I, the Great Depression, WWII, the Red Scare, rock and roll, the first man on the moon, the civil rights movement, Vietnam, Watergate, and the advent of computers. Throughout this time of unparalleled change, Dolph Simons Sr. remained constant on certain themes:

- Lawrence, Kansas, is the best place to grow up, go to college, work, raise a family, and experience the highest quality of life.

- "The editor should never regard his newspaper as a personal plaything because the newspaper primarily is a public service loaded with the responsibility of properly and honestly reporting and interpreting the news of the day."[58]

- "Freedom of the Press is not a freedom for the editor as much as it is YOUR freedom to know what is happening in the world."[59]

- The privilege of living in this country cannot be taken for granted. "We must defend our freedoms. The United States must never lose a war... the results are terrible beyond imagination."[60]

- "We want people to respect us, but we don't expect them to love us. In fact, whenever you find an editor who isn't criticized by many of his homefolks, it is an indication he puts out a weak and innocuous paper."[61]

CHAPTER 5

Ink in His Veins

Lawrence, Kansas, Public Schools

Home Letter from the_First Grade_____ Department of Cordley_____ School
Regarding the Progress of___Dolph Simons_____ Date___

Activity	Description of Work Done and Teacher's Comments	Progress
	Dolph has made satisfactory progress in reading. His home work on the library books has been good and he reads well at school His worst fault is inattention.	

Dolph Simons Jr. 1st Grade Report Card,
Mrs. Jeanette Bowersock, teacher, Cordley School, 1935

It was very clear to the little boy that there should be grass growing where there was mostly dirt around his family's new cabin at Gull Lake, Minnesota. So he took a shovel and pail a long way up the dirt driveway where some small patches of green had sprouted between the tire tracks. He dug them up as best he could, then trudged back down to the yard and lay the sod chunks sparsely on the bare dirt. "I made several trips," Dolph chuckled over his earliest memory. "Well, it bothered me that we didn't have any grass... I wanted us to have a nice yard."

This innate sense of "how things should be" would serve Dolph Simons Jr. well as he honed it (and wielded it) over seven decades of his award-winning career.

Dolph Collins Simons Jr. was the third-generation born with ink in his veins to the Simons newspaper family. He was a sturdy, athletic boy who, by the end of middle school, wished he were taller. He had thick dark hair and wideset, intelligent brown eyes over which arched prominent brows, a throwback to his great-grandfather Adolphus Simons.

Graduate Magazine

K.U., March, 1932

Miss Reineke Photo.

Dolph Jr.—Boy With a Future

Dolph Collins Simons II, two-year-old son of Marie Nelson Simons, '28, and Dolph Simons, '25, of Lawrence, is going to smile his way to fame in the world, for he owns a countenance that is irresistible. If, for any reason, he ever meets a situation where smiles fail he will doubtless crash the line for a gain by sheer force. Alumni looking for a sight of a real American, two-fisted, rarin'-to-go, he-man— but charming—boy, meet young Mr. Simons

"If, for any reason, he ever meets a situation where smiles fail, he'll doubtless crash the line for a gain by sheer force."

Dolph Jr., son of 1928 alums Dolph and Marie Simons, makes the *KU Graduate* magazine.

March, 1932.

As a newspaper kid, Dolph grew up like any other boy except he'd had many interesting and educational experiences beyond the classroom. He was blessed with the social ease and cultured manner of his parents; his enthusiastic interest in people from all walks of life was genuine. He'd strike up a conversation with a university chancellor or the UPS deliveryman with equal zeal. Dolph inherited many fine qualities that lent themselves to newspapering, but some were uniquely and indelibly his own.

"Growing up in this business, I got to meet so many interesting people. I was so lucky," Dolph said. "I was porching papers for the Journal-World when I was eight or nine, and I was also exposed to new ideas and information from such an early age. I was so damn lucky. Pam says 'blessed.'"

Professionally and personally, the Simons were well-informed, industrious people. The hard times that nearly broke ancestor Jennie Bessie Simons' family on the Kansas frontier were long past, but hard work and the value of education were still deeply embedded in the DNA of her descendants.

My parents made it very clear—if you're not in school or out for sports, you were expected to have a job. So after school, or when I wasn't at practice or a game, I worked. By third grade, I had a paper route, but I did a lot of other things, too, including:

Mowing lawns. Some of my customers would let their grass grow so long I'd have to sickle it, then rake it up before I could even start to mow.

Selling the Saturday Evening Post door-to-door. This was a great way to meet people and make a few bucks. I knew every address in Lawrence.

Selling garden vegetables out of our large victory garden— probably 100 by 25 feet. All the money went to the war effort. It was a real learning process to keep a garden productive and growing. Dad used it as a teaching experience for John and me.

Harvesting potatoes. I was stationed at the end of the sorting line at the Heck family farm, catching the potatoes in 50-pound burlap bags that I lifted onto a table to be sewn closed by hand.

Working at the Stokely-Van Camp canning factory. My job was collecting the hot cans as they came out of the cooking delivery line. I used a large strap to collect perhaps 15 to 20 cans at a time then pass them onto a cart. Some of the cans would be so hot they'd explode.

Paving streets in Lawrence. It was a physically demanding job, but I liked it. It put me with a different group of interesting people.

Counseling at Camp St. John's, a military school in Wisconsin. I'd gone there as a camper, and went back as camp counselor in addition to overseeing waterfront activities and various sports. As the saying goes, it's all great fun until somebody gets hurt. Well, I was that somebody. I was in a boxing program and got knocked out by my 6'5" opponent in a championship match and spent the night in the hospital. No hard feelings... we ended up good friends.

Painting and sealing the Memorial Stadium at the University of Kansas (KU).

Working for the U.S. Forest Service at Hot Sulphur Springs, Colorado. I worked at a ranger station clearing trails by hand with saws and axes—there were no power tools, repairing downed power lines, and doing all kinds of things. It was physically hard work. I learned how to run down the steep mountain—to hop and turn ski-style. I loved it. Bob Dole got me that job—I was under-age, didn't have a car. When my parents came out to visit, I hitch-hiked a ride on an 18-wheeler down to Denver to meet them for lunch at the Brown Palace Hotel, but the maître de wouldn't let me in because I wasn't shaven!

Selling advertising for the newspaper. Actually, I think I have done just about every job there was at the paper.

My parents really didn't have to encourage this, I looked forward to working. Of course, there were things I didn't enjoy, like pulling a weighted sled to smooth out the rock and freshly poured concrete streets for the paving finishers on hot summer days. My hands were like hamburger from that. My mother would wrap them every night. It was hard work... same at the cannery and the potato farm. I was just dripping, but I didn't mind. I was proud I could do hard work. I didn't mind being exhausted, that meant you were doing something productive. I never liked sitting around on my ass. I liked working. I still do.

Dolph Simons Jr.

Admittedly, life wasn't all work and no play for young Dolph. From earliest childhood, he enjoyed a lively social life. His mother Marie, a former KU Kappa Kappa Gamma sorority girl, organized a full roster of activities from the printed invitations to the handwritten thank you notes. "Mother usually put on a nice birthday party for me with my classmates around the table," Dolph noted. Two of his best buddies, "Paul Coker and Fred Six were always there."

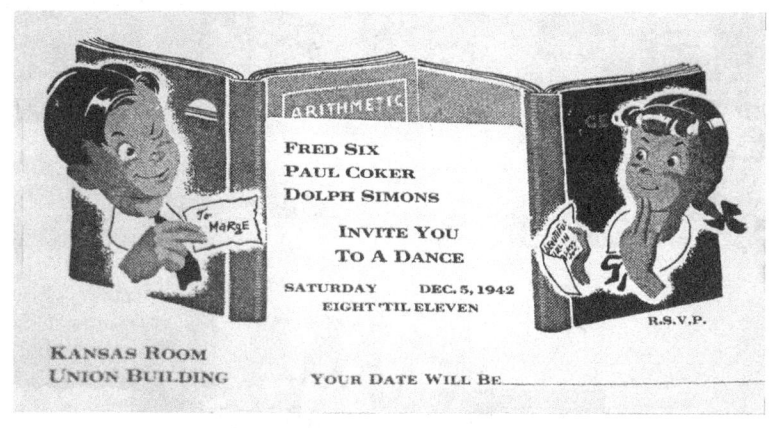

Dolph, Fred, and Paul would remain lifelong friends.

There was a brief, early dalliance in the theatre. Dolph's debut as Humpty Dumpty in a play directed by Fred Six's mother in the Cordley Grade School basement was followed by an appearance as a dwarf in *Snow White and the Seven Dwarves*. However, Dolph's interests lay elsewhere, so that was the extent of his theatrical pursuits.

From Dolph's childhood home on Massachusetts Street, just about everything important in his world was within reach. For a kid, the stately home's "red-tiled roof... fronted by a limestone portico with stone steps, a stone railing, and ornamental limestone posts rising to an arched lintel surmounted by a shaped parapet" (per the property description submitted to the Lawrence Historic Resources Commission)[1] wasn't nearly as wonderful as the basketball hoop and backboard his father installed in the backyard. But the two-story Mission Revival structure was an architectural rarity for that era in Lawrence, and a masterpiece... a fitting home for an editor and publisher of the local newspaper, the *Lawrence Journal-World*.

Dolph's boyhood home at 1509 Massachusetts Street.

The Simons Boys
join Marie and Dolph
in wishing you a

Merry Christmas

For young Dolph and John Simons, this was the center of a neighborhood universe full of families who knew each other. In meticulous detail, Dolph can still recall them.

"The Buehlers were on the left. Their three girls, Beatrice, Phyllis, and Rosemary, always painted their dad's toenails, which we could see from our upstairs window. Their mom was a wonderful high school teacher and their dad was a debate professor at KU. South of our house was the Hunt family. He was a Methodist minister, I think. Their son Bob was one of my heroes. He was a KU basketball player. Many of the KU basketball greats would come visit him and end up shooting baskets in our backyard."

Each family name triggers a unique memory for Dolph who, even as a youngster, had to know the backstory.

"Across the street were the Perkins. Also, the Buhl family who'd moved here from just outside Detroit. Buhl was the Navy ROTC commander during WWII, and Henry Ford II would come visit him. They'd had servants back in Grosse Pointe where they grew up, so apparently, they never learned to cook. My mother taught them some kitchen basics. On one of Mr. Ford's visits, they had my parents over for pressed duck, so Mrs. Buhl must have been a good student."

Next to the Buhls was the Martin family—Mary and Jack. "Mr. Martin managed Sunflower Ordnance Works, the huge munitions plant near DeSoto. It was the largest powder plant in the world at the time, and produced explosives used in WWII. Jack Martin left Lawrence and went on to became president of Hercules Powder company."

Classmate Betty Lou Stephenson lived within walking distance. The day Dolph beat her in a game of marbles, he announced his win proudly at the dinner table. "My dad stopped the conversation dead in its tracks," Dolph remembered. "He said *'You don't win when playing against a girl, and you don't take her marbles. Get up right now, put those marbles in a bag, and take them straight back to her.'* And that's exactly what I did."

Although the Great Depression spanned the first decade of his life, Dolph Jr. was blissfully unaware of it as a child. Dolph Sr. and

Marie Simons were a steady, loving presence that buffered their sons from harsh realities in the wider world. "We had to save everything, turn the lights off when we left a room, things like that. But I was brought up by frugal parents, so that wasn't out of the ordinary," Dolph said. "I know they must have been anxious about things at times, but they kept that to themselves. Mother and Dad made every effort to celebrate our birthdays, have special things for Christmas, and make life feel normal. We didn't miss any meals. Our family was very fortunate."

World War II brought the outside world closer to home. "Most everyone knew someone who'd gone to war. Things were rationed from gasoline to coffee and sugar. Dad would take our cars in to have the tires retreaded because there were no new tires. We planted a huge victory garden, bought war bonds—everything and anything that would help," Dolph recalled. "My mother was involved in collecting things for the war effort. I picked up so much trash and cans for scrap metal. I remember Dad and Granddad guaranteed jobs would be waiting for employees at the paper—no one had to worry about not having a job when they came home from the war."

However distressing circumstances were elsewhere, Dolph had an idyllic adolescence in Lawrence. There was always something to do and friends to do it with, the activities shifting to a more teenage agenda after eighth grade. Of Dolph's many good friends, "Paul Coker, Fred Six, and I maintained a good relationship all those years from kindergarten through college. Fred was a serious student... went on to become a state Supreme Court judge," Dolph noted. "And Paul became famous in his own right."

A physical handicap limited Paul's ability to run. Arrangements were made so he could use the janitor's closet to paint and draw pictures when the other kids were in gym. "He got around... in fact, Paul had the only car in our class. And he became one of the best artists in the country. He did *Mad* magazine, Hallmark cards, and all kinds of movie animation and television cartooning," Dolph recalled. "I got a letter from him not too long before he died in 2022. He wondered what our school superintendent would have thought of what we three had made of ourselves. We sure didn't have a clue back in those days."

Those were the days of awkward high school dances with boys and girls lining opposite sides of the gym. Neighborhood girls who'd been reliable teammates for a pick-up game of kickball were now nubile young ladies strolling on a Saturday afternoon in downtown Lawrence. From their cars parked strategically along the main drag, Dolph, Paul, Fred, Gene Russell, Bob Near, and others watched in a kind of awed bewilderment.

Coming of age in America's heartland was the stuff of movies. The routine of classes, after-school jobs, sports, and homework was followed every evening with dinner as a family for the Simons. Topics on the table included what was going on with the newspaper, KU updates, and events in the community. As with the lesson of the marble game, whatever Dolph and John were learning about life or at school was expanded into further teachable moments over the course of the family meal. "One time, I remember my brother and I were talking about some girl—not very nicely either," Dolph admitted. "All of the sudden, my father hammered the table with his fist as hard as he could. *'I don't want either of you talking about any girl unless you've slept with her yourself! Rumors are terrible. They can ruin lives!'* That's the kind of dad I had."

Dolph's true passion was sports, which began in earnest in high school. To his great dismay, he was not among the tallest, biggest boys chosen to play football as a freshman. This was one of few dark spots on the school years, not counting his recurring black eyes. "I didn't go to opening classes at junior high—maybe even the first year of high school—without a black eye from fights with my brother John," Dolph laughed. "We'd have pretty rough times in our bedroom, but we tried to keep quiet so our parents wouldn't hear. The rule was, I was older so I wasn't supposed to hit John in the face. But he could hit me anywhere he wanted to—and he did."

Of course, Dolph Sr. did hear what his sons were up to, so he arranged boxing lessons to channel their energy more productively. "Dad had a KU student who was a boxer work with us down in our basement. He wanted John and me to know how to take a good hit, get knocked down, and be able to get back up and win a fight," Dolph Jr. said. The training served the brothers well. Although they continued

Dolph Jr. (left) and John Nelson Simons during grade school.

to pound on each other until the bed boards broke, the brothers eventually joined forces and expanded their targets. "If anybody came after one of us, he'd get both of us," Dolph winked.

Lawrence was a great town to grow up in. I thoroughly enjoyed my childhood. I did very well in high school football and was named to some all-state teams. I made good grades—was Phi Beta Kappa, all that. It wasn't because my parents made me study, but the slow infiltration of their influence. From junior high and high school on, I wanted them to be proud of me. I was proud of them. Mother was so gracious; she had a world of friends. Dad was one of only a few small-town newspaper publishers on the Associated Press board.

My brother Dolph was just two years older. He and I never had significant differences in what we thought. We were close. I never felt my parents had anointed him to the newspaper world but not me. Honestly, I was already wondering if I was cut out for that. I figured I'd find something else.

Most of my summers were spent up in Minnesota where I became a fishing guide. That's how I met Dr. John Kirklin, one of the great pioneers in cardiovascular surgery at Mayo's. He suggested I give some thought to going into medicine. I was at an age where I'd not yet committed to my career, and all of the sudden this guy I'm a fishing guide for offers the perfect idea. He got behind me... the rest is history. I became a plastic surgeon and I thoroughly enjoyed it.

With my personality, going into medicine was the right thing to do. It would have been very crowded in the newspaper business. And I don't think I would have been as happy.

I have five children of my own and I try to repeat how my parents conducted themselves. Dad and Mother were as warm and loving as any parents could be. I have no complaints whatsoever with my child-hood, not even about my big brother.[2]

John Nelson Simons

Sunday dinners were usually spent with the grandparents, W.C. and Gertie Simons who lived at The Cedars on Vermont Street just a few blocks away. The aunts, uncles, and cousins were often present, which could, on occasion, spark some hijinks amongst the rabble of youngsters. "Once John was getting picked on and left out. Of course, he was upset," Dolph said. "My dad came to see what the fuss was all about, so we told him. Then Dad took John and me down to the basement for a private talk. He told us we were starting our own secret club, just the three of us. We would have a special handshake and other signals, a motto, and a pledge that only we would know about. Afterwards, we came back upstairs. All the cousins wanted to know what was up, but we just said, 'Nope, we're in a secret club and can't tell you.' My brother and I were walking tall again. That's the kind of dad we had," Dolph said, adding, "And we still have that secret club in the family today. It's still active with exclusive members frequently giving the signal at most any kind of public event."

Dolph's respect and admiration for his dad and mother never dimmed. "My parents were both so smart. And my brother was a brilliant student—truly brilliant in college, and in medical school," he pointed out. "I was the poor student of them all. By comparison to Mother and Dad and John, I felt like the dunce in the corner."

However uneven his academic record may have compared to his brother's, it didn't raise grave concerns at school, with two exceptions. First, with his Latin teacher, Miss Gertrude Ruttan, who "got so upset with me, she kicked the wastebasket across the classroom and yelled, 'Dolph, when are you ever going to figure out conjugation!'," Dolph admitted. With his mother's help, he got through the class.

The second was Chalmer Woodard, his high school football coach who once benched Dolph over a bad report card. "He didn't let me play because my grades weren't good enough. Boy, I can tell you where I was on that bench... the gray bench and the green lockers... the distance from the bench to the locker rooms to the playing field. I remember every single detail," Dolph said. "Woodard was a helluva coach, and a wonderful person, but he taught me more than just football."

Teachers made all the difference. "I had some really good teachers. But when a teacher didn't inspire me, I wasn't a great student," Dolph admitted. "I probably wasn't even a very good student."

Dolph was, however, a standout athlete at Lawrence's Liberty Memorial High School. He was a punter-kicker and guard for the Lawrence Lions—a good one. Good enough to be offered a full-ride to Georgia Tech and other schools (he declined).

The Lawrence Lions went all the way to state and won the championship over Great Bend High in 1946. Dolph certainly earned bragging rights, even if his name rarely made the local paper. Dolph Sr. didn't want to boast in print, but, ironically, "It was when Granddad reminisced that we learned about Dad's gridiron play... his special feats on the field," recalled Dolph Simons III. "Granddad would say something like 'Your dad was a very good football player, he did this or that, but he never wanted to harm another player. He just played tough-nosed football and he excelled at it.' That's how my siblings and I first learned how good he was," Dolph III added. "Dad himself was mum on the subject."

Where there is a jock, there will be girls. Mary or Georgette or someone else was on his arm for dances or an occasional movie, but no one steady for Dolph in high school. Life was full and fun, but he definitely took it seriously. When he famously wrecked two cars on the same icy curve on the same day, it had nothing to do with alcohol or partying, but bad roads on the way to work. "I slid around the corner and smashed right into a concrete pillar. I had to go tell my parents I'd wrecked the car," Dolph explained. "Well, they loaned me Mother's car because I had to have one. Then I went and did the same damn thing again. I thought Dad would have a heart attack, but he handed me his keys," Dolph shrugged. "That's the kind of parents I had."

It took some time for Dolph Simons Jr. to discover the work he was born to do was the business he'd been born into: newspapering. His first inkling of this occurred one Sunday afternoon when he was eleven years old.

"We'd just had Sunday dinner at my grandparent's house like we usually did. I remember I was playing with cars or puzzles on the floor near the dining room... the adults were still at the table talking. All of the sudden, the radio crackled then the announcer interrupted the program. Pearl Harbor had been attacked," Dolph recalled. "It was just shocking. Immediately, Dad said *Let's go... we're putting out a paper.*"

"We'd never published a Sunday paper, but Dad called the team and everybody rushed in," Dolph said. "So, on Sunday, December 7, 1941, the first Journal-World EXTRA edition—our first Sunday paper—was published. Hours after the radio alert, my brother and I were riding our bikes up and down the streets with papers stuffed in our bags, blowing on our dog whistles, yelling "EXTRA! EXTRA!"

Everyone was anxious for news. From the radio reports, they knew what happened, and from the local newspaper, they would learn how it impacted them specifically. Right on the front page of the Journal-World, *"Many Men From Here in Pacific"* provided details about the local boys by location and duty. "One of the most important jobs of the paper," Dolph explained. "is to report on how the news impacts our readers and this community."

That issue of the *Lawrence Journal-World* EXTRA premiered at the same time Walter Cronkite made his on-camera debut covering Pearl Harbor, "the biggest assignment any reporter could have in this war," as Cronkite put it.[3] Dolph remembers feeling much the same. "Even as a little kid, I could see how important our paper was. I was so proud of W.C. and my dad for having a job like that."

Publishing a newspaper was a responsibility, that was clear to young Dolph. Furthermore, being in a newspaper family imposed a code of conduct. "I never wanted to compromise the newspaper

Dolph Collins Simons Jr., Lawrence High Class of 1947

or embarrass my family," Dolph said. "That was always on my mind with whatever I was doing." His brother John concurred, adding, "I just didn't want to disappoint Mother and Dad. They had invested so much of their time in me."

In addition to continuing the work of the *Lawrence Journal-World*, Dolph Sr. and Marie avidly carried on W.C.'s legacy of family values. They went to their sons' games, helped with homework, and included the boys in social engagements and community activities. Doing things as a family was the priority. "A child is really blessed if he gets that time with his parents—if those parents are encouraging and advising," Dolph said. "Dad and Mother set a standard with their behavior. Always do your best, Dad would say. *Give yourself the satisfaction that you did the very best you could.*"

His father's guidance was high-minded but not heavy-handed. "He shared his ideas but didn't beat me over the head with them." Dolph Sr. was always concerned about having undue influence over his son's decisions. In fact, when Dolph Jr. concluded "maybe it was a good idea to go to the University of Kansas, make friends and contacts there," his father arranged to be gone on a fishing trip to Alaska during fraternity rush week. "Dad made sure he wasn't even reachable so there'd be no pressure on me to join Phi Psi, the fraternity he'd been a part of."

In the fall of 1947, with Chancellor Deane Malott at KU's helm, frosh Dolph Simons Jr. pledged Phi Delta Theta and launched into college life. Dolph moved into the frat house on Edgehill Road. He liked his roommates Victor Eddy and Chuck Hall, and being a room orderly to Ray Evans, "Red" Hogan, and Gene Conklin. "That involved making sure their shoes were shined and, on occasion, finding wherever Gene Conklin had been hung up on a hangar in a closet somewhere in the fraternity house." Those were heady days full of new friends and, as always, sports.

As in high school, football brought the best out of Dolph in college. He signed on with the KU Jayhawks who'd made an attractive offer—one that Dolph had to refuse. "My dad wouldn't let me take the athletic scholarship at KU because he didn't want to deny anyone

Jayhawker All-American Dolph Simons

else that resource," Dolph explained. This had an unintended consequence. "The athletic director called me into his office and explained that others felt I was showing off my family's income, which I wasn't. He made me accept the scholarship in my second year."

Without a doubt, Dolph had earned the honor. He was the leading punter in the Big Seven where he also received recognition as a guard.

Athletics were all-consuming for Dolph, but in a good way. "Football was different in those days," he recalled. "There weren't special diets, we didn't have weight rooms or work out throughout the year. Teammates included John Amberg, Mike McCormick, Lynn Smith... our team had many local players. As freshmen, we'd scrimmage against the varsity. The rule was the varsity couldn't leave the field until they scored against the freshmen. They'd have to put up lights around the field the games would go on so long. It was a helluva lot of fun."

By the time he was a senior, Dolph started and played every minute of offense that year, except in three games. His punting average was 46.4 yards, and, as reported in the December 9, 1950 issue of *Collier's* magazine, "many of his kicks were pin-pointed on the sideline stripe." He was named "All-American Specialist" kicker by *Collier's* that year.[4] A photograph of his winning form was taken for a possible (but not chosen) *Sports Illustrated* cover when the National Collegiate Athletic Bureau reported his punting average as seventh highest in the nation.[5]

Dolph Jr. was a guard on the KU football team during the 1948, 1949, and 1950 seasons. In addition, he was the punter for all three seasons. He complained that in those days, punts into the end zone led to a subtraction of 20 yards from the kick's distance. He led the Jayhawks in punting as a sophomore in 1948 with 34 kicks for a 36.9-yard average. In 1950, as a senior, he averaged 41.1 yards on 32 punts, a school record that stood until 1954 when Ted Rohde (43.7) broke it. Dolph Jr. couldn't get his picture in the local paper because his father didn't want to appear to be playing favorites.

The coach all three years that Dolph Jr. played for the Jayhawks was J.V. Sykes. Although Sikes was a good enough coach, visitors were discouraged from watching practice because of Sikes' language and the combative style of practices. If two players got angry at one another, the team would form a circle and the two would have a fistfight.

Dolph recalled that in practice, one of the assistant coaches would spit tobacco juice on his calf where it would run down into his shoe. If he flinched, he had to run laps. "It was awful. It was a different time." He also recalled vividly the day that Sykes screamed and chewed out a player and ran him off the practice field, ostensibly for being a slacker. It turned out the player had polio.

Ralph Gage, Journal-World Managing Editor

His academic record wasn't quite as stellar, but "better than average... with great scholastic improvement during his senior year" according to Chancellor Malott's letter of reference upon Dolph's graduation.[6] "I always did well for teachers who were passionate about their subject and passed that along to the students. I had some incredible teachers," Dolph noted. "Along with Walter Sandelius, who taught political science, I guess Ozzy Backus was among the best of them."

Fluent in Russian, Professor Oswald "Ozzy" Backus had worked in intelligence during World War II.[7] His vast expertise and enthusiasm enriched every lecture. "It was obvious he knew so much from firsthand experience. He established KU's first library exchange system with Warsaw, Poland, and one in the Soviet Union. You knew you would learn something in his class."

There's been much discussion about whether the Greek System really offers anything of value to students. Fraternities and sororities have been criticized for setting themselves up as something special, being too exclusive, and doing nothing but partying. In my time, the guys at Phi Delt were not in college just to drink and carouse. There were freshmen through seniors along with a mixture of WWII veterans. We were all there to get an education and make connections that would help us in the future. It was also a good way to develop friendships with those in other fraternities and sororities. I had the good fortune of becoming acquainted with a number of outstanding young men and women.

Yes, we got hazed. During my freshman year, I frequently showed up in the football shower room with bruises from my butt to my knees from the "boards." It wasn't fun, but if you passed the muster, you had that in common with your pledge-mates and everybody in the house. You proved you were tough enough. Nowadays, there are too many reports of extreme hazing and other initiation rituals that have gotten out of hand. This has resulted in some deaths and the banning of some fraternities from campuses. It's left a terrible stain on the reputation of the Greek system and the positive impact that it can have. It's a shame that something that was once such a positive experience and resource has spiraled down that path.

The Greek system is great when it's done right. A good house mother who cracks the whip and alums who keep an eye on things are a big part of that. I made lifelong friends at Phi Delt. When my roommate Vic got married to a wonderful girl named Carol, I was best man at his wedding. He went on to become a doctor in Hays, Kansas. It's been great to see how the Phi Delts have turned out, and that's true of many fraternities and sororities. There's a good percentage of KU alums from those organizations who have turned out to be very successful in their careers and strong fiscal supporters of the school.

Dolph Simons Jr.

As a course of study, Dolph Jr. felt no pressure to go into journalism. History had a strong appeal, and he could have easily pursued a path into the foreign service or even forestry, based on his successful summer stint in Colorado. Eager to learn and unafraid of

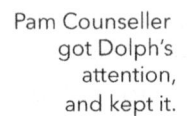

Pam Counseller got Dolph's attention, and kept it.

—World-Herald News Service Photo.

Jayhawk Gridder Turns Scribe

Dolph Simons, who'll be bidding for a guard job on the Kansas football team this fall, is taking it easy while other Jayhawkers toil at manual labor. Simons is serving as a reporter for the Lawrence Journal-World this summer.

"They have been four happy and beneficial years," Dolph wrote for the KU school paper upon graduation, adding, "The future is severe and uncertain."[8]

hard work, he was interested in almost everything. The world was ripe with opportunities. "Dad encouraged me to do whatever I wanted to do," Dolph said. "But I guess journalism came pretty naturally to me." Indeed, for a young man curious about so many things, journalism would serve quite well. Looking ahead to his future, "I couldn't wait... I hated to be missing out on anything, and I liked a challenge."

But the allure of all that dimmed in light of two preeminent developments that engaged all his attention.

The first pressing matter was the Korean War. After graduating from KU with a journalism degree in 1951, Dolph Simons Jr. eagerly enlisted in the Marines.

The second was far more appealing: Pamela Counseller.

Dolph Simons and Pam Counseller's meeting seemed destined, if a bit happenstance. Every summer, the Simons headed up to their cottage on Gull Lake in Minnesota—the same one Dolph tried to landscape as a boy. "I'd invited some fraternity brothers and football buddies up to our place. We were over at the cottage of some friends from Kansas City on another part of the lake," Dolph recalled. "That's where I saw a very attractive girl standing on a nearby dock in a very attractive bikini."

According to the story that's been told and retold in the family for decades since that fateful day in 1950, Dolph announced, "I want to meet that girl."

Pam's account is similar. "My family had a cabin on Gull Lake near Brainerd. The Simons' cottage was in a different bay, so I never met them. But the people who had a place next door to us were from Kansas City. I think Dolph was visiting them when he saw me on the dock... we went from there."

A blind date was arranged after strenuous vetting by various adults who stepped in for Pam's parents, who were out of town at the time. KU Alum and Mayo physician Dr. Claude Dixon was a mutual friend of both the Counsellers and the Simons who vouched for Dolph's character. All that build-up led to "a date so amazing it must have blown my mind," Dolph chuckled. "Honestly, we have both tried to remember where we went and what we did, but neither of us can recall, so it must have been mind-blowing!"

Dolph was indeed smitten. By the end of his senior year at KU, he was ready to get serious and exclusive, although that part got awkward. "On the night after KU graduation, I had a date with Betsy, a

Lawrence, Kansas, Saturday, December 22, 1951.

Society

SOCIAL CALENDAR

Saturday
Marriage of Miss Darlene Schindler and Bill Schaake, 4 o'clock, First Methodist Church.
Marriage of Miss Clara Bell Mar-Lawrence Duplicate Bridge Club, 8 p. m., Castle Tea room.
Mr. and Mrs. W. H. Schindler, bridal dinner for Miss Darlene Schindler and William Schaake.
L. B. Club, dinner at the home of Mr. and Mrs. William Frowe.
keson and Eugene C. Riling, 10 o'clock, St. John's Catholic Church.
Mr. and Mrs. Roland Roney, bridal dinner for Miss Rita Roney and Gaylord Glenn Hunt, The Hearth.
Sunday
Marriage of Miss Nancy Gross and Jerry Zachary, 8 p. m., Danforth Chapel; reception at the Gamma Phi Beta house.

Dr. and Mrs. Virgil S. Counseller of Rochester, Minn., announce the engagement of their daughter, Pamela, to Lt. Dolph Collins Simons, Jr., of the United States Marine Corps. The wedding is planned for February.
Miss Counseller is a graduate of Walnut Hill School, Natick, Mass., and attended the University of Arizona at Tucson. She is a member of Delta Gamma Sorority.
Lieutenant Simons, a son of Mr. and Mrs. Dolph Collins Simons, now is stationed at Quantico, Va. He is a graduate of the University of Kansas, where he was a member of the football team. He is a member of Phi Delta Theta Fraternity, and Sigma Delta Chi, honorary journalism fraternity.

FIANCEE OF LT. DOLPH SIMONS JR.—Miss Pamela Counseller, daughter of Dr. and Mrs. Virgil S. Counseller of Rochester, Minn., whose engagement to Lieutenant Simons is announced today. The wedding is planned for February.

very special, wonderful girl I'd spent quite a bit of time with during my junior and senior years. The next day, I took her to the train station in Lawrence and said goodbye as she left for her home in another state.

Then I immediately jumped in my car and drove over to Topeka to meet another train bringing Pam here to meet my family. I am not very proud of how I handled that, and I've always felt badly for the 'other' girl. But I sure am glad the other 'other' girl said yes when I eventually proposed."

With an easy laugh, outgoing personality, and stunning good looks, Pamela Counseller was a catch. More than that, she was the ideal life partner for Dolph. Pam was comfortable in society and well-grounded by her family. Her father, Virgil Sheetz Counseller, born in 1892, had been orphaned at age nine. He overcame poverty, trauma, and tremendous odds to become a doctor in 1920 at Rush Medical College at the University of Chicago. "My daddy came from nothing," Pam emphasized. By 1924, Dr. Virgil S. Counseller was a Fellow in Surgery at the Mayo Foundation in Rochester, Minnesota. His post-graduate teachers and mentors, Drs. William and Charles Mayo, for whom the clinic was named, took Virge under their wing and into their family. The Mayos and the Counsellers would remain close all their lives.

Virgil married Gladys Britton of Lansing, Michigan, in 1922. Initially, they thought she couldn't have children, so they adopted their first daughter, Virginia. "Then bing-bing-bing, three more of us were born one right after the other," laughed Pam. "Cynthia, David, and me. I was the baby of the family."

"Apparently, they had a perfect life... there was never a harsh word, no one got their mouth washed out with soap or was spanked, and no one lost their temper," Dolph interjects. Tongue firmly in cheek, he goes on, "According to Pam, she had perfect parents, was a perfect child, and never knew strife of any kind until she met me." The story always brings a laugh, but Pam insists it was true.

Virgil and Gladys doted on their four children, and indulged their youngest daughter's love of horses. Charles and Alice Mayo, Pam's godparents, let her board her horse at their farm in the countryside. Pam went to Walnut Hill School for the Arts in Natick, Massachusetts, and Brownmoor School in Scottsdale, Arizona. She attended the University of Arizona, Tucson, where she became a member of Delta Gamma sorority.

Summers drew the Counsellers to their cottage on Gull Lake.

The infamous bikini scene on the dock that got Dolph's undivided attention makes for a good story that gets told again and again, but Pam always has to correct her husband on one point of order: The swimsuit wasn't a bikini.

Their long-distance courtship continued when Dolph left Gull Lake for Parris Island, South Carolina, to enter the Marine Corps. In his absence, brother John was given the not-unpleasant task of keeping an eye on his future sister-in-law. Dolph would later tease, always in Pam's presence so she'd have a chance to retort, "John was smarter than me, and handsomer than me, I think you must have secretly fallen in love with him." Pam rolls her eyes and drags out each word in playful exasperation, "I did not!"

Boot camp at Parris Island lasted three months. "Athletics prepared me well for basic training. I was used to getting hit and hurt," Dolph said. "And I'd had some really tough, critical coaches, so I could handle the demanding drill instructors."

Pam was on his mind, which made for a pleasant distraction. While still at Parris Island, Dolph wrote Dr. Virgil Counseller to ask permission to marry his daughter. "I can't believe he okayed me," Dolph reflected, incredulously. "She was 19... I was 21 and very likely headed to a combat zone." But Pam's parents approved heartily of Dolph, and Dolph Sr. and Marie were equally delighted with Pam. The date was set for early the next year. Invitations went out, and Dolph's grandfather W.C. Simons RSVP'd warmly to the Counsellers, "Pam is a sweet, charming girl, and I am looking forward to the time when she and Dolph will have their home here in Lawrence. I shall be very happy to have Pamela as a member of our family, and I do hope I will be able to attend the wedding."[9] He did.

After basic training, Dolph was sent to Virginia to finish his specialty training at Quantico where he found himself back on the gridiron. "I didn't try out for the Marine Corps team, but my college football experience was in my record," Dolph said. "So I was asked if I wanted to play... well, sir, YES, SIR!" He was a guard and punter for their 1951 fall season. "We were up against other Marine teams and regular college teams. The Quantico Marines Football team had some great players—a number who'd been outstanding college players, several who'd been professional, and others who went onto the pros after the service. I felt so fortunate to be a part of that. It was a great experience."

Once his training was complete, Dolph awaited his MOS: the Military Occupation Specialty code that would include his assignment. His primary MOS was Infantry Platoon Officer, so Dolph steeled himself for news that he'd be headed overseas. Instead, Second Lieutenant Dolph C. Simons Jr. was assigned as public information officer to the El Toro Air-Fleet Marine Force Pacific in California, his secondary MOS. "Maybe my newspaper background played into this, I don't know, but Pam and my mother were sure relieved."

There wasn't much time to get married before reporting for duty at El Toro. "My buddies at Quantico made sure I got an ugly haircut," then Dolph headed north to Rochester, Minnesota, for his wedding.

Mr. and Mrs. Simons' honeymoon was spent driving from Minnesota to California. "Of course, we had to make a stop in Lawrence to drop off my civilian clothing, and give Pam some time with her new mother-in-law," Dolph jokes, his eyes twinkling when he tells the story years later. "I never had a problem with your mother," Pam counters. Dolph pushes back. "Not even the time she surprised

Dolph and Pam were married in Rochester, Minnesota on February 7, 1952.

you by painting the trim in our house in your 'favorite' color?" Pam does a quick eye roll, "Well, she might have asked me what my favorite color was."

The repartee ensues as it has since the beginning of their relationship, playful and familiar. Mother-in-law jokes are Dolph's go-to wisecrack, but it's all in good fun. "Kidding aside, Mother never had a daughter until Pam, and she might have been a bit over-zealous in her attentions," Dolph acknowledges. Pam assures, "We've always had a lot of fun together."

The newlyweds finally arrived at Riverside and settled into the southern California lifestyle. "I was stationed at El Toro Air Base, so we moved into an apartment nearby at Laguna Beach. We lived right at the ocean for about a year and a half. We were madly in love and being on the water was so much fun... we were body-surfing every day," Dolph said. "Actually, I was body-surfing... I don't think Pam was having as much fun as me because she soon became pregnant. That curtailed her surfing."

Lt. Dolph Simons Jr. applied his journalistic chops to the task of media relations and public communications.

Pam enjoyed the perks of an officer's wife at El Toro Air Base.

Dolph and Pam were excited to have a baby. It was a joyful time as a couple, although the contrast to the military realities during wartime was stark. Unlike the esprit de corps America had known during WWII, tens of thousands of U.S. soldiers died in the Korean War that ended in a humiliating stalemate.[10] "Until I went into the service, I didn't really concern myself with world affairs," Dolph admitted. "I watched my first television show when I was at home on leave from Parris Island. My parents were so disappointed because all I wanted to do was watch television while I was there," Dolph said.

News of the world was now directly related to his job. What was happening overseas was on his daily agenda at El Toro. After work, "The 6 p.m. newscast became regimented. TV trays came out so we could watch the news while we ate."

El Toro was the permanent Master Jet Station for the Fleet Marine Forces in the Pacific in the 1950s. As the primary air base for Marine Corps west coast fighter squadrons and helicopters, it was an invaluable asset during the Korean War. As public information officer, Lt. Dolph Simons Jr. served as a conduit of communications between the base and the media, other military operations, and with the public. Dolph would rise to the rank of captain during his service at El Toro. While stationed there, he gained another title as well: Dad.

Pam and Dolph welcomed Pamela Ann Simons on February 2, 1953, at the hospital in Riverside, California. Little Pammie's name came about spontaneously, according to her mother. "I was pretty

Dolph Sr. thoroughly enjoyed squiring Pam and Marie around.

groggy from the medications they gave me during childbirth. After I delivered, a nurse came to get the birth certificate filled out," Pam recalled. Daughter Linda picked up the story that's been well-chronicled in family lore, "...and someone suggested 'Marie' which brought Mom right out of her fog. The only name Mom could think of to counter that suggestion was her own!" Pam shook her head, "I think it was Dolph who suggested my name, which surprised me," she admitted. "And that's what we went with!"

In July of that year, the Korean Armistice agreement was signed,[10] and Dolph's term was up. Captain Simons was honorably discharged. The young family moved back to Lawrence, where the home that had been his grandparents awaited them. Dolph Sr. and Marie had arranged for the purchase of The Cedars after W.C. passed on in May 1952, only months after Pam and Dolph's wedding.

"Apparently, my mother was trying to get it all fixed up for us," Dolph Jr. noted, fleshing out the infamous story. "She got some steel wool and scrubbed the paint off all the interior trim. Then she repainted it and an upstairs porch in colors she thought Pam would like." Such "good intentions" took various forms over the years. Pam acknowledges, "She always meant well." Dolph doesn't hesitate to fill in the gaps. "I know there was a point when Pam got so exasperated, she marched right down to the Journal-World, into Dad's office, and had a heart-to-heart talk. That got back to Mother, who finally got the message."

Dolph Sr. adored his daughter-in-law and his wife, and it showed. "I remember one time my dad came up the gravel driveway in a two-wheeled horse and buggy one snowy morning just to tell Pam Merry Christmas," Dolph said. "He arranged that just for her. That's the kind of father-in-law she had."

Three more children would be born to Dolph and Pam in Lawrence. Linda Kathryn arrived on February 28, 1955; Dolph Collins III on May 8, 1957; and Dan Counseller on June 24, 1961. The household bustled with activity while Dolph Jr. stepped into his role as a newspaper editor and publisher.

The first major step was a big one—4,380 miles away to London.

"This Writer" is Dolph Simons Jr.

With two fingers, Dolph Jr. "hammered on a black 1936 model upright manual typewriter. Often the periods and commas perforated the typing paper, and some keys that had been repaired were out of alignment."

Ralph Gage

CHAPTER 6

The Catalyst

Never argue with a man
who buys his ink by the barrel.[1]

Being born into a newspaper family was definitely an advantage, I was so damn lucky. I like to think I'd have ended up in this business one way or another, although it certainly wouldn't be for my typing skills.

When I started, I worked in advertising, in circulation, and then as a rookie in the newsroom. There were some copy editors in there who must have bitten their lip trying to make my stories hang together.

I want to thank Franklin Murphy, the best chancellor KU ever had, in my opinion, for pushing me to broaden my experience by working overseas. He thought I should see what's out there beyond Kansas. Maybe he thought something would take seed. So I wrote a letter to A.P. Wadsworth, editor of the *Manchester Guardian* in Great Britain, but they weren't hiring. Then I wrote to Sir William Haley, editor of London's *The Times*. He replied positively on November 17, 1955, and that's how I ended up in Europe in January 1956.

It was very interesting to see how things got done at *The Times*. My assignments were general news reporting and as an "expert correspondent" on aviation—my experience at El Toro

Marine Air Base came in handy for that. I covered the landing of a Soviet TU-104 bomber in England— the first time it had been seen outside Russia. Of course when I tried to get on the plane, I got booted off.

Another reporter, David Wood, often took me to the *Times'* reserved box to listen to debates in Parliament. That was a good education. Actually, most of the time I was over there, I did more listening than writing. I was learning about argumentation, the Common Market, globalization, so much... not to mention which were the best pubs in the city. We visited so many historical sites and met such interesting people.

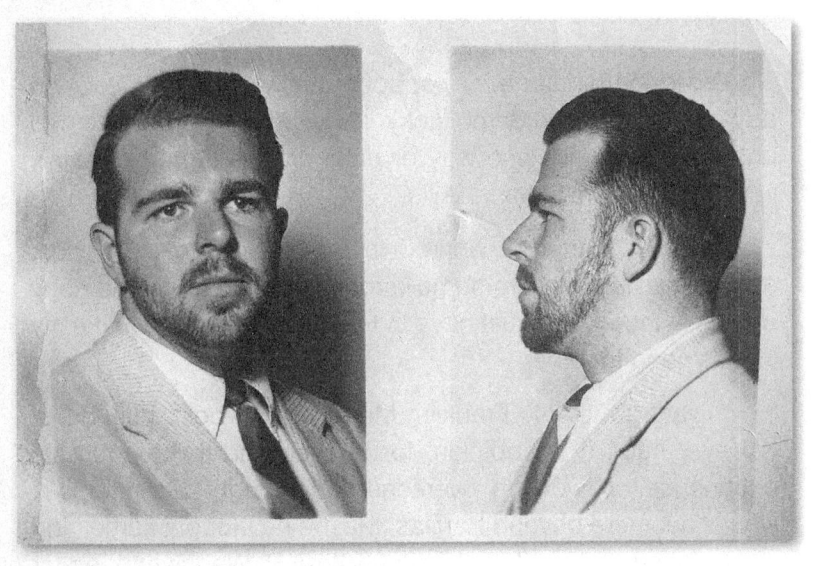

Headed to *The Times* in London: Dolph C. Simons, Jr. Passport Photos

I remember being at the Savoy Hotel for a luncheon when Harry Truman came walking through—he was there doing a press conference. I'd met him in Kansas City seeking his advice about going to work for *The Times*. I couldn't believe he recognized me, and stopped to ask how I was doing. You had to admire that man. He was an ordinary man—a clothing salesman—but he rose to the highest office in the land. I respected him.

Pam and our two small daughters, Pammie and Linda, came along and we lived in a flat in Pitts Head Mews in Westminster. It was an ideal location as we could walk to Buckingham Palace, the Marble Arch, and Hyde Park. It was often cold and rainy. Pam was a good sport about washing diapers in the bathtub, hanging laundry to dry on the radiator pipes, and putting meals together with unfamiliar ingredients.

What I learned in London opened my eyes. My route to work every day took me by Piccadilly Circus and Trafalgar Square... I passed prostitutes along Curzon Street, and would look up at Rupert Murdoch's apartment right above The Green Park. I'd been his guest there, and told him I admired how he fought the unions in London.

I also discovered I had (barely) enough Scottish heritage to wear a kilt of Fraser plaid to the annual Scottish Tourism Board's gathering of the Press Clan in Glasgow.[2] I was representing the London *Times* on that trip, and was asked to make a toast at Cullen Castle, and again at the main government house in Edinburgh.

It was in London where I realized I really liked writing op-ed. In fact, that's where I wrote what would eventually become the Saturday Column, although at that time, Dad published my Times' articles in the news section on page two of the Journal-World.

Experiencing all these new things in Great Britain—looking at the different lifestyles and learning what people were concerned about in that country—it was so fascinating to me. And it prompted me to look for another international challenge. That opportunity came just a couple years later.

The Star in Johannesburg, South Africa, hired me as a political reporter. Conditions in that country were pretty

The family in London.

intense at the time, so I didn't bring my family with me. Politics were rough and tumble—more so than anything I'd seen up to that point. There was an election going on where one politician proclaimed everyone who voted for him would go to heaven, and those against him would go to hell. What I saw there made me think American politics weren't all that tough by comparison. I met the owner/editor of *Die Vaderland*, an

Afrikaans newspaper, and he invited me to write about what I was seeing, so I did.

Looking back, since I was working for *The Star* at the time, I should have asked about contributing a guest article in another paper. A mug shot of me was printed with it, and that didn't go over too well on several levels. I think I violated a policy against writing for competing papers. Plus, some of the other reporters at *The Star* weren't too happy this "guest reporter" didn't get in trouble over that, which I can understand.

Apparently, that wasn't my biggest problem. There was some risk that I might actually get kicked out of the country for criticizing apartheid. "Freedom of the Press" wasn't how things worked in that country, compared to America. I'd written a critical story concerning a bicycle accident where the ambulance picked up the European man who'd been hurt, but left the injured native courier on the curb—he was bleeding from his head but they just left him there. That's apartheid.

Although I didn't get a tongue lashing directly from an editor, I felt the disappointment and perhaps disapproval from him and my fellow reporters. Maybe everybody there was relieved when I went back to Kansas. A number of the stories I'd written were also published in the Journal-World back home, so I received many invitations to speak about my experiences when I returned.

From my point of view, I had to wonder how apartheid was any different from us coming to this country and pushing the Indians off the land we wanted. I wrote comparisons between our pioneers and explorers moving west and settling "Indian" territory and the Dutch pushing north and colonizing Africa. The only difference as far I could see was we landed at Plymouth Rock and they landed at Cape Town.

White Europeans in South Africa were never going to comprise a majority. Tribal people always outnumbered the

European colonists. Killing them or oppressing them was the only way the white minority could survive, so they imposed the rules of "apartheid" (forced separation based on race) to maintain control. The majority were forced, one way or another, to work down in the mines or be in service to the white colonials. The injustice of that made for some tense and violent times.

Pam knew a family from Minnesota who'd moved to South Africa to start a business. They lived adjacent to a large mining operation, and I looked them up and visited on several occasions. The Kenyan Mau Mau uprising of '52 was still on everybody's mind, so I asked them if they were afraid or concerned about living there. They said no, at least they

Simons (right) openly criticized apartheid while reporting in South Africa in 1958.

weren't afraid their "Sally" (housekeepers were usually called "Sally") would kill them. It was understood that their Sally would go next door and kill that family, and that family's Sally would come kill them.

In the hotel where I was living in Johannesburg, I frequently heard the hangars in my closet clinking together. I knew it was from the tremor of gold mining operations underground. I wanted to know what was happening and write about that, so I used my connections and got into a mine near the town of Springs to see what conditions were really like. Mine officials provided me with the gear and I went down to 9,650 feet. I spent the day down there… it was a different world. Upstairs, apartheid was the law of the land—it was how the world worked 365 days a year. Down in the mine, things were different. It was more equal. Everybody had to pull his weight. There was a feeling of "you take care of your job, and I'll take care of mine, no matter what color we are."

Working conditions were harsh. The dangers were immense, so mine safety was the goal. It was extremely humid and hot; the rock was so hot, the farther down you went felt like you were getting closer to hell. I went out into the stopes, sliding on my butt down to the next level, then skidding and sliding down further, hoping there wasn't a pressure burst or falling rock. Explosions happened and miners got killed—this was not unusual. Even more fatalities came from silicosis, the disease caused by inhaling rock dust from the jackhammering and blasting.

It was kind of ironic that up on the surface there was an exercise and playground area for the miners. They were able to enjoy some recreation, and perhaps they did have fun. What I remember mostly is this was where the witch doctors set up shop, ready to tell the miner his fortune. If they predicted bad luck with the bones they threw, that was deadly serious. You'd better buy in… nobody shrugged that off. It was not a show for tourists, it was all business. For those miners, it was what they relied on. It gave them a heads up and they lived by it.

Experiences like this showed me the many different ways people live and why they think the way they do. The more you experience the world outside your own backyard, the more you understand the complex challenges in ways you never imagined. The things I saw in South Africa had a huge impact on me. This certainly made me more aware of how lucky we are in this country, and how we must never take our freedom for granted.

You've got to stand for things that make your country stronger and better. Not everybody is on the same page about what that means, but hell, I think newspapers can and should play a huge role in the process of figuring it out. Looking back, I guess I was figuring out what my part was, and the experiences I had abroad worked better than any classroom for learning it.

After my time in Africa, I had planned to go work for an English-language newspaper in India, but didn't follow through, which I'd later regret. I'd have loved to learn about that country. I hoped there would be many more international experiences for me later. I did try to get a visa from Communist Chinese authorities in 1964,[3] but that didn't work out. I wasn't alone—no visas to bonafide journalists traveling to the People's Republic of China were approved during that era. Several times I worked all my connections to gain permission to go to Russia and observe one of their rocket launches, but got no reply.

At any rate, the fact was, the Vietnam War was intensifying and it was shocking to learn how much of that controversy centered on Kansas. Pam was there with the children, and I needed to get back to Lawrence. Things were really heating up on the home front.

Dolph Simons Jr.

During the 1960s to early '70s, Lawrence, Kansas, was a hotbed of civil unrest. It was as though the city's violent history a century earlier had been smoldering below the surface of the quiet university town. The citizens, city officials, and leaders representing multiple special interests had been able to cushion the edginess, but the pressures of the war in Vietnam and civil rights discord finally converged at KU, splitting into a fissure that spread across campus into town.

Lawrence exploded with radicalized activism.

In May of 1965, KU's staff and students associated with the university's Democratic Society had participated peacefully enough in "teach-ins." These were held simultaneously on 122 college campuses nationwide to discuss the Vietnam war via radio link. But the antiwar zeitgeist elevated across the country. By October 1969, one of the nation's largest protests occurred in Lawrence with 3,500 students, faculty, and local citizens taking to the streets on National Vietnam Moratorium Day.[4] Political and social activist Abbie Hoffman visited campus to support "radicals" demanding the university take an official position on the war.[5]

Racial discrimination was another flashpoint in an arsenal of crises in Lawrence.

Kansas already had ten legal cases before Brown v. Topeka Board of Education rose to the U.S. Supreme Court in 1954.[6] That landmark decision mandated desegregation, but Kansas schools were far from integrated even a decade later.[7] Indeed, African Americans were still not welcome at KU football games, Lawrence's public swimming pool or golf courses. In her 2010 retrospective, *Lawrence Journal-World* reporter Christine Metz characterized Lawrence in early 1970 as a time when "...blacks weren't hired as downtown sales clerks or bank tellers... The city had undrawn lines on who lived where. And as the city's commercial districts grew, residential areas for blacks shrunk."[8]

On a national scale, Lawrence became ground-zero for some of the biggest stories of that time. Buildings at the university were bombed and set on fire.[9] In town, there was extensive property damage to buildings, vehicles, and the local courthouse. The "Weather Underground," a far-left militant organization, sent threats in writing to the KU chancellor and Journal-World demanding Black Panther Angela Davis be freed or "We will blast and shoot our way to freedom! You have been warned!"[10] Clashes between protesters and law enforcement led to physical altercation and death. The exoneration of a police officer for the killing of a KU student further escalated tensions.[11]

The locus of the story was captured every day in the *Lawrence Journal-World*. When Rick "Tiger" Dowdell, a KU African American freshman, was shot and killed by police, the Journal-World published the Kansas Bureau of Investigation's report in its entirety. It was an audacious editorial decision, but typical of the Journal-World's comprehensive, transparent approach.

To manage the coverage, Dolph Simons Jr. found an ally in Ralph Gage. Gage was a KU alum who came to the Journal-World in October of 1969 after serving as a reporter with the *Metro-East Journal* in East St. Louis, Illinois. "I got away from all the racial strife there just in time for all the campus strife here," Gage said.

Lawrence was the scene of so much conflict it made the news coast to coast. It represented "America in microcosm, beset with university turmoil, drug problems, and racial and generation polarization," according to *Harper's Magazine* in 1970.[12] *The Los Angeles Times* reported "The threat of vigilante action hangs over Lawrence, a troubled town in which groups on the left and the right have become increasingly hostile," in December 1970.[13] Times staff writer Bryce Nelson wrote, "It is the jungle in Lawrence... Left-wing militancy and violence at the university and among blacks increases anxiety of those in organizations determined to repress such activity. More activity among militant citizens' organizations increases the fear and armaments of opposing groups."

During this turbulent time, Dolph Jr. had been named president and publisher of the *Lawrence Journal-World*. He was also president of the Kansas Press board and a board director of the national Associated Press. As such, he had an extreme close-up on local coverage with a

Dolph at his desk, circa 1970s.

Dad was known as the "King of Hearts" and had a bounty on him. On his desk was a photo of a group of demonstrators where he'd noted each person who'd threatened to kill him. At dinner time, Dad would ask us kids what we'd do if somebody threw a pipe bomb through our window right now... we had to know where to go.

Dan Simons

simultaneous wide view of its national relevance. Simons exercised every journalistic muscle of his newspaper, deployed every diplomatic skill he himself possessed—and he learned some new ones fast.

Those were challenging times, even life-threatening times... protests were happening everywhere. There'd been demonstrations going on at the university since '65, but the burning of the KU Student Union in 1970 really localized and intensified everything. I was in New York City at an AP board meeting when I saw a large front-page story and photo of the

National Guard surrounding Lawrence High School in one of the New York papers. There were photos of barriers on highways leading into Lawrence that shocked and alarmed me. I got my tail back home then.

A lot of radicals were moving through Lawrence. The demonstrations and violence escalated to the point a young black man from Lawrence, "Tiger" Dowdell, was shot by a police officer. There were a lot of versions of how that happened. There were rumors and then gag orders were imposed. Lawrence felt like a war zone. This was the kind of thing that happened elsewhere, not right here in our pleasant university town. But it was here; it was very real, and it got personal.

I was standing with a group outside the courtroom where witnesses to the Dowdell shooting were being interviewed. A sniper took a shot at us, or maybe it was directed at me, I don't know. Fortunately, nobody was killed or injured, but my thought was I'd sure rather have them come in and talk directly to me than shoot at me to make their point. So I started working up to midnight or later with a well-publicized open-door policy. I didn't want anybody to think I was afraid or intimidated, so I left the drapes in my first-floor office wide open to show I was there and had nothing to hide. I was willing to hear everybody's side of the story.

Late one night, I was there by myself, sitting in front of the window, in came the young man I believed was involved somehow with the fires around town. He wore a dashiki, and walked right in and jumped up on top of my desk like a hellraiser. I just looked at him and said, "OK, Leonard, I know you didn't do it... but I know you know who did. Level with me." He opened his hand and dropped a couple bullets on top of my desk. He wasn't screwing around, and he wanted me to know that. I don't recall feeling afraid, and we just talked. I heard him out and he heard me.

At some point, I had this idea that if the student leaders and town leaders would just sit down together and have a genuine heart to heart, it could help. So I talked various parties into it and arranged for everyone to meet at the Holiday Inn in town. Local law enforcement authorities and the student organizations and the community officials all came and had the opportunity to make their points. The police just put it out there—what would be tolerated and what wouldn't. The students had their say. My hope was that we could minimize differences before they exploded... and help people get more comfortable with each other. Instead of just seeing names in the paper, these people would recognize a person they'd met, maybe even have the potential for on-going communication that would avoid more conflict.

Around that time, Bill Moyers came through Lawrence researching a series he was writing for *Harper's Magazine*.[14] He hung around our newsroom when we were discussing the Dowdell shooting. We had a longstanding editorial policy of focusing on positive stories about African Americans that went back to my grandfather's era, so we wanted to handle this very carefully, very respectfully. When Moyers' story was published in *Harper's* December '70 issue, I didn't care for it. In my opinion, he played up the stereotypes, and I really lost respect for Moyers.

The truth is, I don't know if anybody came out looking all that great during those years.

Dolph Simons Jr.

Some did emerge as bright stars in those dark days, and Dolph Simons Jr. was one of them. "During a harrowing time, Mr. Simons and his staff on the Journal-World maintained that newspaper columns were proper avenues toward dispelling wild rumors and telling the people what was actually happening," said the citation read by Colby College President Robert E.L. Strider, during the presentation of the Elijah Parrish Lovejoy Award to Dolph Simons Jr. in 1972. "That the community was held together when it appeared to be falling apart was due in large part to the role played by the newspaper and its leader," stated Strider.

The Lovejoy Award commemorates America's first martyr for freedom of the press and "courage in journalism." It's one of the most prestigious awards in the field. *Washington Post* publisher Katharine Graham would receive it in 1973 for her role in exposing the Watergate scandal.

In his inimitable fashion, Dolph Jr. used his acceptance speech to assail those who compromise "the credibility of our business" by slanting the news and prioritizing the "sale of girdles and heads of lettuce" over the primary responsibility of fair and accurate reporting. "I am proud of the role of the American newspaper in the present scheme of things," Simons concluded, "but I want it to be better. For, if it is better, life in general in the United States should be better."[15]

And with that, Dolph Simons Jr. summed up his worldview.

Simons could rant, but never just because he had the editorial page at his beck and call. No matter what issue raised his ire, his point was not just what was wrong, but how it could be better. His engagement as editor and community leader during the 1960s and '70s provides often overlooked examples of Dolph Jr.'s unique ability and willingness to step into the fray and defuse an incendiary situation. He had a knack for the rallying cry, but it was shored up with a robust call to action in which he himself would engage in many actionable ways.

The Lovejoy Award cited Simons and his staff for "dispelling wild rumors and telling the people what was actually happening," and for helping hold the community together "when it appeared to be falling apart."[16] Yet Dolph's most important role might have been behind the scenes where his penchant for networking and innovation produced remarkable results.

Dolph contacted the Menninger Foundation, then in Topeka. This organization aspired to create "a better kind of world."[17] Dolph recruited help from Roy and Walt Menninger, experts in psychology and human relations. They agreed to facilitate and lead an initial meeting of the emotionally-charged community groups. That caucus established important inroads that led to ongoing communication (and Dolph becoming a trustee of the Menninger Foundation in 1972).

Then Dolph organized additional meetings to bring the groups together again on common ground. One of his ideas centered on the national fascination with space travel.

Dolph invited Apollo 13 Astronaut Charlie Duke to Lawrence. He took Duke to campus to observe the demonstrations firsthand and "the disgraceful treatment of the American flag." Dolph hoped Duke's presence—a walking symbol of national pride—could alter that mood. That evening, community leaders and students were invited to the Simons' home to meet Astronaut Duke personally, hear his remarks, and ask questions. The dialogue joined the mixed group in a congenial conversation. Later, Duke told Simons the most interesting question he'd been asked was whether he'd like to take some marijuana with him on his next trip to space to see what it's like to be high on the moon.

Lawrence Chamber of Commerce historian Marsha Henry Goff wrote of the gathering, "In one attempt to bring together, in a relaxed setting, representatives of the many factions of Lawrence society, Dolph Simons Jr. hosted an event where a widely diverse group of local residents was given the opportunity to meet Apollo 16 Astronaut Charlie Duke."[18] Dolph's strategy was effective and laudable. Opening lines of direct communication between factions helped heal the rifts that threatened Lawrence's long-term stability.

Simons' mediative mentality was further demonstrated when he invited African American activist Charles Scott Jr. to write a regular op-ed column in the Journal-World. "Those were tumultuous times," Charles Scott emphasized. "I was a college student—right in the thick of it. Dolph Simons Jr. asked me if I'd like to provide my perspective of the Black community, so I did. That lasted about a year. Every week, I got $25 a week to write it. When I wrote *We are an African People*, that got some negative reaction. I was trying to trace the heritage of Black people back to Africa, as many ethnic groups in America had done. I was not saying we weren't Americans, but some people reacted negatively to the article—they felt it was threatening to white people." But Scotts' insights were a much-needed source of education and information... they got printed. "I appreciated their effort to incorporate the Black perspective." [19]

Of such conciliatory efforts, one "constant and dependent reader" of the Journal-World, David Winston Heron, then-director of libraries at KU, wrote Dolph Jr. on December 10, 1970,[20] "to express my appreciation of the low-key and generally helpful way you have handled (things)." Heron believed "that over-reaction inside and outside the University may have contributed significantly to the success of the anarchist element, the anti-intellectual reaction, and the bad press we had statewide and nationwide... I think the Journal-World's handling of it has been both professional and helpful," he concluded.

> *Dolph Simons Jr. "transformed an ordinary newspaper company into a multimedia powerhouse."*
>
> Ralph Gage, Journal-World general manager

To know Dolph Simons Jr. is to grasp the evolving specialization of the Simons as a newspaper family. Each publisher—as businessman, editor, writer, and community leader—brought a unique skillset to the fore. But if W.C. built the engine, and Dolph Sr. engineered the body, then it was Dolph Jr. who ignited The World Company and took it places his father and grandfather never imagined it could go.

Dolph Jr. would shrug off such a claim, and credit his father and grandfather for the newspaper legacy they passed down to the next generation. "Not to disparage that," interjected Ralph Gage, who'd risen to Journal-World general manager, but "Dolph, Jr.'s role was unique as the innovator who transformed The World Company from an ordinary newspaper company into a multimedia powerhouse." And with the advent of cable, Simons shepherded unprecedented advancements in the industry. "Once we converged the media," Gage said, "we had attention from throughout the world."

There was no question Dolph Simons Jr. was driven, and the idea of what he could do next fueled him. On his watch, innovations that broke ground for the *Lawrence Journal-World*, also pushed the leading edge of the newspaper information industry at large. "Every employee at the paper knew his mantra: *Drive with your brights on! It's the only way to avoid the potholes and see what lies ahead*," Gage said.

We always tried to have the latest deadline so we could beat out all the other local papers. We'd hold for a late story or football game on the West coast. We'd call in our press people when we needed to do something special. I was at a meeting in Kansas City when Bobby Kennedy was shot... we didn't have wire photo at the time, so we raced over to the Kansas City AP office to get some photos so the Journal-World could have it first.

Our editorials represented our paper's position or thinking on local, state, or national issues, and didn't go under any one editor's signature. Over the years, Dad, of course, and Bill Mayer, Joe Murray, Ann Gardner, and I would all write editorials. If we got positive feedback about a good editorial, I'd definitely give its author a credit, unless I was the author. I never took credit. We invited and accepted contributed editorials, but there was no guarantee they'd be included. No editorial went without approval by someone in a leadership position. Nothing appeared in the paper that hadn't been read by an editor.

Dolph Simons Jr.

I'd worked for a small weekly in Douglas County. I covered all matters Lawrence and Baldwin City... and I ended up buying that small newspaper company from its owners. A year or so later, the Journal-World decided it wanted to get into the weekly newspaper business. So they started a small, local newspaper to compete with me. We battled it out. For about a year, this little town of 4,000 folks had two newspapers. Finally, the Simons bought me out, then offered me a job. We reached a deal, but I didn't plan to stick around. Once I got there, though, I realized this was a good way to learn about the Lawrence community.

What I really learned was this Dolph Simons guy wasn't who I thought he was. He wasn't telling me to write this way or that way; he was not the "invisible hand." Dolph was just a guy who liked good journalism.

On any given day, it wasn't at all unusual to see Dolph at work, but not in the newsroom—except on 9/11. I'd only started working there the month before, and I got there that morning, Dolph was already in the newsroom directing traffic. He'd made the decision we were going to put out a special edition. I'd never seen him step in like that before, but that was a day that was different for all of us.

Dolph made sure we had almost anything needed to go out and produce good journalism. That's why I grew to like the place, and have been here ever since.

Chad Lawhorn, Editor of the *Lawrence Journal-World*[21]

We tried to present a meaningful and knowledgeable assessment of a situation and how it would impact people. We wanted readers to think about things and know the position of the paper. Hopefully, the paper's track record backed that up with credibility that would give weight to the issue. I'd read the previous day's paper with my red pencil in hand, and mark up what we didn't get right or where we could do better. Also, I'd congratulate a writer or photographer for a particularly good and timely story or photo.

As editor and publisher, I knew I stood in the tall shadow of my dad and W.C., and I worked hard to measure up. They were supportive and encouraging, but they weren't the only ones with expectations of my performance.

Joyce Hall and my dad had been friends, and that relationship helped bring the Hallmark plant to Lawrence. When I was just starting out, Joyce invited me to have lunch at the Crown Room, his private dining room at Hallmark's headquarters in downtown Kansas City. His top executives were there—maybe six or eight people. Joyce said in front of them, "Dolph, I want you to know that these are my trusted executives. They run this company. Today, they may look like a bright shiny penny but if they don't perform, they'll soon look like a thin worn dime." Then he turned to them and said, "Ok, we've got Dolph here. He's got the newspaper in Lawrence, and I hold each of you responsible for telling me if the paper isn't measuring up and we'll do something about it." I can picture that room right now. I can still see him; Joyce Hall had a distinctively long jaw. I respected him, he was a very impressive individual in every respect. I also considered his son Don a close friend and colleague.

I must have been doing something right because I never had another "come to Joyce" meeting. In fact, I thought our Journal-World team could beat anybody—that's how I felt. I'd always say I was willing to put our reporters and our crew up against any other newspaper's in the world. We weren't cocky, but why not be the best we can? We did things in news, features, and photography that others wouldn't do. We had photographers that were great—Richard Clarkson was a junior high kid here in Lawrence who started with us and went on to *Sports Illustrated* fame. Another photographer, Bill Snead, also started at the Journal-World as a high school student and became a top-ranked *Washington Post* photographer, the White House photographer of the year, and a great wartime photographer.

We thought of all our employees as members of a special family. It was an enthusiastic environment… we put out a paper we thought could beat anybody. It's so much fun to know you can pull something off because you've got good people. We'd give our readers one helluva newspaper.

Dolph Simons Jr.

As might be expected of the third-generation Simons brandishing the editorial pen, Dolph Jr. inherited a biological imperative to speak and write his mind. If something deserved praise or a boost, he'd shine a spotlight purposefully on it. "I always want to be for things rather than against things," he emphasized. "But I don't shy away from what needs to be said—even if it isn't positive." Simons famously suffered no fools. This candor typified the weekly opinion-editorials in the "Saturday Column," for which he was best known.

Originally, Dolph's 1956 stories for *The Times* of London were published in the news section of the Journal-World. Over time, his penchant for observation and commentary developed into the Saturday Column, which remained in the news section. "I think Dad kept my column there because that's where readers expected to find it," Dolph Jr. noted, somewhat ruefully. "Looking back, we should have moved the Saturday Column to the editorial section. It was clearly titled 'Commentary,' and it didn't take the place of our editorial, which I didn't always write. I don't know why we didn't move it to the editorial page beyond simple precedent."

The column gained a strong, consistent readership. "Whatever Dolph wrote was usually the buzz around the office water cooler on Monday mornings," retired KU professor Dennis Domer said.

"Whether they agreed with him or not, people sure read him... he got them talking."

From Simons' point of view, it wasn't that everyone was entitled to his opinion but to an opinion, and he wasn't shy about getting the conversation started. Moreover, Dolph's M.O. was not just to get people thinking and talking, but *doing*.

Dolph's "I tell it like I see it" style belied the due diligence he put into his viewpoint. He began each day early—always vying to be the first at the office even if it'd been only seven hours since he left the night before. He read five or more newspapers starting with the Journal-World, followed by *USA TODAY*, the *Wall Street Journal*, the *Kansas City Star*, and the *Topeka Capital-Journal*. At 93, this is still his daily routine at home, with the buzz of television news stations resonant in the background.

It wasn't that everyone was entitled to his opinion, but to an opinion, and Dolph wasn't shy about getting the conversation started.

When drawn to a specific subject, Dolph would tap his vast and diverse supply of human resources for insights, concerns, angles, opinions, related considerations, potential problems, and possible solutions. Those queried could include the nation's top journalists, DC-beltway insiders, politicos, plus the cable guy, his own children and grandchildren (and their dates), and more than one suspected espionage agent (true story). From each, he asks their ideas and perspectives with genuine curiosity.

> *Publishing a paper in a small town is infinitely more difficult than in a large city. You cannot hide behind either your prestige or your anonymity...* "*You live around the corner from the people you rap over the knuckles,*" *Simons said.* "*You want to boost the town but you want to tell what you see, too. You can't run from your hypocrisy.*"

Bill Moyers in *Harper's Magazine* featuring
Dolph Simons Jr. quote. December 1970 [22]

For almost 40 years, Dolph Jr. leaned heavily on Ann Gardner, who'd risen through the Journal-World ranks from reporter to editor of the editorial page. Gardner's perspective was far less conservative than Simons. Their collaboration helped balance the paper's editorial stance by design. "He was respectful of me and would listen," Gardner, a moderate Democrat, affirmed. "He could see I made well-reasoned arguments, and that I had a point."

In the Saturday Column, even though I also carried editor/publisher title, I expressed my personal opinion. It didn't reflect the thinking of everybody in the office. This was clearly *Dolph's* opinion, *his* take on a given situation... and why I thought it was important to talk about it. So there were two different perspectives—the paper's and mine. They weren't always the same view either.

People have asked what business do I have in thinking about what's good for Lawrence, or the university? I'm not the mayor, or on the board of regents or a professor, what right do I have? Who do I think I am that my opinion means anything? Well, if somebody doesn't say something... **if people don't say what they feel they've got to express, then why did our ancestors fight for democracy?**

People can have the opposite view, and they need to express that, too.

For me, when I can get down what I want to say it, I feel relieved. Maybe no one will even read it, but I know I had the courage or the determination to share my concerns. Yes, I had a newspaper in which to do that, but that's the beauty of a newspaper in this country—especially a local newspaper—this is where anyone is welcome to express their opinion in a letter to the editor.

Dolph Simons Jr.

As editor, Dolph Jr.'s approach to the topic at hand was directly related to where it fell on a performance continuum. The high watermark was his father and grandfathers' ideals; the lowest you could go was a flagrant sell-out of the First Amendment. Undergirding that range were The World Company principles welded to his own world view:

- Report the news accurately, fairly, and unmistakably distinct from editorial opinions.

- Never violate a confidence... ever.

- Concerning human relations, treat everyone, regardless of race, gender, creed, or economic stature, with dignity and respect—including and especially the disadvantaged or oppressed.

- In public affairs, expose dishonesty, impropriety, and complacency.

- Hire the absolute best talent you can get your hands on— never a dud. Make their work experience great, and pull every string you can to help them get the next job.

- If you're going to write something negative or questionable, put it in a drawer overnight and look at it again the next morning to see what you think.

- Ensure due diligence and a strong work ethic is employed with everything you do.

- Challenge yourself: Is this the best we can do? How can we do even better?

Throughout that process, Dolph considered what his dad and grandfather would think or do, and whether he was taking himself too seriously. He vetted his intentions with a complicated blend of assurance and denigration—always certain of his duty as editor and publisher, but equally sure someone smarter than him could probably do a better job. He worried about writing without enough background on the subject and missing opportunities to advance the cause célèbre. He was confident but self-deprecating. When meeting Dolph in person after reading his scathing critiques in print for years, many would express surprise at his graciousness and humility. Simons' thoughtfulness was and is bona fide and utterly disarming.

As *New York Times* writer Tim O'Brien put it, "Dolph Simons, who writes a cantankerous Saturday column that draws barbs from

KU was often the focus of Simons' Saturday Column.

Lawrence's liberals, is a gentle, self-effacing man who still serves Thanksgiving turkey to his newsroom employees. He says he considers himself a 'little fish in a big pond' and is reluctant to be seen as a know-it-all by colleagues and competitors in the news business."[23]

Simons could expound on an array of subjects, but bad politics, weak leadership, an apathetic citizenry, and a whole host of KU concerns provided steady grist for his op-ed mill.

Having his by-line under the Saturday Column gave him the freedom to express his own opinions, but that license came at a price. "For years, I couldn't go to the grocery store without getting a lashing. It could be hard on my family, too," Dolph admitted. Still, Simons and the Journal-World stuck its editorial neck out because, as founding grandfather W.C. Simons put it, "We recognize further things which should be done and will be happy to have a part in the doing."[24]

*We never signed editorials in the Journal-World, which we'd take flak for from the community at times. Dolph was very liberal about letting critical letters to the editor be published. We'd get calls: **Who wrote that?** I never had a problem saying that it was the opinion of the paper, not of an individual writer because it truly was a collaborative effort. Neither one of us would point the finger. Dolph said that he* *never identified who had written an editorial, but when he heard a compliment about something I'd written, he might say thank you and give me credit. I always said that I was sure he got blamed for a lot more editorials that I wrote than the other way around.*

Dolph knew I was more liberal than he was, but we worked through it. It was a composite... a negotiation. There were editorials published in the Journal-World that I didn't agree with—but not the ones I wrote and worked with Dolph on. Whatever we came up with together was something I could live with. I think we wrote better, more thought-through editorials because we had that back-and-forth process. Towards the end, Dolph Jr. and I were the only ones writing editorials.

Ann Gardner, former Journal-World editorial page editor [25]

A mash-up of Simons' work illustrates the breadth of experiences and the proclivities "this writer" had:

"The real social outcast over here is the boy with thin hair who shows a tendency to baldness just when he gets enough money to buy a black leather jacket and a pair of Wellington boots."

Writing about the Beatles for *The Times* in London, 1956

"The Vietnam situation is bad, and it **is difficult to see any way for the U.S. to win in this struggle."**

Saturday Column, January 2, 1965

"In a war (with Vietnam) like this, a country like the **U.S. actually sustains the maximum cost and casualties for a minimum gain—a bare minimum."**

Saturday Column, April 20, 1968

"Clinton Reservoir offers Lawrence and the surrounding area tremendous opportunities and assets. **Clinton could be one of the most significant factors in the future development of Lawrence, both geographically and economically."**

Saturday Column, February 24, 1973

"This reporter thinks there could be no better time to express the joys and pleasures which can come from a father-

Dec 17, 1970

Sir:

Just wanted to drop a note and thank you for two things. First, I want to thank Mr. Mayor for the fine job he did in editing my letter of Dec. 14ᵗʰ. I don't know Mr. Mayor but his results show professionalism. Second, I want to thank you for making it possible for me to express a view. By making it possible for citizens to express themselves, you prove that the American "press" doesn't exist for the purpose of selling advertising.

Like many people who are seeking solutions, I just don't have any. As yet, nobody I've been able to think about has come up with anything better than concerned citizens who demand the right of a free press. I don't envy your responsibilities.

Respectfully,
d. Paris

P.S. I often disagree with your editorials.

son business relationship... In this writer's situation, it turned out to be one of the finest, happiest, and most personally rewarding ties any two people could have. Dad was a great companion, teacher, wonderful father, sound, practical adviser, role model, and boss. This guaranteed a wonderful, stimulating, and personally rewarding business partnership of more than 30 years."

Saturday Column (upon the death of his father), February 18, 1989

"This reporter received a phone call from a Soviet official saying they were aware of the delegate who appeared to be missing and he wanted to emphasize that it really wasn't of major concern to the Meeting for Peace group, and/or other Soviet officials. 'You have a lovely city, a lovely state, perhaps he wants to spend more time with you,' the official stated. 'Or perhaps he met a nice young girl and fell in love. Whatever, it is of no concern or worry to us.' This would not have been the case five or ten years ago."

On dicey Russian diplomacy, *Lawrence Journal-World*. October 20, 1990

"Wow, what a park! Last week, this reporter had the opportunity to visit Wrangell-St. Elias National Park. **It's huge, it's beautiful, it's true wilderness, and yet it is doubtful whether many Americans know the location of this 13.2-million-acre park**, the largest unit in the United States' park system."

Saturday Column, August 2000

"**The Dole Institute's focus on the importance of public service could not come at a better time** if it is successful in encouraging men and women of all ages to realize public service is indeed a noble endeavor."

Dedication of the Dole Institute, Saturday Column, July 2003

"**Williams was on a high pedestal in the eyes of most KU fans, and they didn't think he measured up to the image he had created over the past 15 years when he turned in his crimson and blue colors for North Carolina blue.** Chances are, if Williams had it to do over again, he would handle the situation somewhat differently and, after Thursday's going away party at the Lied Center, there may

On a rare vacation, Dolph Jr. at Great Bear Lake, Canada's
Northwest Territories, circa 1990.

be even added questions in his mind about whether he made the right
decision."

KU Basketball coach's decision to bolt to North Carolina,
Saturday Column, April 3, 2003

**"You can't ever be in the hip pocket of a city manager, or a
mayor, or a chamber of commerce, or a football coach, or an
athletic director or a chancellor.** You need to be supportive and
helpful, but you just can't be in their hip pockets. That's just not our
business."

As quoted in "Citizen Dolph," the KU *Daily Kansan* cover story, April 4, 2006.

The "Mid-Career" fellowship at KU is funded by a gift from Dolph
C. Simons Jr. and his wife, Pam. "We believe the opportunity for a
'midcareer' educational experience is going to become increasingly
important in our fast-changing society," Dolph C. Simons Jr. said. **"It
would be like buying a car and never taking it in for repairs or
servicing,"** he said. **"No matter what field or business a person
might be in, it is important he or she have an 'educational
servicing' opportunity to update and broaden their education
and to get their batteries recharged."**

Lawrence Journal-World. January 25, 2006

"Making this event even more unique, not only was the carrier's namesake, the country's 41st president, present, but his son, the country's 43rd president, was the principal speaker... Granted, **there probably were a number of those in the audience who may not have been fans or admirers of George H.W. Bush or George W. Bush, but chances are, even those were emotionally moved by the ceremony itself... their love of this country and its freedoms,** and the thousands of young men and women who will serve aboard this ship."

On commissioning the USS George H.W. Bush.
Saturday Column. January 17, 2009

"Years ago, KU hosted an international group of 'futurists,' a collection of some of the world's greatest thinkers and visionaries...a similar conference should be brought back to campus. Events of just the past several years offer evidence **there is a growing need for individuals with the intelligence and vision to think about the future and the challenges that lie ahead...**"

Saturday Column, February 16, 2013

"The best course of action for the Kochs or their representatives would be to merely ask the Nevada Senator (Reid) to identify and refute the so-called 'lies,' and **if he is serious about the matter, he should back up his claims with specific information.** Or, perhaps the best thing the Kochs can do is not respond... Instances such as this should cause those interested or concerned to take a close look at the individual making the charges and judge the character, record and mission of that individual."

Saturday Column, March 3, 2013

"All excuses, explanations, rationalizations, and justifications aside, KU's academic reputation is sinking. **The current 115th place ranking on the *U.S. News & World Report* Colleges list should be a shocking embarrassment to alumni and friends.** It should, but how many alumni and friends really care? Not too many years ago, U.S. News ranked KU 32nd in the nation among state-aided universities..."

Regarding news of KU being ranked 6th best in the nation for basketball,
but 115th for academics, Saturday Column, September 12, 2015

"Let the battle begin. The semifinal elimination contests have ended, and Donald Trump and Hillary Clinton are now engaged in the championship fight to determine who will take over the world's most powerful elected office, and in effect, determine the future of the United States. **It's likely to be a tough and extremely costly fight with no punches pulled... In one way, the campaign could be described as a contest between fantasy and reality.**"

Saturday Column, June 11, 2016

Biden wins: **So much for draining the swamp.**

LawrenceOpinions.com, November 2020

Upon losing a fantastic KU chancellor candidate Dr. Neeli Bendapudi, Dean of the KU Business School, to Penn State: "Congratulations to those who served on the search and selection committees to find a new president for Penn State University... **Did the [KU] Regents, who had the final vote, have other reasons to eliminate Bendapudi, such as not wanting two women or two women of color to be consecutive leaders of the school?** Bendapudi is a lost treasure for KU and Kansas and hopefully Chancellor Girod will prove to be an inspiring and successful leader."

LawrenceOpinions.com, December 17, 2021

"The pandemic was, and is, a terribly dangerous, deadly virus. There are many who suggest it is likely to remain with us for years... But this writer believes the growing split within our country becoming ever wider... (and) is a more dangerous situation...**This divide is growing deeper with Democrats and Republicans becoming more intense in their mistrust, almost hatred, of those in the other party. Where is the leadership that is essential if this country is to come together?** There is nothing guaranteed about the future of America just because it enjoys a glorious and proud history."

From "Real Danger Facing America" in LawrenceOpinions.com, February 16, 2022

Simons drew supporters and detractors alike, which he took in stride. Christopher Hearne Jr., a one-time *Kansas City Star* reporter turned blogger, was decidedly not a fan, noting, "As for Simons, even a broken clock is right two times a day."[26] His admirers also acknowledged some trepidation. Former KU Chancellor Gene Budig admitted, "I was always a little uneasy on Saturdays when his column could come out, because he was very well known for being very, very critical of chancellors and governors."[27]

For his part, Dolph Jr. remained indefatigably at his post contributing articles and writing over 3,000 Saturday Columns for more than 60 years.

> *Dolph wasn't involved in daily news meetings and didn't edit news stories before they were published. Dolph may have let the newsroom know that he'd like them to cover something, but he certainly wouldn't have wanted reporters to slant any story to conform to an editorial stand. At the J-W, reporters would never have thought to slant a story based on an editorial that they may not even have read! The newspaper's opinion appeared on the Opinion page not in the news columns. We would hope that what appeared on the editorial page also was "fair and accurate" even though it expressed an opinion.*
>
> *The one place that probably created a gray area at the Journal-World was the Saturday Column, which arguably should have appeared on the editorial page, since it clearly was the opinion of the publisher. I'm not sure how the initial decision to put it in the news section was made but it was never a matter of negotiation when I was there.*
>
> Ann Gardner, former Editor, *Lawrence Journal-World* editorial page

My reputation for being overly critical is probably deserved. I know I should work just as hard to say something good, but I'd follow the news, I'd watch this community and the larger world... somebody would confide in me about a situation. Something would happen or not happen that should've happened. Well, I'd write about it, and, if I could, I'd also do something about it. That's really how the "Welcome to Lawrence" project got started, and it's still going on today.

Frank Burge was a trailblazing director of KU's Memorial Student Union building. He turned it into a place where students wanted to be—something was always going on. I wondered why we weren't doing something like that for new faculty, too... not just to welcome new teachers to campus, but connect them to the wider community so this would feel like their home, not just their job. I knew I needed someone at KU to facilitate it, so I brought the idea to Frank and together, we got "Welcome to Lawrence" off the ground. When incoming faculty arrived at the university for the first time, we'd go out and would meet them with an umbrella, park their car, and show them around... introduce them to people. We got the Chamber of Commerce, the mayor, school superintendent, city officials—all those types involved. It turned out great.

That event continued and has expanded into more of a food fair with a tent and stage that draws the whole community. I suppose that qualifies as being positive, but it came from my frustration that the university wasn't actively offering new faculty an experience with the community. Why not? Why can't we do something about that? So we did.

That's not to say the university never did anything. In fact, the faculty there were doing some amazing things, and I thought it'd be great if the community knew more about them. So I invited Chancellor Franklin Murphy to identify 50 outstanding faculty members and we invited each of them to write on any subject they wanted to and we'd publish it in the Journal-World. For every published piece, the author would get a check from the KU Endowment Association. We called it "Opinions on the Hill" and it was really popular.

That project was one of the best things the Journal-World ever did. The locals learned who these professors were. Not just their neighbors who grew their own vegetables and flower gardens, but researchers, scholars, award-winning authors, and renowned experts who lived next door, weeded their own gardens, and walked their dogs. Leonard Krishtalka, director of the KU Museum of Natural History, would often contribute a piece with a far different take on a subject than I'd have. I thought it was great. This really helped with the town-versus-gown situation. Every paper should do something like this—get the teachers to write about whatever they're interested in. Give them a column to write.

That's the benefit of a local paper in a small city or town. Local ownership has a stake in the community and gives voice to the community. Editorials and commentaries are ways to demonstrate how that voice keeps the news and politics local.

For bad or good, I've been that voice, even though it's made me pretty unpopular in certain circles. Others have their own views. I'm not saying I'm always right, but I'm willing to take a stand for what I believe is right. An editor should have the backbone to speak out about what's going on, and a newspaper should have an editorial voice.

In the late 1990s, there was a big initiative to set up St. Luke's Hospital in Kansas City, Missouri, as the premier medical center in this region. It was supposed to be this great deal for Kansas but I wasn't convinced. Several prominent, highly successful Kansas City business leaders were, and pledged millions of dollars to make it happen.

I was hearing from some well-placed industry insiders who shared confidentially what was going on behind the scenes. The plan would leave KU Hospital, Kansas's own academic medical center, twisting in the wind, and the KU regents weren't doing a damn thing to stop it. And anybody backing KU Hospital was supposed to just stand down while St. Luke's was ushered in as "the" major hospital. In case anyone wasn't sure who was going to benefit from that, I didn't hold back from saying so. I even used the term "fat cats," which didn't make my wife very happy.

Dolph Simons always took the time to understand the complex issues surrounding a topic and developed his opinion based on his thorough evaluation. He grasped the significance of proposals developed and the consequences of such proposals.

That is clearly the case related to the controversy related to KU Hospital and St. Luke's. Dolph has always been dedicated to the State of Kansas and served as an important and effective communicator as he protected the interests of the State. He was my strong ally in my attempt to secure KUHS its position as a leading healthcare system in the State. His support was essential to me during this very difficult and highly political time.

Irene Thompson, former president and CEO, KU Health System

If it weren't for Irene Thompson coming in and turning things around as the new CEO of KU Hospital, that venerable institution would have gone up on the auction block.

I knew I was likely to lose some friends over the exposé I wrote. That part still bothers me, especially with these men who'd been my friends and had done so much for Kansas City. My dad's advice always helped—they don't have to like us, but we want them to respect us.

Regarding the St. Luke's versus KU Hospital situation, "It was Dolph Simons' very well-researched and informative columns that exposed the Kansas governor... Indeed, he was virtually the only one...[28] *citizens of the metro area not familiar with Simons' columns remained blissfully ignorant of (the) scam.*

Whatever you think of the Journal-World, from my experience observing Kansas politics from very close up for the past 20 years, is that it was a bright spot in an otherwise dreary world of ass-kissing, press-release-regurgitating "journalism" that should be an embarrassment to the state. I personally think Kansas and KU in particular will soon mourn the loss of the Simons' family ownership of the paper...

John Altevogt[29]

I don't regret what I wrote about that St. Luke's deal because it was true. Our exposé ended up proving that. I think the Journal-World played an important part in helping KU Hospital become The University of Kansas Health System, which is a world-class medical center today.

Dolph was the first to break the story in the Journal-World. He used his influence and shared his wisdom and insight. Dolph said the right things at the right time to the right audience.

Dr. Charles Porter, director of Cardio-Oncology,
The University of Kansas Medical Center[30]

Of all the stories and commentaries I've written over the years, some stand out for me. There's been such a wide variety of them, and they weren't all hard news or commentary. In fact, I did a piece on one of the nudist colonies in Lawrence. Thinking back on that, I remember they were playing volleyball when I arrived... I sure hope I thought to interview someone.

People always opened up with me—whether it was family problems or business problems, or attitudes or information about sensitive situations. I've been given deep confidences, and I've never broken them nor shared the names of people confiding in me. Some have suggested I run for office, and I was complimented, it was nice to be considered, but no way I was going to do that. Putting out the best newspaper we could was how I wanted to be of service. I worry that I haven't been helpful enough... that I've squandered opportunities to be helpful.

The stories I'm proudest of are the ones still happening. KU is an on-going story for me, it never ends. We have a fantastic asset with that university, and I get frustrated it hasn't taken advantage of its opportunities. I can't figure out why so many in KU leadership positions lack the necessary vision, courage, and commitment. They just sit on their butts while we lose valuable ground we once owned.

When the KU chancellor commented that we could expect more students because we won the national basketball championship, I just shook my head. Is that what this is all about? Are colleges and universities here for education or entertainment? Isn't that what we're seeing when more and more money is directed towards athletics instead of academics? I wish to hell we'd get a proper balance there—some equivalent and adequate financial support for academic programs and faculty. Where is the funding for the brightest, most promising students? Or for the students who have special needs or are in some way disadvantaged? The older I get, the more I see the cost to a country that doesn't prioritize education. This bothers me—it's always bothered me. It'll keep bothering me until we fix that.

If someone reads into my criticism that I hate KU, I'd tell them they're dead wrong. I think the record will show we've supported and bragged on the school in the Journal-World year after year for over a hundred years now. Still, there are things that need to be said... that's really my motivation: What needs to be said?

Maybe if I didn't care so much, I wouldn't have so much to say.

On-going and unresolved stories stay on my mind. Conditions at KU and life in Lawrence are on-going stories. Unresolved stories include the water table at the Ogallala Aquifer and getting the Clinton Reservoir built. This is such an important story because the Kansas water supply is not a sure thing, so we can't say it's resolved. For years, I've said fresh water will become our country's most precious natural resource. I think that's becoming clear worldwide.

I'm very proud of the work we did at the Journal-World to keep our eyes on issues like these.

Did it make a difference?

I believe it did… certainly hope so. And it still can, which is why I wish we still had the newspaper. There's so much more we could be doing… I have so many ideas. Even now, I wake up in the morning wishing I could go to the office and put out a good local paper. I think a good local paper makes all the difference in the world.

Dolph Simons Jr.

In the summer of 1970, as we prepared to begin our senior year in high school, my buddy Rob Seaver presented me with a very unusual proposition: Team up with him to write a weekly op-ed column for our hometown newspaper, the **Lawrence Journal-World.** *Most startling, he assured me that we would have the latitude to write about any topics we chose, which opened up a world of tantalizing, if treacherous, possibilities.*

I quickly learned that Rob himself had had this crazy idea of adding some more youthful voices to the paper's opinion page, not to mention the self-confidence to make the pitch directly to Editor-in-Chief Dolph Simons Jr., a friend of his parents and titanic force in the community. But it was Dolph, armed with a clear vision of what he wanted the paper to be, who embraced the idea and made the critical decision to give us the editorial rope to try some exciting things—and possibly to hang ourselves in the process.

Thus began an extraordinary endeavor that would have very dramatic effects on my life from that point forward. The teenagers who agreed to take this on were raw, untested quantities—possessed

Two Centuries Later

By ROB SEAVER
and PAUL CARTTAR

Next week I (Rob Seaver) am leaving Lawrence for Europe, then I will be going to school in the East. Therefore I am ending my writing in this column. Paul will continue dur- establish the solving of this problem as its No. 1 priority.

One optimistic trend is the slow but sure withdrawal of American troops from Southeast Asia. I say this with great

Rob Seaver and Paul Cartter (with glasses) in 1970

of some talents and certainly brimming with unfocused ambition and a sense of grand possibilities but having no practical experience and no clue what it would take to realize the huge potential of this opportunity. Week by week for the next two years, "Two Centuries Later," as we immodestly named the column, became the catalyst for a powerful, accelerated educational process.

Writing initially as a duo then later by myself (after Rob began his freshman year at Amherst College and I trudged up the Hill to KU), I learned real-world truths like how innovative ideas like columns may simply lack someone taking action to become real. I learned practical skills like how to frame sensitive topics, how to develop points of view worth expressing and how to generate 500 succinct, meaningful words even when you don't feel inspired. Perhaps most significant, I learned that I could do this and do it surprisingly well, including embracing full accountability for my opinions, even in the face of aggressive, sometimes unfair push-back.

In short, I experienced the gamut of benefits from taking on a formidable, individual challenge that plays out completely in public in real time in front of parents, teachers, classmates, neighbors, friends, enemies, and total strangers. In ways I could never have anticipated, this prepared me to spot and seize extraordinary opportunities. It better equipped me to build the kind of substantive, value-added life to which even then I aspired.

For this, Rob and I still owe a profound debt of gratitude to Dolph, whose never-wavering support enabled us to make this column our own, despite the belief of some readers (most importantly his father, the legendary Dolph Sr.) that our nascent brains would be more productively focused on the halls of Lawrence High School than those of Congress, or the fields of Douglas County than those of Vietnam.

Paul Carttar, former director of President Obama's Social Innovation Fund, 2010-12; former chief program officer of the Ewing Marion Kauffman Foundation 2003-4[31]

"Dolph's a savvy person," observed Rob Seaver, an artist and international art consultant who grew up in Lawrence and, with Paul Carttar, co-wrote for the Journal-World in his teens. "His detractors tended to view him as a bull in a china shop who was born with a silver spoon in his mouth. The reality was very different. He was— and continues to be—a skilled advocate for what he believes in; and he remains, without a doubt, the most indefatigable and successful promoter of Lawrence in my lifetime."[32]

Those who've admired him are effusive. Dolph's closest colleague and professional wingman Ralph Gage acknowledged, "Everything... I learned everything from Dolph."[33] International terrorism expert and anthropologist Dr. Felix Moos offered, "I would not be who I am without Dolph."[34]

Certainly, there are plenty on the opposing side of Simons' agenda, although even in that circle, it's hard to find anyone openly hostile. They may not agree with him, but they respect him, which has always been Dolph's goal.

Renown historian and author Dennis Domer, a retired KU professor, affirmed, "Dolph was the catalyst. He and I are of different political persuasions, but that didn't mean I didn't respect him, because I did. Whether people despised his Saturday column or not, that column brought us together. They may have criticized him, but they read him. No one ever said Dolph Simons was boring or you never knew where he stood. He pissed people off, but then when you met him, he's gentle, kind, gracious."

Author, award-winning essayist, and paleontologist Professor Leonard Krishtalka admitted, "We differed greatly on certain topics. Very shortly after I got [to KU], I contacted the Journal-World to ask if they'd consider allowing me to contribute with science being my M.O. To Dolph's credit, he encouraged and published a diversity of views across the spectrum. I've easily published 100 or more op-ed pieces in the Journal-World. Although his editorial bent was conservative and that was well known, the paper was ecumenical. For that, I applauded and admired him."

Gene Budig, former Chancellor of the University of Kansas, summed up Simons this way, "To understand Dolph Simons Jr., one needs to remember that he could be a friend and critic, often at the same time. He reacted to important issues with heartfelt emotion."[35]

For Tom Curley, president of the Associated Press from 2003 to 2012, "Dolph was a role model, mentor, and friend. He combined graciousness and generosity with a good reporter's intensity to understand. The result is a classic leader—someone willing to press a vision and capable of rallying people to his side. I enjoyed visits with him as much as anyone in our profession because he knew as much as anyone and was unafraid of making commitments and delivering on them. I loved to visit with him. He always knew things I didn't know. He was a leader, a change-agent, in the best tradition of William Allen White. He was engaged in the larger world but brought it back to the local community. Dolph was a perfectionist."[36]

CHAPTER 7

The Full Court Press

*"There were a lot of important voices
around that boardroom table, but the Simons'
small-paper voice was heard, too. Dolph's consistent call
was for excellence and, more narrowly in AP terms,
for AP to stay true to its heritage of impartiality."*

Louis Boccardi, Associated Press president/CEO (1985 – 2003)

On the morning of May 29, 1972, an editor updated *Washington Post* publisher Katharine Graham on two "incredible events" that had gone on the night before.[1] First, a car driven by someone who'd apparently been drinking went off the road, smashed into the front room, right past the couple having sex on the sofa, then out the back wall of a house. Second, "There were these five men who were caught in Democratic headquarters wearing surgical gloves," Graham recounted with a wry laugh 25 years later in a Freedom Forum interview, adding, "And he told them to me as equal stories!"[2]

The *Washington Post* broke the Watergate story. Reporters Carl Bernstein and Bob Woodward chronicled those events in a manuscript Katharine "Kay" Graham personally handed to her friend Dolph Simons Jr. "I think it was 1974. We were on our way to a newspaper publishers board meeting in Hawaii," Dolph recalled. "Kay asked me if I would jot notes about anything in the book that might be confusing to readers who don't know the news business."

For the next few days, Simons didn't spend much time in the American Newspaper Publishers Association (ANPA) meetings.

Instead, "I sat on the beach reading that advance-copy of *All the President's Men*," Dolph admitted. "I don't recall what edits I scribbled in the margins, but I do remember I could not put it down."

Graham was among many in the newspaper industry who respected Dolph Simons Jr. as a colleague and trusted him as a friend. In Dolph, Graham—a wealthy, astute DC socialite without any "first-line" experience—found an ally in a tough-as-nails business famously intolerant of newbies. He was there to welcome her as the first woman ever elected to the Associated Press board in 1975. He nominated her to the American Newspaper Publishers Association (ANPA) board,

Dolph Simons Jr.'s seat at the table (8th from right) indicates his seniority in 1975, the year Katharine Graham was the first woman and most recently elected director (hence the first left seat) on the AP board.

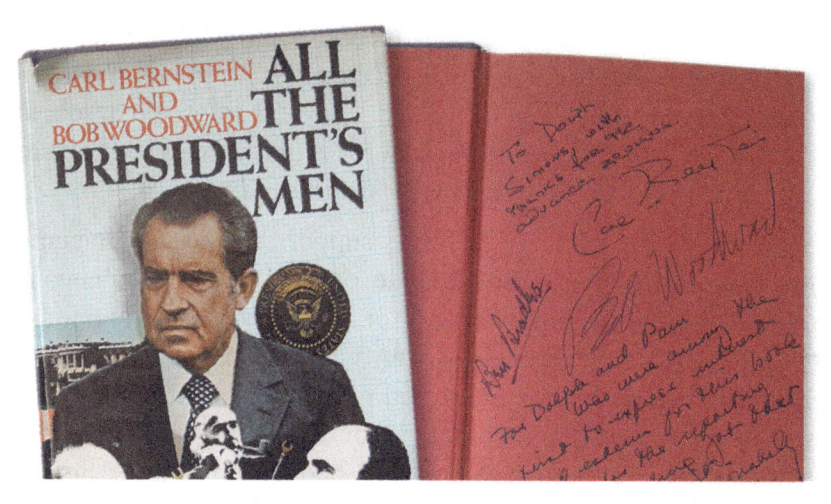

The first edition autographed for Dolph by Katharine Graham, Ben Bradlee, Carl Bernstein, and Bob Woodward.

and shepherded her on other boards and committees, as well as at conventions. "That was before she became the Queen Bee and needed no more help at all," Dolph chuckled. "Kay did an excellent job, and paved the way for more women to move into leadership roles in this industry."

Dolph's support and encouragement weren't unique or exclusive to Graham, just characteristic of who he was. Dolph Simons Jr. brought sincerity and fervor to everything he was interested in, to the delight of his friends and consternation of his foes. His willingness to speak unvarnished truth to power, however awkward or aggravating that could be for some, proved to be an asset in a field full of straight shooters. "The newspaper world recognized Dolph as 'the real deal' and a person in search of excellence," affirmed former-AP President and CEO Louis Boccardi.[3]

> *The newspaper world recognized Dolph as 'the real deal' and a person in search of excellence.*
>
> Louis Boccardi,
> former president and CEO
> of the Associated Press

Straight talk was the Simons' trademark. Nobody knew this better than Keith Fuller, who preceded Boccardi as president of the Associated Press. When the AP wouldn't take the time to police inappropriate use of its own photos by non-AP members, Dolph Sr. unleashed his fury culminating with "This definitely is a threat because we are getting damned tired of all the pussyfooting around that goes on in the handling of Associated Press service."[4]

While The World Company represented a smaller concern compared to media empires in Chicago, New York, Minneapolis, Denver, or Los Angeles, the Simonses brought invaluable perspective to the practicum. They kept things relevant and grounded in an industry dominated by the biggest players. Like W.C. and Dolph Sr. before him, Dolph Jr. was "a committed local editor who could relate to his local audience in ways that big-city editors and publishers simply could not," according to Boccardi. "I can remember Dolph's coming to many a board meeting with tales from the front, so to speak, as he would relate some adventure the paper had been involved in."[5]

In their time, each of the Simons covered not just their local zone, but the full court. They weren't just concerned with their own product, but with the industry's performance. "There were a lot of important voices around that boardroom table," Boccardi said. "But the Simonses' small-paper voice was heard, too. Dolph's consistent call was for excellence and, more narrowly in AP terms, for the Associated Press to stay true to its heritage of impartiality."[6]

Coming from a newspaper family was an obvious advantage for me in many ways. Our name and newspaper were already known and respected, so that opened doors locally and nationally... even internationally.

I probably took it for granted that the way some things are done in newspaper publishing were influenced by my own family. Back in the 1920s and '30s, for example, W.C. was on the national Audit Bureau of Circulations that developed policies for how to measure newspaper circulation and set advertising fees. Things like that weren't standardized yet. Believe me, Granddad was the kind of man you'd want developing a system the industry could comply with because he understood operations in practical, profitable terms. He was also a good writer and reporter.

In 1939, my dad, Dolph Sr., was elected president of the Kansas Press Association. In the 1940s, he was traveling around the world writing news stories that foreshadowed the way embedded reporters function now. Dad's reporting directly influenced our government's view of post-war reconstruction.

By 1950, Dad was first vice president of the national Associated Press, a board he served on until 1960. He was also a juror for the Pulitzer Prize in '61 and '62.

W.C. and Dad took their responsibilities very seriously. This was part of being a good newspaperman; not just putting out a good paper, but making a contribution to the industry. Dad and

W.C. Simons (standing fourth from left) was a member
of the Audit Bureau of Circulation that shaped policy
and practice for the newspaper industry.

KU Chancellor Franklin Murphy (left) and Dolph Simons Sr. (right) welcome Sir
William Haley (center) to Lawrence, the first-ever midwestern visit for London's
publisher of The Times. Photo taken at The Cedars, home of Dolph Jr.
and Pam Simons, circa late 1950s.

Granddad certainly did so in their times. But in the newspaper business, you can't ride anybody's coattails. You have to prove yourself. I was only in my mid-20s, but I was ready to do that.

My first board experience was with the Inland Daily Press Association (IDPA) in 1963. This was an impressive group. Some very big names hoped to be invited to speak at the annual convention. In fact, John F. Kennedy had just given the keynote at their meeting in Chicago in 1957.[7]

The IDPA alliance looked out for the interests of regional and local family-owned papers. They did a survey of all members showing the demographics of each paper and how it performed compared to other publications its size. We'd pore over that report every time it came out to see how we were doing. I developed important, lifelong connections there that opened more doors.

Next, I was named a director of the Kansas Press Association; by 1967, I was its president. All these board experiences helped me establish connections, and become more rounded in different aspects of the business.

Around that same time, my name had been forwarded as a candidate for the board of the Associated Press, the largest news-gathering service in the world. I was nominated to run against a director from a smaller paper in Georgia who was up for re-election. I lost, but barely. Based on that promising start, I was asked if I'd accept a nomination again in 1967, and I did. The incumbent, Fred Seaton, was well-respected and a generation ahead of me. I was nominated as the candidate representing newspapers with circulation under 50,000, and I campaigned hard. Dad put in a good word or two (or three) with his cronies. He had connections from his years with the AP, but I had to run on my own merits. I was young, but I already had quite a lot of board service to show for myself. And I was confident—some might have said cocky—enough to express my opinions. I was very pleased (maybe even a little surprised) to get elected.

At my first meeting, I was somewhat in awe. Many of the "giants" of news in those days could be found sitting around that table. There was Jack Knight, who published the *Miami Herald*, *Miami Tribune*, *Detroit Free Press*, and *Philadelphia Inquirer*. I considered Jack the best newspaperman in the business. There were Bernard Ridder of Ridder Publications, and Harry Byrd who had the *Winchester Journal* and other papers in Virginia and West Virginia. Gene Pulliam was there—he'd been a reporter for the *Kansas City Star* who went on to publish the *Indianapolis Star*, the *Indianapolis News*, the *Arizona Republic*, and the *Phoenix Gazette*. Palmer Hoyt with the *Denver Post* was there, and Paul Miller with Gannett. Paul would be a major influence in my life. I got to know them all, and counted several among my closest good friends.

The AP meetings were fascinating and intense. We were dealing with issues like covering the war in Vietnam, protests against that war, plus civil rights and racial tensions. The

Paul Miller
Rochester 14, New York

Satdy 2/5
Dear Dolph:
I agree with every
last word in your letter,
about Dolph, jr. He is
terrific. He will make
it one day as sure as
I am penning this.
Ask him to drop me

question of whether or not we should pay ransom when reporters were kidnapped was always on the table. The AP was in a no-win position there. If we paid out, it only encouraged terrorists to do it again—and increased the risk for every reporter out in the field. But if we didn't, we seemed cold and uncaring. Damned if you do, damned if you don't... we'd try to negotiate. Sometimes it worked.

My first capital budget (in 1976) was something like $800,000... Within a few years I was scrounging for $16 or $17 million, just to buy equipment. And laptops for every reporter had not yet landed in my lap.

Keith Fuller, AP president/CEO (1976 - 1985)[8]

There were more run-of-the-mill concerns—competition from United Press International (UPI), turf wars with telephone companies, and always rising costs. I can remember the stress over the cost of the first new digital camera we bought when I was on the AP. As the Associated Press was a non-profit organization, money was always an issue.

Still, the AP's primary concern was how to put out the best, most accurate news report. We were the one agency with the responsibility to ensure this standard was upheld. If I was known for anything on that board, it was this point. My strong belief was the AP had to set the gold standard for reporting. It was free of government control, and it had the opportunity to model how reporting should be done. There should never be a reason for anyone to question the integrity of the Associated Press. I hammered on that theme relentlessly.

There were on-going discussions about maintaining impartiality while still trying to be profitable. It takes money to hire good people for your Paris Bureau or report from war

10   Wednesday, September 27, 1972

Kansan Photo by STU BEALS

Simons Addresses Students
. . . said KU vital to Lawrence . . .

Simons Discusses
Journalism's Future

Dolph C. Simons Jr., publisher-president of the Lawrence Daily Journal-World said Tuesday that

He said facsimile printing which made it possible for news to be delivered directly into the

zones and hot spots around the world, or cover the Olympics. Believe me, once you start weighing journalistic standards against increasing your advertising revenue, that conversation gets pretty complicated real fast.

No doubt those same discussions are happening today in AP inner circles. Some things never change even while everything keeps changing. In those days, technology was advancing and television had become such a force. I was there when the first radio manager representing the National Association of Broadcasters came on the board. Hell, we thought of radio as show business, not news. Everything they put on their newscast was from the AP anyway. Of course, we adjusted. Then Kay Graham arrived in 1975 and the conversation changed even more.

Looking back, maybe I should have spread these commitments out a bit, but while I was still on the AP board, I also accepted an appointment to the American Newspaper Publishers Association (ANPA) board in 1971. Then in 1974, I was invited to the board of the Newspaper Advertising Bureau (NAB) which I heartily accepted.

I've been told I was the only person ever to serve on all three of those boards at the same time. I don't know about that, but I'm sure I was the youngest.

The ANPA dealt with the business-end of newspapering including administration and operations. It offered comprehensive training sessions for new people and advanced professional development for those who'd been in the business for years. I presented some workshops and I also took some courses at the ANPA conferences. I remember Barbara Bush came to speak about her literacy campaign at one of the annual events. Everybody wanted the mic at ANPA for their pet project or to spotlight an issue they hoped would get more or better attention in the newspapers.

There was a very active ANPA agenda around labor issues in the industry—unionizing concerns. Also, competition from other sources like magazines, television, and radio. Newspapers used to have 70% of all advertising dollars but that was dwindling fast. A lot of effort was made to figure out how to keep those dollars from going elsewhere. We also had supply chain concerns. For a while, a shortage of North American newsprint meant much of that stock had to be supplied by Scandinavian countries, which no one was very happy about.

The NAB was the lead organization dealing with the fuel that runs this industry—advertising dollars. This was the board everybody wanted to be invited to—a very big deal. The NAB was concerned with keeping advertising dollars flowing into newspapers. Whatever new technologies, new products, or new companies were emerging, the NAB wanted a big piece of their ad budget. The NAB was on top of all that.

Those boards gave me a 360-degree view of the industry, and I loved it. We'd be in meetings all day then go back to our rooms where the conversation would just keep going. *Are truth and accuracy the same thing? Can a reporter be entirely objective?*

We exchanged ideas and discussed what the industry was facing—both problems and opportunities. The so-called "young Turks" on the AP board like John Cowles, Otis Chandler, and me broke tradition a bit and invited AP staffers to join us after the formal meetings for informal discussions. We wanted to know their views from the trenches. At first, staff members were really careful of what they said, but eventually we developed enough trust to speak candidly and in confidence. Not everybody saw eye to eye on the issues, but they usually managed to be friendly about things… usually.

Those were very interesting times. I made such good friendships that lasted all my life, although so many of them are gone now. The Sulzbergers, who had *The New York Times*, were good friends, which goes back to my granddad's day. Arthur Hays Sulzberger invited W.C. to New York City and gave him the full tour of his operation. Granddad was very impressed and commented on the sharp-looking news staff. Mr. Sulzberger just said, "Yes, I know, but I'm concerned that some of them are so open-minded their brains are falling out."

Mr. Sulzberger's son Arthur Ochs Sulzberger was my age. Everybody called him "Punch." He invited me to his house, and over to his sister's place to meet the rest of the family. Later, when Punch's son Arthur Jr. came on the scene, his nickname was "Pinch," as in a small piece of his dad. That generation—including my sons—got to know each other fairly well from spending time together at events. They called themselves the "Nepotism Club."

Another legendary newspaper family we got to know well was the Cowles. They had the *Minneapolis Star*, the *Minneapolis Tribune*, the *Des Moines Register*, *Look* magazine, and half of *Harper's Magazine*. Mr. Cowles Sr. was one of those giants in the industry. He'd invite a group out to Glendalough, their country lodge, to shoot geese or ducks. During one of those weekends, I was sitting in a duck blind with Dwayne Andreas, a good friend of the Cowles. Andreas was CEO and chairman of Archer Daniels Midland, and a real Beltway insider. Kennedy, Johnson, and Reagan all appointed him to special committees or put him on projects that took him all around the world. Carter sent him to Africa. Nixon sent him to Moscow to tell them he was going to open up relations with China. I just sat there listening to all his stories. Finally, I said *Dwayne, you ought to write a book.* He just shook his head because that could never happen. He spoke with the authority of the White House, but they'd deny knowledge of him... that was the deal, he told me.

When Dad was on the boards of the AP and the ANPA, we'd go to events with him sometimes. I remember when Richard Nixon was invited to speak at the ANPA Convention, I ended up in the green room talking to him about the Duke basketball game. I was trying to be real casual, but this was during the whole Watergate drama. Kay Graham was also in the green room. They had to greet one another, it was inevitable, and you could cut the air with a knife.

Dan Simons

In the evening, back at the lodge, you didn't drink too much during cocktail hour because you had to keep your wits

Dolph had great respect for Henry Kissinger,
"he's one of the giants on foreign policy."

Dolph hobnobbing with Nixon and others at an ANPA conference.

about you. At some point, sitting around the table eating and visiting, Mr. Cowles Sr. would ring a little bell to bring everyone to attention. It was time to discuss important issues—and those were some serious discussions. I wasn't about to expose my ignorance, so I mainly would watch and listen.

John Cowles Jr. and his wife Sage were great friends of ours. They'd come visit Pam and me in Lawrence or at our lake cottage in Minnesota. Sage Cowles had been a Broadway dancer from New York. They were both very interesting and deep into the arts. John and Sage raised the money for the renovation of the Guthrie Theatre. After John was fired over a big crisis in leadership at his family-owned paper in the early 1980s, I think he finally felt the freedom he needed to do other things. He bought an old warehouse right in the city and turned it into a dance school and a nice condo where they lived. He helped finance a Broadway show, *The Last Supper* at *Uncle Tom's Cabin*, which toured nationally, and featured the cast taking their final bows in the nude.

At his funeral, John's grandchildren handed out programs they had designed to look like the front page of a newspaper. There was his history, achievements, favorite songs, and hobbies. It was just great. I'll admit, we had serious differences as far as politics were concerned, but he was a hell of an interesting individual and a great friend. I wish I had more friends like John Cowles.

I knew Martin Hayden, editor of the *Detroit News*, and Jack Knight with the *Detroit Free Press*. I wasn't personal friends with John Kennedy, but I knew he was smart—his history went back to his dad and the Kennedy machine. Lyndon Baines Johnson was a strange duck. I knew Alf Landon and his daughter Nancy Landon Kassebaum because the Landons were Kansans. I have a vague memory of meeting President Eisenhower at some function with my dad out in Abilene, Ike's hometown. I did meet Nixon several times—now there was a politician. Trump was one who did things his own way.

I don't think I ever met Ronald Reagan, but I admired him. He was positive, dammit. He wasn't all negative. Kay Graham's editor Ben Bradlee was a real character. He had strong opinions, was tough, and demanded good performance. He was close, close, close to the Kennedys. Ben probably thought of me as a hayseed, but maybe that made me easy to talk to.

Honestly, sometimes I can't figure out why men like Bradlee or Cowles would develop a friendship with me and come all the way to Lawrence to visit. Why this tiny paper in Kansas? Why me? Maybe it was Pam they wanted to see. Most of us brought our wives and sometimes even the kids because social events were a part of that scene. We got to know each other's family, and spent time together—that was good for business and friendship alike.

A number of times, I was invited to a hunt at Wiregrass, Tom Vail's country home in Georgia. Tom had the *Cleveland Plain Dealer*, and he did an amazing job with it. He was also a very dedicated community leader who supported many important endeavors including the Cleveland Clinic. Pam and I were friendly with Tom and his wife Iris, who was from New York City. Anyway, Otis Chandler was also invited on one of the trips, but he was used to big game hunts in Alaska and Africa. The whole small-game (quail, chukars, and pheasant), bird-dogging, fox-hunting, society life the Vails led wasn't his thing. Otis was ready to leave about as quick as we'd arrived. I said *Come on, Otis, you can't leave this soon*, and got him stay long enough not to hurt anybody's feelings.

Of all the friends I made in those circles, I was closest to John Cowles, Tom Vail, Stan Cook, Punch Sulzberger, and Otis Chandler. Otis had the *Los Angeles Times* and saw the role of an editor and publisher pretty much the same way I did.

At one point, Otis and I were both concerned about the SNPA (Southern Newspaper Publishers Association) honchos trying to exert too much influence over the AP board. Wes

Gallagher was AP president then, and he called us into his office to put an end to that dispute. Wes wasn't having it, and that man could make a statement. I tell you Otis and I left there with our tails between our legs!

There was the time Otis and I were at an ANPA meeting in Aruba walking the beach and he said, "Dolph, I want to tell you ahead of time because you're going to be reading about it soon enough." He told me he was buying all of Lyndon Johnson's properties. I assumed that meant a lot of land and a ranch, but it was his businesses, including a TV station. Otis said he considered the biggest asset of the whole deal to be a fellow by the name of Tom Johnson who was LBJ's right-hand man in Washington. Otis brought Tom over to the *Los Angeles Times*, and Johnson stayed on for 13 years as president and publisher, then he went on to CNN. He was a great guy, I liked him. Otis made a good deal.

Otis had me out to his place in California and introduced me all around. He was popular and well-respected in Los Angeles. He was an Olympic athlete; he went to Stanford; and he was very proud of his paper. I could see all that, but I felt there was no way Otis Chandler knew Los Angeles the way I knew Lawrence.

In an operation as big as Chandler's, there's not enough direct contact in the community. I had a closer connection and attachment; I had a greater sense of what our paper needed to do to justify our position within the community. It's just easier to get a feel for that in a smaller city. Maybe I underestimate things in a large city, but I've observed those markets and known those kinds of publishers firsthand. Local ownership in a smaller city or town has a far better chance of its paper being an effective, genuine monitor and historian, referee and superintendent. Otis knew his inner circle, and he had people who knew people. I had the advantage of knowing directly, and often personally, pretty much all the players in Lawrence, and Kansas, too, for that matter.

Dolph finds his dad's name on the seating chart for a 1953 Gridiron Club dinner meeting.

To this day, the bigger mystery is how I also got to know the biggest names in this business all over the country. I was a small fish in a big pond, but I felt comfortable because people were nice enough to visit and exchange ideas. I've always enjoyed visiting and getting to know people. In this business, who you know is everything, so you have to pay attention, which I guess I did. You can always learn something from those you meet, especially if you don't assume you have all the answers. To me, networking isn't taking advantage of a connection because that sounds manipulative, but just being friendly… being helpful.

In its time, the Gridiron Club was probably the most prestigious, by-invitation-only journalistic "insider" network. Dad had been at a meeting or two, and Keith Fuller took me to one of their dinners. At the Gridiron, the rule was no quotes out of the dinner. Everything was off the record… you were honor-bound. If you were invited, you knew not to talk about what was said.

You had to pay attention to how things like that work, and not screw it up. If you talked, or even if your wife talked, you wouldn't be invited back to certain things. Those who knew the ropes brought the others along.

The ANPA network was very good at grooming future leaders. Some of us who'd been around a while would be asked to mentor the younger ones. Jack Knight asked me to take a young Knight staffer under my wing, and he wrote me a kind letter of thanks for that years later. There was even talk of the Journal-World being a formal training center for *The New York Times*, but for the most part, mentoring was informal.

I met Lou Boccardi when he was an AP bureau chief. He was smart, tough, demanding, and had an excellent record within the AP. I tried to get him the president's job, but Keith Fuller, who was a Kansan and close friend, moved into that position. Lou eventually got it though—he became AP president after Fuller retired in 1985.

He worked really hard to know trends... to know what was around the corner. He was unafraid to go after things. Dolph was unusual, fascinating, with a drive for perfection that endeared him to me. He confronted the truth and stepped up.

Tom Curley, Associated Press president (2003 - 2012)[9]

Around the time Lou retired in 2003, I had a call from a headhunter looking for someone who could lead a sizable news operation he wouldn't name. I had a hunch which operation that was, and recommended Tom Curley. I knew Tom from his work with *USA TODAY*. He was one of the first staffers on that paper back in the '80s. We became very good friends. We'd get together when his family would come up to ski near our place in Steamboat Springs. I was really pleased when Tom got the job—which turned out to be president of the Associated Press. He did a terrific job there.

It sounds cocky if I say no one intimidated me, but my reaction to people with the smarts was to get my ass up and learn something more. I've been so damn lucky to know such fascinating, accomplished people... journalists, diplomats, politicians, and presidents. They were my heroes... they inspired me to improve.

Former President George H.W. Bush and Dolph Jr. remained friends since their first meeting in the 1970s.

George H.W. Bush and I were friends for years—since an AP meeting in New York. He had the VIP suite at the Waldorf Astoria and invited Pam and me up for a visit. We hit it off. When President Ford appointed Bush as chief U.S. liaison to the People's Republic of China, we'd get Christmas cards from them with the inscription written in Mandarin, which was kind of fun. George first came to Lawrence when he was head of the

CIA. He visited us at The Cedars a couple times. He loved to play tennis, so I called out to KU and arranged some court-time for him with the KU tennis team. Apparently, the coach put it this way to his team: *I don't care what you did last night or what condition you're in, you're gonna play tennis with George Bush!* I'm sure those young players never forgot that experience.

Actually, anytime I could connect what was going on in the world back to students at KU, I'd pursue that angle. That worked out in a really interesting way some years back. I was in Beijing at a small, but high-powered lunch with some top-level Chinese chatting with the fellow next to me by the name of Henry Yao Wei. Wei was in the inner circle of the Chinese party at the time. He was traveling the world trying to buy land and mines to generate some money for the Chinese government. He would eventually make the mistake of condemning the actions in Tiananmen Square, and then he was out. But not before he asked me if I could help get his daughter Hua to America to attend a university. Naturally, KU was the best school for her, I insisted. So I made some calls, and it all worked out really well. We got Hua to KU by the mid-'70s. She lived with us for a while here at The Cedars. We gave her one of the upstairs bedrooms. I remember Pam helping her untie the corset-like strings to the traditional clothing she had on when she arrived. Pam said, "You're not going to need this in Kansas!"

Hua was very smart and worked her way up to residence in an honor dorm right next to the chancellor's home. She married a nice young man from Bartlesville, Oklahoma.

In 2009, George invited me to the naval base in Virginia for the dedication of an aircraft carrier that was being named after him. I went, and was up early that morning to look around. I mentioned to the hotel greeter this was my first time in Norfolk. She said "Well, sir, anything in this city that's worth seeing is thanks to Frank Batten—he owns our local newspaper."

By God, that was just wonderful. If people in your own community speak of you that way, I don't think there's a nicer compliment a newspaper editor and publisher could be given.

*Dolph served on the Associated Press board of directors from 1967 to 1976 (three 3-year terms was the statutory limit) but in those days one was not appointed. One had to be a candidate and solicit the votes of one's newspaper peers in often competitive elections. I was a junior player in those years. I started working for the AP the same year Dolph joined the board. I noticed that among his best friends on the AP board were big city publishers like the legendary Otis Chandler of the **Los Angeles Times-Mirror** and John Cowles of Minneapolis, who presided over operations that dwarfed the **Lawrence Journal-World**.*

I never had a conversation with them, or anyone else for that matter, probing what it was that opened those doors for Dolph. Here was a man who was almost a textbook example of what one hoped a small-paper editor-publisher-owner would be—deeply rooted in his community, not resting on the history of the business and the voice he inherited but looking constantly to make it better, to renew it and strengthen its place in the community and at the same time open the path to new technology.

I made friendships with some of the directors, and Dolph and Pam were high on that list. That enhanced our lives and still does.

Lou Boccardi, former president and CEO of the Associated Press (1985 - 2003)

In March of 1985, a few weeks before he was kidnapped in Beirut by the militant Muslim group Hezbollah, Terry Anderson was getting on Dolph Simons' last nerve.

NATO Commander General Bernard Rogers was set to give an exclusive off-the-record background briefing on the Suez Canal to ANPA board-members-only in Monte Carlo. Dolph had worked behind the scenes to set this private meeting up, and in fact, was probably the only person in the room who could have pulled off this unusual arrangement.

It helped that Bernie Rogers and Dolph Simons Jr. were old friends and fellow Kansans. Rogers invited Dolph and Pam to West Point to see the cadets. Once, when he was still a U.S. Army general, Bernie stopped by to visit Dolph in Lawrence. His advance team surrounded the house and took up posts inside as well. This made quite an impression on young Dan Simons. "Dad joked with a security detail member that 'my son Dan is pretty fast on the draw and thinks he could outdraw you,'" Dan recalled. "As I was stammering, 'Sir, that is not true! I never said that,' the agent opened up his coat to reveal a serious ability to protect his client. Needless to say, I believed he would win in that contest!"

At the ANPA meeting in 1985, perhaps similarly motivated, Dolph encouraged Rogers to exhibit some of the U.S. military firepower in the Mediterranean. Bernie complied. An aircraft carrier cruised into view from the conference room window overlooking the sea. It was an imposing and impressive backdrop for the general's talk. When he finished, Rogers offered to take questions.

From the back of the room, Terry Anderson, then-AP Middle Eastern correspondent, stood up and started quizzing the general as if at a press conference. It wasn't clear how Anderson, who hadn't been invited to the closed ANPA-session, managed to be there. This was a serious security breach and all eyes were on Dolph to repair it.

"Carol Sulzberger ran over to me," Dolph recalled, "and said '*You have to do something, we promised him (Rogers) he could speak freely— there is to be no press!*'" Simons got Anderson out of the room, then

"I think I might have put in a call to you," he noted in a conversation with Lou Boccardi almost 40 years after the fact.

The former AP president remembered the incident. "Of course I heard rumblings about it because of Terry Anderson somehow being there," Lou replied.[10] Punitive actions were a moot point. A short time later, "Terry was manacled by his captors somewhere in Lebanon for the next six and a half years," Dolph noted dryly.

It wasn't the first time Dolph Jr. was involved in world and national events. There were many experiences, unbeknownst to most of the folks back home in Kansas. Beyond his service on various national boards, Simons was regularly called up from America's heartland to provide thought leadership to the industry at large. Dolph was an invited speaker and contributing writer to trade journals.[11] He was a juror for the Pulitzer Prize in 1977, '78, '80, and '81. He was featured in *Editor & Publisher*, *Harper's*, and *Fortune* magazines, on National Public Radio, and in *The New York Times*.[12]

Not surprisingly, except to Dolph himself, job offers in major markets were forthcoming.

> *I was somewhat aware of the national players in the business with whom Dolph Sr. and Dolph Jr. were involved. They were both good at cultivating those relationships—and that was good for the Journal-World, to have those connections. But it wasn't something the average person in the newsroom would know. I probably knew more because of my daily interactions over the editorial page. It certainly didn't affect the operation of the paper. Actually, those connections almost certainly did affect the paper positively, but they were in the background, not part of the daily conversation.*
>
> Ann Gardner, former Journal-World editorial page editor

Most people in this business are trying to climb the ladder. If you're good, it'll take you as high as you're willing to go. Paul Miller, a man I admired very much, was an example of that. He was the son of a preacher, raised in a small Missouri town.

Paul was a self-made man who rose to president and CEO of Gannett. I first met Paul when he came to KU's journalism school to accept the William Allen White Award back in 1963. Paul was really winning with Gannett—buying other papers and making a name for himself. If that wasn't impressive enough, he flew his own plane to Lawrence, and he brought his own photographer with him.

I remember asking if his photographer Al would be joining us for lunch, but Paul shrugged that off. Al Neuharth wasn't part of the conversation yet, but he soon would be. Later that same year, Al would be running Gannett's operations in Rochester, New York, and soon after that, in Florida.

Paul Miller was president of the AP board from 1963 to 1977—the whole time I was on that board. At some point, he tried to get me to come over to Gannett in a senior executive role. I'll admit, I gave that idea a lot of thought. I'd had similar experiences and opportunities with the *Chicago Tribune* and the *L.A. Times*. Warren Phillips with the *Wall Street Journal* and the Sulzbergers at *The New York Times* pursued me. But every time I considered an offer or opportunity, a man by the name of Bob White came to mind.

Bob White had a paper in Mexico, Missouri, and did very well with it. He got an offer to become president of the *New York Herald Tribune* in 1959.[13] There was a lot of publicity and fanfare when he accepted the position, but then things didn't work out. He came back to Missouri in 1961. What if that happened to me? I sure didn't want to embarrass my family or the Journal-World. I didn't want to try anything unless I knew I could be successful, and I frankly didn't know if I would. I told everyone recruiting me that I'd cut ties with the Journal-World if I came—I didn't want to leave that option open.

*Over the years, Dolph Jr. was offered top management positions at **The New York Times** and in other newspaper groups but declined. He was asked if he ever second-guessed those decisions but said that once they were made, they were made.*

Ralph Gage, remarks made upon Dolph Simons Jr.'s Kansas
Press Association Hall of Fame Induction. 2007

I also didn't know if I could bring myself to leave the Journal-World, or Lawrence. I didn't have any grand plan about moving up to a bigger market, and Pam wasn't a bit interested in that. Just being from Lawrence was nothing to be ashamed of, as far as I was concerned. Putting out a good newspaper in a university town was very challenging and very satisfying. Maybe one of the reasons I was content where I was is that I got to travel to so many places in the world, especially with the Freedom Forum.

The Freedom Forum was one of the best ideas anybody ever had, and the credit for it goes to Al Neuharth.

Al Neuharth succeeded (some say climbed over) Paul Miller in 1973, and he built Gannett into the largest newspaper company in the country. He sure didn't make many friends along the way, but he and I stayed friendly ever since I'd met him in '63. A lot of people thought he was flamboyant, rude, and egotistical. One Gannett trustee, a woman who shall remain nameless, just couldn't stand him. She wrote a scathing letter of resignation from the board in which she called Al every name in the book and said his mother should have run off with the preacher before Al was born. Al thought it was the funniest thing he'd ever read, and gave copies of it to everybody on the board.

Judging by what he (Neuharth) relates, the man who built Gannett into America's largest newspaper chain and created USA TODAY is a conniver, backstabber, and liar, an executive so utterly without principle and so totally self-absorbed and self-indulgent he could startle even the most cynical muckraker. And he's proud of it. To Neuharth, these are traits that separate leaders, and winners, from the plodders of the world. "In my book," he writes, "an S.O.B. is someone who uses whatever tactics it takes to get the job done—to rise to the top."

from *Fortune Magazine's* book review of Neuharth's autobiography,
Confessions of an S.O.B., October 23, 1989.

Probably around 1980 when we were in Switzerland for an ANPA meeting, Al first told me about his idea for what would become *USA TODAY*. He had a KU graduate on board who'd figured out a way to beam satellite pictures so he could create a paper with faster reach and more visual appeal. Al wanted to go straight up against television news, and he was really on fire about it. I told him if he ever came west of the Mississippi, I'd print it for him.

Over a dinner in New York City, I told Kay Graham, Punch Sulzberger, and David Taylor from the *Boston Globe* I was going to be printing *USA TODAY*. They were shocked... *Dolph, what are you doing?! Dolph, why would you risk your good name and reputation on that guy?* They didn't think the idea would last more than a year or two. Like most of the leaders in the industry, they thought Neuharth was nothing but a show-boater. I saw Al as an innovator. He had great ideas, in my opinion, and wasn't afraid to try something new. He sure rubbed some people the wrong way, but Al Neuharth knew how to get things done.

When *USA TODAY* launched in 1982, it knocked the whole industry sideways. By 1984, Neuharth made The World Company one of its official contract printers. We'd joined the Gannett family.

When Al invited me to become a trustee for the Gannett Foundation in 1989, I said *Hell, yes!* I had no idea that decision would take me all over the world with what would soon be known as the Freedom Forum.

It was at one of the first Gannett Foundation board meetings I attended, Neuharth said he wanted to change the organization's name to the *Freedom Forum*. Some were kind of shocked by that—it sounded a bit pompous. What Al had in mind was to create an organization that would promote the principles of freedom of the press and freedom of speech. He established a First Amendment Task Force at the Gannett Foundation in 1990. I was on it, so was Frank Rhodes, the president of Cornell who was considered one of the top five university chancellors in the nation. I admired him. Also, Betty Bao Lord, an author and Chinese culture expert, and a few others. John Quinn, a Gannett VP who'd been calling the shots on the Foundation, drafted the plan that identified the goals of the Freedom Forum, which was officially launched on July 4, 1991.[14] Then we hit the ground running.

One of the priorities was to create forums for discussion of First Amendment principles in places where those ideas had been shut down. We did a fact-finding trip to the Soviet Union in August. Pam and Pammie came with me on that trip. Pam mentioned she wished there was a mirror in our room, and the next time we came back, voila, there was a mirror in our room. Strange things like that happened, so we realized we were being spied on or the rooms were bugged—probably both.

We met with Moscow's underground press and offered support, satellite dishes, and training to help their efforts. Everything felt strained and tense while we were there. Then the Soviet Union's Communist Party attempted to seize control of the country back from Mikhail Gorbachev.

The Russians thought my daughter was a journalist because she had her camera with her everywhere. Somehow she managed to be sitting on the hood of a Soviet tank in the middle of Red Square during that unsuccessful uprising that made headlines all over the world. Not even the U.S. Embassy knew what was going on—communications weren't like they are now. It was actually a strange and dangerous time to be in the Soviet Union.

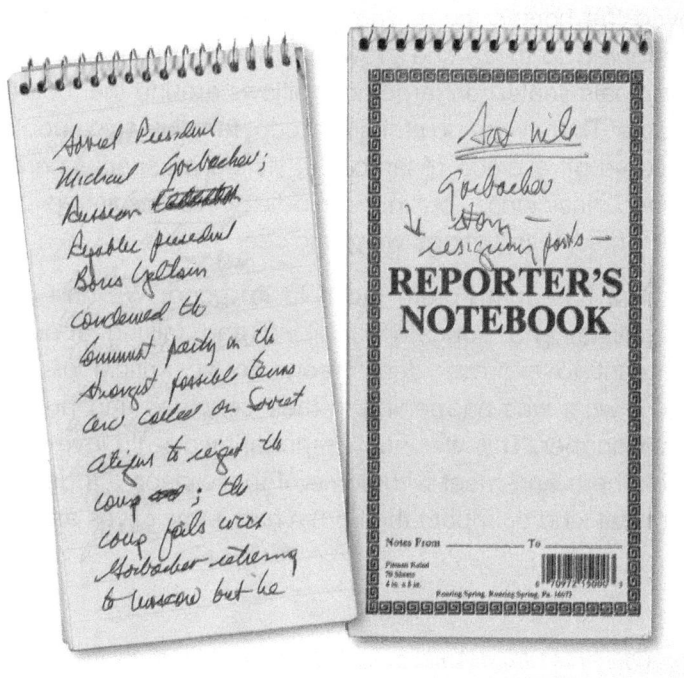

Simons' notes while in Warsaw and Moscow
during the 1991 Soviet coup d'état attempt.

We made it out, and went on to Helsinki, then to Poland where I met and talked with Lech Walesa in Warsaw. We visited London and Berlin.

In the fall of '92, the Freedom Forum went to Mongolia, Hong Kong, Manila, South Korea, and Vietnam. In '93, we went to Mexico. My own observations during those trips made it into the Journal-World. It was such an amazing opportunity to share those international experiences directly with our readers back home—it made other countries' issues all very real.

I have to admit it wasn't all work. There were fabulous meals, informative visits with international officials and U.S. Embassy personnel, and even a drinking contest in Moscow I'm surprised I can remember. My wife Pam came with me on the Mongolia trip. We stayed in yurts in an outpost. She loved the horses there. They were small, wild-looking things compared to those she grew up riding in Minnesota. We ate our meals seated on large floor pillows around the food in the middle. There were no utensils except for a knife you could use to carve off a piece of lamb. We visited a school where they trained musicians... out in the middle of this desolate place. So many fascinating things we got to see.

The Freedom Forum did a lot of good. We had writers, journalists, and educators thinking and talking about what it meant to express ideas freely—to be critical or excited about what was happening in their countries and put that in a newspaper. This was such important work. I'd love to travel back there and meet with some of those people today... find out what kind of impact the Forum had in their lives and work.

One of the First Amendment Taskforce initiatives was to expand its Communications and Media Center offerings. As part of its mission to foster First Amendment principles worldwide, it committed to the development of "television-radio techniques" and state-of-the-art facilities that could "project conferences" to larger audiences.[15] *In 1990, that was a reach-goal for an organization chiefly associated with newspaper publishing, but it remains an important and impactful achievement. Its voluminous record of journalistic history includes, among other things, a June 12, 1997 videotaped Newseum interview with Katharine Graham, retired publisher of The Washington Post, who died three years later in 2001. In it, Graham discussed the infamous break-in at Democratic Headquarters on the 25th anniversary of Watergate.*[16] *By June of 2012, that interview had been viewed over 77,000 times. Many such Freedom Forum resources are still accessible at www.freedomforum.org.*

The Freedom Forum did some pretty impressive things in this country, too. It established the Newseum in Washington, DC, in 1997. This was a huge newspaper museum dedicated to First Amendment freedoms and the evolution of journalism. It was such an amazing idea, and I'm so sorry it wasn't sustained. Apparently, it never made any money. But you really had to hand it to Neuharth. That guy could piss people off, but he was a visionary. After he died, Gannett headed in a different direction, but there's no way anybody could say Neuharth didn't have a tremendous influence over nearly every aspect of this business.

Things like the Freedom Forum were really exciting to me. If I could see how something could make a difference for the better, I've always wanted to be a part of that.

*I was teaching at KU and directing its Center for Asian Studies when I first learned Dolph was friends with the editor of the **Korean Herald**, one of the English-language newspapers in Korea that sent some of their journalists to the KU School of Journalism. Dolph was involved in that. In my view, he was the one person who had one foot on Lawrence, and the other foot on the national/international front. He knew all the players; it was quite impressive. We became good friends, and had many conversations about many things including national security issues.*

In the early 1970s, I'd held the Admiral Ricketts Chair at the Admiral's College for Comparative Cultures at the U.S. Naval War College. After 9/11, Kansas Senator Pat Roberts had just become the chair of the U.S. Senate Intelligence Committee. Dolph knew him well, and set up a meeting so I could share my concerns with the senator about U.S. national security and terrorist threats, as well as the general state of U.S. Intelligence capacities and personnel. Dolph and I encouraged Senator Roberts to sponsor a bill that would prepare young Americans, primarily college students, for Intelligence-focused careers in the U.S. Military and the U.S. Foreign Service, which he did.

The Pat Roberts Intelligence Scholars Program (PRISP) was a bill passed in 2004. In 2010, President Barack Obama signed legislation making PRISP a permanently funded program.

Dr. Felix Moos, University of Kansas professor emeritus of anthropology and East Asian studies, and national and international security studies and terrorist threats consultant [17]

Every person can make a difference, at least they should try. Maybe we start out our careers thinking we will, then somewhere along the way, we lose sight of that. This is why one of my big themes is mid-career training. In the newspaper business, most don't have time to even think about anything except what they have to get done that day. The idea of learning more about your field, or learning some different aspect of it can recharge your energy.

This brings me to another great idea that I'd put on par with the Freedom Forum, and that's the Nieman Fellowships. The Nieman Foundation is associated with Harvard's Journalism School. I received an invitation to apply for a Nieman Fellowship. I'd have a stipend to cover a year off work while I focused on mid-career training. Pam was included—we could take any courses we wanted. There was even a babysitting stipend. I couldn't take the time to do it, but I did agree to join their advisory group to select the Nieman scholars and oversee the Nieman program at Harvard.

That was a pretty heady experience. The fellowship candidates were mid-career journalists who'd been on a police beat or whatever, and they'd come to Harvard for a year to learn more or different topics. I was being exposed to some amazing people. Ellen Goodman was one of them—she was big in television. To get to sit in and be a freeloader with these Harvard professors plus free tuition, housing, and every class open to you… imagine. All the Nieman Fellows had impressive records, and they just wanted to improve themselves. It was an absolutely fantastic opportunity.

The Nieman Foundation published the *Nieman Reports* quarterly in those days, and I was invited to contribute my piece on "What Is the Role of the Daily Newspaper." It was in the same issue as Daniel Ellsberg's commentary on his case that landed *The New York Times* in court—the Supreme Court—and Ralph Nader's commentary on the problem with media.[18] Like I said, it was a pretty heady experience.

Creating that experience was what I had in mind when we established the Simons Fellowship at KU in 2005. I wanted it to be for individuals not connected to academics who were interested in experiencing the intellectual life of a university. KU got a matching grant from the National Endowment for the Humanities, and we've been able to offer a total of $25,000 to support a fellowship for a short period, from one month to a whole semester.

This project hasn't turned out exactly the way I hoped it would, but I still strongly believe in its purpose. The way things are changing in the newspaper business, if you're going to stay informed you have to have access to something like this. It's about improving yourself... being more effective and staying current. I'm still a very big proponent of mid-career training. I'm also in favor of a good education that prepares you for a career, including the things you learn outside a classroom. Hell, we should continue to learn new things all our life long.

If, as the playwright Arthur Miller put it, "A good newspaper is a nation talking to itself," then its voice must be recognizable to be understood, and credible if it's to be believed. An independent, locally-owned, small city or town newspaper has a distinct advantage in this regard. It is the record of the collective voice of a community—pro or con, proud or embarrassed, angry or pleased or confused, deceased or newly born. These are the voices of real people with a personal stake not only in their shared quality of life, but sometimes even the survival of their community.

The newspaper that records those voices keeps the conversation real and locally relevant. In the board rooms of the Associated Press, the American Newspaper Publishers Association, the Newspaper Advertising Bureau, and other organizations, directors relied on those perspectives to ensure the integrity and relevancy of the national conversation. Keeping a seat at those tables for three generations takes brains and backbone, but also a sense of calling or duty to this work. These attributes W.C., Dolph Sr. and Dolph Jr. possessed in spades. Senator Pat Roberts could have been describing all of them when he summed up that calling this way: "I don't know what it is that Dolph Simons hasn't done for the community of Lawrence in every aspect, and for that matter our state, and for that matter our country."[19]

CHAPTER 8

Above the Fold

The history of the Simons family
and the paper is inextricably linked
with Lawrence itself, which was still a young city
*when the family first printed the **Lawrence World** in 1892.*
And while active local ownership can be a double-edged
sword, they are generally regarded as good stewards.

Deron Lee, *Columbia Journalism Review* [1]

What does it mean to be human?

With few exceptions, every student in Judith Galas' class at Bishop Seabury Academy in Lawrence dreaded that writing assignment. Several of Dolph Simons Jr.'s grandchildren took the class and remembered Ms. Galas famously handing back papers to be rewritten if the scholar didn't do the theme justice. Dolph's son Dan recalled his kids laboring through the drafts. "She really made them work," Dan admitted. "That was the point—making her students think hard about the question. It was good for them. She was a very smart teacher."

"I think I would have enjoyed that assignment," Dolph said. "I wonder how I'd answer it now?" To find out, Dolph tracked down Ms. Galas and invited her to The Cedars for lunch in December 2021. Galas, who'd been a financial reporter for Knight-Ridder earlier in her career, was delighted to accept. The two talked shop, then explored the subject at hand.

Judith said, "I'd just shown the documentary *Leo the Man* to one of my classes. It was about Leo Beuerman, who was somewhat famous in Lawrence. Leo was a severely disabled man who got around in a small, wheeled cart. He had jerry-rigged a contraption to lift the cart up to his tractor. Every day, he drove that tractor into town and sold pencils to make a living. Leo was an extremely independent man—a real survivor. He died in the late 1970s."

Dolph nodded. "Leo was something. He set up shop on a main corner of downtown. Some people felt awkward. They'd avoid him... just walk around him like he was pitiful, but that man was made of sturdier stuff than a lot of them," Dolph said. "He wasn't sitting around waiting for a handout, he was industrious. Leo even put an ad in the Journal-World to drum up business, although we wouldn't let him pay for it."

```
                                    Leo Beuerman
                                    1800 West 27th Street
                                    Lawrence, Kansas 66044

Journal World
Lawrence, Kansas 66044

Dear Sir:

I am planning to run the following advertisement in your paper
real soon now or as soon as I hear rom you. I do not know
what your advertiseing charges are on this.

The advertisement:

      REMEMBER ME? I use to drive a little

      REMEMBER ME?  I am that little crippled guy you saw
      drive a tractor, I had to quit driving. I now sell
      at a discount all magazine subscription of public in-
      terest. Write me for prices on magazines you want.
      (This special offer is for one month only)
      Leo Beuerman, 1800 West 27th Street, Lawrence, Kansas
      66044.

What is your charges to run the above advertisement once every
three days for for some time? Also, what will be your charges
to run the advertisement for one week daily?  If your charges
are not to high, I'll run the advertisement often, providing of
course it brings me any orders.  Do you think its okay and
will get me orders?

                              Yours very truly,

                              Leo Beuerman
                              Leo Beuerman
```

"Your grandson Dan was in my class," Judith responded. "After I showed that movie, he volunteered he already knew about Leo because his dad (Dan Sr.) and uncle (Dolph III) were regularly sent by their dad over to buy pencils from Leo. Apparently, Granddad wanted to teach his sons to be helpful and respectful—and to appreciate how lucky they were. I was very impressed that a father would intentionally send his sons to this encounter. It says a lot about the father and the sons."[2]

As an allegory, the Leo Beuerman story certainly stands on its own merits, but it also illustrates the intersection of concerns for the Simons as a newspaper family. How, as parents, they raised their children... how the children behaved... how parents and elders functioned as community members, and how the Simons operated their local business were all inextricably connected. In many ways, their lives played out on a very public stage.

Certain expectations came with growing up in a newspaper family. Doing something notable wouldn't necessarily make the news if it could be perceived as the Simons' using the paper to brag about themselves. Dolph Sr.'s vigilance in this regard resulted in only three Journal-World mentions of his son's award-winning football career over the four years Dolph Jr. spent at KU—and two of the three were his name listed on the team roster.[3] Given that Dolph Jr. was good enough "to have his picture on the cover of *Sports Illustrated* or *Time*, but Dad got bumped for the Korean war," according to daughter Linda Simons de Menocal, Dolph Sr.'s restraint doesn't seem justified.

However, "If your teenage shenanigans caught up with you, anything that made the police blotter would definitely show up in the paper," Dolph Jr. pointed out. "I didn't have a lot of sympathy for anyone asking us not to print something sensitive or embarrassing because we wouldn't make exceptions even for our own family."

Dolph Simons III admitted his teenage antics once made page three fodder, although he was better known as the captain of his prep school football team. Dolph III had the kind of good looks and amiable nature that endeared his future mother-in-law, Tinka Flickinger McCray. She knew the Simons family, and made a point to show her daughter Lisa their Christmas card. Noticing teenaged Dolph, "Lisa said, 'hmmm, he's not bad,'" Dolph III recounted the tale.

Lisa McCray eventually called and asked for Dolph. "Dad answered the phone," Dolph III said. "I think he wanted to hear her pitch so he stayed on until she asked him out on a date before pointing out 'oh, I think you want my son.'" Decades later, the story still gets a grin from both Dolphs. "A sense of humor definitely runs in the family," Dolph III acknowledged.

So do a resilient moral fiber and determination that have been apparent since their ancestor, Governor William Bradford,[4] arrived on the Mayflower in 1620. These traits manifested in strength and courage for Civil War widow Jennie Bessie Simons, who kept her young family from starving on the Kansas frontier. Each of her children went on to lead remarkable, successful lives, including W.C. Simons, who began the family's award-winning newspaper empire.

Such a legacy is a great gift to those who inherit it, but, as the saying goes, to whom much is given, much is required. In one way or another, this heritage—and the expectations imposed on them as a newspaper family—challenged each of them to consider *what does it mean to be a Simons?*

For the Simons, there has always been a crosswalk between family values and newspaper policy, but "It all really comes down to the golden rule," Dan Simons said. "We were always taught to treat people the way you want to be treated." This was how Dolph Jr. and Pam Simons raised Pam, Linda, Dolph III, and Dan. It was understood this applied personally and professionally. In fact, Dolph Simons Sr., a.k.a. "Grampy," had included the golden rule in The World Company's employee manual back in the 1950s, and before him, W.C. Simons built the business on moral high ground.

W.C. Simons always aspired "to see the other man as he is, rather than as he appears to be."[5] As a kind of mission statement, it served him well; although for the observed, it could cut both ways. "My grandfather, W.C., was stern but compassionate," Dolph Jr. said. "He knew right from wrong and believed his responsibility as editor and publisher was to take a stand on things as he saw them."

So strong were his convictions, W.C. would go nose to nose over ethical issues with the opposition, politicians, subversive organizations, or even a competing newspaper edited by his brother-in-law, J.L. Brady. Indeed, his handling of the complicated business/family dynamic speaks volumes about putting a noble theory into practice.

Although Simons and Brady had launched their newspaper business together in 1891, they separated operations in 1905 when The World Company purchased the *Lawrence Daily Journal*. Brady took over that paper, publishing as The Lawrence Journal Company. Simons continued with The World Company that published the *Lawrence Daily* and *Weekly World*. Whether their split was a divide-and-conquer attempt to buy out the competition, expand the family's business interests, give Brady room for his increasingly divergent agenda, or to cut ties that had been painfully stretched by the acrimonious divorce[6] of W.C.'s sister Julia from Brady, it isn't known. Whatever the impetus, Simons and Brady were now functioning independently and competing for advertising dollars and subscribers. Those weren't the only demarcations.

W.C. Simons published "a decidedly Republican paper,"[7] whereas Brady's stance and strategies with his *Lawrence Journal* were less certain. In a letter to W.C. in December, 1923, he reflected on his "hopes of anything under the sun as long as it was big." He aspired to politics and was famously "opposed [to] tight lacing [and] the use of cosmetics"[8] for women. However, his journalistic intent was, at times, questionable. Professor Dennis Domer, author of a seminal series on Lawrence history, noted that Brady gave KU journalism students free rein with his Saturday paper in April 1908, "for unknown reasons." The students had a field day with it. "Beer Sold Here," their ensuing exposé of gambling, drinking, and houses of ill repute in the East Bottoms of Lawrence, "rocked the foundations of polite society."[9]

The students "laid bare" the shocking news that "many of the houses are owned by Police Judge Louis Menger." As unsavory connections between life in the Bottoms and certain upstanding members in the community became clearer, the entire fiasco backfired on Brady. Presumably under pressure from Menger or his operatives, Brady recanted the story, then "criticized the students for using bad judgment, denied that a liquor problem existed, insisted that Lawrence was a clean city, and asserted that it was a mistake to have given the paper over to the students in the first place."[10]

Meanwhile, Simons' *Daily World* went "on record as standing fairly and squarely behind the boys in their statements." W.C. Simons railed on the "cringing cowardice"[11] of Brady's paper in "not exposing vice and corruption, but covering up and making excuses for them."[12] Future Pulitzer Prize-winner (and former KU student) William Allen White, editor of the *Emporia Gazette*, agreed "the students did exactly the right thing."[13]

The students were vindicated by the resulting arrests and convictions of numerous parties named in their article, which prompted another about-face from Brady. Domer wrote, "The *Daily Journal* congratulated the students" and "admitted it had not done its job." Even the *University Daily Kansan* credited "the World on its conversion."[14]

W.C. Simons maintained his vigil against vice in the Bottoms. A year later, he tried to quash efforts "to swell the ranks of those favoring a wide-open town"[15] during a mayoral election in April. A die-hard prohibitionist, Simons supported temperance candidate William H. Carruth to no avail. Independent candidate J. D. Bishop won handily with help from the endorsement of "Aunt Jane" Williams, the "Queen of the Bottoms," who delivered the bootlegging society vote and "seems to have won in the court of public opinion rather easily in 1909 against W.C. Simons..."[16] And so it would go as Simons continued his righteous, if uphill, battle against "the dark corners of town" that threatened a virtuous Lawrence. It was abundantly clear W.C. had found his own voice as editor, and he wasn't afraid to use it. He'd certainly earned the right.

W.C. "Collie" Simons had been only 18 when his mother, Jennie Bessie, purchased the *Salina Daily Republican* and made her new son-in-law, J.L. Brady, its editor in 1889. For the next 16 years, Collie remained subordinate to Brady until their 1905 split gave W.C. sole control of The World Company. Simons didn't hesitate to put that in writing. On November 28, 1905, W.C. incorporated The World Company and "Resolved, that we do hereby give full power and authority to W.C. Simons as President and General Manager of the Company" with Gertrude R. Simons as secretary.[17]

One has to wonder about W.C.'s reaction to the idea of sharing the masthead with Brady again when that issue arose unexpectedly on February 17, 1911. A fire destroyed the Bowersock Building that housed Brady's Journal offices and printing equipment on the first floor. The elimination of competition could've been a boon to The World Company, but W.C. Simons wasn't the sort of man who'd take advantage of the situation.

Even so, Simons surely felt some reticence to attach his name to Brady's, an editor he'd previously described as "cringing with cowardice" over the East Bottoms debacle. But W.C. didn't hesitate— he did the right thing. Just three days after the fire, the newly-merged *Lawrence Journal-World* hit the streets. Its masthead featured both Simons' and Brady's names, but there was no mistaking W.C.'s preeminence. The consolidation was announced as a win/win decision for the newspaper and merchants of Lawrence. Over the next few

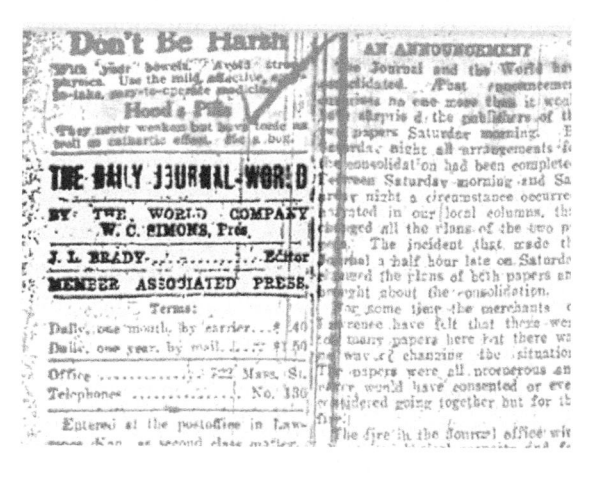

years, W.C. kept the positive spin turning, and emphasized the good aspects of the situation.

Indeed, for the rest of his life, W.C.'s narrative characterized the merger as a collegial work-around, but this version was likely crafted with judicious restraint. Circumstantial evidence suggests the stress of sharing the leadership role is what eventually prompted Simons to seek out a like-sized newspaper for sale in Arkansas, and then he put it to Brady in no uncertain terms. "W.C. made him a buy-out deal. Either Brady would take his proceeds and move to Arkansas or Granddad was prepared to go himself," Dolph Jr. said. "Fortunately, Brady took the offer and headed to Arkansas, or things might have turned out very differently for our family. I have to believe Granddad was glad to have his paper back. This experience probably had a lot to do with my dad's advice to never have more than one man running the shop. I'm sure he got that from W.C."

W.C.'s skill and authority in newspapering transferred readily to the leadership and guidance of his family—and family always came first.

As the "little man" of the family since he was seven years old, Collie Simons assumed his patriarchal duties early on. His siblings sought his counsel all their lives about business opportunities (which sometimes involved W.C. loaning necessary funds) and in personal matters. When his older sister Julia was paralyzed with grief over the death of her granddaughter in 1926, W.C. gently counseled her:

> *Compare your loss of little Sally, as dearly as you loved her, with the death of Papa. Mama loved him as tenderly as you loved Sally, he was her idol, her husband, the father of her large family of children. The one who had provided for her, and here she was left with five little ones. Think of her, inexperienced, with no idea of business, facing the world and keeping her family together. She was not conscious of doing anything heroic, but she kept her family together and made it possible for each member to make and hold a*

place in the circles in which they have lived and moved. Supposing
Mama had given up to her grief and decided there was nothing
worth living for, where would we have been?[18]

Those thoughts surely came back to W.C. two years later when
he and Gertie lost their own son in 1928. The youngest of their five
children, John Louis was 13 years old the day he came home from
school early because he didn't feel well. He went upstairs to rest, and
never woke up. His death from an unknown cause "came suddenly and
without warning," W.C. wrote. His heartbroken parents established
a memorial fund at Cordley Grade School in honor of John Louis
Simons, a "sturdy and loving child—with a love for music and the
rare sense of perfect pitch."

Somehow, as it does, life went on.

In 1930, W.C. gave a talk to the "Saturday Night Club"
comprised of Lawrence's movers and shakers. In it, he pondered
whether "education today offered any easier manner of learning the
character and background of men than the hard way in which I learned
when I came to Lawrence, not knowing a solitary person in the city,
or county, aside from the members of my own family."[19] While Collie
didn't receive a traditional classroom education, that hadn't limited
his vast intellect and varied interests as a grown man. W.C. was an
autodidact who read voraciously. He more than held his own with a
fascinating array of people he would come to know, and the world
into which his own children were born was one of comfort, privilege,
and intellectual stimulation.

The family lived at The Cedars on an acreage at the edge of
Lawrence. It was originally built in 1877 by William Crutchfield, a Civil
War veteran, as a "fowl ranch" known for its Wyandotte chickens.
After the Simons bought it from Crutchfield's estate in 1917, Gertie
immediately set about remodeling and modernizing the house with
electricity, indoor plumbing, heating, and the addition of two good-

Generations of Simons lived here at The Cedars. Photo circa 1930s

W.C. and Gertrude receiving guests at their 50th wedding anniversary.

sized porches.[20] A barn out back sheltered some serviceable animals, but farming was never a primary goal, to the great relief of their son Dolph, who opined, "The worst job in the world is milking a cow with a wet tail on a cold morning."

The Cedars, a large, lovely two-story white-frame structure with a graceful, wide front porch, had a warm, inviting feel to it, notwithstanding the number of people who died there including William and Anna Crutchfield, Gertie's mother, young John Louis, and W.C.'s sister Etoile, whose large body became wedged against the door when she collapsed and died. It was and is a happy home where the Simons have gathered for four generations for Sunday dinners, holidays, formal dinners, and social events.

Back in the day, the Journal-World's society column provided interesting tidbits about life at The Cedars. A stray dog having puppies under the porch (December 1942) and a lilac going into a second full-bloom in September (1946) were noted. When Mrs. W.C. Simons hosted a Mother-Daughter Picnic on the lawn with Haskell Indian School girls as special guests, it made the front page on May 20, 1920.[21]

W.C. and Gertie Simons were gracious hosts. They instituted this important aspect of Simons family culture, then Dolph Sr. and Marie, and Dolph Jr. and Pam, took hospitality to the next level.

In the late 1940s, the Simons became the go-to hosts for certain KU VIP events because it was against university policy to serve (and pay for) alcohol. "It was against my granddad's policy, too," Dolph Jr. noted. "W.C. was a complete teetotaler. Once, Dad and Ernie Pontius, our advertising manager, were having a drink after work at the house when Granddad stopped by. Ernie knew W.C. would disapprove, so he slipped his drink behind his back. Of course, Granddad knew what was up and told him, 'Ernie, never do anything you have to hide. Pull that drink out and drink it if you must.'"

Dolph Sr. and Marie stepped up with receptions at their house, offering wine or cocktails with the tastefully limited two-drink convention of society. Dolph Jr. said, "It was an important support to the university, and it grew into an amazing experience for our family as well. Of course, W.C. wouldn't have approved of the alcohol, but he definitely would have enjoyed the company."

Dolph Sr. and Marie were consummate hosts. Conversant and cultured, their combination of style, charm, and intellect found its ideal expression in the social scene. Marie was an excellent pianist, and Dolph, who also played, was ever ready for a duet. Whatever stereotypes their international, east or west coast guests may have heard about Kansans were eclipsed by the entertainment, stimulating conversation, and sophisticated gourmet fare served at the Simons' perfectly appointed Duncan Fife table.

When it was their turn to take the primary hosting role, Dolph Jr. and Pam reveled in it. One evening in particular showcased the "best of" both generations as hosts. "We were having a black-tie dinner party here at the house, and it was definitely a black-tie crowd—a very formal, very nice, dressy dinner party," Dolph Jr. said. "One of the VIP guests hadn't arrived from Kansas City, and that went on and on... I kept making excuses and was wondering how long I could delay the dinner. So I called Mother and Dad, described the problem, and asked what they thought I should do. They'd already gone to bed but said, give us a minute, we've got an idea. Just a little bit later, they pulled up

Self-taught player Dolph Sr. often joined his classically-trained wife Marie at the piano. The Simons were consummate hosts and ready entertainers, circa 1985.

in black tie and gown and made huge apologies for being held up. The guests who were late never showed up, but my folks saved the day, or night in this case."

> *Why not a course in "Personal Conduct and Manners" for all underclassmen, in which young people would be taught the fundamentals of being a gentleman or a lady? I can see where the school would contribute substantially to the well-being of the individual, and to society as a whole, if it would teach young men the importance of being correctly clothed, in manners of approach, a good handshake, correct use of table silverware, acts of courtesy due a lady, the handicaps attendant with dirty fingernails and uncombed hair, and accepted customs related to personal correspondence.*

> Dolph Simons Sr. from a talk delivered to the Saturday Night Club
> January 23, 1943.

Dolph Sr. and Marie could always be counted on for knowing the right and proper thing to do and doing it. "Grampy was the kind of man who wore a suit or sport coat to a basketball game," Dolph III noted. Marie was similarly inclined in dress and formal manner, eschewing even nicknames like Grandma or Grammy. Her grandchildren called her by her first name. "Marie was always dressed—heels with a dress or lovely slacks. She wasn't showy but dressed," Linda recalled. "She'd come out for a visit in white pants, or a dress with gloves on, and she'd just start weeding the garden with an air of 'Well, somebody has to do this!' We always knew they loved us, but they were formal—not touchy-feely people." Dolph III added, "Except for when I got some poison ivy and Marie threw me in the bathtub and scrubbed me head to toe with Tide!" Linda chimed in, "Same with me except she used Oxydol!"

That Dolph Sr. wrote at least one edgy novel but never showed it to anyone suggests there was more going on behind the starched curtains. His book, *Wanted; Loving Care*, featured a protagonist who was the local newspaper editor and part-time preacher struggling with mid-20th century moral dilemmas including his own murderous rage over his unwed daughter's pregnancy. "Apparently, Dad tried to get it published, but that didn't happen," Dolph Jr. said. "He never shared the book with me, and didn't talk about it."

Pam and Pammie with baby Linda, circa 1955

As Dolph Jr. and Pam increasingly stepped into their roles in society, their growing family had to be factored into the schedule. Four children might have clipped the wings of another couple, but Dolph and Pam adapted by bringing their brood with them. There weren't many "grown-ups only" activities for this generation of Simons. Pammie, Linda, Dolph III, and Dan were routinely included in whatever was going on, including business trips.

> Pam and I have lived in this house since I got out of the service—soon after W.C. passed on. All these years later, I can still see him and Grandmother sitting in the living room reading. The house was lit by gas then, and W.C. was always concerned with whether the light was good enough to read by. The red room that's now a study used to have Grandmother's harpsichord in it. The master bedroom upstairs used to be a porch where

W.C. slept on hot summer nights—those were the days before air conditioning. Actually, he'd sleep out there on cold nights, too, now that I think about it. The bedroom on the northeast corner that became my daughter Pammie's room was where my brother John and I would sometimes sleep over. We'd have fights until we broke the slats in the bed. There were a few horses and farm animals that my dad had to care for when he was growing up here, and Granddad kept bees. Where we have a swimming pool now is where they used to butcher pigs. This home was where everybody gathered for the big events. Sunday dinners here with my grandparents were a wonderful tradition.

Pam and I moved here in 1954, and we raised our family in this house. She remembers having to put wet towels around the windows and doors during the dust storms. Pam loved horses, so we had a couple of ponies out at the small barn that's a pool house now. She rarely had time to enjoy them with four young children to keep an eye on—they certainly kept her busy. I'd later learn that Dolph (III) told his little brother Dan he had to learn to jump out of the second-floor window in case of a fire. Dan remembers this very fondly (wink wink). The kids had a large yard and nearby stream to play in, and fields to roam. Haskell was right across the street so they'd go over for the Pow Wow events every year.

We had so many visitors over the years, including some who weren't invited. One night, I awoke to the sound of our piano being played, and upon going downstairs to investigate,

We had two Shetland ponies and an Appaloosa-type pony, and a quarter horse named General Jeb that was just for mom.

They all ended up moving on, but I think that was the result of horses not getting the necessary attention. Mom went to horseback riding camps and grew up with that, but I think life got too busy with four kids to maintain her passion while raising a family.

Linda Simons de Menocal

The Simons at Thanksgiving time 1960
Left to right: Linda, Dolph Sr., Dolph III, Marie Simons, Pammie, and John N. Simons.

Standing left to right: Dolph Jr., Pam, and Dolph Sr.
Seated: John holding Dolph III, Pammie, Marie, Althea holding John Jr., and Linda.

I found a young Haskell student at the keyboard without a stitch of clothes on. I'm not sure how she got in there, but her boyfriend skinny-dipping in our pool outside probably had something to do with it. Pam heard this as well and came down the steps not far behind me. I didn't want her to be alarmed, so I calmly said, 'Pam, look, we have a visitor.' I suggested to our guest that she leave, but she said it was too cold outside. Well, there was no way I was driving a naked girl back to school—what if we had a wreck? So Pam came with me. We got her into the car and drove her back to campus in our pajamas. When we returned, her boyfriend was gone. Those two were harmless, unlike the guy who came in here one night brandishing a knife. I managed to talk him out of it—and out of the house.

Mostly, the people who've come were invited, and they came back again and again. Between W.C., my parents, and Pam and I, our guests have included one of the Wright brothers, a Russian cosmonaut, an American astronaut, George Bush Sr., Walter Cronkite, Ann Landers, Ben Bradlee, Sir William Paley, and so many more.

My brother John, who'd become a very successful plastic surgeon and counted a number of Hollywood and senior Washington judges and politicians as patients, was here for a dinner the same evening decathlete Rafer Johnson was a guest. Pam must have been out of town, and I realized too late we were lacking a bouquet for the table. John came to the rescue and constructed a centerpiece out of breast implants surrounded by a number of votives to add sparkle. As unforgettable as that was, it did not make "most memorable" event. There's a tie for that title and Pam wins for both of them.

There was an editor I knew from working in South Africa who came stateside and called me up to make good on my *stop by if you're ever in Kansas* offer. He'd arrived right as Pam was getting home from the hospital with newborn Linda in her arms. She gave me a look that said HOW COULD YOU?

In long white gloves, the glamorous Mrs. Dolph Simons Jr. mingles with newspaper royalty including the Wes Gallaghers and the Paul Millers at the 21 Club in New York City in 1968.

Who could blame her? She was a great sport about such things normally, which brings us to the next most-memorable event. Pam was very pregnant while hosting a party at our house, and while she was carrying a tray from one group to another, her water broke. Pam laughs about that now and reminds me that I always liked her to be entertaining.

When I think about who has played a helluva role or inspired me in my life, there are so many names but I have to say Pam has been the most important one of all. She let me spend so much time at the office. I'd be out of here at six in the morning, home for dinner, then back to the office afterwards. There were plenty of nights I wouldn't get home 'til 12:30 or 1:00 a.m.

More and more, I think about the adjustments Pam had to make to marry me. Her family in Rochester was so closely tied to the Mayo family—they were her godparents. Virge, her dad, was Dr. Virgil Counseller, the surgeon who headed the department of obstetrics and gynecology at Mayo Clinic. At that time, Virge was the only doctor at Mayo's who was board-certified in three specialties—just a top flight individual. He was a kind, gentle man, and Pam's mother, Gladys, was polite and refined. Pam had a very upscale lifestyle growing up. Everything was calm and peaceful. That's just not a real world, at least it's not the world she found herself in when she moved to Lawrence.

I doubt many patients can just call their doctor directly day or night to complain or tell him he did their surgery wrong or left a scar, but if you're a newspaper publisher, you're right in the middle of that all the time. You can't walk the aisles of a grocery store without getting told what the paper is doing wrong. Any time Pam would answer the phone, it could be someone with something bad to say about the paper. She handled it well. She did a great job adjusting from her pristine environment of her youth to the sometimes gritty world of a newspaper family.

Pam often traveled with me on work trips. She got to know the other publishers and their wives—she was completely comfortable with the social scene, which was a big asset for me. Pam is gracious but tough. She's been through a lot—won four battles with cancer and had total shoulder and knee replacements. She never lost her cool, although I've heard her use certain words under her breath on rare occasions and I'd ask *what would Gladys think if she heard you say that?* In recent years, Pam has shocked me with some very specific language about where my head is located or what I could do with it... she's full of all kinds of suggestions.

The truth is, I've been lucky in my marriage and lucky in my children.... blessed is Pam's word, and she's right. We have been very blessed with a full life and a happy home.

Our home has been remodeled and expanded to accommodate our family and the guest list, but I think it retains its original charm and character. Pam and I are up in our 90s now and don't entertain as often, although I think we had 86 people here for our 2022 Christmas party. My best friend, Bob Trapp, makes that all possible. I've known Trapp since mom hired him back when he was just getting Trapp and Company started. He's the pro—even worked at the Reagan White House and the U.S. Embassy in London. He did their parties. Trapp has been a part of some very important events, and he knows everybody. He's certainly been a big part of this family. He's one who can always make Pam smile.

"Many people came to our house. We were always encouraged to engage in conversation and learn from these journalists, dignitaries, and world leaders," Linda said. "We were definitely not excluded as kids—our parents wanted us to be exposed to all kinds of people." Dolph III has vivid memories of those experiences. " We were allowed to hang out with whoever was here. Dad wanted us to be a part of that.

Bob Trapp and Dolph, Christmas 2021 (Photo: L. Seaver)
below, Pam Simons managed Columbine Cablevision in Colorado.

He wanted us to know what was going on. I remember listening to this Russian cosmonaut talk about his experiences."

As the eldest, daughter Pam remembered more than Linda about their first overseas trip. "Linda was still a baby when we got to live in England while Dad was working in London at *The Times*," she recalled. "I was only three, so some memories are a bit fuzzy. My nightie caught on fire when I got too close to a heater. I don't remember that, but they do! We had a nanny who was Welsh, so I'm told I was talking with a bit of an accent early on."

The summer she was nine, Pammie flew with Grampy Simons up to Minnesota. "We were in a small plane, and the door flew off," she said. "Apparently, that didn't faze me. We landed in Nebraska, got the plane fixed, then we took off again." Pam proved to be an

At six, Pammie was already mingling politely in adult society.

Pammie, Linda, Dolphie, and Dan Simons, circa 1962

intrepid traveler. "Dad took Linda and me to London, and I got to go to Switzerland with him once. I remember we took an evening cruise and I ended up talking with a Chinese couple. I enjoyed that." She also made the Freedom Forum trip to Russia and Poland with her folks in 1991. "We were the first people Lech Walesa talked to in Warsaw. I was always taking pictures. In Moscow, the Russians thought I was part of the press crew," Pam said. "It was wonderful to grow up with a world view."

Dolph III and Dan also made numerous trips with their dad, and hung out with what "We jokingly called the 'Nepotism Club' because there were third, fourth, even fifth generation newspaper families represented there," Dan said.

For the Simons kids, growing up in a newspaper family definitely had its perks, but there were also disadvantages. As the son of the local editor himself, Dolph Jr. knew the pressures all too well. Just as everything the Simons did could reflect on the newspaper, so, too, could anything published in the newspaper—for better or for worse—impact members of the family.

"There were a lot of people who hated the paper and the Simons, and were very vocal about it," daughter Pam admitted. "We had to get used to that treatment. Our family wasn't liked by everybody, so we had to develop a pretty thick skin."

Dan had a similar experience in school "My political science teacher said *I don't care what you do, Simons, you're never getting anything higher than a C in this class because I hate your father and your newspaper.*"

Linda commiserated. "In any small town, there's jealousy and resentment. If your father is writing opinion editorials that are going to piss people off, that can be a trigger. I don't think I ever actually felt disliked. Only once when I was in high school did this present much of an issue for me. This teacher was pointing out things on a map, and he singled out one spot in Lawrence and said *This is what we call 'Snob Hill,'* and I realized it was our house."

Dolph III, Pam, Pamela Ann, Linda, Dan, and Dolph Jr., circa 1974

from left: Dan de Menocal, Linda holding Emily, Dan and Trish Simons,
Dolph III, Pam, Marie and Dolph Sr., Dolph Jr. and Pam Simons,
at Christmastime, 1986

Everybody knew my dad had the paper, and there I was taking journalism classes. My professors did what they could to minimize it, I guess, but the Journal-World was often used in the classroom as an example of "poor journalism." It was rather upsetting.

What I learned on the job was important preparation for the real world, but maybe I should've paid attention more at school. It's been a helluva challenge. I know I could have been a better editor. I honestly don't know if I've ever done anything that gives me the feeling I've done a great job that couldn't have been improved on. I wish I'd done a better job with a talk at Colby College up in Maine. I was no scholar, but there I was, speaking to faculty, alumni, and students at a very nice school that was giving me an honorary doctorate.

He was always mindful of the community and constantly preached to his sons and company managers the word from his forebears: "You take care of Lawrence, and Lawrence will take care of you."

Ralph Gage

Nowadays, I spend more time wondering if I could have been a better son and husband and father.

As a son, I never wanted to do anything to embarrass my dad or the paper. The flip side is, once I had children of my own, I knew the same pressures affected them. As a publisher, I wasn't conflicted, I knew what I had to do; but as a father, I worried a lot about how this life impacted my kids. I didn't groom them to become journalists. Pam and I encouraged them to do whatever they wanted to do with their lives. Growing up, they all spent time working at the newspaper or the cable operation. They all delivered papers, climbed poles, or wired houses. So they've lived it... they know the business, which is both good and bad.

One of the bad things about this business is you have to be prepared to lose friends. Maybe that's why we are so close as a family. Family must come first. Like Linda says, family is everything.

All four of our children are so different. I know Pammie had other opportunities—including an offer from HBO—but she took over our cable operations in Ft. Collins so we could expand in Colorado. She's the most devoted aunt our grandkids could ever have, taking them on trips and all that. She keeps an eye on Pam and me, and comes back here often.

Linda climbed poles and installed cable for a summer as a teenager, but her career took her back east. She made her mark with Yankelovich, Skelly, and White, an opinion research firm in New York City. She met Dan de Menocal from Rye, New York. He proposed to her at a Halloween party when they were dressed up for a three-legged race so she couldn't get away. They made their home back east in Bedford, New York, with a summer house on Nantucket. They have three wonderful children. They're very involved in their church and community, but Linda still gets back this way several times a year.

Both boys have stayed closer to home, and worked at the newspaper and cable operation with me.

I've worried that it's been hard on Dolph III to carry that name. Sometimes I wonder if he felt like he had a choice about his career. His people skills have been so important to the paper. He's easy-going and approachable—he truly has a gift. He could have been a preacher. We were very fortunate he and Lisa stayed here in Lawrence. They had four beautiful daughters. One of them, Jennifer, was born with some serious medical problems. She couldn't walk so Dolph just carried her and held her wherever they went. I don't think he could've been a more devoted father.

Dan didn't take school very seriously until he met Trish. They met when she snapped the band attached to his sunglasses to wake him up in a class he was sleeping through in college. Trish was going to graduate before him. She told him she wasn't going to wait for him, so he got his grades up fast. Dan brought many new ideas to our cable operation and made it one of the finest in the nation. We did things nobody else had ever done before. There were so many more things he wanted to try. He was like a pole vaulter always ready to take the higher leap. Dan and Trish have two great kids who've grown up nearby.

Both Dan and Dolph check in on us regularly.

I think Dolph grew up thinking his father and grandfather were the important journalists—not him. His mom and dad were really strong. Everything was perfect—the right this and the right that. His mother was extremely beautiful. His dad was a perfect gentleman all the way. His brother John was a brilliant doctor, and Dolph stayed behind to take on the newspaper.

He puts himself down—I've listened to that all these years. I tell him oh quit that, stop it. In his industry, Dolph was the voice from the Midwest... he was so well respected. I doubt people in Lawrence realize what a power he was in journalism in America, but that's so often the instance. You're never a hero in your hometown. In my travels, I'd run across people who worked for him and they had such wonderful things to say about him.

This is true in his family as well. I can truthfully say I don't know if I've ever been around parents whose children loved and appreciated them the way Dolph and Pam's do. They've had their ups and downs and their problems, but Dolph does guide that family through them. This is a remarkable American family.

Bob Trapp[22]

These are only a few of the stories. There are more... I should know many more. I have to face up to it, I was so

> involved or committed or determined to make a success of the paper, maybe I didn't spend as much time with my children as I should have. I sure wish I had. I'm continually surprised to learn from my kids the things they did that I wasn't there to see… and they want to know what I was doing that they never knew about.
>
> That's really why we did this book.

For all the excitement of big trips and world travel, Linda admitted, "One of my absolute favorite things to do—usually on a Sunday afternoon—was get in the car to drive around and see what was happening in our own town. We had a station wagon, and I'd be in the far back because I was the only one who didn't throw up. Often, Dad would take us around campus or West Lawrence just to see what was going on… what was being built, what was being torn down. Whoever was around would pile into the car and we'd always end up at the DQ."

As parents, Dolph and Pam were proactive in encouraging their children's curiosity and providing structure for how to explore their world. Dolph III said, "We were coached on how to act—how to have fun but not be disruptive." His sister Pam agreed, "Dad and Mom were 'no means no' kind of parents. If you were out of line, you'd be set straight." If the kids were too loud or unruly, "Dad would bide his time 'til the time he slammed his hand on the table," Linda recalled. "That got our attention."

Dolph tended to be the stricter disciplinarian, but Pam had her ways. "Mom was known by everyone as 'Saint Pam.' She'd forego whatever she wanted to do in favor of doing for others," Linda said. "Mom did spank us, and wash our mouths out with soap if we needed it, but she was not an argumentative person in any way. If you didn't get up when you were called, Mom would start playing Rachmaninoff loudly on the piano. If that didn't work, you'd get the wet-washcloth treatment," Linda laughed.

While her husband focused on the paper, Pam wrangled the kids, managed the social calendar, and ran the household. As the wife of an important man in the community, she was very visible herself. "Every newspaper publisher's wife plays a role—they have a certain framework. They're expected to entertain, to join civic groups," Dolph III said. "Mom enjoyed it, but I wonder if she got tired of it sometimes."

Dolph and Pam had a traditional arrangement, typical of the times, but Linda pointed out, "Mom was not subservient to Dad. They were equals within their own track." Pam understood her husband's commitment to the paper, and supported it. "Well, I knew what Dolph's business was. It meant he had to be available to the paper 24/7," Pam explained. "But he found time for the family. He was almost always home for dinner."

The Sunday dinner tradition at The Cedars continued with Dolph and Pam. Daughter Pam mused on the menu, "Mom made cheese souffle and we've all tried to do that ourselves. Pot roast was my favorite. Dad always loved her Hungarian goulash. We had to wait for him to get home before we could eat, and sometimes he was late. Dad always sat at the head of the table, and would go around asking what we'd done that day. You sat up straight, used your manners, and you had to say something—you knew it was coming!"

> *Anytime there was a siren, fire, whatever, we were going! Dad would hop in a car and we'd jump in the back. We were definitely siren chasers, and were never kept from the action as kids. We weren't kept from anything because we were kids—we were always included. We always had dinner together, and everyone had chores associated with that. What was cool to me was that my dad knew everything going on in town. When he'd sit down, we'd get an update on what building was going up, which politician was doing whatever, he knew what the hell was going on. I thought that was cool, and that's why I wanted to get into the business.*

Dan Simons

Sporting events—especially KU basketball or football—were greatly anticipated by the whole family. "Those were fun social times with my folks," Dolph III said. "Dad was working all the time, and in every newspaper family, the publisher has to divvy up the pie. The bigger slice is work, not family." His sister echoed that reality. "I didn't realize 'til Linda had kids and we were hauling them over to Paul Bunyan Land near Brainerd, Minnesota, that Dad had never been on any of those trips when we were growing up," Pam noted. "He was always at work."

He didn't take vacations often, but when he did, Dolph Jr. was having fun—strenuously—with his kids, and, eventually, grandkids. The Simons owned a house in Steamboat Springs, Colorado, that was base camp for ski adventures, but their cottage on Gull Lake in Minnesota saw the most action. "When Dad was there, it was go! go! go!" Linda said. "Waterskiing, fishing, going out on the boat. Sometimes we'd go up to Ernie's for lunch, which was a treat because we didn't go out to eat a lot when I was growing up."

The Gull Lake cottage had been built by Dolph Sr. in 1932. The Simons spent time there every summer since Dolph was a toddler. "When I was one or two, my parents took a vacation up in Minnesota and stayed at a resort. When I was two, they decided they wanted a cabin of their own," Dolph Jr. recalled. "Dad made a deal with some guys from Lawrence to come up and build it. Dad did all the cooking without electricity. We slept on mattresses on the floor. In 1937, we finally got electricity, that was the same time when we found out mother's dad was dying so we had to leave and drive back to Nebraska."

The cabin has been expanded, and a guest cabin built, but "the original part still looks like it did," Dolph noted, adding, "I wish we had more space, more space between us and other people." He and younger brother John grew up swimming, fishing, and sharing adventures. "John and I loved to fish. We got to know Gull Lake so well we offered our services as fishing guides," Dolph Jr. recalled. "John even had business cards made advertising his 12 years' experience on the lake... he was only 15 at the time."

The Counsellers had their lake house there, too, so Pam's childhood summers were also associated with the 9,947-acre lake. "Dad would drive us up and drop us off around Memorial Day and pick us up at Labor Day," daughter Pam said. "We spent the first half of the summer at Mom's family place, and the second half at Dad's family's house."

For one golden week every August, Dolph Jr. joined his family at the lake. "That's when we saw him the most," Linda said. "I don't think he got much rest! We begged Dad to take us skiing morning and night."

Convening at the lake in August became the tradition for grandparents, parents, kids, spouses, and grandchildren. At the annual gathering, the agenda shifted from the family business to family bonding. "The newspaper never came up," granddaughter Emily de Menocal said. "On family vacation, we weren't seeing the successful newspaper publisher, just our granddad."

The next Simons generation included Linda and husband Dan de Menocal's Emily, Crosby, and Jane; Dolph III and wife Lisa's Kate, Elizabeth, Jennifer, and Whitney; Dan and wife Trisha's Briahn Marie and Dan Jr.

With the family's expansion, membership in the secret club begun by Dolph Sr. back in the 1930s also grew—with diligent vetting. Dan emphasized, "We still have relatives and once-removed cousins who've tried for years to learn the name of it, the secret sign, and the response signal. There are family members and others who try to learn. But there's no automatic entry, not even by marriage. Anyone marrying into the family is eligible, but that individual must apply with suitable humility to be considered."

In the summer of 2022, Crosby's new wife Courtney was inducted. Through tears, she delivered a moving acceptance speech reminiscent of an Oscar winner who genuinely never thought she had a chance. "She won some extra points for that," Dolph Jr. nodded.

As a rite of passage, the secret club was de rigueur, but bonding took many forms. "One of Trisha's favorite stories of Grampy Simons is from the gathering up at the lake," Dan noted. "My grandmother Marie was the family disciplinarian—in a loving way. She made sure things were the way they should be—this was a woman who ate fried chicken with a knife and fork. Anyway, one time she called dinner and sent Trish to go find Grampy. At that time, the driveway was deep sand. Trish found Grampy sitting in back, as he often did, watching a turtle lay eggs there. He invited Trish to watch with him but she said, 'We're going to be late and I'll get in trouble.' He just calmly said, 'No, you're not, you're with me.'" Days at Gull Lake began with a big breakfast. Granddaughter Jane de Menocal said, "Every morning,

The family at Gull Lake, 2014. Back row left to right: Linda Simons de Menocal, Trish Simons, Pam Simons, Dan Simons, Dolph Simons Jr., Pamela Ann Simons, Lisa Simons, Dolph Simons III. Middle row: Dan de Menocal, Briahn Simons, Whitney, Elizabeth, and Kate Simons, Emily de Menocal; seated: Dan Simons Jr., Jane, and Crosby de Menocal

Granddad fries bacon and eggs, and makes tote-toties, which are these little pancakes. I'd come down and he'd be standing at the stove in his robe cooking for everybody." Whitney Simons explained, "Everyone comes together at the main cabin. Granddad always serves Nanny her breakfast before anyone else. When we're all there—aunts, uncles, cousins—we go slow through the morning. We come together over the food, which is a lovely tradition."

The day's activities revolved around the lake. Plus, talent shows, campfires, skits, hide-n-seek, and trips to the local antique or second-hand stores are always in order. For Kate Simons, "Just being together—whether that's all 17 of us or just the cousins—is what I find most enjoyable. We can be loud sometimes. There's almost never a dull moment!"

The Simonses' unique version of Bingo developed over the course of 50 years. "Granddad always calls out the numbers and letters, and we recite the sayings that go with certain ones," Kate explained. "He'd announce 'B-4,' and we'd all respond in unison, 'NOT AFTER BUT BEFORE!' Granddad would call, 'B-9' and we'd say, 'NOT MALIGNANT BUT BENIGN!'" Crosby de Menocal added, "When we were younger, the prizes included huge bags of candy—Twizzlers, Thousand Dollar bars, Milk Duds, and Dots—and, of course, toothbrushes! There were fun T-shirts, pencil cases, Minnesota Twins and Vikings merch." Aunt Pam curated the prize bags, adding knick-knacks from her travels.

All the grandkids eventually became members of another exclusive Simons' club, one even friends were eligible to join. Dan explained, "It's a lesser club, the Gull Lake Walleyes. It started because the kids were always complaining about wearing life jackets, so the adults said, ok, then show me you can swim." The successful candidate was one who could swim three quarters of a mile out to Birch Island. A pontoon boat full of cheerleaders paced alongside the swimmers. "Grandad swam it with all us grandkids—even some of my aunts and uncles joined in," Kate recalled.

Even for those fully ensconced in the Walleyes, swimming out to the island continued as an annual tradition. "My best time was 16 minutes when I was training for Lake Placid Ironman USA in 1991," Dan noted.

At the close of day, the grandkids climbed up to a large loft of bunks for bed. "Dan would go up there and tell bedtime stories featuring each kid," Dolph Jr. recalled. "Dolph (III) would try it, but

Kate, Whitney, Elizabeth, Dolph III, and Lisa Simons in Spain, summer 2017

Dan and Trisha Simons with Briahn and Dan Jr. at Gull Lake, August 2020

he'd fall asleep. Then the kids would call to the adults downstairs, 'Uncle Dolph fell asleep again!'" Jane de Menocal loved her uncles' stories. "Uncle Dolph would start his stories by stomping up the stairs hitting every stair hard! We always knew his scary stories weren't that scary," she remembered. "And he would always fall asleep before the end!"

Letter to Dad
who "doesn't want anything for Christmas, dammit!"

A child always thinks her father is infallible, the best. It is only when we become parents ourselves that we understand we can only attempt to measure-up. Looking back as you probably do with your father, and he, his, I think you and I are both lucky enough—blessed enough—to know we had the best father. Being the best parent is not easy to replicate on a daily basis, but you gave me the confidence to know what was right... to know what Mom or Dad would do.

A father/daughter relationship is different than that of a father and son, and very different from a mother and her daughter. I look to Mom for my feminine side (and, boy, is she the personification of a MOM). Mom's many attributes have shown me graciousness, organization, leadership, loving-all kindness, child-rearing (a huge category), how to throw a party, recipes galore, personal style, decorating, putting up with a husband, not throwing the children down a well, loving/needing dogs and horses—sometimes all on the same day! Mom has done this without complaint and so very effortlessly.

This particular Christmas letter is ALL ABOUT YOU! It's about how you look out for, care for, fight for, pave the way for, keep tabs on, and worry about others. I know you are always wondering if there is more you could do—from your parents to your employees to your longtime friends and business associates; for the widows, your brother, your wife, your children and their spouses, to nieces and nephews—the list keeps growing.

The generosity-of-you is the embodiment of love. I feel it. I know it.

It's about how you fight to make things right, to make things better. You know how things should be in business, in town, in the country and the world. You speak out (or write out, I should say). You make calls. You follow up. You give concrete suggestions. You're tireless and driven. And, dammit, with your tongue clenched between your teeth, you make it happen (or call them the fools they are— politely stated—if they don't listen)!

You taught me to fight... to be inquisitive; to step up and make a difference, to never give up, to make the most of each day. I may not save the world, but I try in my own small sphere.

No one, and I mean no one, could have a father who included his children more. You read the paper to us before we could read. You took us on road trips all around town and all over the country. You taught me to punt a football in the side yard, and you took us to ball games. You brought us along to national conventions (both political and business). If you were doing it, you figured out a way to involve your children. All this while you were at the office every day, Saturdays and Sundays included.

Look back, remember… we've had wonderful times. We love each other fiercely. We find the fun. I am so proud to have you as my father. I'm proud of your accomplishments, inquisitiveness, and leadership, but most of all, for being my father.

Linda Simons de Menocal, excerpts from her 2020 Christmas Letter

Dolph reading the news to Pammie (standing) and Linda circa 1962.

The retirement years finally offered Dolph Jr. the opportunity to indulge in unfettered time with family—to their great delight. "Every year, without fail, we would all come to the lake," Linda affirmed. "The kids are very close because they've had this experience as cousins every summer. Like everyone else, we do have our squabbles, but how many families spread all over the place make the time to vacation together, and get together two or three times a year? Dad is interested in all of us—he's such a cheerleader. He always knew the answers to everything... 99% of the time, he knew all the answers to my life. We're his everything, and he and mom are our everything."

The gathering at Gull Lake was the main event, but there have been other epic experiences. Kate remembered when, in 2018, "Granddad extended an invitation to all us grandchildren to go to Alaska fishing with him. He'd been going up there for a long time. Not only did I get to fish with him, but with my dad, too. It was so fun to experience that all together."

Jane de Menocal considers the Alaska trip her "favorite memory" with her granddad. "The look on his face every time I came back after a day of fishing... I always named all of my fish and had stories about them that would just make him so happy," she said. "He was excited for me being so happy!"

Alaska showed Whitney Simons a new view of her grandfather. "We went to Good News Lodge. I think that was the first time I had intentional time—time for extended conversation—just with my granddad. Prior to that, I got bits and pieces. At Gull Lake, there's always a big group so it's hard to find one-on-one time. Now I saw this 90-year-old man traveling to Alaska—still sufficient and capable. He doesn't want help from others. I watched how he carried himself, his confidence. I saw how he engaged with the fishing guides and the owner. Going out fishing with him, sharing a meal, hearing stories of how he grew up—that was wonderful."

Her grandparents' views on religion were especially important to Whitney. "One of my first memories about Nanny was she'd always give me an angel, or a Bible, or a book about God. She referred to God at times I myself wasn't into it. But later, when I became a Christian,

I thought about how many times she must have been praying for me. That is so cool looking back... seeing her faithfulness," Whitney reflected. "When I went to Alaska with Granddad, and had that personal time with him, he shared what he believed about God and Jesus, what his passions are. I got to know his personality. It was the first time I saw his deep caring side... his heart."

Dolph Jr. flanked by a few of the grandkids on the Alaska trip, from left: Briahn Simons, Elizabeth Simons, Emily de Menocal, Jane de Menocal

As grandparents, Dolph Jr. and Pam were very present for the Simons and de Menocal kids. Once she landed the job she'd been pursuing, Jane de Menocal said, "Granddad called me every day to see how things were going.... He wanted to know what I was struggling with and what I was doing best. He wanted me to keep a journal, and I agree with that."

Emily de Menocal chimed in, "He's always asking questions. Anytime we had a new boyfriend or girlfriend, Granddad had to get the story on them." When things got serious enough to bring someone special out to The Cedars or up to Gull Lake, "Granddad wanted to make sure the guy had good values, a strong background," Emily explained. "The first time I brought my husband Stefan up to the cabin, he got the inquisition. And he nearly killed himself swimming to the island."

Whitney Simons thought "It's cool to have a granddad be such a big part of his grandchildren's lives."

As heirs apparent, the fifth generation were coming of age as the family business was waning. "I do remember thinking, gosh, who is going to take that on?" Whitney admitted. "No one in my generation seemed focused on that career choice."

Dan's daughter Briahn came up with the idea for a teen board that the Journal-World launched in 2002. It was an innovation that appealed to the younger demographic, but not something Briahn intended to pursue professionally.

Briahn Simons was a high school freshman when she suggested a Teen Board for the newspaper in 2002.

In fact, the Simons' grandchildren weren't pressured to carry the newspaper forward. The message they got was pure encouragement to follow their own dream.

"I love the beach, which is one of the reasons why I moved from Kansas to Charleston in 2010," Elizabeth Simons said. "I found my passion in hospitality, and attended the College of Charleston where I graduated with a degree in Hospitality and Tourism Management and a minor in Studio Art."

Kate Simons got her journalism degree from KU, but "on the strategic side—public relations, advertising, and marketing. For two summers, I interned with [The World Company's] magazine division, *Sunflower Publishing*, when the Simons still had ownership. That was fun," she noted. "While I was in J-school, sometimes I wondered if anyone there knew I was a Simons. I certainly didn't get treated differently."

Dan prepared Briahn and Dan Jr. that they might. "You're never going to be alone at a party. Someone is gonna come up and say you suck OR I love what your paper says," Dan said. "I warned my kids because some people hate our family."

Linda Simons de Menocal had similar concerns for her son. "When Crosby left New York to attend KU, I told him not to let anybody know he was connected to the Simons because he'd get slaughtered."

(from left) Stefan and Emily de Menocal Dixon, Jane de Menocal, Linda Simons de Menocal, Dan de Menocal, Courtney Pfortmiller de Menocal and Crosby de Menocal, 2021

Undaunted, Crosby dove in. "The Simons are taught to be tough-skinned," he said. "You just have to get out there and do it." The family name didn't set him back, quite the opposite. "Post-college, I was job-searching back in New York when Granddad called to say how a friend of his was visiting at the lake," Crosby recalled. "Granddad showed a furniture piece I created while I was still at KU. Grandad's friend took an interest in the piece, and was curious to meet me." Crosby flew back to Kansas for an interview which led to an internship. "That turned into an all-around finishing school for everything real estate and development," Crosby explained. "I ended up working with them for about six or seven years, before stepping away to start my own construction company."

Although Jane de Menocal grew up on the east coast, she chose to move to Kansas to pursue a career. Proximity to her grandparents was a factor, but not to open doors professionally. She just enjoys time with them. "Granddad is so invested when he's talking with you. His words are worth listening to—even when he's saying something funny under his breath or a joke, it's hilarious!!" Jane said. "It's just this feeling in your heart when you see Granddad and get to talk... it's so heartwarming."

Traditionally, newspapers were folded for display with the biggest front-page stories positioned "above the fold" for maximum visibility. As a metaphor, that pretty much captures the exposure of a newspaper family—with the unspoken imperative to live a life above and beyond reproach because people were watching (and reading).

In the Simons family, this expectation was anything but unspoken. It was communicated very directly, and reinforced with cautionary tales like the implosion of the Hearst family in California and the Binghams in Kentucky who ended up in a litigious screaming match over power and money troubles.

Plenty of families feud, but when the family is eminently in the public eye, their lives are inherently above-the-fold fodder. Dolph Sr. pressed this point in no uncertain terms—the Simons family must never be that newspaper family. They must "always be kind and considerate," especially to each other.

"I can remember Grampy spoke to us very seriously about this," Linda said. "That influenced our adult relationships as siblings. I think Grampy and Dad worried unnecessarily about this. We were

buying power due to inflation.

    Please always be kind and considerate of your mother, ~~and do everything possible to avoid any serious disagreements among yourselves.~~

      With love—

        Dolph Simons

Not only with regard to "your mother," but at every turn,
Dolph Sr. counseled kindness and consideration.

raised as a family that supports each other, and honors our parents... our father and grandfather. We would never act in that manner. Even when Dad's gone, we'll still be all for one and one for all."

Whitney Simons would add a sense of pride in the family is a big part of what it means to be a Simons. "I just feel so honored by what my grandfather has achieved, and what they stood for," she said. "Family is a priority for Nanny and Granddad, so it became a priority for everyone else."

In all that goodness, there may be clues to the mystery Dolph Jr. ponders.

"Most every living thing has an ability—a richness of abilities all its own. If you say being human means to have a life—well, plants and trees have life. What do we really know about their lives? Can you say only humans know right from wrong? Who's to judge this? Who could tell you if your answer is right? A minister? The best mind at a university? A chemist or farmer? Maybe OBGYNs have a slant on this because they've seen birthing a thousand times and that has to have an impact," Dolph said. "The truth of the matter as I see it is it must be up to each individual to come to the answer in and of themselves."

CHAPTER 9

Convergence

We were doing great things. That was getting noticed and we were winning awards. In 2005 during our print-video-internet heyday, The New York Times hailed us—a small family-owned business from Kansas— as "The Newspaper of the Future" because we were dominating multi-platform distribution in the early days of the internet.

Dan Simons

A special *Lawrence Journal-World* edition featured the converged news center in 2003.

For W.C. Simons, the challenge had been to start and sustain a newspaper company during the days when "the wild, wild west" aptly described both the state of Kansas and the newspaper business from the late 1800s into the first part of the 20th century. He wrote, "Rebelling against such condition of affairs, I came to the conclusion that the newspaper business should be a respectable one."[1]

> *"Others are more laudatory but equally cautious about Lawrence's online innovations. 'Nobody else is close to doing what they've done,' said David Card, a new-media analyst at Jupiter Research."*
>
> from Tim O'Brien's "The Newspaper of the Future." *The New York Times.* June 26, 2005

Dolph Simons Sr. continued his father's work with an emphasis on newspaper publishing as a democratic right and responsibility. "We who work at newspapering should not consider the First Amendment to the constitution as a grant of special privilege; rather, we should accept it as a responsibility to serve," he wrote. "We should forever remember that the people have the 'right to know' and that it is our obligation to keep them informed, even if at times it appears the public doesn't want to learn."[2]

Dolph Simons Jr.'s name was added to the masthead of this well-respected enterprise in the late 1950s. His leadership spanned an era of unprecedented social change and technological advancement. There would be no more business-as-usual for newspapering. Undaunted and risk-tolerant, Dolph Jr. was the Simons for that job. His view was "I would rather try something new and fail than have someone else try it and succeed."

Dolph's sons Dolph III and Dan, and daughter Pam, worked their way up The World Company ladder and stepped into management roles just in time for the sea change in the industry that would separate the entrenched from the agile. Pam shouldered general manager duties for the company's Colorado expansion with Columbine Cablevision in 1978. By 2004, Dolph III was president of the company's Newspaper Division, and Dan was president of the Electronics Division.

The Simons took their position at the leading edge of changing times, merging their traditional newspaper with entirely new modes of mass communication in a process that would be called "convergence."

Convergence wasn't a buzzword in the industry when The World Company began its metamorphosis in the 1970s. In fact, most of the buzz was from an increasingly stressed newspaper industry wondering how it would survive the shift to new and different sources of news. Technology was ushering in the digital age and newspaper publishers had to adapt or die.

In a *New York Times* cover story, "The Newspaper of the Future," Tim O'Brien wrote, "Although journalists may cringe to hear it, the near-term battle for corporate survival is likely to be waged and won primarily by inventive business and advertising teams at media companies." O'Brien spotlighted an exemplar in his June 26, 2005 article. "The Simons family, through The World Company, enjoys an unfettered and often-criticized media monopoly in Lawrence. But the family has used that advantage to cross-pollinate its properties, ranging from cable to telephone service to newspaper and online publishing, and to take technological and financial risks that other owners might have avoided."[3]

Over the 60 years Dolph Jr. spent in various executive roles for The World Company, change was perpetual, pervasive, and exponential. Existing leadership models "weren't built for this kind of 3-D change," according to the Harvard Business Review.[4] Fortunately, nobody told Dolph Simons Jr. that.

Dolph's well-known "drive with our brights on" mantra wasn't just to see what was coming at The World Company, it was the business model driving the company proactively toward the future. Simons' high octane mix of audacity and instinct fueled it, and he attracted world-class talent like former UPI photojournalist and White House photographer-of-the-year Bill Snead, and tough-as-nails journalist and general manager Ralph Gage to take the journey with him. Gage said, "Dolph was always pushing to get us into something more... into something new. There was never a dull moment."[5]

Indeed, Dolph was "not resting on the history of the business and the voice he inherited," former AP President Lou Boccardi emphasized. "He was looking constantly to make it better, to renew it and strengthen its place in the community and at the same time open the path to new technology."[6]

The World Company functioned with rare nimbleness for a company more than a century old. When Rob Curley stepped into a newly created position as World Online General Manager, he told media watchdogs at the Poynter Institute, "To create the kind of journalism I wanted to create, this might not just be the best place in Kansas to do it, but it might be the best place in the world."[7]

The first idea of a cable system for Lawrence started in the early 1960s when this writer attended an ANPA meeting in New York. I think the speaker was John Walson who set up an early cable system in a hilly, rural area of Pennsylvania. Walson, who had been a lineman for Pennsylvania Power & Light, owned the appliance store in Mahanoy City. He got permission to run some coaxial cable up a tower on the highest hilltop to capture the signals, then fed the clearer images via cable to customers who'd purchased a TV from his store.[8] This was early cable television, and I saw the potential for Lawrence.

I returned home thinking about the possibility of the Journal-World building a cable system. Bill Daniels had been pioneering this out in Denver, Colorado. I invited him to come and explore the possibility of a partnership with us in Lawrence. He brought a group of his associates and toured the city to assess the quality of Kansas City and Topeka television signals in various parts of town. Daniels concluded there were too many rooftop antennas already in operation, so he didn't think cable TV in Lawrence would be a viable venture.

Even though Daniels was not encouraging, I told The World Company leaders I thought it would be wise to proceed and enter the cable business.

Dad was always concerned with how it would look if we owned more than one media company, which is why he gave up the radio license in Lawrence he'd acquired back in the 1940s. But times had really changed, and we had to change with them. We had to diversify. Somebody was going to do this if we didn't, which was a big part of why we went after the business—not to corner the market, but to adapt to the times. Were we going to watch a competitor come in and beat us at our own game? Dad could see the point, but he wondered what this was going to cost... and frankly, so did I. There were so few cable operations out there, and none our size or in our region yet. We were definitely the pioneers. This was a major investment, so Dad was cautious but he said, "If you think it's the thing to do, go ahead."

In 1968, the Lawrence City Commissioners heard our cable television proposal. After a number of meetings and discussions, a franchise was granted to The World Company to build and operate the system. Back then, John Malone, who would become one of the country's most successful cable owners, had a company in Philadelphia that designed, engineered, and built cable systems. John agreed to build our Lawrence plant that would be engineered to carry a maximum of 13 off-air broadcast signals from Kansas City and Topeka. We called our new enterprise Sunflower Cablevision and started laying cable that same year. By the end of '71, we opened for business at our location at Seventh and New Hampshire Streets.

Our cable operation was unique—I believe the Lawrence installation featured the first earth-receiving station west of the Mississippi River. Another thing we did differently was run Sunflower Cablevision our own way—not just as a community antenna. We wanted to be about Lawrence, not just provide clearer images on a TV screen plus dozens more entertainment programs. So, in 1971, we came right out of the gate with live coverage from 6News Lawrence supported by a fully-staffed newsroom covering city commission meetings, KU sports, area high school games, local events, charitable fundraising endeavors, weather—we even had a call-in music request program. We offered advertising services and unlimited ability to support local programming. Our first manager was Max Falkenstien, a Lawrence native who had been with Topeka radio station WREN, and was the voice of KU Jayhawks for 60 years.

Lawrence was clearly ready for that because we started out without a single subscriber, but had 1,800 by late January of '72—before we'd even done any promotion. By May, our cable subscriptions had risen to 2,800.[9] The only person more relieved than me was Dad who came to my office almost every morning before he'd even taken his overcoat off to ask, "When do you think we'll see some black ink?"

Our number of subscribers and advertisers kept growing, and the technology kept improving. This made it possible to add an ever-increasing number of traditional network television channels as well as a wide variety of sports networks and more special interest programming. We'd figured out our model, and felt ready to replicate it.

In 1978, we won the cable franchise for Ft. Collins, Colorado. That was a big deal because we were up against some very heavy hitters including Bill Daniels and John Malone himself. I always enjoyed beating the big boys, and that's exactly what we did in Ft. Collins. Malone and Daniels weren't prepared to lose to a small family-owned company out of Kansas. They had a few choice words for me as we left the city council meeting the day we won that license.

We called our new venture Columbine Cablevision. My daughter Pam went out to oversee the plant construction and operations. She did a helluva job and had great ideas. The city commission really gave her a beating, and then she had a pretty serious ski injury on top of that. Ralph Gage went out to take the pressure off her, along with my son Dan. Dan stayed on and ran things with Pam. We considered other opportunities to continue expanding the cable business, but decided to focus on really innovating things underway in Lawrence.

What they did with cable—to have a full-fledged local news operation within a local cable station—that was an example of a truly pioneering, out-front broadband operation.

Ann Gardner, former editor, *Lawrence Journal-World* editorial page

By 2003, Sunflower Cablevision had evolved into Sunflower Broadband. We had a highly-trained work force of more than 200 supporting our cable news programming, local and long-distance telephone service, more than 300 channels, high-speed cable modem internet access, and all digital services.

In 2004, Sunflower and Journal-World news and advertising departments converged into a joint operation. These were two highly competitive newsrooms that enabled us to provide 24-hour news coverage of Lawrence across two platforms. Then we added online operations to maximize news formats for subscribers and advertising options for our customers. We won many national awards including the Cablefax 2010 System of the Year.[10]

*"Then there is that word that sends panic into the heart of the most intrepid reporter...**convergence!***

One of the most daunting challenges facing (Journal-World) Managing Editor Ric Brack as he moved into his job, was how to overcome the natural antipathy that traditional newsmen felt towards interfacing with their TV brethren. "Working closely with TV was a big change for us," says Brack. "It had been ingrained in our minds that we were to compete with TV. Competition is good. Suddenly we went to sharing everything. Now we were going to tell our 6News people not only what we were going to cover, but maybe cover it ourselves. We had an example in the past few months where one of our reporters wouldn't even tell us the story he was working on, because he was afraid we would break it on line. We had a discussion with him. Since then it's gotten a lot better, and the thing that helps now is the public gets to see the face of the person who writes for the paper. We now have stories in the paper by 6News reporters. The challenge was to get people to trust and respect each other. Getting everyone in one newsroom has been a big help. We have a writer, Mark Fagan, who we call "the converged reporter." He realized that in many ways the TV people have it a lot tougher. If you are a newspaper reporter, you pick up the phone, take notes, and write a story. In TV, that's not a story. That's getting ready to do a story. After our people have done a few stories on TV, it's no big deal. I think attitudes around here have changed a lot."

Dirck Halstead from "Driving with Your Brights On: A 20,000 Circulation Daily Takes Care of Its Community (and Convergence)" for www.digitaljournalist.org, 2003.

It makes me very proud when I look back at what we did. We were so far ahead of that game, but we had to be. I'm not saying I was a futurist, but I could foresee how cable could weaken the role of the newspaper. It was up to us to decide what we were going to do about that, which took us from being strictly a newspaper business to being in the information business. We applied the principles we followed at the Journal-World to this new cable platform. Eventually, we converged our newspaper, cable news, and online services, and provided local and long-distance phone services, which hadn't ever been done before in this business, as far as I know. Dan had so many innovative ideas—we were constantly breaking new ground. It was so much fun.

Building excellent cable systems over 40 years was a challenging and enjoyable experience. Such good memories were made with a lot of great people, many of whom went from their employment with us onto highly successful careers in television, cablevision, and information services throughout the country. In this writer's opinion, we gave area residents ways to explore the wider world while, hopefully, inspiring them to become more involved in their own community.[11]

Dolph Simons Jr.

Most of the industry was still cave-painting the concept of convergence when The World Company launched Sunflower Cablevision in January, 1972. In May of that year, Kansas City Mayor Charles Wheeler brought members of his city council and cable television study committee to Lawrence to consider the feasibility of cable.[12] It would take five more years before major markets like Kansas City or Miami would get their cable systems fully up and running, in 1977 and 1979, respectively.[13]

Cable offered a whole new world of programming with new networks for "sports, programs for children, families, women, minorities, etc. aimed at specific interest groups."[14] This brought the Simons "a lot of offers to expand what we were doing with Sunflower to other markets, but we were very cautious about growth," Dolph Jr. explained. "We didn't do cable like everybody else was doing cable. Our emphasis was always on the community—not just delivering a bunch of entertainment channels."

After I finished my degree at KU, I went to work for Dad at Sunflower Cable. My title was director of special projects, although I don't know if any of us knew what that meant. It was early in the cable industry, and there wasn't much programming out there, so we kind of had free rein to create things. We had a bit called the "Fearless Football Forecasters." I'd be behind our cardboard set dressing. We started doing a music request line with some guys in production spinning records to a moving, psychedelic backdrop. This was way before MTV, but I'd had this idea about editing video to popular songs, although it never went anywhere. I do remember when one of our production guys, I think his name was Randy Mason, actually got an invitation from MTV to audition for one of their new "VJ" positions. He didn't get the job, but we were all so excited and wondered if MTV found out about him from watching our primitive version of the music video.

Pamela Ann Simons

As founding member of what would become the National Cable Television Cooperative, Dolph Simons Jr. was one of the elder statesmen of cable during what CableCenter.org called "a franchise frenzy" in large cities nationwide in the late '70s.[15] To put events in context to time, consider that newly-established ESPN was striving for recognition in 1978 when it came to Simons to ask if he'd set up a meeting with Big 8 Conference leaders at the Lawrence Country Club. Simons agreed, and put his neck out for the fledgling sports network— to no avail. Ralph Gage recalled how that went down. "ESPN wanted the Big 8 to become a showpiece conference for a relationship with their then-new cable TV network, but KU and Conference leaders decided ESPN was kind of a fad and didn't pursue the opportunity."[16]

The Simons, however, were early adopters. Staying ahead of the competition was key because it provided "a great opportunity for (our) cable and newspapers to get together and create content that no one else could match," said Dan Simons,[17] who was director of The World Company's new ventures in the '90s.

It would be years—decades even—before other media markets would converge platforms in comparable ways to what the Simons were doing. In fact, as late as 2018, Michelle Holmes, then-vice president of content for the Alabama Media Group, noted in a roundtable discussion of the future of newspapers sponsored by The1A.org, "My company (the Newhouse Company) was really out-front in recognizing the trends of newspapers and the opportunities that existed in the digital space"[18] as of 2012. That year, the Alabama Media Group reduced printing their newspapers to three days a week "which really allowed a ton of room to begin to think—years before many other news companies in American really had the luxury to start thinking about how to serve our readers in a digital space—and our advertisers," Holmes said.[19]

In contrast, The World Company had successfully converged their newspaper, internet, and cable news platforms by 2000. In 2005, Rob Curley, then-director of new media for The World Company, told NPR reporter Rob Folkenflik, "We believe that journalism has been a monologue for so long and now is the perfect time for it to become a dialogue with our readers. We want them to think of this as their paper, not our paper."[20]

With Columbine Cablevision, another opportunity for innovation presented itself—upgrading and expanding the technology at Colorado State University in Ft. Collins. "I wanted to take advantage of what you could do with cable and medicine," Dolph Jr. said. "So we partnered with CSU, then wired every building—the entire campus. All the veterinary students could watch every operation. We were doing things there we could have been doing at KU, but they declined, which was very short-sighted of them and frustrating. We had a better cable system than Los Angeles or Chicago, but KU wanted to try things their own way."

It was a missed opportunity. There weren't many of those, although then-COO of The World Company Ralph Gage cited another one. "When applying for the cable television franchise in Loveland, Colorado, Dolph Jr. went head-to-head with cable magnate John Malone in a session culminating in a heated debate about censorship and the First Amendment. Dolph Jr. carried the vote of the city's advisory committee, but the city eventually awarded the franchise to a Florida company."[21]

"Actually, we were up against Malone and the company from Florida," Dolph Jr. explained. "The committee approved my application, which didn't make Malone very happy. He said, 'Well, you think you're looking pretty good now, don't you?' Yes, I told him, but your shorts are looking pretty dirty."

The group from the Florida firm "made a lot of promises, and put on quite a dog and pony show," Dolph recalled. "They pulled up in an 18-wheeler painted with the new name they were proposing for the franchise—and they were in costume. They won the contract, but their proposal was dressed up in promises they never delivered on.

In the end, Loveland had a basic operation. That's how the game got played—some of these folks would say whatever it took to get the contract, and fall flat on their faces when they couldn't deliver."

As with all aspects of oversight and management of The World Company, Gage continued to be Most Valuable Player, even with something as novel as converging media. His field guide to the industry, "Navigating the Road to Convergence," was published in *Nieman Reports* in 2005.

Navigating the Road to Convergence

by Ralph Gage

In 2000, we decided to combine our newspaper and cable television news operations, putting print and broadcast reporters side-by-side in a newsroom, along with a small but growing staff in our Internet operation. To do this, we gathered as much information as we could about newsroom convergence by talking with people at the *Chicago Tribune* and working with Jimmy Gentry, who was then dean of the William Allen White School of Journalism and Mass Communications at the University of Kansas. We traveled to Tampa, Florida to see its combined newspaper and television operation, and our architects and newsroom managers came along when we went to the *Orlando Sentinel*.

Once the lessons were absorbed, we bought an old Lawrence building, which is now listed on the National Register of Historic Places, and remodeled it as our News Center. It became the hub of our multimedia newsgathering operations and the place from which storytelling for our community emerges.

There was hesitancy and uncertainty in the minds of our news staff as we set out to make these changes. For years these reporters and editors had operated in competition, yet now they were being asked to meld into one multimedia organization. The mortar that would hold them together was prepared in a series of small group "convergence sessions" in which the company's owners and top managers shared with employees the history of the company and stressed the necessity and opportunity for the company to serve the community better by competing with the media from nearby metropolitan areas instead of among themselves. They also offered assurances that the proposed changes had their enthusiastic endorsement.

Groups of newsroom staff members—selected by me in consultation with managers—were launched into a week of exercises designed to help them to analyze how job duties could be shared. Multimedia assignments were created to help acquaint them with one another and with each other's responsibilities and prepare them for the time when they'd be working together. They were helped in overcoming their concerns and fears by the values they shared, such as honesty, accuracy and fairness, and by their day-to-day operations of planning stories and meeting deadlines.

Included, too, in these small groups were production staff, employees from the business office, circulation and advertising. Almost all of the departments of the broadband company and newspaper— managers and hourly employees alike—were represented in the training effort so that everyone would have some exposure to the change in operating philosophy. The intermingling of employees also gave staff members the opportunity to gain an appreciation of the company's various components, but the primary intent of these training sessions was to focus on how the news staffs would operate in the converged company.

The training process stretched over a year because we did not want this transition to strain the news departments, which were short-handed when colleagues were excused for the convergence training. As each group went through the training, members provided ideas that were then incorporated into it, as well as leadership for the next group; this slower paced, learn-as-you-grow strategy provided additional opportunities for larger numbers of "competitors" to blend more easily into a single organization. At this time, too, print, TV and Internet news managers were working together to plan the layout of the News Center that would combine what had been separate facilities into a converged newsroom. Technology issues—our TV staff used PCs while our print and online people used Macs—were addressed with the creation of an Internet-based assignment system that enabled everyone essentially to be on the same platform.

In August 2001, news staff from television, newspaper and online physically moved into the News Center and began to deal with challenges that arose. Now the job of the newsroom leaders changed from designing the workspace to dealing with the staff issues that surfaced within it. When newspaper staff were uncomfortable with appearing on television, they were not forced to do so, and TV staffers who didn't feel comfortable writing for the paper weren't forced to do that. Workloads were stabilized to assure that multimedia responsibilities would not overwhelm any individual staff member, yet everyone was encouraged to look for ways to contribute that took advantage of the converged newsroom. When reporters found documents to support their reporting, they would be scanned and used on the website. If a tape recording was made of an interview, key quotes would be extracted and used to enhance the website display of that story. As time went on, peer-to-peer training helped integrate more of reporters' work into multimedia presentations.

Soon the work of our reporters and editors was being featured in textbooks, and they were being invited to share their experiences at major industry seminars and conferences. Faculty from the University of Iowa and Kansas State University came by to study what we were doing, and the Associated Press managing editors sponsored credibility studies examining facets of our operations. Recognition of this kind offered a real boost to our small media company and reassured our newsroom staff of the value of their innovative work. Internally, the company recognized its top performers with a special round of pay increases.

During the past five years, newsroom leadership skills have evolved as the expectations of reporters' and editors' multimedia engagement have increased. Participation in these new approaches to storytelling is part of each of our employee's annual review process. Three phases of leadership emerged as a part of our convergence efforts:

1. The first phase laid the groundwork. A more collegial style encouraged rather than demanded participation. It facilitated efforts and was more project centered.

2. The second phase involved less hands-on management. It became what we termed "organic" convergence.

3. The recently instituted third phase puts in place a manager with clearly defined authority. A managing editor for convergence can now make news decisions across all media. He doesn't need to encourage; he can command. This ensures that we do not miss opportunities that "organic" convergence might have overlooked or passed by. The authority and responsibility vested in this new leadership position demand a vision that transcends any one medium and a vision to maintain the company's role as the community's historian, storyteller and whistleblower. It definitely requires the gift of encouragement.

Training for employees is being reinstituted at a time when news staff know that the expectations for their involvement in multimedia storytelling are increasing. We are instituting more frequent online chats with print reporters and pushing responsibility onto newspaper section editors and others, not simply leaving it to our online personnel. We also want photographers, no matter which is his or her primary medium, to be able to produce images for all media. In other words, it has become time to step up the pace. And we are paying particular attention to evaluating which medium works best with what kind of stories, or part of a story, and then having our coverage reflect those findings.

One recent example of news presentation involved this summer's release of local census data. The Journal-World reporters did an in-depth look at the numbers in the course of examining local government policies likely to be impacted by the surprising decline in the city's population. Our TV reporters used this news

Convergence created a multimedia platform for The World Company.

as a peg to tell the story of a family who moved from Lawrence to a small town nearby; their circumstance and concerns illustrated some of the factors influencing the census numbers. On our website we created an interactive database to help readers and viewers navigate through graphs of these trends; we also gave online visitors an opportunity to post their comments and offer feedback and tips to the news staff.

Convergence is neither easy nor simple, and the commitment to it must be renewed daily. In the transition to convergence, we've lost no staff member, but as we seek applicants for jobs in our multimedia newsroom we emphasize an expectation that employees bring a multimedia background. We seek versatility in our new employees and also look for an eagerness on their part to join with long-time staffers who have achieved status in their professional lives because they were "early adopters" of our convergence efforts. Today, in our News Center, print reporters also report and present stories on television and TV reporters and anchors produce stories for the newspaper. Their early embrace of multimedia storytelling has made them leaders within our newsroom; among them is Joel Mathis, who is now our managing editor for convergence. These multimedia staffers are paid better than one-dimensional peers at other news operations our size, too.

Our print circulation climbed steadily as we ventured into convergence. In measuring our cable television viewership we found that our local news programs beat the networks. We are in 80 percent of the households in our core market, which has a low satellite dish penetration compared to other markets. Our company also has the highest penetration of cable broadband Internet customers in the nation. Our main Web sites record about 30 million page-views each month; Internet traffic has increased beyond our expectations, and this means we've virtually sold out of advertising "space" on our Web sites. Our experience with newsroom convergence also moved us into other "converged" efforts involving advertising, the business office, and human resources.

Convergence is expensive. As a private company, our financial circumstances are not revealed to the public, but we have invested significantly, especially for a company of our size. In 2005 our online revenues were just under one million dollars—profitable for the first time. The early years are ones we consider a long-term business investment. We expect profitability going forward and intend to capitalize on the abilities of the Internet to deliver customers for our advertisers.

What's next? More convergence, of course, combined news staffs in a more integrated, efficient fashion. Even given an expanded region for our efforts, our focus remains intensely local, which is what our surveys tell us our readers and viewers want.

Doubtless the road ahead will have unexpected twists and turns; we intend to drive it, as we always have, with our brights turned on. Only now we will be delivering information in many different ways and letting consumers decide on the delivery method they prefer at the time they want to access our product. No longer is this a one-way street: While they are choosing how to absorb what we can offer, we'll be listening carefully to them and to our newsroom staff to figure out new and better ways of interacting with one another.

Ralph Gage for *Nieman Reports*, December 2005,[22] used with permission

From the mid '90s into the early 2000s, The World Company added numerous subsidiaries and created new businesses to support its convergence including:

- WorldWest LLC was a vehicle for newspaper expansion.

- The World Online provided website development and hosting.

- Mediaphormedia was its project to monetize web-based production system, Django, the software framework developed for The World Company by two Journal-World employees in 2003.

- World GeoSolutions and Bullseye Media provided sophisticated tools to help target demographics for advertisers seeking specific audiences.

- Sunflower Publishing was launched to serve the magazine business, publishing high-end products like Kansas tourism and Colorado hunting magazines.

photo courtesy of JOURNAL-WORLD

JOURNAL-WORLD DIRECTOR: Dan Simons, director Web site design, cable modem Internet access, *of new ventures, helps the Journal-World in Lawrence,* personalized Web content and computer repair and Kan., *into the 21st century with new services such as* installation services.

Dan Simons was director of new ventures for The World Company when he gave an interview to *The Inlander* newspaper in April 1997. He'd go on to become president of The World Company's Electronics Division in 2004.

- Geeks on Wheels, mobile tech-support, served local customers, also Ft. Collins, and was trialed in Detroit.

- KTKA, the ABC-affiliated television station in Topeka, was acquired through a newly-created subsidiary in 2005.

- The Care Car, a complete mobile medical office in a van that traveled to rural communities and sent information via signal transmission directly to the hospital.

Newspapering remained an important part of the mix. The World Company created WorldWest LLC in 1994, with Dolph Simons III positioned for leadership of operations. WorldWest invested in small papers in New Mexico, Arizona, and Colorado. The New Mexico properties ultimately were spun off, and attention returned to Kansas concerns. The company started a paper in Baldwin City, later acquiring a competing newspaper there. It also acquired newspapers in Tonganoxie, Eudora, De Soto, Basehor, and Bonner Springs-Edwardsville, all in Kansas. It launched papers in Lansing and Shawnee, but as the media landscape changed, the Lansing, De Soto, and Eudora papers eventually closed.[23]

"During a local election, a list of questions (6News/Journal-World) reporters had asked of all candidates as part of a voter's guide were posted online. That allowed voters to answer the same questions themselves. Then they could use an online tool to find the candidates whose answers most closely matched their own—an example of civic journalism on steroids.

The paper also routinely files local freedom-of-information requests and uploads piles of public records to its Web site. In 2003, World installed about 30 wireless hot spots around Lawrence. That same year, it began sending daily content to cellphones. For example, subscribers can have real-time scores and statistics from the University of Kansas's football and basketball games delivered on demand.

The company has begun offering daily "podcasts" of news and other information to Apple iPod owners or anyone else carrying an MP3 player. It plans to offer a service that automatically loads information onto a docked MP3 player in the early-morning hours before students head to school."

Tim O'Brien, *The New York Times*, 2005

With Dad and Ralph, there was a constant push for excellence. If we were going to commit to this cross-platform installation, which was beneficial for the user because it gave them what they wanted— video with a print story—we just wanted to do it the best way possible. A lot of people came—as far away as from the Netherlands and Japan—to see how we did convergence because we were doing it well. We had broadcast, cable, print, and we put them all into one unified newsroom. We were the seventh newspaper to ever put our content online. KUSports.com won best website in the nation. We weren't trying to win awards, just put out a good product. We were just early adopters with great people who tried real hard.

Across all products—cable, HBO and the other subscription services, phone, and internet—we were going gangbusters. We were innovating on so many levels. We had a need for a more user-friendly website framework, so our own people developed a software they called Django,[24] and we made it free and open source. It's still used all over the world. We were always higher with subscription saturation because we kept our prices low and had great customer service. When other cable companies first offered phone nationwide, a saturation goal was maybe 18% whereas we were reaching 30%. In our cable market, DISH had horrible numbers, and Direct TV had maybe 300 customers in Lawrence because most in the community were already subscribed to our Sunflower cable which meant they got 6News, a value-added local news broadcast. I think we provided a good product for our community. We had 80% saturation of cable customers—that was unheard of. We were well ahead of average subscription rates for all our services. I'm proud of those achievements.

As a fourth-generation Simons at the helm, the pressure to achieve was real. "Working for your father is the hardest thing you'll ever do—and the easiest. In both directions, you don't want to be the employee who disappoints his boss/Dad, or the Dad/boss who has to be a hardass to the employee who's your son. If you're the kid, you have to earn the respect of the other employees so you've got to pull your weight. This work ethic was instilled in every one of us.

Dan Simons

During this time of vigorous growth, The World Company made a strategic decision—the third of its kind since 1892. In 2004, "Senior management changes at Lawrence's 112-year-old World Company put the family-owned operation in the hands of its fourth generation."[25] Dolph Jr. was still editor and chairman, but his two sons would share overall responsibility for the direction of the family business. And there were now two divisions: Dolph Simons III would be president of the Newspapers, and Dan C. Simons was the new president of its Electronics.

Dolph III was "complimented to have my father's vote of confidence in assuming this new role of leadership." The promotion could have felt like a fait accompli, but what Dolph III hadn't foreseen was how well he fit into the leadership dynamic. "As a kid, I'd fold the papers while watching Gilligan's Island. I had 70 papers, and from my Firestone 3-speed bike, I'd porch my papers right out of the bag. You never forget your route," Dolph III said. "Back in the day, you'd have to go into everyone's house with your pad, and tear off their receipt and give it to them. Going into everybody's home—they had different smells and you got a feel for America that way. The smell of

In 2004, a Journal-World subscriber could have read news of
World Company management changes online at LJWorld.com.

food, the different lives they were living. Paper boys had a chance to
understand people... in the five minutes you were there, or a bit longer
for a chitchat, you began to develop certain social skills."

Dolph III's people skills proved a distinct advantage. "He had the
ideal personality for a local paper," Dolph Jr. said. "Dolph has a way of
making folks comfortable. That was a real asset for us, particularly in
advertising and circulation where a lot of business is conducted over
a cup of coffee or on the sidelines of a ball game."

Dolph Jr. was generous with praise for Dan's leadership as well.
"Dan was always full of ideas about what we could do," Dolph said.
"He started out climbing poles and laying cable, so he learned from
the ground up. Dan and Pammie put together a call-in show with her
stack of records. Dan had the first idea of a telethon. Dan was behind
so many things we were able to do with our cable business."

Winning awards was never the goal, but recognition followed The
World Company nonetheless. Dolph Simons Jr. invested heavily in
excellence, putting quality over profits. By many industry-standards,
he achieved it. "Dolph is among the most future-oriented people in
the industry," Tom Curley, then-president of The Associated Press,
told the *Digital Journalist* magazine in 2003. "He is constantly on a
search for the ways to improve his operations."[26]

As such, *Editor & Publisher* magazine recognized the Journal-World as one of "10 That Do It Right" in 2004 (the *Los Angeles Times* also made the list).

In 2005, Dolph Jr. was recognized by the Cable Television Center as a "Pioneer" in the industry for Sunflower's free public access airtime, weekly cablecast of Lawrence City Commission meetings, and live nightly newscasts"[27] before the Cable Act mandated public education, and government use channels in 1984.

Also in 2005, The World Company's 6News Lawrence earned that year's Walter Cronkite Award for Excellence in Television Political Journalism.

Simons wasn't motivated by accolades and made no effort whatsoever to document them, but to his credit, Ralph Gage compiled a fairly comprehensive awards list[28] in 2011:

- Sunflower Broadband was one of 50 companies, technologies and people considered to be "a breed apart" in the broadband business, according to an industry publication.

In a 1976 letter, Dolph Sr. admired Walter Cronkite for "not pussyfooting" around with his news coverage. "He had a good nose for the news," Dolph Jr. acknowledged. "And you'd learn something whenever you had a chance to visit with him."

Donning red heels in support of a local charity fundraiser:
(left to right) Dolph III, Dolph Jr. and Dan Simons in 2012.

- Sunflower was one of four cable operators named to the CED Top 50. The others: Rogers Communications Inc., which is the No. 1 cable company in Canada, and Comcast Corp. and Time Warner Inc., the two biggest operators in the United States. CED is the common name for *Communication Engineering & Design* magazine, which is considered the industry's premier trade publication. Also named to that list were Microsoft Corp., Google Inc., Sprint Nextel, and others.

- In December 2003, Sunflower Broadband was honored by being named System of the Year by CableFAX's *CableWORLD*, a leading trade magazine in the cable industry.

- NPR called Lawrence, Kansas, the "Convergence Capital of the World" in 2005. Reporter David Folkenflik of Morning Edition came to the Journal-World offices for a tour. World Online General Manager Rob Curley explained that the print, broadcast, and online newsroom wasn't divided by medium but by "beat, so all the political reporters are sitting together, all the courts and cops reporters—print and television and online—are sitting together."

- World Company website creation and management from The World online, the "people who dare to go anywhere and know how to get there," produced two websites singled out as the best in the nation at the Newspaper Association of America's 11th Digital Edge, i.e., "Edgie" awards for 2006 in Orlando, Florida.

In other Edgie categories...

- Lawrence.com was named the best entertainment website among newspapers circulation 50,000 or less. It also ranked first for best design and site architecture.

- LJWorld.com was named the best overall news site among newspapers 50,000 circulation or less.

- Other top winners in their respective circulation categories were the *Washington Post*, *Modesto Bee*, and the *Minneapolis Star Tribune*.

- The Judges noted:

  "This year's list of winners includes sites that have made an impressive habit of consistent excellence, such as washingtonpost. com and Lawrence.com."

- Select comments from Edgie judges...

  "Repeating as the winner in the Best Overall News Site category, LJWorld.com continues its reign as a strong, clever news provider that has earned its reputation for interactivity, responsiveness and innovation."

  "What makes Lawrence.com so special? Start with the useful and authoritative content, such as ultra-timely 'Restaurants Open Now' list, move on to fantastic online radio station, head toward the terrific band listings, and catch your breath with the extensive video offerings."

Dan Cox, director of World Online, said he and his team were gratified by the awards. "It's an honor to be recognized for our efforts," Cox said. "We work hard to build the finest websites possible for our news community, and our readers. We are dedicated to continue providing meaningful, informative content and interaction to our readers."

- The Associated Press Managing Editors honored the Journal-World with its national Convergence Award for a series of stories about mining's legacy in Kansas in 2007.

- The company was a leader among cable companies in moving into internet and telephone operations, and that was one reason *Communications Technology* magazine named it its "System of the Year" in 2010.

> *"I'm just stunned to hear our team's efforts mentioned as consistently great with the likes of the* **Washington Post***," Dan Simons, president of The World Company's electronics division, said in 2006. "That is amazing and this isn't a contest of lightweights; 187 of Americas best newspapers compete for the awards. Some companies build products to win awards, we build products for the reader and advertiser. In my mind, it is that focus that separates us from others. I'm proud of our team."*

Convergence was a wild ride, but The World Company reached the Information Age well ahead of the pack with its principles intact. "It's fun to be on the forefront rather than the last one in," Dolph Jr. said. "You just hope you've done your homework. We knew we had to perform or we were going to look pretty silly—and I always had the sense W.C. and Dad were watching. I wish they could have seen how it all turned out... we were successful, and I think they would have been proud."

CHAPTER 10

The World Company

Act like there's a competing newspaper hard at work right across the street. That's always driven us, but I think the bigger motivation has been that we just loved what we were doing. I still wake up in the morning full of ideas about what we could be doing.

Dolph Simons Jr.

A panel from The Assemblage by Robert Shneeberg, 1985

As a name, "The World Company" might have seemed a tad aspirational to the citizens of Lawrence in 1892, but the gutsy new business would more than earn its ascendancy over the next 125 years. It was a family business that valued relationships. "At the Journal-World, they always seemed to put the employees first, at least that's how I felt," said Rich Salierno, who managed newspaper distribution. "I'll give you an example... I remember one time Dolph III came back to where I was working and said, 'You ready to go?' 'Go where?' I asked. He said, 'C'mon, we're going to St. Louis to watch the national championship game.' So I texted my wife and she gave me the go ahead. Dolph and I jumped in the car, drove four hours over, talked about life, then drove four hours back. Just us. Things like that... I still miss the 'family' there." [1]

Congeniality typified the culture of The World Company, but that didn't equate to relaxed standards. It was a good but challenging place to work. That atmosphere attracted people who took the work seriously, and produced award-winning products. "Awards are not to be coveted but built upon," Dolph Simons Jr. often said. Doing your best work was the point—not getting famous.

Nevertheless, the Simons had clout in newspaper publishing, although "Dolph never flaunted it," said Ann Gardner. As such, few people in Lawrence were aware of the Simonses' far-reaching influence across the industry at large. The uninitiated could hardly be blamed for wondering how a comparatively small press in a sparsely-populated flyover state came to such prominence in the newspaper publishing and cable industries. Certainly, solid midwestern values and a herculean work ethic were evident in each generation, but there were specific qualities—some insightful, others inciteful—that brought the Simons to the fore of their field.

The World Company remains one of the longest family-owned newspaper businesses in the country. [2] Their staying power, Dolph Simons Jr. believes, was rooted in "What we stood for... we've always strived to be true to our principles."

What the company stood for was built into the masthead of its flagship, the *Lawrence Journal-World*:

- Accurate and fair news reporting.

- No mixing of editorial opinion with reporting of the news.

- Safeguarding the rights of all citizens regardless of race, creed, or economic stature.

- Sympathy and understanding for all who are disadvantaged or oppressed.

- Exposure of any dishonesty in public affairs.

- Support of projects that make our community a better place to live.

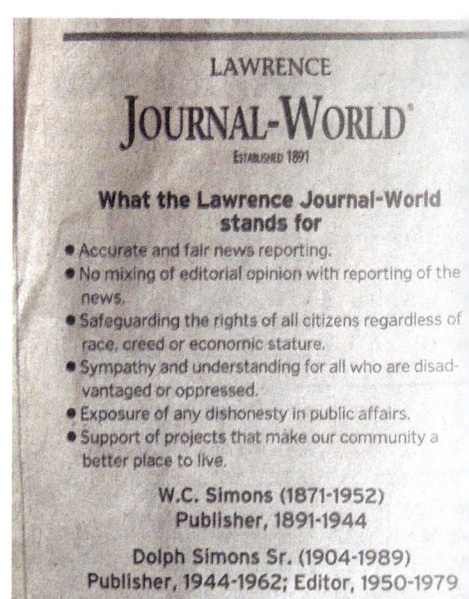

These theoretical principles were applied with diligent practice over decades.

During that time, the business would define, refine, innovate, and expand its deliverables—and mechanisms for delivery. The Simons' operations grew from frontier newspapering to a fully-integrated publishing, broadcasting, telephony, and online centrifuge of information-sharing across the Midwest and West. "We have always been about providing news and information," Dolph Simons Jr. said. "That took many forms as we kept up with the times and technology."

In 2005, NPR reported on The World Company in "Lawrence, Kansas, Convergence Capital USA"[3] noting the Journal-World "is providing a model for how the media may operate in the future." The Simons were ahead of the times, according to Louis Boccardi, former president and CEO of the Associated Press. "All of that may seem primitive now in the world of digital newspapers, Twitter, Facebook, TikTok, etc., but Dolph and his folks were looking ahead with their cablevision startup in Lawrence."

For Crosby de Menocal, great-great grandson of W.C. Simons, "Learning about my family is like taking a class in history or at the journalism school," he laughs. "I could've studied it in college, but it's more fun just to hear Granddad's stories over the Thanksgiving dinner table, or really, anytime we gather. He is interesting. He knows so much, so many people, so many subjects—and not just superficially. There is always something interesting being discussed at my grandparents' house."

The *Lawrence Journal-World* carried on the work of the Kansas *Herald of Freedom*.

With each innovation, the Simons brought integrity, continuity, and nimble adaptability to the quickly-changing platform and mercurial news environment.

Whether the focus is journalism, history, business or political science, any study of the evolution of The World Company begins on the plains of Kansas.

Highpoints and Tipping Points

1873 Although Adolphus "Dolph" Simons had done well and was offered partial ownership of the general store where he was manager and bookkeeper in Owatonna, Minnesota, the job felt "too confining." In spite of his failing health, he moved his wife, Jennie Bessie, and three young children to greener pastures in Dakota County, Minnesota. He'd move farther into western Minnesota the next year for the same reason—there was opportunity ahead.

This drive to take on the next challenge would characterize his descendants for the next 150 years.

1887 The Simons' first foray into the newspaper business was Jennie Bessie Simons' investment in the Houston, Kansas *Weekly Gazette* in 1887. W.C. recorded this astonishing development in an autobiographical sketch he drafted (but never published) many years later: "My mother bought for me a one-half interest in the weekly Gazette published for a short time at Houston, Kansas."[4]

Whether it was her idea or future son-in-law J.L. Brady's, something about newspapering obviously appealed to Jennie. However it happened, no doubt Jennie Bessie thought this could be her 16-year-old son Collie's ticket off their failing farm in Hodgeman County. Unfortunately, Houston, Kansas came to a dead end. Its local post office was discontinued the same year she made the investment; Houston would become a ghost town.

No copies of the Houston *Weekly Gazette* appear to have survived.

1888 Newspapering still seemed viable, so Jennie Bessie Simons purchased the Salina *Daily Republican* next. Her oldest daughter Julia's new husband James Leeford (J.L.) Brady, left his job at the *Jetmore Advance* to take over editorial responsibilities straight away. W.C. "Collie" Simons, now 18, learned the ropes and reporting strictly OJT (on-the-job training). This proved to be the vehicle that moved the Simons family off the ill-fated farm in remote western Kansas.

A peer review in the December 20, 1888, *Abilene Reflector* was generally optimistic with just the slightest underpinning of snark:

> *"The Salina **Daily Republican**, under the editorship of J.L. Brady, made its first appearance yesterday. It is a right, seven-column folio, con-taining the same telegraphic matter as the Reflector, only published twelve hours later—on the following morning. The editor says he has purchased a cemetery lot to be ready for any demise that may take place. We hope he will not need it. Salina should stand by what she has so long been wanting—a good, bright, newsy daily."[5]*

By 1890, W.C. was working on the local paper in St. Joseph, Missouri, when opportunity beckoned him back to Kansas.

Daily Republican.

TERMS:

Daily, one week, by carrier	$0 15
Daily, one month in advance	50
Daily, one year, by mail	5 00
Weekly, one year	1 50

By The Salina Republican Printing Co.

J. L. BRADY, Editor.

This paper is published every day in the week except Monday. It contains all of the telegraphic news several hours ahead of any other paper.

Office in Ober Block, Third Floor.

A NEW DEAL.

The subscription books accounts since July 2nd, 1888, press all clear mater'al, etc., of the REPUBLICAN has been sold to Mrs. Jennie B. Simons. The management will not be changed. Mr. Brady will be retained as editor of the paper. A complete new dress

December 1890 – March 1892

A month after Brady, W.C., and Louie Simons arrived in Lawrence, Kansas, in December 1890, they leased *The Daily Record* and pub-lished with only Brady's name on the masthead from No. 5 East Henry Street. A subscription was 15 cents a week for daily porch delivery or $1.00 yearly for the weekly.

Brothers W.C. and Louis Simons

Always the most politically-inclined of the three, Brady wasted no time wielding his editorial voice. In the February 8, 1892 issue, he took issue with his rival, Col. C.E. Learnard, editor and proprietor of the *Lawrence Daily Journal*, for "squeal[ing]" and exhorted Learnard to "express himself in polite though forcible English, otherwise he will use ordinary bar room billingsgate, and in the use of the latter, we can hardly hope and certainly shall not attempt to compete..."

By March 1, Brady and Simons had established The World Company because, per W.C.'s reflections written for the Journal-World in 1931, "We liked the name *world*."[6] Then they launched their own independent paper, the *Daily World*, on March 2, 1892. Editor J.L. Brady and Business Manager W.C. Simons shared the masthead.

The *Daily World* worked aggressively on circulation. It ran a special Back-to-School promotion on August 27, 1892, that offered to purchase school books for any students who secured new subscribers.

To all BOYS and GIRLS as Scholars in the Public Schools of Lawrence, beginning September school term 1892.

NEW BOOKS will be required of ALL SCHOLARS in every grade of the Lawrence Public Schools and the WORLD WILL FURNISH THEM TO EVERY GIRL AND BOY FREE OF CHARGE. No money will be required... all that will be required of each scholar is the exercise of a little energy.

*PROPOSITION to students in 1st thru 8th grade, any boy or girl securing new subscribers to the **Daily World** would have all books purchased new by the World.*

Journal editor C.E. Learnard apparently didn't appreciate the competition. He wrote "...it must be acknowledged that Mr. Brady, in this enterprise, indicates that he has more nerve than judgment, yet the JOURNAL sincerely hopes that he may be able to make a success of the hard work he has undertaken." Learnard went on to speculate on the political leanings of the World, then closed dismissively, "Generally speaking, it does not appear that there is a crying need for another paper in Lawrence, but as this country is a free one..."[7]

In 1895, The World Company purchased Learnard's *Daily Gazette* for $2,000. Thereafter, the paper's pedigree was proudly added to the masthead:

*The World was established in 1892 and has always done a good business. **The Record** was established in 1889, and was published for four years. It was purchased by the Gazette in 1893, and was run under the name of **Daily Gazette** until 1895, when it was purchased by The World and consolidated with the **Daily World**. This gives the **Daily World** the advantage of three successful newspaper properties, and gives the largest circulation in Lawrence.*

1900 - 1905 Early in the new century, the *Daily World* raised its subscription to 25 cents a month for carrier delivery six days a week, and 50 cents for the weekly by mail. The office could be reached by telephone at number 136.

When we purchased the Journal in 1905, it was necessary for us to borrow quite a large amount, and much to my chagrin, I learned that the credit of newspapers that time was on a par with that of the livery barns. Rebelling against such condition of affairs, I came to the conclusion that the newspaper business should be a respectable one. That the credit of the paper should be as good as that of any other business concern, that the plant should occupy as good a building as

W.C. Simons, circa 1905

that occupied by a bank, and that the newspaper man's home should be as good as that of the banker's.

Two things were necessary to prepare the way for the transformation. One was for the newspaper man to pay his bills promptly, and in order to do this, he must collect promptly the accounts due him. It took about thirty lawsuits, all of which I won, to prove that a debt owed to a paper was just as much of an obligation as a note owed to a bank. With this fact established, we were in a position to be lenient and extend necessary credit to our patrons.

I learned one day many years ago that four children had died of an ailment that had not been understood. We had an expert obtain swabs and found it to be diphtheria. We came out in a top head story that made every parent and every physician alert to the conditions confronting them. There was but one more death. But one of our advertisers thought we were running trade away from the town and tried to start a boycott. We successfully met the issue by asking the merchant to tell us just how much trade he should have to warrant the unnecessary death of a child.

I feel that perhaps I have had a real part in bringing the newspaper business to a higher standard. The boys born with silver spoons in their mouths could not possibly have felt the same interest in the matter that I did.

W.C. Simons, from a talk given to the Saturday Night Club (undated)

Having bought out his brother Louis, W.C. was now the majority owner and shareholder. He borrowed enough money to buy old rival C.E. Learnard's *Lawrence Daily Journal* for $18,000 in 1905. J.L. Brady took over its operation and began to publish the Journal independently of The World Company.[8]

1911 The *Lawrence Daily Journal* operated out of the Bowersock Opera House building at the corner of Seventh and Massachusetts Street. *The World* was operating nearby at 722 Massachusetts. On February 17, 1911, a fire destroyed the Bowersock building—the Journal's newspaper offices and most of its equipment along with it.

Thanks to a swift merger of Brady's and Simons' papers, no time was lost. Just days after the fire, the first issue of the newly-minted *Lawrence Journal-World* was published on February 20, 1911. The

The Lawrence Journal offices on the building's ground floor were also destroyed by the Bowersock Opera House fire on February 17, 1911. (Photo courtesy Kansas Historical Society)

Simons (third from left) and Brady (third from right) merged their operations in 1911 creating the *Lawrence Journal-World* that operated out of 722 Massachusetts Street.

masthead made it entirely clear, "This paper is a straight Republican paper, one that gives the news without bias or color."

1914 - 1915 W.C. Simons bought out J.L. Brady in December 1914, and gained complete control of the company. Brady moved to

Arkansas with his proceeds to purchase a paper W.C. had located for him. According to Kansas City's *Weekly Gazette Globe* on December 31, 1914, "Editor Brady Sings His Swan Song Before Leaving Kansas.

> *With this issue of the Vine, I am bidding good bye to the field in which I have labored so long. I have fought the battles for the people whether they have realized it or not and I have steadfastly defended against the many new foibles and innovations of our government. I have opposed tight lacing, the use of cosmetics, the initiative and the referendum. The good old ways of my father have been good enough for me and rather than stand the constant agitation for reform I have decided to move to some spot where a man can go about the routine of his daily business without having to undergo the mental gymnastics necessary to keep up with things around me and I cannot forever keep on. I cannot forever keep trying to keep my readers in the paths of rectitude. The Vine has ceased clinging and I bid you farewell."[9]*

Only Simons' name appeared on the January 1915 masthead that provided two phone numbers for the Journal-World—one for news, one for business.

As president, editor, and publisher, W.C. set an edifying (if somewhat preachy) tone with his first editorial in January 1915, (only a few days after Brady's "swan song"):

> *It is one of the grandest things in life that one can begin all over again. No matter what a botch he may have made of things, there is ever present the opportunity of making a new start, in which one may make good. Of course, it is best to start clean and stay clean, but the next best thing to having kept yourself pure from the start, is to keep yourself pure from now on. It may be that the burdens you have carried have left their impress in humped shoulders and bowed head, or hard lines may have furrowed their way through your forehead and cheeks, but in spite of all that you can start again and still make good.*

1917 - 1918 The World Company covered the biggest of world events and the smallest of local news, including this tidbit about the heir-apparent of the family business:

1920 - 1925 A 1925 *National Printer Journalist* article about the *Lawrence Daily Journal-World* noted "While it is a Republican paper, it is independent in its policies. A Democratic meeting will secure as fair a news story as that of Republican. A few years ago, the Socialists of the City, a few hundred in number, sent representatives to the Journal-World to see what it would cost them to publish the national Socialist platform. The publisher, realizing that any price in accord with advertising rates of the paper would seem prohibitive to the group, offered to run, and did run, the platform one time for nothing. As a result, at the following meeting of the Socialist union, resolutions of appreciation were adopted, which were, it proved, of greater value to the paper than would have been the price for the space." [10]

Dolph Simons Sr. was coming of age professionally. During the summer break from college in 1924, he interned at the Associated Press offices in Chicago. Dolph's initiation into national news came by covering the Leopold-Loeb trial. Local Lawrence news was equally intense as the KKK harassed Journal-World employees and attempted a boycott of the paper.

1925 The World Company's location at 720 Massachusetts Street featured restrooms on each floor and showers in the basement for "all around efficiency."

When someone hears a cock and bull story, he waits to see if it appears in the paper, and if it does not, he decides that it is not true. That kind of confidence puts a tremendous weight of responsibility on the publisher, but it is worth maintaining.

W.C. Simons (in his undated talk about Lawrence history)

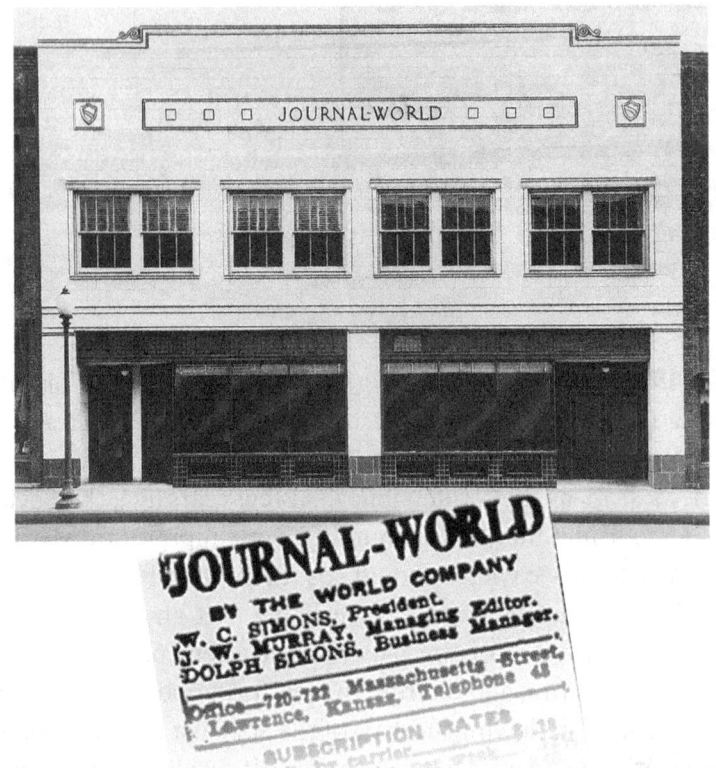

1928 By 1928, Dolph Sr. joined his father, W.C., on the masthead as Business Manager.

The Journal-World cost 13 cents a week by carrier.

In the 1920s, carriers picked up copies of the paper in front of the ticket office of the Kansas City and Kaw Valley Interurban Rail Line at 636 Massachusetts Street. The train and streetcar depot were located next door. The railroad made daily round trips between Lawrence and Kansas City with stops in Tonganoxie.[11]

Being a Journal-World carrier was a good gig. The Simons hosted a regular banquet for the boys who "were just a little startled by the flash light, but it didn't affect their appetite," W.C. noted under the photo taken of one of the dinners.

1930 In March, The World Company's next generation was secured with the birth of Dolph Simons Jr. to Dolph Sr. and Marie Simons.

1932 W.C. Simons was a board member of the Associated Press of Kansas, which brought him inside larger conversations being had in the industry at the state and national levels. His authoritative nature and redoubtable integrity made him an ideal director when he was appointed to the National Audit Board of Circulations in 1932.

1936 The World Company operated a commercial printing department and bindery. Supervised by W.C.'s son-in-law, O.W. Maloney, husband of daughter Janet, the department published several magazines and provided printing supplies throughout Kansas and surrounding states.[12]

Somewhere in the U.S., the manual upright typewriter that Dolph Simons Jr. would use to bang-out editorials with two-fingers over his entire career—up to 2023 and counting—was manufactured.

December 7, 1941 The *Lawrence Journal-World's* first Sunday EXTRA edition—prompted by the attack on Pearl Harbor—was published.

1944 National loyalty was a major concern during WWII that continued into the '50s with the Red Scare and McCarthyism. The Simons family did not shy away from addressing that head-on for The World Company. First Amendment concerns notwithstanding, neither W.C. nor Dolph Sr. could understand the hesitation some had expressed about signing a public oath of loyalty to the United States of America.

The directors of The World Company put their names to it on November 28, 1944.

Dolph Sr. stepped into his father's shoes as publisher of the *Lawrence Journal-World* in 1944. The newspaper's wide circulation inspired its slogan, "The most familiar sight in Douglas County."

Eager to make his own mark, Dolph explored diversification. He secured a radio franchise in the '40s, but in a classic Simons' turn at the fork of integrity versus enterprise, "Dad gave it up," Dolph Jr. said. "He just didn't feel it was right to corner the news market.

In a play on the Journal-World slogan, the Editors Simons are presented as "the most familiar sight in Douglas County."

Dolph Simons and W.C. Simons, circa 1940s

1945 During the second World War, Dolph Sr. introduced a popular weekly column called "Dear Buddy." It was full of local news of home so family members could cut it out and mail it from "The Folks" to their sons overseas.

Folks at home could clip out "Dear Buddy" and slip it into a letter to loved ones stationed far away.

Weather and local sports updates were mixed with tidbits like "George G. Clevenger is celebrating his 98th birthday today... that's a lot of years" and "If this much talk of cigarette shortage should get to the rationing stage, we really would be in for some fun... last night at the Eldridge coffee shop we saw several grandmoms with fags and thought how funny it would look to see them puffing away on pipes."

1947 At U.S. Secretary of War General Robert P. Patterson's invitation, Dolph Simons Sr. traveled with a tour of Ally-occupied Germany and Austria. Dolph published his straight-forward account of the conditions, and his report became a popular reference handbook of the War Department.

1948 In his December 14th editorial, W.C. reflected on the newspaper's service to its readers: "We have watched with pleasure the growth and improvement of everything in connection with the Home Town, but we recognize further things which should be done and will be happy to have a part in the doing. I am grateful to the people individually and to the community as a whole."

1949 On the heels of his successful trip in '47, Dolph Sr. was the only civilian to accompany Admiral Louis Denfeld, chief of naval operations, and Vice-Admiral Robert B. Carney, deputy chief of naval operations, on a Navy inspection flight around the world. Dolph visits 22 countries in six weeks, and publishes *A Globe Circler's Diary*, an account of the conditions and cultures experienced during his 35,000-mile world tour.

Dolph Sr. was the first Simons to serve on the Associated Press national board of directors.

1950 Publisher of the Journal-World since 1944, Dolph Sr. became its editor in 1950. He was the first Simons to serve on the board of the national Associated Press (AP), to which he was elected first vice president in 1950. Dolph Sr. remained on its board until 1960.

1951 Sporting a new masthead design, the Journal-World celebrated its 60th anniversary in 1951. The World Company averaged about 70 employees a year with an annual payroll of $240,000.00 including about 30 newspaper carriers.[13]

Journal-World offices at 722 Massachusetts Street, circa 1950

Ruth Love was one of those employees. She reflected on the paper's 60th anniversary in 1951 with specific appreciation for its founder. "Mr. W.C., as he is affectionately called by employees, has always made a practice of employing department heads in whom he has confidence and then leaving the running of the departments up to them. Without bossing, he still plays a large part in the daily schedule... he's in the office every day... always available when an employee has a problem... invaluable aid to reporters when they are writing about the early days of Lawrence because of his store of historical knowledge."

1952 W.C. Simons would pass away in May of 1952.

1953 The 1953 employee manual, *Working for the Journal-World*, provided "a clear understanding of the conditions of employment and extra benefits." These included sick pay, paid vacation after a year's employment, life insurance, health insurance, workmen's compensation, retirement plans, and double-time pay plus shorter hours when working on holidays.

In it, Dolph Simons Sr. encouraged anyone to drop by his office if they had questions about the policies outlined in the booklet, noting "the door is always open." The most important policy of all, he emphasized was "The Golden Rule: treat the other fellow the same as you would want to be treated if you were in his place. That applies to everyone from top to bottom, and there can be no better rule for all of us to follow."[14]

Dolph Simons Sr. attended the 1952 Republican Convention as a member of the press corps.

1954 The Journal-World celebrates its 100th birthday on September 25. "The *Herald of Freedom*, the first newspaper published in Lawrence, is a direct forebear of the Journal-World. More than 40 newspapers have been consolidated into the present paper which goes into 9,600 homes each day."[15]

1955 Construction on the new *Lawrence Journal-World* headquarters and printing operations began 100 years to the day from the inaugural issue of the Kansas *Herald of Freedom*. The Herald, the first newspaper in Lawrence, was subsumed by the *Lawrence Daily World*, which merged into the *Lawrence Journal-World*. On January 27, The World Company moved into new offices as construction was completed at Sixth and New Hampshire Street in downtown Lawrence.

The commercial printing department and bindery of The World Company were among the largest in the state of Kansas during this decade, producing leather-bound books, periodicals, and thousands of smaller orders for individual companies. There were three automatic magazine presses doing color work with speeds ranging from 2,100 to 5,000 printed sheets per hour, and a folder that could fold 4,000 sheets per hour. There were stitching machines, gold stamping presses, punching machines, paper cutters, and numerous other pieces of equipment required for printing and publishing.[16]

The World Company also offered complete mailing services and maintained addressograph equipment and thousands of mailing plates for several magazine publishers.

Rich Clarkson began his career as a photographer at the Journal-World shortly before graduating from KU with a degree in Journalism in 1956. From there he went on to the *Topeka Capital-Journal*, then the *Denver Post* before becoming *National Geographic* magazine's director of photography in the 1980s. He was best known for more than 30 covers on *Sports Illustrated* and photographing six Olympics.

This was also the year Lawrence High School student Bill Snead got his start in photo-journalism mixing darkroom chemicals for the Journal-World under Clarkson's tutelage. Snead went on to become UPI Saigon photo-bureau chief during the Vietnam War, and an award-winning photographer for the *Washington Post* and *National Geographic* magazine, among others. His illustrious career would come full circle when he returned at his friend Dolph Simons Jr.'s request, to his beloved hometown of Lawrence to become editor and photo editor at the *Lawrence Journal-World* in 1993.[17]

1956 - 1958 Dolph Jr. was busy earning his journalistic stripes on the other side of the pond when he first made the masthead as "Associate Publisher" in July 1957.

His stories for London's *The Times* in 1956 and the *Johannesburg Star* (South Africa) in 1958 were reprinted in the Journal-World. They were the genesis of what would become his regular op-ed "Saturday Column" that would continue running for the next 65 years in the *Lawrence Journal-World*.

1959 Dolph Simons Sr. awarded the William Allen White Award of Merit. Fellow editor, publisher, and friend W. L. White of the *Emporia Gazette*, wrote, "If Dolph Simons, in spite of his editorial halo and his purple toga as publisher, still has the respect of the working press, it is only because he has always been one of them." Simons is also voted 2nd vice president of the Associated Press board of directors.

With circulation on the rise, the Journal-World ordered a new 40-page newspaper press that would be built by the Goss Company, the world's largest manufacturer of rotary press equipment.

Since 1954, the number of carrier boys had risen from 21 to 103.[18]

1960 The new Goss press was installed, enabling the Journal-World to produce 40,000 complete papers per hour. It is 56 feet long, 11 feet high and weighs 50 tons. Featuring the latest technology, one mile of rolled newsprint could pass through the press each 4.5 minutes.

1961 Dolph Simons Sr. invited to serve as juror for the Pulitzer Prize.

1964 The price of daily delivery went up to 35 cents per week. The masthead indicated Dolph Jr. was now vice president and publisher by October 1964.

1965 When Dolph Jr. was at a meeting of the American Newspaper

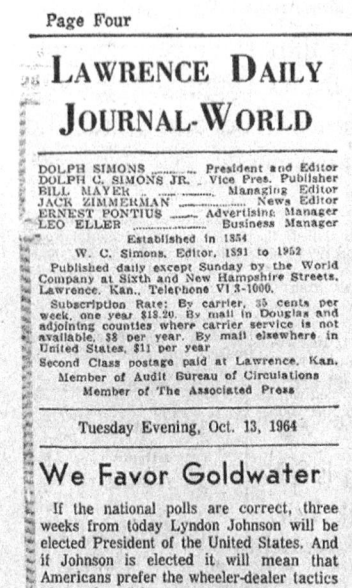

Page Four

LAWRENCE DAILY JOURNAL-WORLD

DOLPH SIMONS .... President and Editor
DOLPH C. SIMONS JR. .. Vice Pres. Publisher
BILL MAYER .... Managing Editor
JACK ZIMMERMAN .... News Editor
ERNEST PONTIUS .... Advertising Manager
LEO ELLER .... Business Manager

Established in 1854
W. C. Simons, Editor, 1891 to 1952

Published daily except Sunday by the World Company at Sixth and New Hampshire Streets, Lawrence, Kan., Telephone VI 3-1000.

Subscription Rate: By carrier, 35 cents per week, one year $18.20. By mail in Douglas and adjoining counties where carrier service is not available, $8 per year. By mail elsewhere in United States, $11 per year

Second Class postage paid at Lawrence, Kan.
Member of Audit Bureau of Circulations
Member of The Associated Press

Tuesday Evening, Oct. 13, 1964

We Favor Goldwater

If the national polls are correct, three weeks from today Lyndon Johnson will be elected President of the United States. And if Johnson is elected it will mean that Americans prefer the wheeler-dealer tactics of Lyndon Johnson to the unsophistication

Publishers Association (ANPA) in New York, he had the first idea of starting a cable franchise after listening to a speaker describe how he ran coaxial wire up a high tower to help deliver TV customers reasonably clear signals. Dolph returned to Lawrence and started making plans for how to do this in Lawrence.

1966 Dolph Jr. was director of the Kansas Press Association, and its president by 1967.

1967 Efforts to establish a union at the Journal-World came to a vote on January 30, 1967. Fourteen people voted for it; 29 against, and one challenged vote out of 45 eligible voters. This was the first and last attempt to unionize at The World Company, and no one was fired.

> *I've worked in places that are so closed minded, they don't listen to any suggestions. But Dolph was never like that, and Ralph (Gage) wasn't either.*

Rich Salierno, former Journal-World distribution manager

In 1967, Dolph Jr. was the youngest person ever elected to the Associated Press's national board of directors.[19] He would be reelected each successive term for the next ten years.

Dolph Jr. was often the youngest member of the boards on which he served including the Lawrence National Bank board shown here, circa 1961.

Three generations, Dolph Sr., Dolph Jr., and Dolph III, circa 1967

1968 In August, Dolph Jr. was in Chicago to cover the controversial Democratic National Convention of 1968, "among the most tense and confrontational political conventions ever in American history."[20] Although he'd covered the convention scene before, "This one went to a whole different level," Dolph said. "I'd arrived early and stayed there all night—I didn't go back to my hotel until the next morning because I didn't want to miss anything. There was an angry mob just outside the convention center on Michigan Avenue. Some of them were dropping bags of urine on the crowd below the view deck. It wasn't exactly a riot, but things were very tense."

1969 As of December, Dolph Jr.'s title was president and publisher of The World Company. Dolph Sr. was editor. The price of delivery had risen to 43 cents a week.

After robust recruiting by Dolph Jr., Ralph Gage, a KU J-school alum who was working on an East St. Louis paper, signed on with the Journal World as a reporter covering the KU beat. Gage would rise through the ranks from managing editor, assistant to the publisher, general manager, to chief operating officer (for The World Company) in 2004, as well as serving as director of special projects.

> *We thought of Lawrence as kind of a peaceful college town, but arrived just in time for all ROTC protests, the burning of the Union... certainly not what we anticipated.*
>
> *I didn't imagine staying for my whole career, but it was exciting. Dolph [Jr.] was always pushing to get us into something more... into something new. There was never a dull moment.*
>
> *My own father died when I was five or six years old, so Dolph was like a surrogate father. When my mother was dying from liver cancer, Dolph tried to be very reassuring and positive. I certainly remember those conversations.*
>
> Ralph Gage, May 27, 2021

1970 The civil rights movement across the country that led to "Days of Rage" on the KU campus in April put Lawrence in the spotlight, and in a declared state of emergency.[21] Dolph Jr. was at meetings with the AP board in New York City when scenes of the National Guard patrolling the remains of the arson-burned KU Memorial Student Center splashed across the front page of every newspaper and evening news broadcast. He was on the first plane home.

1971 The first liquor advertisement in the *Lawrence Journal-World* appeared on December 3. "That was not an easy decision," Dolph Jr. recalled. W.C. Simons was a teetotaler with a strict policy against accepting advertising dollars from alcohol vendors. "We held the line on that for 20 years after Granddad passed," Dolph said. In the end, lifting the prohibition against liquor sales was just a business decision.

Dolph Jr. was appointed to the ANPA board on December 10, 1971.

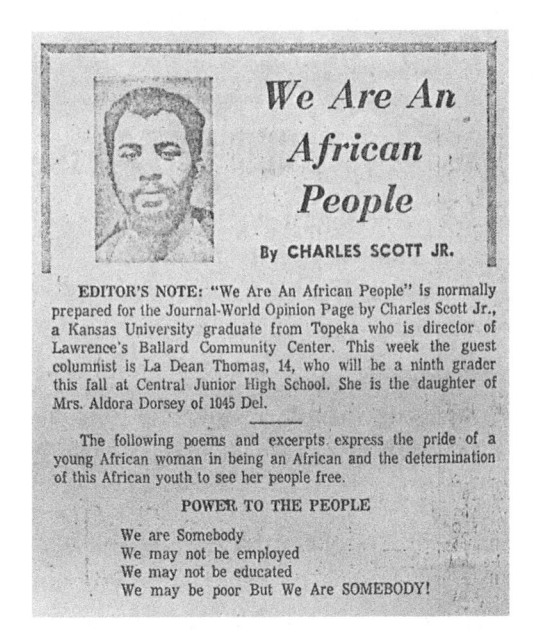

We Are An African People

By CHARLES SCOTT JR.

EDITOR'S NOTE: "We Are An African People" is normally prepared for the Journal-World Opinion Page by Charles Scott Jr., a Kansas University graduate from Topeka who is director of Lawrence's Ballard Community Center. This week the guest columnist is La Dean Thomas, 14, who will be a ninth grader this fall at Central Junior High School. She is the daughter of Mrs. Aldora Dorsey of 1045 Del.

The following poems and excerpts express the pride of a young African woman in being an African and the determination of this African youth to see her people free.

POWER TO THE PEOPLE

We are Somebody
We may not be employed
We may not be educated
We may be poor But We Are SOMEBODY!

In 1972, "Dolph Simons Jr. asked me if I'd like to provide my perspective of the Black community, so I did," Charles Scott Jr. said.

The World Company sought and received the franchise to operate a cable television company—putting them years ahead of other markets including nearby Kansas City.

In 1972, its new subsidiary, Sunflower Cablevision, began serving its first cable television customers in Lawrence.

1972 From 1972 to 1980, Dolph Jr. served as director of the ANPA (which later became News Media Alliance). In 1975, he was elected national secretary of the 1,100-member American Newspaper Publishers Association. He was simultaneously a director of the Associated Press, the Newspaper Advertising Bureau and a trustee of the Nieman Foundation at Harvard University.[22]

1974 On May 20, The World Company converted from hot metal to photo-composition and offset printing. This was a vast improvement over the cumbersome processes of old that began with handset type in W.C. Simons' days, followed by linotype that continued into Dolph Sr.'s era. "Offset was so much better and cleaner—and safer," Dolph Jr. said. But there was a steep learning curve for longtime staffers who had to learn the new process. In his letter to stockholders on January 14, 1975, Dolph Sr. wrote:

> *"To be completely frank, we made the changeover differently than most plants we know about. Elsewhere, owners have trained new people for the work, and then, when the changeover came, the composing department was operating largely with newly*

trained typists and compositors, and old members of the force were terminated. Because of our interest in our regular staff, we arranged it so that everyone would have an opportunity to show talent and desire to justify continuation on the job.

In most cases this has worked out well for both the employees and the company, although we earnestly believe our profit for the year would have been higher if we had trained new people. On the other hand, old friends and trusted employees are terribly important in the long run."

The transition was managed without missing a beat. The Journal-World's Goss offset presses would continue to run seven days a week, 365 days a year.[23]

As a matter of course, a six-week supply of paper and ink was always kept on-site in case railroad strikes or other supply chain interruptions risked going to press. "We never missed an issue," Dolph Jr. stated. "Even when weather conditions kept employees from getting home, we had a plan. We'd go to the store and buy everything we needed to feed everyone at the plant. Hell, we'd put on lunches or dinners just for the fun of it sometimes, too."

That tradition extended back to W.C. Simons' era, and Dan Simons remembered how he was trained for the company's holiday giving. "Ernie (Pontius, advertising director) taught me how to load the fruit baskets—we started with 52 and ended up with over 500."

1977 Dolph Jr. became a juror for the Pulitzer Prize. He would continue in this role several more times in 1978, 1980, and 1981.

Journal-World secretary Dorothy Fritzel's shopping list for an "Impromptu luncheon" for 200 at the plant.

Ann Gardner, a 1975 KU J-school grad, was recruited by Ralph Gage this year. "I covered all the little towns around Lawrence—there were probably seven or eight of them. I kept track of their city council and school board meetings, farm issues, weather, and local news," Gardner said. "After a year or so, the Journal-World wanted to expand their Sunday Features section. So I moved over to that and became co-editor with another woman for several years." Ann would eventually become editorial page editor, a title she held for 30 of the 40 years she worked for The World Company.

We used to have a rule that nothing went into the paper that wasn't reviewed and copyedited. A good copy editor is so important. My dad was a great writer and editor. I would often ask him to read a column I'd written. He'd say you should think that over again... put it in the drawer and see if you still feel the same way tomorrow. I did a lot of that. Nowadays, I ask Dolph (III) and Dan to read the editorials I write for the blog.

I did not hold back on my opinions about things that were going on in Lawrence or at KU... or anywhere else. There were people who canceled their subscription to the paper because of something I wrote... I wonder how many did that. My dad's editorial stance was to take a positive slant, but I don't know if I did as good a job at that as I should have.

What I was for was making Lawrence the best place to live, and I felt it was my job to point out what we could be doing to make things better. Why wouldn't we want to improve our quality of life? People didn't have to agree with me about what that would take... many didn't. But I just couldn't stand by and watch the leaders and politicians screwing things up or dodging the issues. If they had a point of view that ran counter to mine, we were open to publishing it. We criticize others so they can criticize us. We ran more letters to the editor that were critical of us than the other way around, by far. We sure didn't toot our own horn. Our views weren't perfect, but we owned them.

> I recruited and interviewed all our reporters, and I'd tell them the rules. Complacency and dishonesty were the cardinal sins. We should operate like there was a competing newspaper across the street. It's so different now. So many papers have died—there used to be so much individual ownership. Kansas had more newspapers per reader than any other state in the country.
>
> To me, the primary role of the newspaper business is to inform, enlighten, stimulate a desire for improvement, and to help bring about constructive changes in our society through a well-informed and engaged citizenry. Perhaps newspapermen should think more often about the role of the newspaper. Perhaps we need to do more frequent soul-searching about our goals and our performance. If we in the business have fuzzy thoughts about our role, how can we expect the lay person to understand what we are trying to accomplish?
>
> Dolph Simons Jr.

1978 The World Company expanded its cable operation to Colorado, launching Columbine Cablevision in Ft. Collins. After directing special projects for Sunflower Cable, Pam Simons heads to Ft. Collins to start-up operations at her dad's request. "When I first started, I was on the only woman on the Colorado Cable Association board of directors. I'd attend cable conventions and be the only woman there, unless I brought our advertising manager with me," Pam said. "Then there'd be two women there."

The Journal-World began publishing a Sunday edition in November. As quoted in the *University Daily Kansan*, Dolph Jr. said, "We felt if we were going to serve the public with a complete newspaper, we had to go to a Sunday edition." This decision was consistent with industry trends at the time.[24]

1981 Rich Salierno hired on at the Journal-World, beginning a tenure of more than 30 years during which he had numerous titles.

"Depended on the day... if somebody wanted something done, they'd say go see Rich," Salierno laughed. His role as Distribution Manager was outsourced in 2014—a sign of the times. Salierno went on to work at the *Kansas City Star*, which he described as "a totally different world. At the Journal, they always seemed to put the employees first, at least that's how I felt. Dolph Jr. and Ralph Gage always had their door open, and you could go in and talk about a problem. Ralph might tell you that you were the problem, but then he'd help you fix it."

1984 The World Company became an official printer and distributer of the groundbreaking new national paper, *USA TODAY*, in April of 1984. It was a controversial move in the industry, according to Dolph Jr., because the old guard "made fun of what Al Neuharth was

Dolph Jr. and Al Neuharth worked together on *USA TODAY* and the Freedom Forum.

trying to do—like it was just a huge ego trip for him," Dolph explained. Allen Neuharth, the paper's publisher, wasn't an industry insider and he didn't get a lot of respect. "What he was trying to pull off was an untested approach to covering the nation with a TV-style news-paper," Dolph said. For some, it was an affront to how things had always been done or should be done, but as Dolph saw it, *USA TODAY* was the wave of the future.

Industry-wide, the Simons name had always imbued respectability, so more than one of his colleagues with the ANPA and AP took Dolph Jr. aside to advise against sullying his reputation with Neuharth's upstart enterprise. Dolph waved them off, "Al was onto something. The guy had brains and guts. I admired him."

Dolph had taken The World Company on a transformative journey of its own since the late '60s, so he wasn't shying away. "My dad trusted me. He knew I wouldn't do anything to embarrass our own paper."

It proved to be a good call for the Simons. *USA TODAY* changed the newspaper publishing landscape forever, and that connection positioned The World Company among the most progressive operations in the industry.

> *"Thank you for the card. You don't realize what you've done for me as a young boy giving me a chance and becoming a man working for your family for almost 50 years. I'll always be in your debt."*

to Dolph Simons Jr. from Billy Porter, former Journal World employee, 2022

1985 The Assemblage, created by Robert Shneeberg, an artist and Hallmark cards designer, was displayed on the lobby wall of the Journal-World office. It was composed of more than a ton of type, type cases, engravings, and tools formerly used in producing the newspaper and in its commercial printing operations that had been rendered obsolete through modernization. Commissioned by The World Company, it featured numerous images and names of individuals who had been prominent in Lawrence history—even the KU Jayhawk.

1987 Ann Gardner was promoted to editor of the editorial page this year. "I had to really give them credit for giving a 30-something woman the editor job. It was an older-male dominated environment, and it must have been a leap for them to put a woman in that role," Ann said. "Both Dolph Sr. and Jr. wrote editorials, so there was a negotiation period because sometimes I'd have to advocate for something I wrote. Sometimes I'd talk to them first about a topic. We'd have some lively discussions. I'd question, explain, and maybe push a little—but I always knew it wasn't my call to make. Not often, but maybe a dozen times in all those years, I couldn't live with the changes they'd make to an editorial, so we'd nix it entirely."[25]

1988 The World Company tripled the size of its facilities with a major expansion of the Sixth and New Hampshire Street offices that were originally opened in 1955. Instead of relocating for the build, "We were making every effort to remain downtown," Dolph Simons Jr. said. Four buildings at 616, 620, 622, and 626 Massachusetts Street had to be torn down to accommodate the 21,506-square foot production

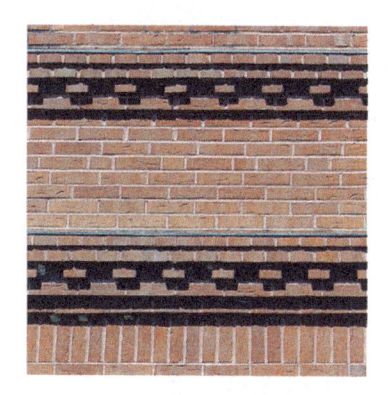

(opposite page) The Journal-World facility tripled in size in 1988.

(left) Marie Simons' touch showed up in the brickwork of the new plant.

facility. It was the largest single business/industry development in the history of Lawrence to date.[26]

Marie Simons was particularly interested in the aesthetics of the design. "Mother worked so hard to get the mortar a certain color, and the coursing of the brick a certain way," Dolph Jr. recalled.

1989 Dolph Simons Jr. was named to the Gannett Foundation board of trustees by its chair Al Neuharth, president and publisher of *USA TODAY*. Neuharth announced the Foundation would change its name to the Freedom Forum.

1990 A subscription to the Journal-World was $6.80 every four weeks by carrier or $88.69 per year by mail. Circulation was about 20,000.

The '90s were a time of expansion and innovation for The World Company. If Dolph Jr. was the visionary, then Ralph Gage was the guy with boots on the ground making it happen. "At some point I seemed to be responsible for all the entities the Simons owned," Gage said.[27] In addition to being general manager of the Journal-World, Gage was secretary of WorldWest Limited Liability Company, and had various roles with World Company enterprises including Orbiter LLC, KTKA-TV in Topeka, the area weeklies, magazines, and Mediaphormedia. "Mediaphormedia was our project to monetize our web-based production system," Gage explained. "Many people representing various companies encouraged us to take the step because they were interested in acquiring what we had developed. So we did, and it remained viable long after we sold it."[28]

Employee turnover wasn't an issue for the Journal-World where the culture was more familial than corporate. Staff knew each other at work and around town.

Journal-World employees gathered for an update from Dolph Jr., circa 1990s.

1991 The early association with *USA TODAY* Publisher Al Neuharth led to Dolph Jr. joining the board of the Freedom Forum (formerly the Gannett Foundation) in 1991. The Forum's fact-finding mission that year took the board to the Soviet Union and Poland. The next year, Simons and the board would visit Indonesia with the Forum. Wherever the Freedom Forum went, its goal was to foster discussion of First Amendment principles, particularly in lands with government-controlled media.[29]

Dolph Jr. congratulates new Kansas City Mayor Emanuel Cleaver (on left) in 1991.

1992 This was a big year for *Lawrence Journal-World* golden boy Bill Snead who was named the White House News Photographers Association's Photographer of the Year, and a runner-up for a Pulitzer Prize in news photography for his coverage of the war in the Balkans. At this pinnacle, he took a sabbatical from the *Washington Post* to teach a course at the University of Kansas that Dolph Simons Jr. helped facilitate.

1993 At Dolph Jr.'s invitation, Bill Snead stayed on in Lawrence, training Journal-World's photographers and assuming management of the newsroom. "He was so damn talented, I couldn't believe we got him back," Dolph Jr. said. "We've had so many incredibly talented photographers at the Journal-World. Snead was one of them—he supposedly got the first picture of the Beatles in America. Another was Richard Clarkson, who had more *Sports Illustrated* covers than anybody. He was temperamental as hell, but God he was good."

Another big event happened in 1993. On October 16, the *Lawrence Journal-World* flag looked like this:

The next day, it looked like this:

The new design reflected the findings of a market research study Dolph Jr. commissioned by Clark, Martire, and Bartolomeo. "They surveyed the Lawrence community to learn what we should be doing with the Journal-World," Dolph explained. That information directed a brand-new approach to a modular layout and "news you can use" with emphasis on local stories.

Ann Gardner remembered the process of incorporating that strategy into a new look for the newspaper. "When we decided to redesign the Journal-World, Dolph, of course, wanted only the best, so they hired Mario Garcia, a very well-known designer who had redesigned papers like the *Washington Post* and *Miami Herald*. Mario spent weeks with us doing the design, much of which is still in use by the Journal-World."

On October 17, 1993, the Journal-World premiered its new look—and price, up from 50 cents the day before to $1.00 an issue. The focus was on encouraging direct communications with frontline staff identified by name, department, and phone number under a large, bold header on page 4a inviting readers to **call us...** The masthead was on page 14a. The type was bigger, there was more color, and the valuable space "above the fold" was packed with story leads that continued inside the paper.

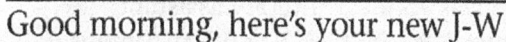

1994 WorldWest Limited Liability Company, was founded by Dolph Simons Jr. on April 12, to publish newspapers in Arizona and Colorado. The World Co. acquired Raljon which owned papers in Colorado, New Mexico, and Arizona.

1995 The last afternoon edition of the Journal-World was produced on Friday, August 18. Its first morning edition was printed on Monday, August 21.

After 67½ years at The World company, Dorothy Fritzel retires.

Dorothy Holcom of Girard, Kansas, was just 22 years old when she took a job at the Journal-World in 1937. Fresh out of business school, she was well-prepared for her new position as secretary to W.C. Simons, editor and publisher of the paper. In 1938, Dorothy married John Fritzel, and gained the last name she'd be known by for the next 67 years as a mainstay of The World Company. She was utterly devoted to the work and the Simons family. Dolph III fondly remembered her smile when he or anyone in his family walked by her desk. She'd look up and say "Love and kisses from your 'amanuensis'!" Indeed, she was an ideal "literary assistant" for W.C., Dolph Sr., Dolph Simons Jr., Dolph III, and Dan Simons. The Simons would all rely heavily on Dorothy Fritzel to keep the Journal-World administration running in greased grooves.

Pleasant, thoughtful, generous of spirit, and one who "always spoke of the good in every person," Dorothy was by all accounts much more than a secretary. She was a consummate professional and an adroit manager of people, paperwork, and projects. There was "never a more dedicated person to a job or family," according to Kathy Underwood, who worked closely with Fritzel at the Journal-World. "She did indeed love the Simons."[30]

"Dorothy kept a 'red book' with details on everything we did as a company... and as a newspaper family," Dolph Jr. explained. "Dorothy even kept track of everything that happened in the Simons' family. Every anniversary, every new baby, and major event. She'd remind you to make a doctor's appointment for your next physical."

Fritzel was a meticulous record-keeper, although she was the only one who knew how to use her filing system, Underwood acknowledged. Dorothy was also a flawless typist.

"In those days, we didn't have copy machines, so every letter or document had one or two 'onion-skins' over carbon-paper beneath the stationery as she typed," Dolph said. These carbon-copies—without a single typo or correction—and subsequently photocopies—remain in files dating from the late 1930s. Boxes full of Fritzel's voluminous files are a silent, fascinating testimony of the leadership of each Simons at the helm of The World Company.

"She was the perfect secretary," Pam Simons stated. "And she was stylish—always in heels." Dorothy Fritzel's high heels were her style signature. Every single day, she came to work in high heels. "My mom Marie was the same way, and some have said this was Dad's influence," Dolph Jr. mused. "Dad thought women should dress a certain way, and Dorothy and my mom were shining examples of that look."

Dorothy's sense of fashionable and appropriate attire extended even to what certain people were wearing to the office. "Oh, she wouldn't hesitate to ask me if I thought I was dressed properly for whatever was going on that day," Dolph laughed. Dorothy exercised a subtle but significant influence over Dolph Jr. "Every spring she would suggest he might write a nice editorial about the arrival of spring, wonderful weather, beautiful flowers blooming, etc.," Kathy Underwood noted. "This was her way of getting him to write something positive vs. negative. Dolph Jr. could get 'his needle stuck in the groove' as Dorothy would put it." Dolph Jr. readily admitted "Dorothy kept a close eye on him. She'd remind me what I had on my calendar, and ask if I'd replied to so and so yet."

Dorothy's husband John had a dairy operation, and the Fritzels were very much a part of the Lawrence community. "She'd share story ideas or her opinion on whether we got a story right or missed something important," Dolph noted. "We knew her family, she knew ours. We were as close as family. There may have been people on staff who wouldn't come to Dorothy about something out of fear she'd share that with Dad or me, but she wasn't a gossip. She was a gatekeeper. She'd keep people who wanted to just cause trouble away from W.C., Dad, and me. Dorothy was a great keeper of secrets."

Dorothy remembered employee birthdays, whose child was in a school play, the flowers for funerals, and what to buy in large quantities for a spontaneous employee luncheon. Her people skills were phenomenal—she'd go out of her way to do something nice for someone. "I remember Dorothy brought a six pack of light beer for George Bush when he was in town and spent an afternoon playing tennis with the KU team," Dolph III said. "And I'll never forget her constant reminder not to end a sentence with a preposition!"

After her husband died in 1977, it took some convincing to get Dorothy to move from their lake house in the Lone Star area back into town. Eventually, she conceded, but there was no moving her again in later years from the upstairs apartment where she'd settled. "She insisted on keeping that place and climbing those stairs," Dolph III said, shaking his head.

"Dorothy was tough in her own way," Dolph Jr. acknowledged. "Most people didn't know that about her, but W.C. sure did. My granddad was well-known for judging a man by his handshake, so one time this vendor who filled the soda machines in the plant decided to make an especially strong impression with W.C. It must have been a bit too aggressive, because W.C. just flipped him right on his back. The guy wouldn't let go of Granddad's hand, and they both ended up on the floor. Just about that time, Dorothy Fritzel came through the door and saw the struggle. She whipped off her high heels and started beating the poor vendor with them to defend W.C.," Dolph laughed. "I'll tell you what, that's more than a secretary right there. That's family."

1996 Columbine Cablevision, the Simons' cable franchise in Colorado, is sold to TCI; the Simons narrowed their focus to Kansas operations.

1997 WorldWest purchases Yampa Valley Newspapers in Craig and Hayden, Colorado.

1998 News that a "Simons-led group buys mall" makes the Journal-World front page on December 29, 1998. The site of the former Lawrence Riverfront Plaza Factory Outlets will become part of an expansive convergence of The World Company's print and cable operations by 2001.

1999 First issue of the *Baldwin City Signal* was printed. The *Tonganoxie Mirror* is purchased on September 2, and its first issue published on the 8th.

Lawrence's stately old 1906 post office, vacant since 1965, was purchased by The World Company with the intention of making it the new center of its operations.

2000 The World Company purchased the *Eudora News* and *DeSoto Explorer*. First editions printed on March 2.

The Journal-World sported a new narrow web design.

2001 The World Company acquires *Bonner Springs Chieftain*, *Basehor Sentinel*, and *Tri-County Chieftain*.

The World Company's massive renovation of Lawrence's historic former post office into a state-of-the-art news center was recognized with Kansas's top historic preservation honors. The architecturally unique structure gained a new life with restoration, remodel, and an addition that connected it to the existing Journal-World plant next door. When work was completed, the building was re-named The News Center. In it, the offices for the news staffs of the Journal-World, 6News Lawrence, and World Online were combined in a novel shared-space bullpen that encouraged cross-media collaboration as The World Company converged its print, cable, and online platforms.

The tragic events of 9/11 hit close to home with a story about George de Menocal who was on the 99th floor of the second tower at the time of the terrorist attacks. He was one of only three who were that high in the structure who escaped. A reinsurance executive by trade, de Menocal is the brother-in-law of Linda Simons de Menocal. That connection led to sharing his first-person perspective with Journal-World reporters for the special edition on the events. It was among the best local-angle stories in the country and ran exclusively in the *Lawrence Journal-World*.

On 9/11, I was already at the office with the television on over in the corner when the first plane hit the North Tower at 7:46 am

CT. I watched the live coverage of the second plane flying into the South Tower of the World Trade Center from our newsroom. The clouds of smoke, the panic—I felt the shock like everyone else. No one knew yet what we were seeing—we couldn't believe what we were seeing. The first reports suggested a small plane had flown into the building, but I knew it was a jet. Then the second jet confirmed that. I just kept thinking *why would anyone do that?*

We didn't know about Al Qaeda yet, or that my daughter's brother-in-law George de Menocal was on the 99th floor of the South Tower. That was the second Tower hit—between the 77th and 85th floors—but the first one to fall. George was one of only three from his company on that floor who got out. As he came running down the stairs, he met women who were panicked, screaming, and uncooperative when he tried to help them. Finally, George said, "I know how you ladies feel about your pocketbooks... I'm going to take yours if you don't come with me right now." That got them going. George ended up with a woman on his back and another under his arm. When they reached the mezzanine level, the firemen held them back because the "jumpers" were killing people by landing on them out there. So, George and the others had to keep running down to the underground concourse to escape.

George de Menocal shared his story with us, giving the *Lawrence Journal-World* arguably the best local angle feature on 9/11 in print or online across the whole country. George heard from friends all over the world after we published that story.

Dolph Simons Jr.

2003 The World Company, now housed in its "magnificently refurbished"[31] news center that was the old Lawrence post office, had all its newspaper, broadcast, internet, and telephony divisions

operating under the same roof. Convergence was the name of the game in the new millennium.

Sunflower Cablevision was now Sunflower Broadband delivering unprecedented innovations to the industry. This was the year software engineers at The World Company created and introduced the Django web framework that enabled easier, more user-friendly development of secure and maintainable websites worldwide.

Django was created by Journal-World web programmers Adrian Holovaty and Simon Willison with help from Jacob Kaplan-Moss who was hired early in Django's development. Holovaty named the framework after his idol, guitarist Django Reinhardt.

The World Company was humming. *USA TODAY*, the *Kansas City Business Journal*, *University Daily Kansan*, *Pitch Weekly*, and other periodicals were being printed by a new subsidiary, Sunflower Publishing, in the World's commercial printing division. There were now 600 employees, and rounding out its deliverables were seven weeklies outside Lawrence for Eudora, DeSoto, Tonganoxie, Baldwin, Bonner Springs, Basehor, and Shawnee.[32]

2004 With the appointment of Dolph Simons III to president, Newspaper Division, and Dan Simons to president, Electronics Division, The World Company welcomed the fourth generation to the C-suite.

In July 2004, the Journal-World was recognized by *Editor & Publisher* magazine as one of "10 That Do It Right." (The *Los Angeles Times* also made the list.) The magazine cited the company's "gutsy" decisions to take chances on cutting-edge technology and

(from top) W.C., Dolph Sr., Dolph Jr., Dolph III, and Dan Simons

its strategic moves involving the convergence of cable television, newspapers, and internet operations.

Ralph Gage named chief operating officer; Patrick Knorr named director of strategic planning; Joe Ryan named director of operations; Rob Curley named director of NewsMedia.

The World Company's 6News (part of Sunflower Broadband) earns the 2005 Walter Cronkite Award for Excellence in Television Political Journalism.[33]

The first issue of the *Lansing Current* is published on November 4.

2005 The World Company made the front cover of *The New York Times* that described the company's multimedia platform as "The Newspaper of the Future." In it, Dolph Simons Jr. explained the new mindset of his converged company. "I don't think of us as being in the newspaper business. Information is our business and we're trying to provide information, in one form or another, however the consumer wants it and wherever the consumer wants it, in the most complete and useful way possible."[34]

In recognition of its groundbreaking efforts at convergence, the National Cable Television Cooperative named Dolph Simons Jr. a "Pioneer" member of the industry in 2005.

The Suburban Newspaper Association honors the *Lawrence Journal-World* with its Newspaper of the Year award. The LJWorld. com website is named the best overall news site among newspapers with 50K (or less) circulation.

The Craig (Colorado) *Daily Press* won the Inland Press Association's award for Community Leadership for papers with less than 10K circulation, demonstrating the best commitment to its community through outreach, editorial leadership, and devotion to readers.

> "The World Company created a web publication called Lawrence. com in 2003. It was intended to be a hipper, pop-culture alternative to its own more conservative, prim and proper-toned daily newspaper.

World Online General Manager Rob Curley was encouraged to cut against the newspaper's own grain. 'Before we even launched the site, Dolph told me, Rob, if I like anything or appreciate anything about Lawrence.com, you've probably failed.'"

excerpted from David Folkenflik, NPR's Morning Edition, April 12, 2005[35]

Dolph Jr. oversees the acquisition of KTKA-TV in Topeka.

Django was released publicly under a BSD license in July 2005.

2007 Suburban Newspapers of America honored Dolph Simons Jr. with the Dean S. Lesher Award, given for Lifetime Achievement.

The World Company's broadcast and video production entities included 6News Lawrence, and Sunflower Broadband Channel 6, Free State Communications and Studios, and KTKA ABC/Topeka.[36]

The Associated Press Managing Editors honored the *Lawrence Journal-World* with its national Convergence Award for a series of stories about mining's legacy in Kansas.

The Suburban Newspaper Association again names the Journal-World as Newspaper of the Year (and again in 2009 and 2010).

Sunflower Broadband's rapid implementation and achievements in on-demand television advertising have led to industry recognition at the Society of Cable Telecommunications Engineers' Cable-Tec Expo 2007 in Orlando, Florida.

2008 The World Company wins four Media Innovation Awards at the annual Newspaper Association of America's Marketing Conference including Best Overall News Site: LJWorld.com. This is more recognition than any other company had ever earned to date.[37]

Last edition of the *Lansing Current* is printed.

2010 Sunflower Broadband is sold to Knology, a Georgia-based cable interest. The sale included 6News.

Lawrence Journal-World named "Newspaper of the Year" by Suburban Newspapers of America.

2011 The death of Osama Bin Laden was the banner headline of the Journal-World on May 2, 2011. Inside the cover were local reactions to the news from Kansas state representatives, senators, and local citizens including Ron Holzwarth, who posted this comment: *"We used to have a saying out in western Kansas: after you cut the head off a rattlesnake, you don't have to worry about him anymore."*[38]

Television station KTKA in Topeka, which had been acquired through a subsidiary of The World Company, was sold in 2011 as the company shifted focus to its print and digital operations.

2014 With the decline of circulation and ad sales across the industry, the writing was on the wall for newspapers, and The World Company was no exception. In 2014, printing operations that had been rolling since 1891 in Lawrence came to a halt. That function was now outsourced to the *Kansas City Star* press for both the Journal-World and *USA TODAY*, and to other print shops in the region for the smaller papers.

Printing of *Tonganoxie Mirror*, *Shawnee Dispatch*, *Bonner Springs Chieftain*, and *Baldwin City Signal* all shifted to Independence, Missouri, facilities for the first time.

However, the end of that era wasn't the end of The World Company.

In true Simons' fashion, the company adjusted to the times. Among other innovations, the "Dolph C. Simons Jr. Family Broadcast Studio" was launched at The University of Kansas Health System in 2014. Thanks to a major gift from the Simons, this state-of-the-art studio raised the bar on in-house production across the healthcare industry nationwide with its cloud-based technology. KU Health System used the Simons Studio to produce informational videos, host news conferences, and broadcast live events for internal and external communications.

2016 It was the end of an era. On June 17, 125 years after W.C. had ambitiously named his new venture The World Company, the Simons family announced the sale of the *Lawrence Journal-World* and its other papers to Ogden Newspapers of Wheeling, West Virginia.

Dolph Jr. had resisted offers to buy the company when he could have tapped out profitably, but it was never about the money for him.

In the end, "decades of major economic and technological assaults that destroyed the longstanding economic underpinnings of local newspapers" left a "news desert"[39] where local papers had once thrived nationwide.

"Dolph shielded the staff from a lot of the chaos as things started going downhill," Ann Gardner pointed out. "The cable station was subsidizing the newspaper, and after the cable enterprise was sold, the paper wasn't able to produce a profit. He had such high standards and wanted it to be the best paper it could, and he tried everything. But the financial model just wasn't working... and Dolph couldn't accept the kind of compromises it would have required to keep it in the black. They had to sell."

Also in 2016, the Simons' WorldWest, LLC, which owned newspapers in Arizona (the *Payson Roundup*) and Colorado (the *Steamboat Pilot* and *Today*, and the *Craig Daily Press*), announced their sale to White Mountain Publishing and Swift Communications, respectively.

2019 The World Company corporate offices at Sixth and New Hampshire Streets moved to new location at 901 Kentucky Street in Lawrence.

2020 Never one to sit it out, Dolph Simons Jr. launched an op-ed blog www.LawrenceOpinions.com in January. He was 90 years old.

In March, COVID-19 hit hard, and for the next 24 months, the nation struggled through a pandemic that shut down or curtailed normal activities both locally and worldwide. People were clamoring for news, and the media was struggling to find accurate information to share. The Medical News Network, a groundbreaking innovation spawned in the Dolph C. Simons Studio at KU Health System in 2014, responded with a live, hour-long interactive program Monday through Friday. Viewers could post questions on featured topics to physicians, frontline caregivers, recovered patients, medical researchers, infectious disease experts, hospital leadership, and elected officials.

This "Morning Media Update," broadcast live from the Simons studio, was picked up by CNN and livestreamed by other news agencies

nationwide achieving 10,998,075 total impressions—national and international—for a broadcast and digital news reach of 24.5 billion in just the first six weeks of its broadcast.[40]

Having the infrastructure already in place at the Simons Studio uniquely positioned the Medical News Network to provide breaking medical news. "Other news outlets were scrambling, but the Simons Studio proved to be the perfect tool for sharing critical information

in a timely way," said Jill Chadwick, Medical News Network Director. "There wasn't anybody else in healthcare communicating or sharing vital information the way we were—not one other hospital in the country or the world, for that matter."

On May 16, the front page of the Journal-World announces the newspaper will cease publication of all Monday print editions as of May 25.

On Sept. 28, the newsroom staff of the now Ogden-owned Journal-World publicly announced its plan to unionize as the Lawrence Journalism Workers Guild, or LJW Guild.[41]

On Dec. 28, 2020, the guild voted to be represented by the United Media Guild, Local 34067 with The NewsGuild-CWA,[42] ending the 125-year run of union-free operations during the Simonses' ownership of the *Lawrence Journal-World*.

2021 These writers...

I never knew W.C., but know of him through stories. I understand that Dolph Sr. once took his keys away and threw him out. I've heard Dolph Sr. had a temper, although he kept it under wraps. I never saw a temper display. He could be tough. But I have to say that the family always seemed to be united and never pitted one against another.

Dolph Sr. was a prototypical gentleman. He always wore a jacket and tie—even to baseball games. Dolph Jr. was not such a fashion plate. If he's got frayed cuffs, he doesn't pay attention to it. Dolph Sr. was quite a businessman. He was chair of the Federal Reserve Group in Kansas City. Dolph Jr. was more of a newsman, that was his baby.

In my opinion, Dolph Sr. published a pedestrian paper... an ordinary newspaper. Dolph Jr. really wanted to put out the best newspaper we could operate. It wasn't about the business; it was about the newspaper. The World Company didn't really take off until Dolph Jr. took control. He had a vision—he wanted to be the best. His dad was more focused on the bottom line. There were years and years when Dolph never asked for a budget—he just wanted a good newspaper, and as long as we had the wherewithal to pay for it, we would. Dolph Jr. was focused more on the news product than the bottom-line costs.

When we were building the cable company in Lawrence and again in Ft Collins, Dolph Sr. would be scrutinizing the bottom line, analyzing costs, wanting to know when we'd turn the corner. After he passed away on Valentine's Day 1989, that influence was no longer a major factor. As long as we were making money—and we were—Dolph Jr. could focus on putting out a good product—an exceptional product with all the staff and the space that he wanted. If he wanted to buy a press, he'd buy a press. If he wanted to hook up with **USA TODAY** *and print it, we'd do it. And we did.*

Dolph Jr. was the visionary. He's so self-effacing... he won't acknowledge it. But he was a driving force behind everything that happened here.

reflections by Ralph Gage, May 2021

2022 In his September 2 blog post at LawrenceOpinions.com, 92-year-old Dolph Simons Jr. posted a question everyone was asking, "Aside from the Civil War days, has this country and its citizens ever been as divided as they are today? Not just "divided" but angry, mad, frustrated, and afraid of what is happening to this country?"

Blogging might not be Dolph's preferred medium, but he adapted. Given the state of the nation, and his journalistic birthright, having a say is, in no uncertain terms, his *raison d'être*. So he writes.

"What can be done to lower political temperatures and avoid another civil war? All Americans—Democrats, Republicans, conservatives or liberals, blacks, whites, or whatever colors, young or old, gay or straight, should realize there are far too many citizens who hate this country and will do most anything to achieve their goal."

In his signature style, Simons points (and pounds) his finger at the problem over the keyboard of his old manual typewriter. And true to form, he does not raise the issue just to rant, but because he has an idea. Shouldn't The Dole Institute take this issue on in the furthering of its mission "to promote political and civic participation as well as civil discourse in a bi-partisan, balanced manner"?

"Well, if you've got a problem with something, you have to do more than just complain," Dolph said. "Things are a lot more productive if

"Citizen Dolph" has definite opinions on the duty of a citizen to his community, according to the Daily Kansan, and likely all Kansans. April 2006

you offer a solution… some ideas to offer. I still have so many ideas… I wake up with new ideas every day."

2023 Dolph Jr., as a trustee of the Dole Institute and board member for other community organizations, continues his advisory role with his aspirations for Lawrence, Kansas, the nation, and the world. He publishes his first book, *This Writer*, a chronicle of newspapering and the role of a free press in shaping democracy, and the story of his family.

CHAPTER 11

The End of News as We Knew It

*I fear the public often does not realize that
the First Amendment was not designed to set up special privileges
for reporters and editors, but rather, it was designed to ensure
a right for the public, a right of the people to be informed about what
is going on, a right for the governed to have someone watching and
reporting on the action of those who govern. The First Amendment's
reference to a free press is for protection of the public, not to put a
protective fence around a publisher or editor or reporter.*

Dolph Simon Jr.[1]

By the time a news story reaches the public, it's supposed to have been vetted by a process that assures, among other things, its accuracy, context, and relevance. Over the last 250 years, that process has been honed by a journalistic mission to uphold the First Amendment. If this process is compromised or threatened, it is, ultimately, the public that suffers. But that wasn't going to happen on Dolph Simons Sr.'s watch, if he could help it. So he didn't hesitate to step up when prompted by events that began with a grisly discovery on November 8, 1977.

When the battered body of an 84-year-old woman was found in her Lawrence home shortly before noon that day, police on the scene suspected foul play.[2] Law enforcement officials would provide no details to *Lawrence Journal-World* reporters, pending notification of next of kin. Yet the victim's name, the time and likely cause of death, and other pertinent details were leaked selectively or "released in dribbles" by sources inside "officialdom," Simons learned. As editor of the Journal-World, he had a problem with that, along with certain other behaviors of various elected officials. What he did about this serves as a primer on the role of a local newspaper in a community.

On November 9, Simons sent a sharply-worded letter to Police Chief Dick Stanwix and Sheriff Rex Johnson. It certainly got their attention, although neither of them deigned to reply. Instead, it was Douglas County Attorney Michael Malone who penned a trifling response. Although horrifying, the case itself didn't remain in the headlines long, which was beside the point for Simons. He seized the teachable moment with the strong muscle of a free, independent press.

"I think the fact that you answered my letter, although it was not addressed to you, is a big part of our problem today," Simons wrote Malone. "Obviously, someone has downgraded the positions of police chief and sheriff, as far as filling their public responsibilities, and you have accepted the post of 'czar'..."

Over several pages,[3] Simons castigated Malone's affronts to the "public's right to know" including the violation of three principles straight out of the Journal-World's canon:

Accurate and fair news reporting: *"We are the purveyor of news, and you are the elected prosecutor, not the official 'news bureau'..."*

Safeguarding the rights of citizens: *"...the people will not accept any ideas that the chief of police and the sheriff have been muzzled... (or that) they are now supposed to be puppets."*

Exposing dishonesty in government: *"I sense the creation of a closely-knit committee which is determined to keep the public in the dark as much as possible—not only about crime but about the personal work habits, absenteeism, and neglect of some of those involved."*

Simons was clearly provoked, but his words represent more than a rant. He was doing his job in the great lineage of independent newspaper editors and publishers from Kansas's William Allen White, who won a Pulitzer Prize for the *Emporia Gazette* in 1923 for his spirited writing on Freedom of Speech, to Iowa's Art Cullen of the *Storm Lake Times* whose 2017 Pulitzer for Editorial Writing explored how big topics like immigration, agriculture, and the environment play out in a small community "in the middle of nowhere." The strong editorial voice of a local newspaper makes the news relevant to a community— and it can make a community relevant to the world.

Read: Strong editors produce good newspapers, and good newspapers provide an important public service.

Newspapers don't just disseminate information; they help ensure the *function* of news in society. As Princeton University Professor Paul Starr described it in the *Columbia Journalism Review*, "More than any other medium, newspapers have been our eyes on the state, our check on private abuses, and our civic alarm systems."[4]

It was this cause Simons served, like his father, W.C. Simons, before him, and his son, Dolph Jr. who would don the mantle after him. This watchdogging role, combined with fair and accurate news reporting, constitutes a free press—the most fundamental expression of a democratic society.

> *Newspapers don't just disseminate information; they help ensure the function of news in society.*

Confidence in the free press is greatest when citizens know and trust who's doing the news reporting and watchdogging in their own community. "Americans continue to hold local news in higher regard than national news across a variety of metrics... regardless of political party affiliations" according to a Gallup Poll in 2022.[5] The relevance of news intensifies when it's localized to a community. And when a community rallies to address the problems and possibilities the news raises, that is democracy in action.

"Local newspapers cover county government, city hall, and beyond that, they publish local news of the community—school board meetings, the obituaries, weddings, and all these indispensable parts of a shared experience. Members of a community are also voters who need knowledge about local and state news so they can make wise decisions about whom and what they'll vote for or against," said media executive Tom Johnson, former president of CNN and publisher of the *Los Angeles Times*. "The Simons and the *Lawrence Journal-World* played a crucial role in that process."[6]

Although research shows this kind of civic information has earned the greatest trust, it is increasingly inaccessible to communities nationwide.

When Simons wielded his mighty pen against "officialdom" in 1977, there were 1,761 newspapers across the country.[7] Circulation was 114 million large and small, weekday and Sunday newspapers[8] nationwide, according to the Pew Research Center. Circulation peaked in 1984 for dailies, and in 1993 for Sunday papers[9]—combined at almost 126 million (not counting weeklies), give or take over that nine-year span. Only three years later in 1996, newspapers by day, week, or on Sunday began a decline that's continued unabated.

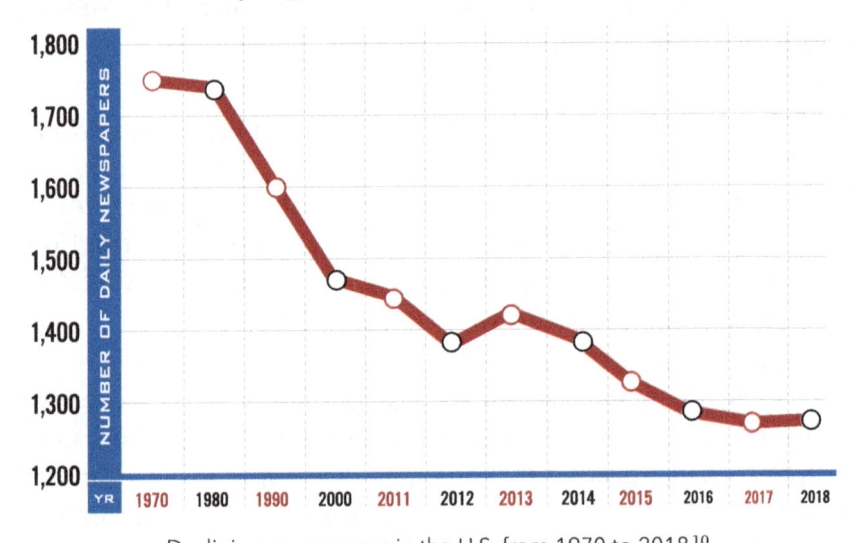

Declining newspapers in the U.S. from 1970 to 2018[10]

By 2018, at least 70 million Americans lived in a community without a newspaper or a community at risk of losing theirs, according to Josh Stearns, director of the Democracy Fund.[11]

Ironically, even though research shows newspapers remain the most trusted source of information and news,[12] the very technological advances that launched the "Information Age" also sounded the death knell for the newspaper industry.[13] By 2020, the number of newspapers still circulating across the country was under 40% of its 1980s high,[14] with locally-owned, independent newspapers among the highest casualties. In a country once thriving with local and national coverage, the loss of newspapers across the board but especially in rural areas contributed to "news deserts" where there was no ready access to local or even national news.

Of the remaining news sources, the 2022 Gallup poll indicated a majority of Americans continue to "have more trust in local than national news to give them information they can use in their daily life."[15]

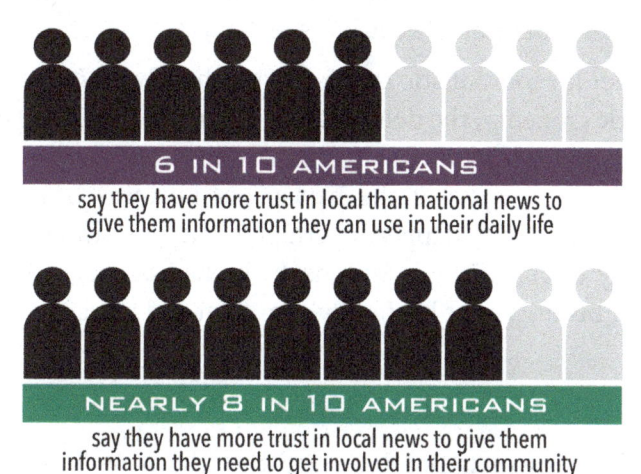

6 IN 10 AMERICANS
say they have more trust in local than national news to give them information they can use in their daily life

NEARLY 8 IN 10 AMERICANS
say they have more trust in local news to give them information they need to get involved in their community

Gallup Research in 2022 showed a majority of Americans still trust local news sources most for information relevant to their daily lives. Published by the Knight Foundation, used with permission.

Research continues to show a clear demand for local news, but that hasn't stanched the industry's bleed-out. The near extinction of locally-owned papers and ensuing industry-wide crises "arose because the news media's commercial imperatives never fully aligned with democratic objectives,"[16] according to Victor Pickard, author of *America's Battle for Media Democracy*.

Simply put: the business model failed.

It sounds simple, but the problem was complex. "It costs money to produce a good paper—a lot of money if it's a great newspaper because that takes the highest quality people you can hire. You have to make sure you can cover the cost of doing that," Dolph Simons Jr. explained. "I always felt we had to deliver the best newspaper we could," said Simons. "We've tried to help Lawrence become a better town and to be honest with our community. That's the role of a newspaper in this country... that's our responsibility under the First Amendment."[17]

Simons worries that the emphasis on the business model has gutted the altruistic purpose of news reporting, and is drawing the wrong kind of people to the field, especially profit-driven corporate owners with no journalistic agenda. "So much has changed, and not for the better, I'm afraid," he acknowledged.

Whether it's journalistic mission drift, the advent of the internet, an apathetic citizenry, the demographic and psychographic shift from traditional print readers to digital natives, or some combination of factors, the collapse of the newspaper business has no simple explanation. It didn't happen overnight, but over time, it became increasingly clear to Dolph Simons Jr. he had to make the hardest decision of his life about his family's 125-year-old newspaper.

The first inkling Dolph Jr. had that the news business as he knew it could be in trouble was back in the mid-1970s. The industry hadn't even reached its circulation peak, but Simons was "driving with his brights on" and he saw big changes ahead. In 1977, the Midwest Research Institute invited him to share his futuristic ideas about "Newspapers in the Year 2001" for its Midcontinent Perspectives lecture series. Although he didn't have the vocabulary for them, Dolph Jr. predicted certain advancements with surprising accuracy:

- *"Information storage systems will be able to cut and edit stories without any human intervention."* (artificial intelligence)

- *"News cameras will no longer require current photo chemical processing, no film developing, no waiting for the negative to dry to print. The picture will be fed instantly from the photo electronic cell onto a viewing screen; editors can look at the picture, improve the quality, store it for future use, or use it immediately."* (digital photography)

- *"Major information storage systems in most newspapers, and in regional centers, where hundreds of 'pages' of information will be stored. This information will be updated and corrected continually, and at some future date, newspaper 'subscribers' will be able to plug into the system for whatever they desire, at whatever time they wish."* (the worldwide web)

The future looked bright, but there were fast lane changes coming from broadcast competition. "When I was on the board of the Newspaper Advertising Bureau back in the '70s, we spent a lot of time looking at the grim statistics at our meetings." Seventy cents of every potential advertising dollar had always belonged to newspapers, but those budgets had begun hemorrhaging across television and radio. "I think most of us saw the writing on the wall—or maybe I should say screen," Dolph said.

Most did, but not everybody. Some very big players missed the danger signs or were in denial as electronic media overtook even the most visually-compelling of print publications. In 1970, media magnate Gardner "Mike" Cowles told the *Los Angeles Times*, "We have no thought of closing *Look*." [18] The bi-weekly magazine folded in 1971.

Simons wasn't resting on his laurels. He reacted by proacting— the Journal-World would change with the times. For a century-old newspaper business, The World Company proved surprisingly agile. Its expansion into cable in Kansas in 1972, and in Colorado in 1978, was phenomenally successful. Both newspaper and cable systems were getting attention and attracting lucrative offers from buyers all over the U.S. Dolph sold the Colorado operation, Columbine Cablevision, in 1996.

The sale freed Simons up to focus on the Lawrence mothership. In 2003, The World Company opened a cutting-edge News Center in downtown Lawrence. Its merged newspaper, cable, and internet platforms were unprecedented in the industry, earning Lawrence recognition as the "Convergence Capital" of the nation in 2005. Dolph Jr. realized "We were doing better than just about anybody else. Per capita, we had more cable customers, more newspaper subscribers, and more local news content than ever." He was quick to add, "But we weren't trying to do more and more just to be the best, we were responding to our customers who wanted more ways to get news and information."

It was an expensive endeavor. As president of The World Company's Newspaper Division in 2003, Dolph Simons III had a close-up view of the multi-dimensional dynamic. "Of course, everybody was worried about advertising dollars drying up, which had always been a bigger source of income than reader revenue," he noted. "I think everybody in the business was losing money." Dolph III was not wrong.[19]

Ad revenue was dropping fast for newspapers industry-wide—from $60 billion to about $16.5 billion between 2010 and 2017.[20] Many owners laid off staff, cut costs, and down-sized before finally selling out to commercial ownership that wasn't mission-driven. This pattern changed the business in seismic ways. Instead of journalists with their shoulders to the plow, the field of newspapering was a commodity bought and sold by off-site chains, entertainment conglomerates, and hedge funds.

Increasingly, First Amendment values ceased to drive the agenda. Worse still, the "'existential threat' to journalism... is that people don't really care where the news comes from," stated David Carr, the former *New York Times* columnist.[21]

Dolph Simons Jr. couldn't disagree more.

> Every poll shows the country's belief in the press is dropping, dropping, dropping. Other research shows people trust newspapers more than ever. Who's telling the truth? Maybe it's in how we ask the questions... or answer them. I truly believe people care a lot about the accuracy of the news they're getting, but don't always recognize when it's not accurate.
>
> An informed citizenry is the only hope we have for a free country. Whether at the county courthouse or in Congress, if the public is in the dark and not kept informed by honest reporters, the country is... damn near all is lost.
>
> There are corrupt politicians... both Republicans and Democrats. A free press was envisioned as a way to call that out; this is how democracy works. What can we do about this today?

It's been sad to witness the death of newspapers. It used to be so different. I'll never forget the dinner at the Gridiron Club when a senior member at the head table asked us all to rise so he could propose a toast to the current president for the job he's done leading our country. This man was well-known for being from the opposite party, but he had respect. In those days, it seemed like everyone had more respect. The news business was like that once, but no longer. It was more civil then, and in many ways, this country is lesser for it today.

It solidified this was about learned family values. Journalism was discussed and respected by the younger generation. Looking back on it now, it showed what was important then and how with the loss of family-owned/controlled media came the loss of accountability. It didn't really matter if you were a huge East Coast company or a small Midwest independent. We knew each other beyond the confines of the office and we could share with each other our thoughts of how things were being covered. Sure, the business model changed, but when accountants took over as publishers and CEOs, we lost the familiar care for the product's integrity.

Dan Simons, speaking on the value of the Nepotism Club
to a younger generation of newspaper-owning families.

The country needs more sources of accurate news, and that takes people with backbone and finance. You can hope and hope and hope, but if you don't have the money to pay for it, you can't do much. It takes more than a vision; it takes funding to maintain a quality source of information—to make it attractive, timely, and accurate. Maybe there will be more weeklies or bimonthlies. Those can do a damn good, deep analysis of the news. That's what you have to have to hold people accountable. But I don't see local papers coming back the way they were, I hope I'm wrong. I don't know if there will ever be a revival.

I remember reading something Kay's son Don Graham (of the *Washington Post*) wrote about local newspapers being rarer than whooping cranes. The few that are left... I don't know how they're holding on. At one point, I got a call about buying up seven of Gannett's papers. I declined, then the man wanted to know if I knew anybody who'd want to buy them. So I did make a few calls but got nothing but emphatic NOs.

Nobody's buying newspapers anymore, except maybe Alden Global Capital or Jeff Bezos. Bezos bought the *Washington Post*—why? To champion the First Amendment? Was that an ego trip or in order to influence the public, or both? Kay Graham, Jack Knight, and John Cowles would roll over in their graves.

It's even harder to sell a local paper. And if somebody does come in and take over the local paper, the first thing they do is fire your best people. It happened to us.

Deciding to sell was a debate within the family and staff. Ralph Gage and my son Dan, in particular, warned me they thought newspapers were on their way out. I didn't want to see it. At one time, I was getting calls weekly about selling the paper— we were in demand. *The New York Times* had a full-page feature on the Journal-World and me—about having the answers about the future of news and information. Well, we had some answers, and we were riding pretty high in those days, but we weren't cocky. We had great people—absolute professionals. The offers were coming in, but we'd never consider selling. It was actually me—I was the one who said no.

My view was quality made the difference. I believed we could survive by putting out the absolute best product. We had a helluva paper and broadband operation. Looking back, I don't know what we didn't do to diversify ourselves from being a traditional newspaper to becoming a multifaceted information business. We did everything and more, and we did it well. But doing it well was expensive. We were losing a million dollars a year on 6News television alone. That wasn't because there weren't a lot of viewers, there were. There were also a lot more ways advertisers could spend their available budgets. The field got bigger and they had to sow their seeds a lot thinner to cover it all.

It was probably around 2005 when Dan put the argument down on paper, titled it *Deep Holy Shit Thoughts by Dan*, and gave Dolph (III) and me a copy. There it was in black and white—the cost of continuing operations or selling. We'd reached the point where I had to take the advice I was being given.

The question was which goes first—the paper or cable? Dan, Ralph, and others thought it best to sell the paper first. But Dad (the old fuddy duddy) thought the paper was more important to the town than cable. I don't think I ever said they *had* to do this or that, but they knew I hoped we could keep the paper alive and fulfill its obligation to this community.

So in 2010, we decided to sell Sunflower Broadband. We had dinners here to meet the people who were interested in buying it. There was a man from Georgia who brought his wife. She said, "I want you to know my husband is the most honest man in the world. You can trust him—his word is his bond. You'll never have to worry." She couldn't have laid it on any thicker. Well, he said things that were terribly important to me because of our employees, their hard work, and vision, so we ended up selling to him. It was rather naïve of me to have believed everything the new buyer said. Sunflower Cablevision changed dramatically in many ways after we sold it.

It must have given him a great deal of pain to see the love of his life—the newspaper business, the industry—slipping away. It must have hurt a great deal to see that happen. To Dolph's credit, and I imagine he was responsible for this, he must have negotiated a hands-off policy with the new owners. It's a shrunken version, but it still is the only source of local news.

Leonard Krishtalka, Ph.D., anthropologist and author

When it came time to sell the paper, we looked at a lot of potential buyers before choosing Ogden Newspapers, a group from West Virginia. They were an old newspaper family business, owned by the Nuttings, and known nationally. The KU chancellor thought they were good people, and we wanted owners who were about newspapers, not banking.

"We should have done it years earlier, but Dad was worried about our community going without a paper. He could have sold for a helluva lot more money years earlier, but he wouldn't do it. We were losing a million a year on cablevision news—but it was important. It differentiated us. Then the first thing the new owners did was close that out."

Dan Simons

Bob Nutting assured me there would be minimal changes to personnel, so we inked the deal in 2016. I called a meeting and was standing up there with the new buyer and all the employees. I said we're all family. I hope the best for you, and thank you for

The sale of the Journal-World marked the end of an era in Lawrence.
(Photo: L. Seaver)

what you've done for our town. I introduced Bob Nutting, the new owner from Ogden. He made some remarks. I didn't feel good about the situation, but it was what it was.

Then the next day, Kathy Underwood, my secretary, told me they started letting people go immediately. They fired some of the best people, and took the newsroom down to nothing. Their business model was very different from ours, that's the reality of it. They got rid of our old post office building we'd remodeled into the News Center with that huge balcony and a peak-ceiling sky roof. Everything was white marble, all the artwork, these big blown-up period photos we'd hung. Gone. They moved the Journal-World offices over to a shopping mall. I'm glad W.C. and Dad didn't live to see that, but that's the reality of the newspaper business today.

We've covered an interesting span of newspaper history. I know that era is not coming back, but what do we have instead? What are you going to do if there's no local paper willing to take on elected officials or question its university chancellor, regents, or the quality of education? Where's the editor willing to step on toes, or get involved? It's getting more and more difficult to get young, intelligent people who want to run for a public office. You have to give up your privacy, and time from your work and family. You could lose customers or create enemies. Everything is so contentious people are afraid to say or do anything. Without a local newspaper, you may not even know what's going on with things you care deeply about—enough to run for office so you could make an impact.

I'm sure if we still had the paper, this is the viewpoint we'd be expressing. Today, the Journal-World will include a syndicated piece, but seldom carries locally-written editorials.

I think the public today has far more access to far more information than just from the "news." Something happens in Afghanistan and you have ten different ways to learn about it in ten second's time. We think that means "well-informed," but in truth, the consumer has become far more compartmentalized. The conservatives tune into conservative channels, and the liberals tune into their shows. No one is looking at the opposing view. I guess everyone is more skeptical and the news media isn't giving us much reason to trust. How do you know what's fake or biased?

You have to have common sense, but it'd sure help if reporters were doing a better job. Today, some notion of "freedom" gives some reporters the idea that they can report however they want. Where are the facts? Did the reporter even talk to more than one person, or the person in charge, or check the source? I can tell in the first line or two of a story what the reporter's bias is. I can see it based on the wording and placement of the headlines and positions of the stories. What you're getting is the slant they want you to see. A reporter will say something happened when he or she should be saying it was "alleged" to have happened. Where do they learn to be reporters—where did they go to school? Where was the editor sending the story back until the reporter got it right. That's how it worked in newspapers; I don't see how it works now.

I just don't get it… what stands for "news" now.

I wonder what W.C. or Dad would have done in my shoes. They'd be shocked and puzzled. I think they'd wonder whether we'd met our own expectations—or if we curved or dodged because of pressure? I don't think either one of them would've compromised or made exceptions. They'd faced challenges of their own. My granddad started with absolutely nothing. You have to appreciate what he went through… Dad, too. The struggles they had—all the troubles and problems in a brand-new town, two world wars. They faced them. That means a tremendous amount to me, and it makes me wish I could have somehow solved the problems we faced.

I certainly wanted to make W.C. and Dad proud of what we made of their accomplishments. I think it would make them sad that we couldn't keep it going… we didn't have the smarts or the backbone or the commitment. I think back on all of it, and wonder how we could have done something different. Hell, we did do a lot of things different, but it is what it is.

Dolph Simons Jr.

It was really hard for Dad to sell the paper, but I keep reminding him that Grampy's first question every morning was "Are we in the black?" My granddad was a businessman and he'd have looked at the numbers and changes in the industry, and reached the same conclusion about selling. It had to be done. If anything, he'd have reached that conclusion sooner than Dad did.

But Dad was right to fight until the bitter end. Or as he would say, he fought and fought and fought until the very bitter end.

Linda Simons de Menocal

There's a lot at stake for a community when it loses its local newspaper. The implications have been studied by researchers, academics, journalists, politicians, and pundits. Here's a curation of some of the most important lessons learned.

- The function of a properly managed newspaper created the vital lubricant for a functional government, political discourse, and economy even in the most small and medium-size American communities. As its role devolved to become "properties" traded by Wall Street, so went effective discourse in our communities.

  Doug Phares, former (and final) Director, Inland Press Association, 2022.[22]

- The loss of local news may have cost lives during the pandemic because it paved the way for misinformation to take hold and hindered journalism on breakdowns in the official response.

  from "Local News Initiative" in the *Medill-Adenauer Report*. Northwestern University. 2021.[23]

- A good local paper is one everybody reads. Even if they argue and disagree with the editorials, they're reading it, they're discussing what's in it. It's an information source to keep the conversation going... to give that commonality... without it, the community has less to share. There's less that binds their cultural dynamic. Perhaps this is taken over by aspects of social media, but it's not the same. Social media is scattered, diverse, and not functioning the way a local newspaper did to unite a community. A local paper may not unify everyone in thought on politics or various topics, but it does bring people who are living in the same place together in a conversation about their shared experience.

  Leonard Krishtalka, Ph.D., anthropologist and author. 2021.

- "When more journalists were working at the local paper, more candidates ran for mayor. If a newspaper hired one more staffer for each 1,000-person circulation (or 10 staffers for a paper with a circulation of 10,000), the number of candidates would increase by an expected factor of 1.23, all else held constant. When there are fewer reporters covering an area, fewer people run for mayor, and fewer people vote. Put another way: When newspaper staffing levels are higher, voters have more of a choice in who leads their city, and more of them feel like showing up to choose."

  Sarah Holder, "As local newspapers shrink, so do voters' choices." in *Bloomberg*. 2019. [24]

- If a county/municipality doesn't have a local newspaper, there will likely be a higher interest rate charged by a lender because the risk of "bad actors" in local government going undiscovered by the local press is an identified factor. "When a lender is more nervous about lending to an inefficient government, then they're going to have to ask for a higher interest rate on the money they're lending to compensate for that risk."

  Dermot Murphy, Finance Professor, University of Illinois/Chicago. 2018.[25]

- When it comes to local politics, though, the local newspaper remains the predominant source of information about local government, whether that be school boards, city councils, mayors, county commissions. And over the course of the last 20 years, and it started even before then, we've seen a steady decline in the availability of local news. The problem with the increasing dominance of national news over local is that local news has more credibility and trust among consumers, according to research. So its loss erodes community cohesion.

Jennifer Lawless, University of Virginia Law professor, excerpted from her report on the crisis in local news. Northwestern University, 2021[26]

- I could not have written my most recent novel about this sensational story that happened in 1871 without the *Lawrence Journal-World*. The newspaper provided a minefield of information—not just about the trial, the murder, but the personalities of the people involved. The hero of the novel is the first woman reporter who wrote for the *Kansas Tribune*.

Leonard Krishtalka, Ph.D., anthropologist and author. 2021.[27]

- "There's so much misinformation out there now... unhindered by any editor. At least when Dolph was editing, you knew who to take your issue with the news to. Without local newspapers, you don't have evidence. It's gone. We've lost about 75% of the information we routinely got from the Simons."

Dennis Domer, retired KU professor and author.[28]

- When people lament the decline of small newspapers, they tend to emphasize the most important stories that will go uncovered: political corruption, school board scandals, zoning board hearings, police misconduct. They are right to worry about that. But often overlooked are the more quotidian stories, the ones that disappear first when a paper loses resources: stories about the annual Teddy Bear Picnic at Crapo Park, the town-hall meeting about the new swimming-pool design, and the tractor games during the Denmark Heritage Days.

These stories are the connective tissue of a community; they introduce people to their neighbors, and they encourage readers to listen to and empathize with one another. When that tissue disintegrates, something vital rots away. We don't often stop to ponder the way that a newspaper's collapse makes people feel less connected, more alone. As local news crumbles, so does our tether to one another.

Elaine Godfrey, *The Atlantic Magazine*. October 2021.[29]

"Dolph Jr. announces the sale of the newspaper to employees."

I've asked you to gather here this morning to let you know we have made a decision. After 125 years of family ownership, we have decided to sell the Journal-World.

Over the years, I believe we have published a damned good newspaper with a tremendous group of associates. The Journal-World has been an industry leader in many respects. We are proud of its record and know the many accomplishments and awards could not have been achieved without a superior group of associates working with us.

It's been an extremely difficult decision for a stand-alone, family-owned newspaper. But due to the tremendous changes taking place in the business, and the technological developments in news delivery, we recognized it was time to sell. Ironically, our present paid circulation numbers are down, but today we actually have more than three-times our newspaper readership—at or above 90,000 unique daily visits on our website. Unfortunately, website viewers do not generate advertising dollars compared to the printed version of the Journal-World.

We considered ways to reduce expenses, but that would have cost us quality. We weren't willing to do that. Obviously, we could close shop, but we didn't want to do that either. We could find a buyer who we believed would be able and committed to carry on the role of the Journal-World. In the end, what drove our decision were three ultimate goals: To keep the Journal-World going; to do what's best for our employees; and to act in the best interests of Lawrence.

With this in mind, we have selected Ogden Newspapers of Wheeling, West Virginia, to take over the paper. They are good operators and good people. Ogden Nutting, the father, has been running Ogden newspapers for the past 40 years and his sons Bob and Bill still call him the boss. However, Bob is chairman and president of Ogden newspapers, and his brother Bill is vice president. Bob is deeply involved in various environmental and educational programs, schools, colleges, civic affairs, museums, and has served as chair of the Association of West Virginia Independent Colleges and Universities. Highly respected by those in the newspaper business, Bob is also chair and principal owner of the Pittsburgh Pirates, involved in the Nature Conservancy, and he is a pilot.

At this time, Dolph and Dan would like to make a few comments.

Final papers on the sale are expected to close August 1, and until that time, we will continue to run and operate the paper.

Bob, I know we are handing over a good newspaper and a damned good crew in a very special town with the potential for a great future. We believe you and your company will be good owners and operators of the Journal-World.[30]

We are losing our community and our democracy... we don't understand each other because we don't know each other anymore. Last time I asked the William Allen White School of Journalism at KU, there were no more scholars looking at the significance of local newspapers. There's no professor in the history department focusing on local history. The person who runs the Humanities Center said he was embarrassed that KU had no one looking at local history. As a historian, the newspapers allow me to present who we are—who we really are. And who we were. In fact, I quote W.C. Simons back in 1891 when he wrote about the mayor... who he disagreed with, who he agreed with. I go all the way back to 1855 with a quote—it's all there. What am I going to quote from 2016 on? What is there to find about the community—just the high points as they see them, and there's no photography. I'm doing what I can in the last years of my life to write this stuff hoping my generation is making its contribution to local history. I know the next generation will need to do it, too, but they'll have to look somewhere to find it. Our local history is incomprehensible.

Dennis Domer, Ph.D., historian and author

Within days of the sale of the newspaper, Ogden began eliminating employees. There had been approximately 250 on staff at the time; by 2023, only about 20 people remained. It was a bitter pill to swallow, made worse by the fact that there was nothing Dolph Jr. could do about it. It had never been Journal-World culture to run a skeleton operation, even under dire circumstances. During WWI and II, his grandfather and father held jobs open for employees serving in the military. Simons' anguish persisted, but an unexpected source of consolation came from W.C. Simons himself.

Boanerges

Just how Grandfather and my father happened to get into the breeding of fine horses, I do not know. When Goldsmith's Volunteer became the leading trotting bred Hambletonian stallion in America (in the 1850s), one of his outstanding sons was Volunteer Jr. and Grandfather had Tempest and Harry, two beautiful mahogany bay stallions, which were equally well bred. At that time, Papa owned Flora, a mare of fine qualities and breeding; and two young mares, Minnehaha and Bird, who were sired by Volunteer Jr. He also had two stallions, Boanerges and Black Tiger, whose pedigrees we used to have but which have been lost through the years.

Minnehaha and Tempest had been exhibited by Papa at the Minnesota State Fair, where Minnehaha won first place as a three-year-old mare, and Tempest second as a three-year-old stallion. It was said that Tempest should have been given first place also, excepting for some small thing which I have forgotten.

My father, Adolphus Simons, died on October 29, 1877. Shortly prior to that time, Flora had been overdriven and died, so Mama brought the stallion Boanerges, and Minnehaha (which we shortened to Minnie), Bird, and Black Tiger with her to Kansas. During the several weeks that the family remained in Larned, while houses were being built on our claims in Hodgeman County, our horses were stabled in a livery barn owned by a man named Stokes. He saw great possibilities in Boanerges, so the horse was left with him for training as a trotter. In a short while, Boanerges was making such a record he promised to become famous.

Then the livery barn burned, the only animals saved being a team owned by a star route mail carrier who was dangerously burnt in rescuing them. Every effort was made to save Boanerges, and he was brought to the door twice, but turned back into the barn.

There was no insurance. The loss was very hard on Mama, who had hoped to dispose of the horse at a big price because she desperately needed the money. However, this may have had considerable influence in shaping our lives. I always liked horses, could ride them well, liked to race, and with a little encouragement, might easily have followed that sort of life.

We had a tendency to value our horses high and refuse good sales. It taught me the lesson that the time to sell is when you have a buyer who is willing to pay you at least a fair price. The man who holds property too long does not profit as he who sells quickly, taking a smaller profit and then going on to make more deals. You seldom go broke selling at a profit.

W.C. Simons, circa 1938, personal memoirs

Some 85 years after W.C. had written "Boanerges," and eight years after the Journal-World had been sold, Dolph Jr. read his grandfather's crisp, sepia-toned pages. They'd been discovered in boxes in the basement in 2023, which in itself was miraculous. It was a story he'd never heard before, in fact, no one in the family remembered hearing it. Such an unusual bit of family history with a takeaway message that seemed destined to finally reach him. When you must, *the time to sell is when you have a buyer willing to give you a good price.*

"I can't say it makes me feel good about letting the Journal-World go," Dolph Jr. reflected. "But I've always wondered what W.C. would think about us selling the paper. It's strange to say, but his story made me think he'd understand."

If Simons ever comes to peace with letting the newspaper go, it won't be an indication he's got nothing left to say, or that his news days are behind him. On any given day, Simons—age 93—is still focused on what would make a great paper. As he reads each of the five newspapers he subscribes to daily, and monitors the news channels, he maintains a running commentary. He can be critical, but more to the point, he's calling out the next line of questioning the reporter should pursue, another story angle to be explored, or what his contemporaries Chandler or Knight or Neuharth would think about what their papers are up to now.

At some point, Simons will shake his head in frustration then slap his widespread hands flat on the air in front of him as if it were a desk, or he a conductor stopping a discordant orchestra. He re-tunes his thoughts and with a blend of exasperation and excitement, he looks up and begins to describe what he'd do if he still had the paper... how fun it would be. "There are so many things that could be done," he says, "that *need* to be done."

CHAPTER 12

Op-Ed on Life

"The words of love that I wrote years ago are just as living today as when they were written, but other things have grown old, changes have come about, until the things which told of material matters are of no value. So perhaps you will find it through life. It is really love, cooperation, and goodwill that are worthwhile."

W.C. Simons to his wife, Gertrude, and children in 1936[1]

Imagine the great plains of the American west as W.C. Simons described them long ago. "The buffalo grass is green... with winding creeks heavily timbered and dark masses of verdure almost constantly in view... everywhere was a wealth of wildflowers."[2] With no foreknowledge of the disasters that would soon befall her, the beauty of springtime in Kansas in 1878 must have given the young widow Jennie Bessie Simons hope, and she claimed it. The effort would cost her nearly everything except what was most important—the love and dreams she had for her children. That was enough to keep her going.

With family as foundation, that determination and drive is the real through-line of the Simons story. It explains the weathering of many storms across the decades and generations for both the business and the family.

The Simons built their newspaper and information business with righteous intention. Having set an ethical gold standard, W.C.'s stewardship influenced even the emerging newspaper industry from 1890 into the 1930s. He left The World Company in the capable hands of his son, Dolph. From the late 1920s into the early '70s, Dolph's journalistic aptitude and business acumen met with serendipitous timing—those 50 years were newspaper publishing's finest hour.

Dolph Jr. came of age professionally during those decades. He was the right Simons for the job ahead. From the late '60s into the 21st century, he expanded the award-winning enterprise and led it into the digital age with invaluable support from the next generation—his daughters Pam and Linda, and sons Dolph III and Dan.

A correlation can be drawn between the 2016 decision to sell the family's newspaper business and Jennie Bessie Simons giving up on what she hoped would be a land legacy for her children in 1888. When faced with untenable circumstances, it always comes down to doing the right thing for the right reason. Family is always the right reason.

Knowing and then doing the right thing usually brings closure to such complex considerations, but for Dolph Simons Jr., the deliberation of selling or not selling—and almost all other matters— can continue. In fact, probing each point and nuance of his choices and actions over the course of 90 plus years isn't driven by self-doubt as much as Dolph's propensity to wonder how he could improve things—starting with himself.

By extension, Simons scrutinizes what KU could be doing better, what newspapers and the media should be doing better, what leaders and politicians must do better, and how the world would be in such better shape if everyone tried harder. He loves few things better than a robust discussion of potentialities like those at KU's 1968 "Man and the Future" conference he co-hosted. A brain trust including anthropologists Ashley Montague and Loren Eiseley, inventor and idea-shaker Buckminster Fuller, science fiction writer Arthur C. Clark, and psychiatrist Karl Menninger, was convened to explore the vast possibilities for the future. Dolph Simons Jr. was rapt, "I'd like to have KU renew that Futurist conference with a collection of the world's foremost visionary thinkers. Wouldn't that be fantastic?"

Simons never lacks for ideas on specific improvements. His perseverance on this topic has been a recurring theme in his opinion editorials. Dolph could come off more critical than aspirational at times, but not even his critics accused him of pussyfooting around the biggest issues of the day. Since launching his Saturday Column back in the 1950s, Dolph Jr. spared neither friend nor foe in pursuit of his primary passions—patriotism and protection of the First Amendment; the sanctity of democracy; innovation; appreciation for his hometown and state; and how to make Lawrence, Kansas, and America even better.

After decades of deep-diving into each topic, he's still got questions, but certain answers have emerged and endured.

Dolph Simons Jr. at The Cedars, 2022. (Photo: L. Seaver)

I don't know how much time I have left, but I can still get excited about what's to come. There are so many ideas we should be pursuing in this country—and right here in Lawrence. Why aren't more people getting on board? We can't stay behind the times… let's stop this "fly-over" attitude.

Years ago, Palmer Hoyt, who was the editor and publisher of the *Denver Post*, put together a special train trip for VIPs-only. It was one of the most sought-after invitations in the whole business and I got one thanks to Dad. Each train car was filled with the corporate leaders and executives from every important company nationwide. Hoyt wined and dined them. He took them to Cheyenne Frontier Days. It was great, just incredible. Every VIP on that train got an impression of Colorado and the front range that encouraged the expansion of their industries into that region. And the guy behind it all was a newspaper man—Palmer Hoyt.

I'd like to get Kansas City to buy into this idea. We'd get railways, airlines, and sightseeing buses to participate in a two- or three-day event where leaders from across the entire country came to Kansas City. We'd have tie-ins with the Nelson Art Gallery, MRIGlobal (which used to be Midwest Research Institute), a bank such as Commerce Bank, the Kaufman Performance Center, the KU Health System, the Linda Hall Library, the American Royal Rodeo, maybe a ball game—Chiefs or Royals—a whole package of sponsored events with every damn good restaurant and hotel pulling out all the stops with meals and banners. The whole thing would celebrate why Kansas City is such a great town, and Lawrence ought to be the perfect example of a satellite relationship. Bring them in, make transportation easy, and show them what they're missing by flying over.

If a Kansas City bank would make something like this happen, the dividends would be great. Why don't people do things and have fun doing them? It's frustrating. If Charlie Kimball were alive today, we'd have a meeting and dream up a plan that would make a lot of sense. It'd be a winner for Kansas City, and we'd figure out how to capitalize on that for Lawrence.

That's what Miller Nichols (a major Kansas City developer) and I had in mind when we were talking about starting a town. I knew where the new highways were going to be built through eastern Kansas, and this town would be designed as an amazing satellite community between Kansas City and Lawrence. It'd be mainly built like a circle with a massive technology and business center at the hub, then various arcs expanding outward with houses, shopping, schools, restaurants, and golf courses. Public transportation would be accessible throughout—everyone could access everything easily. The model could work in lots of places. Nichols and I were talking about this years before wireless free internet was invented.

It's just so much fun to think of what we could be doing to solve the problems every state is facing. That's what my "Big Eight" conference focused on. I've been so lucky to participate in many dialogues about these challenges, and I wonder what improvements might have come out of these gatherings if they were still happening today.

I know I spend a lot of time thinking about what ought to get done, but I probably spend more time worrying about what

Dolph Jr. at top, Dolph Sr. and W.C. center, John Simons at the tiller, circa 1940

Dolph III top, Dolph Jr. and Dolph Sr. center, Dan Simons at the tiller, circa 1985

I could or should have done. I could have done more with the breaks I had and opportunities that came my way. Pam says I'm too hard on myself, but if I'm going to be critical of others, I have to take a look at my own performance first. I had a lot to measure up to with role models like W.C. and Dad.

Looking at that picture of them with John and me at Gull Lake, I can put myself right back in that fishing boat. I can remember what we were talking about. It makes me wish I could talk with them all now and ask what they think of what's going on in the world. We recreated that photo back in the '80s with Dad and my sons. I've been looking at a lot of old photos for this book. There have been so many great times. I wonder if I appreciated them as much as I should have?

I write letters almost every day using my old typewriter. If I have something to say to Rupert Murdoch or Elizabeth Dole, I'll write them. I wrote to the widow of a friend of mine to explain this to her—the conversations I'd have with her husband if I could. I can pull it all up—the discussions at an ANPA board meeting, or with Al (Neuharth)… the things Kay Graham would say, or some point Dad or W.C. was making. I could pick up right where we left off with a topic. Sometimes I wonder if I listened well enough.

Maybe I overthink things, but when you live this long, you certainly have a lot of things to think about.

"Thank you for the nostalgic letter, Dolph. It made me think of how unusual our lives have been. Yours, mine, and Fred's. Who would have imagined the future of those three little boys from Cordley Grade School? Miss Simmons would be proud. It's been a helluva run for us all."

Paul Coker, 2022

Even now, when I turn off Massachusetts Street onto Vermont Street, I'll go back to a day I was walking by myself down that same street back in college. It's a very specific memory. I'd just finished playing a football game and was re-living the game in my mind, knowing I'd screwed up. If I'd tried harder, I could have made that block that would've made things better for the team. Why do I still think about that now? What can I do about that now? Or about the old pear tree down at the end of the yard? When my grandparents lived in this house, I mowed this whole yard by hand for them. I was always tired from sports or my other jobs, and never felt like moving all the limbs to get up close around that tree. Dad always said do your best even if it's just for the satisfaction of knowing you've done your best. So I did move those branches and mow close around that tree.

Those two memories play off one another. Did I do my best? This is something I think about a lot. Did I try as hard as I could? Not just in school or sports but in my work, was I fair in what I wrote? How could I have made my point better? Is there a difference between truth and accuracy? How do we perform in a manner that justifies or affirms the right of a media organization to function as the First Amendment dictates?

There are so many things I still wonder about. I'm politically conservative, so that's my perspective and those are my values. We should have pride and enthusiasm about how lucky we are to live in America. Sure, we've got problems—who doesn't? Where are the community leaders who are going to fix them? Anymore, people don't run for city commissions or leadership positions because they don't want to step on toes or make people upset.

I'd like to see compulsory community service. I think it'd be good to do that after high school and before college—in the forest service or military or something—get their heads screwed on straight. The military can be a good place to learn discipline and responsibility; to take and give orders. You learn a lot living with different kinds of people than you've ever known before. Have those drill instructors work you over… no screwing around. Become a person who has earned respect.

When I grew up, I had high respect for leaders who'd earned it. In my mind, if you were on the city commission or school board, that was something. Today, people aren't choosing to go into public service, or a lot who do are in it for ego or money. I'll tell you, Washington changes people. They're seldom the same person after a term or two in Washington. I've seen it... hell, we've all seen it.

We've lost the narrative of our country; things aren't looking good for us. They're looking worse, in fact. But Dolph brought out that opposition in understandable ways. I don't know too many Republicans I'd care to sit down with, but Dolph is a really unusual man in our country today. We desperately need people like him. But we don't have ways for those voices to reach us—that's what we've lost when we stopped publishing local newspapers.

Dennis Domer, Ph.D., author and historian

I worry about complacency in this country. People are laughing things off as if we'll just look back at this time and wonder why we ever worried. It seems like that feeling is growing right at a time we should be more concerned than ever. Take Black Lives Matter—there's every reason for African Americans to be concerned about their lives, due to history and how they were introduced to this continent and the role they played; how society placed them. African Americans came as slaves and workers until people woke up and said this isn't right. It's been a long time since Martin Luther King's "I Have a Dream" speech, and the Black medalists who raised their fists on the podium at the '68 Olympics—one of the strongest, most visual statements that their race wouldn't take it anymore. Then Kaepernick wouldn't stand for the National Anthem during a football game. Congress wasn't even focused on these issues, but things like that get our attention.

Until the athletes got involved, a whole lot of people weren't listening. Athletes might have been the most identifiable "face" of the issue until a policeman held his knee on George Floyd's neck and a 17-year-old girl captured that on video.

We are experiencing a confluence of all those things exposing the rawness and deep feelings that still exist. Having experienced the civil rights movement of the 1960s in a very direct way, it's shocking to learn we haven't gained more ground since then. The country is going to have to learn to play by new rules. Destructive riots are not the answer. The media must start reporting the facts and identify opinions as editorial or commentary.

Where is the leadership that is essential if this country is to come together? There is nothing guaranteed about the future of America just because it enjoys a glorious and proud history. Where is the leadership, the individual who merits the support, trust and confidence of the public? Without such leadership, the United States at local, state, and national levels, could soon become a relic of its past, no longer the shining star of democracy and freedom.

How do we fix all that's wrong with public education—the inequity, the privilege? I've been in a privileged class... I'm so privileged. I know that. Even though I wore a tie 12 to 14 hours a day, six days a week for 55 years, I recognize I inherited many privileges. My great-grandmother Jennie Bessie struggled, so did my grandfather W.C. I've been the beneficiary of that and so much more.

Dolph still lives with this notion that his dad and grandfather were the important ones.

Bob Trapp, Dolph's best friend

I could have grown the company more than I did, but I didn't want to get too deep in debt, and place the company in a potentially dangerous position. Both W.C. and Dad were always mindful about too much debt. Maybe I didn't have the smarts, or the business mind that my dad had. He was better at most everything he did than I was, as far as writing and business. It's true. I'm not saying that in a phony way.

If there's such a thing as destiny; if you follow the road map presented, when you're given certain opportunities, I don't know if it's being lazy or afraid if you don't take them. Maybe it's just being content with where you're at. I've been content with my job but never content with the state of the world.

Some have said I'm too critical or negative, but my whole point was if I knew something wasn't good for Lawrence, or Kansas, or America, I never hesitated to write about it. I wasn't trying to make anybody mad, but I knew there were times I did disappoint or anger people.

Dolph reviews an 1854 copy of the Kansas *Herald of Freedom* that's been boxed away in the family archives. Most of these primary sources will become part of the Simons Collection at KU's Spencer Library. (Photo: L. Seaver)

There was a story I wrote that still haunts me. Kansas Governor George Docking put highway funding above education back in the 1960s, and I quoted then-KU Chancellor Franklin Murphy saying the newly paved interstate would be filled with KU faculty using it to go to work for other universities in other states. He didn't tell me that in confidence, and quoting him wasn't wrong; it was factually correct. Franklin was a great friend and mentor, but I didn't run it by him before going to press—I wouldn't have done that for any official. To protect the chancellor or, in some ways, the governor, would have been against our editorial policy, so we printed the story. But then Franklin called me and said, "Oh, Dolph, what have you done?" He was so disappointed in me... I can't tell you how bad I felt.

By publishing his remark, the consequences were so unexpected—it became the political straw between Franklin and the governor that broke the camel's back. Franklin Murphy ended up resigning. He went on to become chancellor of UCLA, so things turned out ok for him, but what a loss for KU. It might have been my fault, but I did what I knew was right as a newspaper editor and publisher. Knowing it was the right thing to do made me feel better about the outcome, somewhat.

So many years later, I'm still second-guessing this decision. If the same thing happened today with an esteemed chancellor in that situation, if I'm being perfectly honest, I'd still make that choice. If you're going to be true to yourself as an editor, you have to be willing to lose your friends—at least that's how it works in the newspaper business. This is a business that stands for honesty and accuracy. But it still bothers me how that all went down with the best chancellor KU ever had whom I still admire so much to this very day. Franklin passed on in 1994.

Critics have said my opinion could influence the whole newspaper. I worry there were times this might have been true. The critics could probably say "who's he kidding?" when it came to fairness. Developments could happen, situations could change and I could see a different view of whatever I wrote about… little shitty things like parallel parking versus angled parking downtown. A strong letter to the editor—which I have been happy to publish—often helped me see things differently. Anybody who's read me closely over the years knows I've had to change my stance at times. Dad, Ralph Gage, and Ann Gardner saved my ass a thousand times—helping me get something said right. I'm sure Ann had to bite her lip a lot. She certainly helped harness my runaway ideas.

Some of the best ideas I've admired most include:

- The Freedom Forum. This wasn't just Neuharth flying his flag, and it wasn't just a vehicle to sell USA TODAY. Al started the Freedom Forum back in the '90s to carry the message about the importance of a free press—whether the underground press of Moscow or going to Beijing where we supplied satellite dishes to get more information into certain areas. It's petered out since Al's death.

- The PRISP Bill. The Pat Roberts Intelligent Scholars Program. I'm really proud of a federal bill which was conceived in my office with Senator Roberts and Anthropology Professor Felix Moos. It allows our diplomats and military leaders to become more knowledgeable about representing our country. They need to know language, culture, and history in analyzing, listening and reporting back to our elected officials. It passed the House and Senate with a unanimous vote, and codified in 2004.

- The Newseum. Another Neuharth project. It was right in downtown DC. It got everybody's attention with its display of all these newspaper front pages and this big wall in the entryway hammered out the importance of the free press/freedom of speech in the Constitution.

- The Dole Institute. I've been on this advisory board for years, and remember the post-election roundtables in particular. They brought in the campaign director for Barack Obama, pollsters, national reporters, fundraisers, intelligence specialists for the United States and people who played major roles in various elections. They'll just admit, "We ran out of money" or share some insights into what was behind some of the strategic decisions. You got a peek behind the scenes.

- The Midwest Research Institute (now called MRIGlobal). It was a combination of defense department, economic development, pharmaceuticals. This showed what could happen if we put these efforts together. Charlie Kimball— and he was one I go to for advice on just about anything— chaired the MRI. Charlie was a dreamer. He could inspire and motivate. You'd go there and get your batteries charged. He was a person who made you believe you could make a difference.

- The KU Endowment Association. When I was its chairman, one of my ideas was to take some of our meetings out around the state. People shouldn't have to come to Lawrence to kiss the ring of the chancellor. Instead, we'd take a group of trustees to showcase the faculty around the state. People got excited. It sure got the Alumni Association off their asses.

- The Big Eight Conference of University Cities. I'm really proud to have been a founder of this event. Charlie Kimball was president of Midwest Research Institute at the time, and he was a lot of help getting this off the ground. We got eight similar-sized towns that had universities to get together to discuss how we all solved our problems. Community leaders including mayors, chancellors, police chiefs, superintendents of schools all convened to discuss similar challenges we faced from the various points of view. Columbia, Missouri was there; also Norman, Oklahoma; Lincoln, Nebraska; Boulder, Colorado; and Manhattan, Kansas. We were able to get that idea off the ground and it was very effective for a number of years. We should still be doing that.

- International Association of American Universities. I'm not sure I've got that name right, but KU belonged to this great program that doesn't exist anymore, at least not in the same way. It provided opportunities for professionals, scholars, writers, and even reporters to have international experiences or to study abroad. Then they'd come back to a participating U.S. campus and share their insights into what was happening where they'd been. I was fortunate to be invited to participate at KU and learned a helluva lot about what was happening in the world. I remember Smith Hempstone in particular. He was a *Chicago Daily News* reporter then—this was before he became U.S. ambassador to Kenya. His talk was of great interest to me since I'd work in South Africa early in my career. It was a fantastic program overall, and I hope something like that still exists.

- The Nieman Foundation. Mid-career training at its best. I think it's extremely important to get the best possible education—and that doesn't just stop after college. Go back to school. Get some mid-career training and keep learning, especially if you aren't excited by your work anymore. Don't be a sloth or a lardass—do something about that. Make a contribution to your community for the satisfaction it gives you. That's been a major theme for me.

My granddad and dad had their own particular interests. W.C. had a strong faith, and Dad was fascinated with so many things. He was frequently asked for his advice or help by chancellors, and at other times, he would go up to the chancellor's house just to be on hand—particularly when there were demonstrations on its lawn. It's interesting to see how each of us write about similar situations. We all seemed to have certain subjects in common.

Dolph maintains his loyalty to the manual typewriter. Whenever an ink ribbon needs replacing, secretary Kathy Underwood scours the antique stores. (Photo: L. Seaver)

W.C. Simons

- *It was 40 years ago today that this writer, then 19 years old, arrived in Lawrence. Together with his brother, L.A. Simons, three years younger, he had driven down from St. Joseph, Mo., and the trip, which may be made easily now in a little more than two hours with an automobile, required two and a half days with a horse and phaeton over almost impassable mud roads of that time.*
  (Editorial, December 14, 1931)

- *The United States, which for years has been the ideal of all nations, is in a sorry state. It has a government today of which no one can be really proud. The PAC (political action committee) swung enough votes to Roosevelt to give him a fourth term. They're a selfish,*

ruthless lot of men whose domination is extremely dangerous to the life of the nation, and to the happiness and well-being of her citizens.
(Speech to the Saturday Night Club, December 16, 1944)

- *Something that is of importance to me is the lack of interest and failing on the part of so many people to take a part in making Lawrence a better city. Perhaps it has always been so in Lawrence, and every other community, but I feel we have too much smugness and self-satisfaction. Too many people, who have been endowed with security by their forebears, show so little interest in wanting to make our town and our University a better city and a better school. I want Lawrence to be a prettier town and a happier town. We must have citizens who will devote their talents and long hours to matters of government and industry, but we also need people who will constantly be working toward a more attractive town and a more tolerant and congenial community. If we like our home town of Lawrence, it is because those who lived before us took a deep interest in making it a better town. Are we going to do the same thing for those who follow us?*
(Notes on his 67th Birthday. W.C. Simons personal files at
The Cedars. July 1938)

Dolph C. Simons Sr.

- *This editor visited KU last week. We arrived on the campus when a student had just shot and wounded another student with a .32 caliber... that evening, another small fire was discovered and put out... the university's computer center was damaged with a bomb explosion. Our opinion is that only a handful of individuals (and perhaps non-students) are responsible for the arson, bombing and shootings, not the 18,000 students there working to become better citizens...*
(Editorial, December 16, 1970)

- *Visitors who have come from afar to attend the Eisenhower homecoming will see much more than the general and the welcome extended to him. They will have the privilege of viewing the Kansas countryside at its best... the discovery of Kansas always holds the*

possibility of a thrill for people who didn't know there was much of anything beyond the Alleghenies. Some of the visitors from the East may make that discovery when they come out to see Ike.
(Editorial, 4 June 1952)

- *Surely, no other small city in the entire U.S.A. offers more in "extras" for good living than Lawrence.*
(Letter about Hallmark Cards opening a plant in Lawrence. November 4, 1957)

Dolph C. Simons Jr.

- *This writer has had the good fortune to work with a tremendous group of individuals here at the Journal-World. It has been a family environment with talented reporters, photographers, sales people, pressmen, circulation and business specialists, and great secretaries. All of us are proud of those who had long careers here, as well as those who accepted offers to move to highly successful careers elsewhere.*
(His last Saturday Column, July 30, 2016)

- *It is difficult to have a respectful visit among a group of people relative to the merits of former President Trump and current President Biden. Even long-time close friends find it difficult to exchange views about current events without damaging treasured relationships... this writer believes the growing split within our country is becoming even wider due to the lock-downs, mandates and quarantines. This is a more dangerous situation than COVID-19 or the variants which may evolve in the future.*
(LawrenceOpinions.com, February, 2022)

- *Living in Lawrence has been a joy. It's been a great community in which to live, work, and play. It has most everything a city planner could desire: a great location, a sound supply of water, good work ethics and practices by a majority of its residents, a fine state-aided university, honest city government, an excellent transportation system, easy access to a major airport and world class healthcare.*
(the Saturday Column, 2016)

Today, we're at a real crossroads with so called "traditional values" but W.C. and Dad had very similar thoughts and worries on that topic in their day. I wonder what today's futurists think will unfold for us 100 years from now? Equipment will be different but what about the people? Will we just order the baby we want? That kind of takes the fun out of it.

Being a family man has been a great joy and a challenge for me. In all the letters I've been writing my kids and grandkids, I say if marriage is in the cards for you, then look your damnedest to get a good partner. Pray for good health, and take care of your

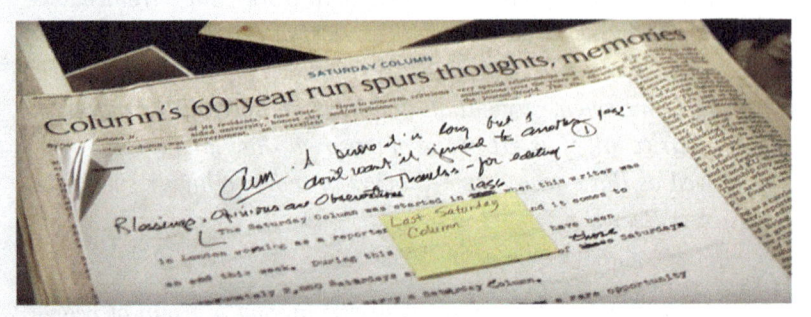

"It is difficult to imagine a more interesting, challenging opportunity than I have had." Dolph Simons Jr. in his last Saturday Column, July 30, 2016.
(Photo: L. Seaver)

health. If you have children, spend as much time as you can with them. The clock is ticking… you can't get that time back. Also, don't be an overbearing parent, but offer an encouraging word or a helpful thought. You think it won't count, but it does.

I've spent hours and hours trying to recall things in my life, things I'm so appreciative and thankful for, things I've been so lucky or blessed with; but I just end up concluding I should have had the backbone to do more. I heard a sermon in which the minister talked about wearing cheaters—those eyeglasses that help you see—but in this story, the cheaters make you see yourself for who you really are. That message stuck with me. I can spend a lot of time asking myself if I was the kind of person I should have been.

My grade school, high school, and college years were happy ones, although I wish I'd been a better student. Maybe I couldn't have been. If I did have the ability, I sure wasted it. I blew a lot of it. Over the years, I've gotten to know people who are so smart and have accomplished so much. Hell, it's intimidating, but it doesn't bow me to my knees. It inspires me. It makes me wish I'd done better in school. I wish I had taken more writing courses. In journalism school, you learn libel, slander, and the six W's, but what I'd say to J-school kids today is to focus on learning a lot of things beyond journalism. Learn history, foreign languages, psychology, business. Become a well-rounded person, that's what this field needs.

It could also use a conscience.

Dolph Simons is a man who takes standards seriously, whether vetting the details of a front page exposé, or enforcing the rule that gentlemen wear jackets at dinner here in the Adams Alumni Center. The story is still told of one high level administrator who wrote to complain that she and her husband were turned away because he appeared in South American dress shirt rather than a jacket. As the driving force behind this center's creation, and himself a frequent lunch and dinner host to Al Neuharth, Don Hall, and other luminaries, Dolph stood firm in defending the rule and the staff for enforcing it. After all, he noted, this was not a Faculty Club but an Alumni Center—a magnificent expression, in brick and stone of the unwavering loyalty KU graduates feel toward their alma mater.

His own allegiance to the place was to have historic consequences, and a continuing impact that no plaque or sculpture can fully communicate. I hope no one here will take offense if I point out that long before he was editor of the **Lawrence Journal-World***, chairman of The World Company, an AP director, Pulitzer Prize juror, pioneering cable TV entrepreneur, National Parks Conservation Association trustee, bank director, hospital board member, or reporter for* **The Times** *of London; before he married his beloved Pamela and became the vastly, justifiably proud father of Pam, Linda, Dolph*

III, and Dan—all of whom it bears noting, attended KU—before he was grandfather and pater familias to this astonishing brood, Dolph Simons Jr. was a KU alumnus. He has spent most of his life since 1951 giving back to the school that gave him a degree in journalism. And before, during, and since his days as a Jayhawk in training, he was something else, something even more central to his character and his contributions.

He was his father's son. "The prevailing characteristic I remember in Dolph Sr. was that he was a selfless person," recalls former Chancellor Archie Dykes. "He wanted others to succeed. And if they were successful, then he'd be successful." The elder Mr. Simons came by these sentiments naturally, as a paperboy working for his journalist father, and as an AP reporter in Chicago, before rising through the ranks at the Journal-World, all the while supporting and expanding KU, and serving on the executive committee of the Endowment Association for more than forty years. Helen Spencer's name is on the art museum, and quite properly so, but Dolph Sr. was instrumental in its creation—one of many campus landmarks and programs that bear his stamp. "Anyone who has had the privilege of living here this long under the shadow of Mount Oread is a lucky person," he observed. "I am grateful for the great joy the university has brought into my life."

When Mr. Simons joined the Endowment Association in 1939, the organization boasted assets of $67,000. By the end of his life that figure had grown to $220 million. Yet his greatest legacy, to KU and to Lawrence, was a son who would emulate the father's commitment to both. Like the father, the son would become the first citizen of his community, at once a cheerleader and a friendly critic, a booster alive to imperfections as well as possibilities, a visionary and a pragmatist. In a profession transforming itself through technology, he has never lost the human touch. He would embrace the new ways without relinquishing the old values that have guided the Simons school of journalism since 1891. Dolph Sr. may have found time atop all of his other responsibilities, to be a banker as well as a one-man chamber of commerce. But he knew instinctively that a newspaper deals in the currency of Trust. With every edition it must be renewed, through local controversies and national challenges alike.

Next to their families, the Simons men most loved KU—and yet their love was not uncomplicated, nor did it ever degenerate into uncritical acceptance of the status quo. They cherished this university because it was set on a hill, in more ways than one. Because they looked up to it, they accepted the mandate to ensure, when the time came to hand the baton to the next generation, that KU had not simply grown under their stewardship, but that it had grown in stature and aspiration alike. Whether reporting the news or making it, imagining KU's future of fulfilling its promise, they led by example, voices of conscience, catalysts for excellence.

Such men are the true public servants on which a free nation relies to defend its shores, advance its ideals, and fulfill the dream of a republic that would govern itself by enshrining service before self. Thank you, Dolph (Jr.), for all you have achieved, and for all you have given; above all, for insisting that KU live up to its highest traditions, even as it justifies the pride of its most demanding, and affectionate, alumni.

Richard Norton Smith, Pulitzer-nominated author, historian, and former Director of the Dole Institute, speaking at a KU Adams Alumni Center event commemorating the Simons in 2014.

I've never had a crisis of faith. I've asked the Lord to help me be a better person, to help the family on trips, to help Pam out, things like that. For a certain period of years, I was totally out of it, but I'd hear about other people's experience with faith, and check back in. I admit, I think a person is foolish to think everything on earth just happens randomly, that there isn't a pattern or design. I believe there is a plan. The miracle of birds or trees or even people... I still can't even figure out the magic of rain.

The one who really tries to nail me on this stuff is my granddaughter, Whitney. She'll poke you in the chest and ask directly how are you living your life? To me, it's a puzzle. The way I see it, if we listen, the Lord has given each of us a punch-list. Beyond that, what does it mean to be religious? If you follow the golden rule— all that kind of stuff—do you need more religion than that?

I never got any strong message from Dad or Mom about this, but I didn't ask them. I wonder if W.C. ever pressed them about young Dolph having better attendance at church. I was encouraged to go to the Baptist church because my grandparents were there. At some point, probably during college years, I sang in the Episcopal choir, of all the dumb things (me singing, not Episcopalians). Mother did want me to have a strong church affiliation before I went into the service, but we never discussed why. This left the door open for me to form my own views. The way I see it, I'd rather be open to new ideas and different philosophies than just see everything in black and white. Being rigid can create problems.

The Things Dad Won't Tell You!

Dad gets things done. He is rarely idle. But if he appears relaxed, don't be fooled, his mind is whirling with what to do or take care of next. He loves making things happen, learning more, meeting new people, maintaining connections, supporting others, work, family, and having fun!

Not a day goes by that Dad doesn't ask himself how can I help, who should I call? Then he acts on it. He makes the connections; he follows up. He makes a difference for others. He doesn't let a friendship, an institution, association, or family member fade away. He cares... he keeps at it.

He'll chat with you about anything, but invariably, he'll turn the subject back to you. He wants to know what you're interested in. If he can help you achieve a goal or solve a problem, he'll give his time and attention to it whether you're his daughter's date, the repairman, his old friend, or a visiting dignitary. He'll ask as many questions as he needs to get a true bead on your personality, job, or outlook on life. Then he'll be your best cheerleader, and not quietly! He'll write you, call you, then write and call you again offering praise, encouragement, and assistance. He makes things happen!

Indeed, in any endeavor—academic, the arts, sports, work, leadership, or volunteerism—excellence and effort win his approbation. The point is if you gave it your all, even if you weren't declared the winner, that stick-to-it-iveness counts with Dad. Taking pride in yourself and achieving your goals is important to him. However, while winning is big with Dad, handling a loss (particularly a loss by one of his sports teams) has not been one of his better attributes.

Dad loves all kinds of work, physical or mental. "Don't just sit on your butt" has been a phrase heard often in our family. Whether it's a thank you note to be written or a tree that needs to be watered, he doesn't procrastinate. Work gives him great satisfaction. He reads voraciously. Acquiring knowledge is his favorite "work." He knows so much about such a wide array of subjects, people, institutions— and not just superficially. His mind continues to overflow with almost everything he's ever learned or about people he's met—he remembers it all, still at age 93!

For all his seriousness as a businessman, Dad loves making people happy and having a good time. He revels in family silliness, throwing parties, laughing, Dixieland bands, telling good jokes or tall tales, and remembering when. If you're his friend or a member of his family, the emotion he might conceal, but what we feel in full, is his love. He loves because he cares so damn much!

Linda Simons de Menocal

There's so much tension in the world today. Our ancestors also faced wars, droughts, pandemics, and government corruption, but somehow America bounced back. I'm not saying we solved all our problems, but our forebears kept working on it. They paved the way.

It's important to be open to different perspectives, or at least to recognize if you're being closed-minded. Look at education— what we taught or didn't teach, what we left out of a textbook. There have to be new ways to see old problems. Should we go into space? Is there life out there in a different universe? Should the Supreme Court decide if we pay college athletes? Who gets to make decisions about a woman's reproductive rights? What should we focus on? I guess that depends on who you ask.

There are so damn many things going on, and people who don't see eye to eye. I have to believe W.C. and Dad would be shocked at the contentiousness of it all. Have we become a world built just to pay lawyers?

We can do better than that. We need to be respectful of each other; to keep lines of communication from dissolving. How in the world can we get anything done without working together to solve our problems? How can we plan for the future?

It's understandable that many are frustrated, disappointed, worried, or angry about current conditions, but there's every reason to believe this country can and will regain the excitement, energy, and commitment that made the United States the world's greatest, freest land. If excellence and achievement are rewarded; if we don't get infected from partisan politics; if we can get people engaged in their community, state, or national governmental bodies, the future of our country and its citizens is almost unlimited. That's the American spirit, and that spirit is a powerful, protective shield.

I believe the strength of that protection is directly tied to a free, honest media that merits the respect of the public. That's the best possible force to keep this country on track.

Should a drooling, senile old man get to weigh in about any of this? Well, I'm 93, but I'm not that old. I have an opinion, and I'll express it. Who gives a damn what I think anyway?

In 1944, towards the end of the second world war, W.C. wrote:

> *Step by step we doubtless could go back to the very beginnings of time were we able to do so, and still we should find that ambition, self-reliance, courage, and a willingness to work in all of those whose blood, ever so diluted, still flows in our veins. The world has not been made great by a set of weaklings who have ridden through on the backs of suffering humanity, but by those who were giving their best to their everyday tasks, and somehow and in some way carried on under crushing difficulties. We are the heirs of worthy ancestors and we must not let them down.*

Granddad was 72 years old then, and as his writing indicates, he just kept getting wiser as he got older. Same with Dad. We've got some wonderful tape recordings of him talking about his experiences hunting and fishing... he's giving little pointers along the way. Dad and Mother moved to Arizona where they kept busy with things that interested them, which was a lot of things. Dad took up painting and he really enjoyed it. We have some of his artwork framed around the house. Although he seldom came to the office anymore, Dad kept checking in on the paper, contributing occasional editorials, but he had a life.

That's inspiring to me... to stay engaged in life while you're still alive. And if you're still alive, then you damn well better act like it. Make a contribution. Hell, if I feel any guilt about not performing in the past, shouldn't I just do a better job with the days I've got left? We're all going to be ancestors eventually—shouldn't we try to be worthy?

Not long ago, I cracked open a Chinese fortune cookie that said "To love what you do, and feel that it matters... how could anything be more fun?"

That's me in a nutshell... the wisest thing I know can be found in a fortune cookie. Pretty fitting—I've been so damned lucky.

Of course, Pam would say blessed.

Dolph Simons Jr.

Dolph Simons Jr. at the empty Journal-World plant in 2022. (Photo: L. Seaver)

Authors' Notes

This Writer could not have been written without the help and interest of many, many individuals including personal friends, co-workers, close associates in the newspaper and wire services fields, professionals from various academic and media-oriented organizations, as well as from libraries, museums, and historical societies. This book has been put together using voluminous family scrapbooks, photographs, stories, vignettes, newspaper clippings, and personal mementos that have been saved since as far back as the Civil War.

However, there are three individuals who, by their actions, beliefs, and careers, provided the greatest inspiration for this book: Jennie Bessie Simons, W.C. Simons, and Dolph C. Simons Sr. Their personal stories are entwined with the historic role and importance of the newspaper in the development of this country.

My great-grandmother Jennie Bessie, pioneered in Hodgeman County, Kansas, in 1878. Her faith in the Lord got her through her struggles and she was able to provide a good education for her five children. It was Jennie Bessie who invested what little she had in a small newspaper for her 16-year-old son Collie, introducing him to his future occupation.

W.C. "Collie" Simons, was the eight-year-old "man of the house," plowing unturned prairie land in the failed endeavor to farm drought-ridden Kansas. By 1891, when he was just 19, my grandfather moved to Lawrence, Kansas, and started a newspaper. There were already eight other papers in town—

his would succeed. Granddad was a gifted writer and observer with a strong moral compass that influenced the family business for generations.

W.C.'s son, Dolph Simons Sr., was a unique man, a hard worker, smart, an excellent writer, editor, a top businessman, and a true, visionary leader who was content to remain behind the scenes. Vitally interested in the welfare of the University of Kansas, the agriculture community, and politics, he was committed to putting out a good newspaper. He also was a great father and boss from whom I inherited the family business that was respected throughout the industry.

Newspapers were the glue that held people together and documented their effort to make a better future for themselves, their community, and the nation. I am humbled and grateful for the opportunity my family has had to participate in something so important. And I'm thankful to my wife, Pam, and children Pam, Linda, Dolph III, and Dan for the support and sacrifices they've made being part of a newspaper family, which isn't always easy. My daughter Linda has been the impetus for documenting this story, and I'm grateful for her encouragement.

This story could not have been told without the long, hard exhaustive work of Leeanne Seaver. She is a champion researcher, a gifted writer, and a joy to work with. She was hooked by the Jennie Bessie story and couldn't let it go until she followed the next three generations and the evolution of the *Lawrence Journal-World*.

Dolph C. Simons Jr.

P. S. A suggestion to those thinking about writing a book about family history: Put the date, the place, and the names of the individuals in the picture on the back of the picture. The "who, what, when, where, and how" all are important and, like it or not, memories fade.

The authors at work at The Cedars, September 2022. (Photo: Kristi West)

Without question, the Simons' story is so big, it would take several books to cover it, and each could be found in a separate section of the library from American Government to History to Journalism to Women's Studies. That's right, Women's Studies. There's enough diverse material here to develop a compelling curriculum—or prompt a Netflix series.

While *This Writer* tells the story of a Civil War widow sod-busting on the high plains, it barely touches on her daughters' fascinating lives. One became a supervisor of the famous "Harvey Girls," traveling in her own train car throughout the west during the 1920s. She went onto the University of Chicago where she earned a Ph.D.—one of only three women among 85 men in the program.

Those are just two of the early Simons women. There are more with remarkable stories going back to Alice Bradford in 1620. She was the wife of Governor William Bradford of the Plymouth Colonies— and W.C. Simons' sixth great grandmother. More than 350 years later in 1978, Pamela Ann Simons became one of the first female general managers in the country to run a cable operation.

Indeed, practically every stone unturned on the long journey of the family's history could lead down another intriguing path. This book focuses on 125 years of their story that paralleled, intersected, and influenced the evolution of the newspaper industry in this country.

As always happens when a story wants to be told, the right people and information serendipitously show up, and the scattered threads of the story somehow ravel back together. Sometimes, that took the form of a photo, or a letter or clipping so old and crisp I hesitated to unfold it. One time, it was the volunteer guide at Ft. Larned Historic Site named Canvas who manually entered the coordinates of an 1878 land claim into my cell phone navigation app. Thanks to this savvy digital native, I was able to find the limestone foundation blocks that are still visible at the remote, unmarked site of Jennie Bessie Simons' homestead about four and a half hours southwest of Lawrence.

The foundation of Jennie Bessie's homestead is still visible in May 2023.
(Photo: L. Seaver)

However, most of the time, it was Dolph's keen memory, with the occasional boost from his family and friends, that helped connect various points. Lou Boccardi, in particular, provided invaluable expertise and insight to help me get the story right. I'm indebted to

Dennis Domer, Rob Seaver, Paul Cartter, and Ann Gardner for their input and intellect. Kristi West was not only a most resourceful, enthusiastic research assistant, she was lots of fun. I could always count on Kathy Underwood to find an obscure detail or document in the office files. Laura Adams and Bob Ball gave the manuscript an exhaustive and much-needed tech-edit. Linda de Menocal has been not only a creative collaborator but a damn fine proofreader. Honestly, I could go on and on with the names of those who deserve thanks (and I will).

Mostly, I want to thank Dolph for trusting me to help make this book happen. Thank you, dear friend, for the keys to your kingdom of incredible primary source treasures; for gentle, constructive feedback and encouragement; for the happy hour limes and the 11 p.m. bacon run. With all my heart, thank you for the privilege of participation in this epic story which is as important as it is big.

This Writer weaves real people through events that have helped define the United States—and there's so much going on here about what goes into being "united" as states. To understand how this country came to recognize itself as a new nation is to grasp the role of a local newspaper—how important that function was and still is.

Local newspapers bring us into the story... joining us in a shared experience that transforms individuals in a community. The more we are associated in community, the more that shared experience matters to us—and we matter to it. What comes of that dynamic is nothing less than democracy in action.

There's reciprocity involved here that needs what a local newspaper delivers: a mechanism for knowing each other's story, and understanding why it matters. With fewer and fewer local newspapers to reflect that back to us—even as the mass media blasts more and more messages at us—is it any wonder we struggle to recognize ourselves as a nation today?

The hours and hours spent pondering such problems with Dolph Simons Jr., whose wisdom is second only to his sense of wonder, gave me a new perspective on how all this works. Albeit, we ended up with more questions than answers, but that's a kind of progress in my book—to ask better questions. History shows us again and again that there are those who rise to the challenge of solving them. My own Dane, Dakota, and Makena Seaver give me reason to hope.

Leeanne Seaver

Acknowledgements

If you've ever wished certain people could know what an important impact they've had on your life, you can understand the motivation for creating this list. We would like to acknowledge some people (living or not) who've played a part, whether directly or indirectly, in the creation of this book. These individuals have provided support, guidance, or inspiration. We want to sincerely thank them by name.

Laura and Paul Adams, Forrest (Phog) Allen, John Amberg, Neil Armstrong, Oswald Backus, Neeli Bendapudi, Jim Betterman, Bernice Black, Clay Blair, Louis Boccardi, Ben Bradlee, Gene Budig, Warren Buffett, George H.W. Bush, Paul Cartter, Jill Jensen Chadwick, Otis Chandler, Ruth Clark, Richard Clarkson, Paul Coker Jr., Stan Cook, Virgil and Gladys Counseller, John Cowles Jr., Tom Curley, John Dennis, Martin Dickinson, Dallas Dolan, Robert and Elizabeth Dole, Dennis Domer, Archie Dykes, Victor Eddy, Ray Evans, Bob Fenimore, Kathleen Oswalt Forsythe, Dorothy Fritzel, Keith Fuller, Ralph Gage, Judith Galas, Mario Garcia, Ann Gardner, Mike Getto, Clifton C. Gillespie Sr., Jack and Lee Gillespie, Suzanne Goff, Mike Gorton, Katharine Graham, Henri Medinilla Grau, John Hadl, Don Hall, Charles Hall, Roby Harrington, Deborah Harsha, Bob and Maryann Hayward, Paul Henson, Tom Johnson, Charles Kimball, John (Jack) Knight, Maude Kreamer, John Kreamer, Leonard Krishtalka, Chad Lawhorn, Eppie Lederer (a.k.a. Ann Landers), Canvas Lovesee, Laura McFarlane Lunde, John Malone, Bob Marbut, Bill Mayer, Paul Miller, Sue Clark Moore, Felix and Ling Lung Moos, Billy Morris, Thom Mozloom, Jeremy Mulderig, Franklin Murphy, Alan Mulally, Al Neuharth, Robert Nordyke, Mike Ort, Warren Phillips, Paul Plutnicki, Charles Porter, Liane Quinn, William Reed, Frank Rhodes, Bernard Rogers, Ian Saffer, Rich Salierno,

Albert Salisbury, Walter E. Sandelius, Dwight Sargent, Gayle Sayers, Luke Saylor, Charles Scott Jr., Jim Seaver, Rob Seaver, Tom Seaver, Gerald F. Seib, John N. Simons, Fred Six, Lyn Smith, Richard Norton Smith, Bill Snead, John Stewart, Wade Stinson, Arthur O. Sulzberger, Davis Taylor, Irene Thompson, James Thompson, Bob Trapp, Kathy Underwood, Bob Vosper, Chalmer "Woody" Woodard, Arthur Weaver, Jon Wefald, Clarke Wescoe, Kristi West, William Allen White, Beth Whittaker, Odd Williams, Erin Wolfe, Tom Vail, Elaine Bickle Zdrojewski

This list may be overly long, but it's hard to know where to stop. There are so many who led the way... who taught, challenged, and encouraged us. It's been heartwarming and humbling to reflect on the role each has played. We are so very grateful.

Epilogue

We grew up with stories... stories at the nightly dinner table with Mom and Dad, or Sunday dinners with our grandparents, or while out fishing for walleye or on long car rides. News stories, people stories, or stories of family lore, the many remembrances grabbed the attention of the youngsters we were.

Time advanced and our memories of those fascinating stories started to fade. They could not have been passed down to succeeding generations with the same nuance or accuracy of Dad and Grampy. Thus, a request to Dad to write them all up—just 300 words or so on different vignettes for our children and grandchildren to know more about their forebears and what life was like when he grew up in Lawrence.

Dad had been going through boxes handed down from his parents (which had been handed down from their parents.) He was finding memorabilia which also told stories—more stories! So, ever the journalist, Dad did us one better. He brought in a pro: Leeanne Seaver!

The narrative throughout this compendium is all Leeanne. Not just the eloquent writing, but all the source work. As might be expected in a family that deals in information, voluminous amounts of letters, photographs, speeches, and official documents ad nauseum were kept. My great-grandfather, W.C. Simons, had documented our genealogy and written down many of his childhood stories of sod-busting on the plains of Kansas, so there were some amazing primary sources. While all office documents and photos were saved in meticulous order, the family memorabilia were not. Leeanne spent hours, weeks, months sleuthing, reading, organizing, synthesizing over 150 years crammed into boxes, scrapbooks, letters, school programs, newspaper clippings, Christmas cards, loose photos, handwritten notes, etc. She doggedly chased down facts and verifications. She was the one who insisted this project was more than a personal memoir only the family would read. She turned it into a chronicle of multiple generations in newspapering.

Leeanne brought to life a multitude of facts and nuances (personal, family, and professional) about our parents, grandparents, great grandparents, and even some earlier ancestors. She interviewed first-person sources in the newspaper industry, historians, friends, and community members. She even drove to southwestern Kansas to locate my great-great grandmother Jennie Bessie Simons' 1878 homestead in remote Hodgeman County and found what remained of its block foundation!

Among the most exciting documents discovered were Jennie Bessie's diaries, begun during the Civil War, which sat unnoticed on a bookshelf at The Cedars for decades. Many thanks are given to Beth Whittaker, Erin Wolfe, and team who transcribed and digitized these priceless artifacts which are now a part of the Simons Collection at the University of Kansas Spencer Library. Such a gift to our family!

As we children know, Dad would never want the spotlight. He never looks for nor wants accolades, but we insist it all be included. His story is fascinating. We've learned more from Leeanne's interviews than he ever told us himself. We hope the reader finds his inquisitiveness, compassion, leadership, energy, professionalism, accomplishments, writings, and vision to be compelling.

We especially enjoy his love for family, generosity of spirit, cheerleading our accomplishments, pushing us to excellence, and always, always, his supreme happiness when we're all together.

Thanks, Dad! We love you!

Linda Simons de Menocal

The Simons Timeline[1]

1866 On July 3, Adolphus Ezra "Dolph" Simons and Jennie Bessie Gowdy are married at 8 a.m. at her parents' home in Waukegan.

1871 Their first son, William Collins Simons, is born in Owatonna, Minnesota, on July 8. He is "Collie" to his family; he'll later change his name to *Wilford* Collins Simons.

1873 Although he's been successful as a store manager and bookkeeper, Adolphus "Dolph" finds the work "too confining" and moves his family to greener pastures in Faribault, Minnesota.[2]

1877 "Dolph" Simons succumbs to the ill-effects of his Civil War soldiering days, dying on October 29 at Faribault, Minnesota.

1878 In March, Jennie Bessie Simons, now a widow, moves her family to their claim in Kansas; going with her two brothers and parents. They settle in Hodgeman County on the western plains.

1882 Final proof of Mrs. Jennie B. Simons' land claim is published in Public Notices in the *Jetmore Reveille* on May 16.

1887 Jennie Bessie Simons purchases for her 16-year-old son Collie a one-half interest in the *Weekly Gazette* published for a short-time in Houston, Kansas. The town's two-year-old post office shuts down the same year.

1888 In the spring of the year, Jennie Simons relocates to Salina, Kansas, where her children will have access to a better education.

Jennie B. Simons finally receives her Civil War widow's pension in August.

The *Salina Republican* noted on Friday, August 17, 1888, that "Mrs. Jennie B. Simons has purchased the residence of Paul Jordan, at 217 Ellsworth Avenue."[3]

W.C. enters Kansas Wesleyan University in Salina on a part-time basis, and begins writing for the *Salina Republican*.

1889 Jennie B. Simons purchases the *Salina Daily Republican* on April 8.

"The subscription books accounts since July 2nd, 1888, press and all clear material, etc., of *The Republican* has been sold to Mrs. Jennie B. Simons. The management will not be changed. Mr.

Brady will be retained as editor of the paper. A complete, new address will soon be here and things will boom. *The Republican* has come to stay."[4]

1890 W.C. Simons is working at the *St. Joseph Herald* in Missouri.

1891 On December 14, W.C. Simons, with his 17-year-old brother Louis A. Simons and brother-in-law John Leeford Brady, establish The World Company with $50.00 of L.A.'s capital. Their offices are at Seventh and Massachusetts in Lawrence.

As partners, J.L. Brady, W.C. and L.A. Simons lease the *Lawrence Daily Record*, but opt not to renew after three months.

1892 J.L. Brady is editor and W.C. Simons is publisher of *The Lawrence Daily World*, their own, newly-launched independent paper.

1893 On December 27, the land in Hodgeman County that Jennie B. Simons abandoned in 1888 goes up for public sale due to non-payment of taxes.

1894 W.C. Simons and Mary Gertrude Reineke are married on November 14 in Kansas City, Missouri.

1895 The World Company purchases the *Lawrence Daily Gazette* and consolidates it into the *Lawrence Daily World*. The masthead now claims "the widest circulation in Lawrence."[5]

1904 W.C. and Gertrude Simons have a son, Dolph Collins Simons, born on November 24 in Lawrence, Kansas.

1905 *The Lawrence Journal* is purchased by The World Company.

1906 Marie Nelson, future wife of Dolph Simons Sr., is born in Omaha, Nebraska, on July 16.

1911 After operating independently but with joint ownership, the *Lawrence Daily Journal* and the Lawrence *World* merge when a fire destroys the Journal offices and equipment. W.C. is publisher, J.L. Brady, editor, of the *Lawrence Journal-World*. The offices are located at 722 Massachusetts Street in Lawrence.

1914 In December, Brady sells his stock in the Journal-World to W. C. Simons, and immediately relocates to Ft. Smith, Arkansas, where he'd purchased a controlling interest in the *Times-Record*.

1915 W.C. Simons is now sole owner of The World Company, and editor and publisher of the *Lawrence Journal-World*.

1921 Jennie Bessie Simons dies at the home of her daughter, Julia, in Chicago on November 17. She was 85.

1924 During summer break from KU, Dolph Sr. is working as a cub reporter for the Associated Press in Chicago where he covers the Leopold-Loeb murder trial.

1925 Dolph Sr. graduates from the University of Kansas with a degree in Liberal Arts, enters the *Lawrence Journal-World* business on a full-time basis.

1928 Marie Nelson, a Kappa Kappa Gamma sorority sister, graduates with a teaching degree from KU.

1929 Dolph Collins Simons and Ann Marie Nelson are married on February 16 in Auburn, Nebraska.

1930 Dolph Collins Simons Jr. is born on March 11 to Dolph Sr. and Marie Simons in Lawrence, Kansas.

1932 Pamela Counseller, future wife of Dolph Jr., is born August 31 in Rochester, Minnesota.

Dolph Jr.'s brother John Nelson Simons is born in Lawrence.

W.C. Simons continues to serve as a member of the Associated Press of Kansas, and the Audit Bureau of Circulations.[6]

1933 On January 6, Louis Adolphus "L.A." Simons dies in Kansas City.

1937 Dorothy Fritzel begins employment as Dolph Sr.'s secretary on November 9.

Dolph Simons Sr. becomes a Chamber Leader with the Lawrence Chamber of Commerce.

1939 Dolph Sr. is now president of the Kansas Press Association,[7] and on the board of the KU Alumni Association.

1942 Dolph Jr., age 12, earns his Junior Lifesaving Certificate. By 16, he received his Red Cross Senior Lifesaving Certification.

1943 Sister of W.C. Simons and former wife of J.L. Brady, his business partner, Julia Simons Brady Hoinville, age 76, dies in Chicago.

1944 Dolph Sr. becomes publisher of the Journal-World. He is also a delegate to the Republican National Convention.

1947 From May to June, U.S. Secretary of War Robert P. Patterson does a reconnaissance of occupied Germany and Austria, bringing Dolph Simons Sr. and 11 other newspaper men along to observe. Simons' report, "Germany and Austria, May to June 1947," will become an important resource for the US military.

Dolph Jr. graduates from Lawrence High School where he was a football star and editor-in-chief of the school newspaper. In the fall, he heads to KU where he'll become an All-Star kicker on the football team, and become associated with Phi Delta Theta and Sigma Delta Chi fraternities.

1948 Mary Gertrude Reineke Simons dies on October 30 in Lawrence, Kansas. She was 73.

1949 On the heels of his successful trip in 1947, Dolph Sr. is invited to accompany Admiral Louis Denfeld, chief of naval operations, and Vice-Admiral Robert B. Carney, deputy chief, on a Navy inspection flight around the world. He chronicles his observations in "A Globe Circler's Diary," which is widely distributed by the U.S. War Department.

1950 In November, W.C. Simons establishes the Jennie B. Simons Memorial Fund at KU in memory of his mother. His gift of $1,000 (worth over $12,576 in 2023 dollars)[8] will finance the construction of an exhibit of pioneer life in the university's Museum of Natural History. "The memorial to Mrs. Simons is doubly welcomed by the university," Chancellor Malott said. "It will help preserve the memory of an aspect of early Kansas life unknown to the current generation. It also is an expression of the loyal support local citizens have given in making KU a great institution."

Dolph Sr. elected president of KU Alumni Association.

Dolph Sr. is elected first vice president of the Associated Press. He will remain on the AP board until 1960.[9]

Publisher of the Journal-World since 1944, Dolph Sr. became its editor in 1950.

Having been named "All-America Specialist" by *Collier's* Magazine, Dolph Jr. earns Big Seven recognition as right guard and kicker on KU's football team.

1951 Dolph Simons Jr. graduates from KU in June with degree in journalism. He promptly enlists in the Marine Corps.

1952 Dolph Sr. is a member of the press corps at the Republican National Convention.

On February 7, Dolph Jr. and Pamela Counseller are married in Rochester, Minnesota. They set up housekeeping in Laguna Beach, California, near where Dolph is stationed at El Toro Marine Air Facility.

At age 80, W.C. Simons dies on May 15 in Lawrence, Kansas.

1953 Dolph and Pam have a daughter, Pamela Ann Simons, on February 2 in Riverside, California.

Dolph Jr. is honorably discharged from the Marines with the rank of captain.[10] He and Pam move back to Kansas.

1955 Dolph Jr. and Pam's second daughter, Linda Kathryn, is born on February 28 in Lawrence.

Rich Clarkson begins his career as a photographer at the Journal-World shortly before graduating from KU with a degree in Journalism in 1956. From there he went on to the *Topeka Capital-Journal*, then the *Denver Post* before becoming *National Geographic* magazine's director of photography in the 1980s. His photos will grace more than 30 covers for *Sports Illustrated* and chronicle six Olympics.[11]

While still a student at Lawrence High School, Bill Snead is mentored by Clarkson, learning the ins and outs of the darkroom and working as a cub photographer for the *Lawrence Journal-World*. Snead will go on to become an internationally-known, award-winning photojournalist.

1956 Dolph Jr. moves to London to work as a reporter for *The Times*, accompanied by wife, Pam, and their young daughters, Pammie and Linda.

Dolph Simons Sr. receives KU's "Citation for Distinguished Service to Mankind," in 1956. The citation read, "Catalyzer of opinion and generator of positive action for progress, Dolph Collins Simons merits the Citation for his professional career, his public spirit, and his devotion to his alma mater."

1957 Dolph Jr. and Pam are back in Lawrence. His name joins the masthead of the *Lawrence Journal-World* for the first time.

Pam and Dolph's son Dolph Collins Simons III is born on May 8 in Lawrence.

1958 Only briefly back in Kansas, Dolph Jr. leaves Pam and kids behind to become a reporter at the *Johannesburg Star* in South Africa. He publishes eye-opening accounts of apartheid before returning to Lawrence.

1959 The William Allen White Foundation Award for Journalistic Merit is presented by William L. White, son of the namesake, to Dolph Simons Sr.[12]

On October 20, Dolph Sr. is bestowed the 32nd degree as Free-Mason, and recognized as "Knight Commander of the Court of Honor."[13]

1961 A son, Dan Counseller Simons, is born to Dolph Jr. and Pam on June 24. Dan's future wife Trisha Malson is born on October 24 in Akron, Ohio.

1961 – 62 Dolph Sr. is a juror for the Pulitzer Prize.

Dolph Sr. is vice-president of the Eisenhower Foundation.

Dolph Jr. is president of the Lawrence Rotary Club.

1961 – 65 Dolph Jr. serves on the KU Alumni Association board of directors.

1962 Dolph Sr. is director of the Federal Reserve, Kansas City Bank.

Dolph Jr. named publisher of the Journal-World, a title he'll retain until 2004.

1963 Dolph Sr. is elected deputy chairman, Kansas City Federal Reserve Bank.

KU School of Business names Dolph Simons Jr. to its advisory board.

1963 – 66 Dolph Jr. is director of the Inland Daily Press Association.

1966 Dolph Sr. receives the 1966 Minnesota University Award for Distinguished Service in Journalism at an Inland Daily Press Association luncheon in Chicago.[14]

1966 Dolph Jr. becomes director of the Kansas Press Association, and its president in 1967.

1967 Dolph Simons Sr. is named chairman, Kansas City Federal Reserve Bank which serves a seven-state area.

Midwest Research Institute names Dolph Simons Jr. to its board of trustees.

On April 11, Dolph Jr. is elected president of the Lawrence Chamber of Commerce.

1967 – 70 Dolph Jr. is president of the board of the William Allen White Foundation.

**1967
– 76** Dolph Jr. is a director of the Associated Press.

First cable license granted to The World Company for Sunflower Cable.[15]

1968 Dolph Simons Jr. is a director of Commerce Bank in Kansas City, Missouri.

**1968
– 69** Dolph Jr. continues as president of the Kansas Associated Press board of directors.

The World Company establishes Sunflower Cablevision in Lawrence in 1968.

1969 As of December, Dolph Jr.'s title is now president and publisher of The World Company. Dolph Sr. is editor.

Dolph Sr. works with Phillip Godwin, Lawrence Memorial Hospital chief of staff in the late 1960s, to start its endowment.

1970 The Journal-World runs full capacity on its press for the first time.

1971 Dolph Simons Sr. is elected chairman of the Kansas 4-H Foundation.

First liquor advertisement in Journal-World appears on December 3.

Dolph Jr. appointed to the American Newspaper Publishers Association board on December 10.

Sunflower Cable begins serving its first customers in Lawrence.

In the *Junction City Union*, an editorial written by John Montgomery on December 21, suggests Dolph Simons Jr. as candidate for governor of Kansas. Simons will decline.

1972 Dolph Jr. receives an honorary doctorate and is recipient of the Elijah Parish Lovejoy Award from Colby College, Waterville, Maine.

Dolph Jr. serves on the board of Lawrence Memorial Hospital from 1972-1974. He also is a former board director of Oread Laboratories Inc., a Lawrence-based pharmaceutical company.

From 1972 to 2004, Dolph Jr. serves as trustee of the Menninger Foundation of Topeka (later in Houston, Texas), which promotes psychiatric health and provides psychiatric treatment.

The Nieman Foundation at Harvard designates Dolph Simons Jr. as a member of the Nieman Advisory Committee. Dolph's functions include selecting Nieman Fellows who will be supported for mid-career training.

1973 Dolph Jr. is re-elected to another term on Midwest Research Institute.[16]

Future President George Bush, then America's ambassador to the United Nations, is a guest of Dolph and Pam Simons at The Cedars. Bush spoke at the Annual Meeting of the Lawrence Chamber of Commerce on April 14, 1973. He is also the guest of honor at a luncheon in the Student Union, hosted by Dolph Jr.[17]

A Watkins History Museum Fund Drive, chaired by Dolph Simons Sr., raises $296,887 to renovate the building and endow the museum with an operating fund.

1974 Dolph Jr. named Outstanding Kansas Publisher by KU's Kappa Tau Journalism Society.

Dolph Jr. is appointed to the Newspaper Advertising Bureau Board on October 6.

On May 20, the World Company converts to offset printing.

Dolph Sr. receives the Fred Ellsworth Award for significant service to KU.[18]

1976 Dolph Jr. receives KU's Fred Ellsworth Award.[19]

Dolph Jr. is board secretary of the ANPA from 1976 to '79.

1977 Dolph Jr. becomes a trustee for the KU Endowment Association, which he'll serve until 2004. He'll join its executive committee in 1985, and from 1994 to 2004, serves as its board chair.

At the VII Session convened by Midwest Research Institute on April 21, Dolph Simons Jr. delivers the keynote, "Newspapers in the Year 2001." More than 20 years before the internet is established, he forecasts an "information line allowing occupants to receive news, advertising, and other information in many forms" in addition to power, water, and telephony coming directly into homes.

Dr. Virgil S. Counseller, father of Pam Counseller Simons, dies on October 26. He was 85.

1977, '78 Dolph Simons Jr. is selected as juror of the Pulitzer Prize.

The World Company establishes Columbine Cablevision in Ft. Collins, Colorado. Pamela Ann Simons assumes general management duties. She is one of the first women in management in the budding industry.

Dolph Sr. retires. His title shifts to chairman of the board on the masthead.

Dolph Jr. is named editor of the Journal-World on December 15, and appears as editor and publisher on the masthead.

1979 Dolph Jr. serves as a member of the Central Governing Board for Children's Mercy Hospital in Kansas City, Missouri, until 1986.

1980 Dolph Simons Jr. serves as juror of the Pulitzer Prize again, also in '81.

Dolph Jr. receives the Distinguished Service Citation from KU, the university's highest honor.

1982 Dolph Jr. is national president of the KU Alumni Association from 1982 – 83, and will remain on its executive committee until 1987.

1983 At a Journal-World luncheon on June 15, Dolph Jr. announces a contract with Gannett is underway to publish *USA TODAY*.

1984 The World Company becomes the official printer of *USA TODAY* on April 2.

Dolph Jr. named trustee of the Haskell Foundation, which raises money to support Haskell Indian Nations University. He serves from 1984 to '94, and helps organize a congressional reception to demonstrate local support for Haskell during its centennial commemoration events in 1984 and '85.

1985 Linda Kathryn Simons marries Daniel Crosby de Menocal on May 4 in Lawrence.

Dan Simons and Trisha Malson are married on November 16 in Ft. Collins, Colorado.

On April 10, Dolph Simons Sr. named Citizen of the Year by the Lawrence Chamber of Commerce.

1986 Dan and Linda Simons de Menocal have a daughter, Emily Collins de Menocal, on August 5.

1987 Daniel Crosby de Menocal Jr. is born to Linda Simons de Menocal and Dan de Menocal on December 5.

1988 Dolph Simons III named operations manager of Journal-World.

1989 Dolph Collins Simons Sr., age 85, dies at his home in Arizona on February 14. He is buried in Lawrence, Kansas.

On March 24, Briahn Marie is born to Dan and Trisha Malson Simons.

Dolph Simons Jr. joins the Gannett Foundation board of trustees.

1990 Dolph C. Simons III and Lisa McCray are married.

USA TODAY recognizes Lawrence as "Most Valuable Site" with top performance in all the paper's production network.

Dolph Jr. named as trustee for the Kansas Nature Conservancy, which works to preserve natural lands in the state. He serves on the board until 1997.

In February, the Dolph Simons Jr. family commits $1 million to KU's Campaign Kansas fund drive in memory of Dolph Simons Sr.

1991 On the occasion of the 200th anniversary of America's Bill of Rights, Dolph Simons Jr. delivers a keynote speech, "A Century of Newspapering: The Simons of Lawrence," at the XII Newcomen Society Gathering, with co-presenter David Anderson, Ph.D.

Dolph Simons Jr., as trustee of the Freedom Forum, goes with its first delegation to eastern Europe with meetings in Warsaw and Moscow in July. Wife Pam and daughter Pam Simons go with him.

On June 13, Katherine Flickinger Simons is born to Dolph III and Lisa McCray Simons.

Dan Counseller Simons Jr. is born November 21 to Dan and Trisha Simons.

1992 Dolph Jr. becomes a trustee with the National Parks Conservation Association, which works to preserve national parks, and continues to serve this non-profit organization until 2005.

Elizabeth Counseller Simons is born to Dolph III and Lisa Simons on July 10.

1993 The new design of the *Lawrence Journal-World* debuts on October 17.

Kathy Underwood starts working as assistant for Dolph Jr.

Dolph Simons Jr. honored as "Distinguished Citizen for Public Service" by Baker University.

Recently retired from the *Washington Post*, Bill Snead returns to Lawrence at Dolph Jr.'s invitation and takes over as editor of the newsroom.

Jane Brookings de Menocal is born to Dan and Linda Simons de Menocal on June 12.

1994 Dolph Simons Jr. elected chairman of the KU Endowment Association. He also begins service as a trustee of the Nelson-Atkins Museum of Art in Kansas City, Missouri, which he will continue until 2004.

On November 15, Jennifer McCray Simons is born to Dolph III and Lisa McCray Simons.

1995 Dorothy Fritzel, longtime secretary to W.C., Dolph Sr., and Dolph Jr., retires.

Dolph Jr. buys a house in Steamboat Springs.

From 1995 to 2004, Dolph Jr. is chairman of the Lied Board of Governors, which helps oversee the Lied Center for the Performing Arts at KU.

On December 3, Linda Simons de Menocal is featured in *The New York Times* for her work in re-establishing the local Bedford, New York newspaper. "Against All Odds, a Community Paper Emerges" tells the story of her endeavor that results in a merging of two local papers into the *Bedford Record Review*.

1996 Dolph III and Lisa Simons have a daughter, Whitney Collins Simons, on October 10.

The Dolph Simons Biosciences Research Laboratories are dedicated in a ceremony on May 6 on the West Campus of KU. The "Simons Laboratories" add nearly 49,000 gross square feet to the existing operating complex that's linked to the McCollum Research Laboratories.

2000 On June 6, Jennifer McCray Simons dies of a medical condition present since birth.

2001 Renovations of the old Lawrence post office are nearing completion for its transition to The World Company's converged News Center.

2003 On October 25, at age 97, Ann Marie Nelson Simons dies at Lawrence Memorial Hospital.

The Journal-World is selected as recipient of the Jim Batten Media Leadership Award, named in honor of the former Knight-Ridder chairman.

Developers at the Journal-World develop the Django web framework.

The Robert J. Dole Institute of Politics is dedicated at the University of Kansas in Lawrence, featuring the Simons Media Room, the gift of the Dolph Simons Jr. family.

2004 Dolph Jr. joins the board of advisors to KU's International Center for Ethics in Business.

A Kansas Bioscience Authority is established by the legislature to marshal the state's technology, pharmacology, energy, oil and gas, agriculture, and aviation resources to attract corporations to Kansas. Dolph Simons Jr. is appointed to its board by Ken Glasscock, then-Kansas speaker of the House. The brainchild of Clay Blair, a Johnson County developer, the project draws major businesses and thousands of new jobs to McPherson, Sterling, Overland Park, Manhattan, and more cities across the state.

Dolph Simons III named president, Newspaper Division.

Dan Simons named president, Electronics Division.

Dolph Simons Jr., in partnership with KU Anthropology Professor Felix Moos, encourages Senator Pat Roberts to sponsor a bill that would prepare students for careers in foreign service. The senator agrees, and the Pat Roberts Intelligence Scholars Program (PRISP) passes in 2004. In 2010, President Barack Obama secures permanent funding for the program.

The Journal-World's campaign raises $150,000 for new Kansas University marching band uniforms in time for the 2004 football season.

2005 Dolph Simons Jr., one of the founding members of what is now the National Cable Television Cooperative, is recognized by the Cable Television Center as a "Pioneer" member of the industry.

A Simons family gift of $8.5 million is given to the KU Endowment Association and the Douglas County Community Foundation.

The Lawrence Kiwanis Club presented Dolph Simons Jr. with its "Substantial Citizen Award."

A gift from the Simons Family, with matching funds from a National Endowment for the Humanities Challenge Grant, provides $25,000 per recipient. Candidates must be experienced and accomplished individuals outside academe who seek the opportunity to engage with humanities-based, KU higher educational learning for a short period before returning to their occupations. In turn, the university will benefit from the professional perspective of each selected applicant. In line with the wishes of the donor, applicants cannot hold an academic position or otherwise work at an institution of higher education.

2006 The Lawrence Chamber of Commerce honors Dolph Jr. with its Citizen of the Year Award, and Baker University gives him their Outstanding Leadership and Achievement in Business Award.

The Kansas Sunshine Coalition for Open Government gives Dolph Simons Jr. its first "Above and Beyond" award because of initiatives the paper led for open government.

The *Lawrence Journal-World* wins the American Planning Association's 46th annual Journalism Award competition in its circulation class for "Mapping the Future," a special section published in December examining Lawrence's growth opportunities.

2007 Dolph Simons Jr. is inducted into the Hall of Fame of the Kansas Press Association.

On October 4, Dolph Jr. received Dean S. Lesher Award for Lifetime Achievement from Suburban Newspapers of America in Philadelphia.

Bill Snead retires as executive editor of the *Lawrence Journal-World* where he had first started his award-winning, international career.

2008 The World Company is winning major awards for innovation and technology from the Newspaper Association of America's Marketing Conference including Best Overall News Site: LJWorld.com.

2010 Dolph Simons Sr. named to Lawrence Business Journal Hall of Fame. (Posthumous)

2011 Dolph Jr. receives the Ralph Casey/Minnesota Award at an Inland Press Association ceremony on October 18 in Chicago.

A capstone gift from the Dolph Simons Jr. family has fulfilled a $1 million challenge grant from the Andrew W. Mellon Foundation for the Spencer Museum of Art at the University of Kansas.

2013 Ralph Gage retires.

Dolph Jr. receives the 2013 Huck Boyd Leader of the Year Award in Community Newspapers from Kansas State University.

2014 The on-site printing of the Journal-World newspaper ends, with printing moving to the *Kansas City Star's* production facility in Kansas City, Missouri. Production, editing, and administrative functions remain in Lawrence.

The "Dolph C. Simons Family Broadcast Studio" at The University of Kansas Health System is launched, thanks to a major gift of over $500,000 from Dolph Simons Jr. and family that funded the cutting-edge, cloud-based technology that made this broadcast facility possible.

The Medical News Network begins broadcasting from the Simons studio at The University of Kansas Health System.

2015 Dolph Simons Jr. Family makes a lead contribution to KU's Spencer Library and Museum, enabling fundraising efforts to meet and exceed the $5,000,000 goal by more than $2,000,000 additional dollars.

The University of Kansas Health Systems gives its Catalyst Award to the Dolph C. Simons Jr. family, and inducts them into its Hall of Fame.

2016 On June 17, the Simons family announces the sale of the Journal-World after 125 years of ownership to another long-running family-owned company, Ogden Newspapers of Wheeling, West Virginia.

Dolph Simons Jr. family contributes $100,000 to the Lied Center at KU.

Bill Snead, *National Geographic* and *Washington Post* award-winning photographer who got his start the *Lawrence Journal-World* dies in February.

Dolph Jr. is named to the advisory board of the Robert J. Dole Institute of Politics.

2017 After nine years of service, Dolph Jr. steps down from the board of the Douglas County Community Foundation.

2019 On May 1, The World Company offices move from the historic post office to a smaller location on Kentucky Street in Lawrence.

2020 In January, www.LawrenceOpinions.com is launched. Dolph Simons Jr. continues publishing editorials on this blog. He is 90 years old.

2021 - 23 Dolph Simons Jr. finally acquiesces to pressure from family and friends to document the family's history. He enlists help from writer and biographer Leeanne Seaver, and together, they write this book.

Bibliography

In addition to more than 50 unique oral history interviews conducted by Leeanne Seaver, this bibliography draws from the Simons Collection at KU's Spencer Library, plus an even larger archive of over 150 years of this family's own records kept at The Cedars, which, since 1917, has been the Simons home in Lawrence, Kansas.

The contents of this varied assortment range from W.C. Simons' rare books collection to Marie Simons' voluminous scrapbooks to long-time secretary Dorothy Fritzel's famously comprehensive, well-preserved "red books." Her work diaries captured decades of events and notable dates for The World Company and the Simons both professionally and personally. Add to this the copious writings of Ralph Gage, Dolph Simons Sr., and Dolph Simons Jr. Additionally, W.C. Simons' seminal family history, *From the Landing of the Pilgrims*, as well as his and Dolph Sr.'s many essays and prepared speeches, were as historically insightful as they were literary. Along with hundreds of newspaper clippings from various epochs (although often undated), reams of letters, cards, and notes of various family members and friends, this astounding trove of resources defied restraint. Yet the goal was always clear—share the story of this remarkable American family whose lived experience was inseparable from the rise and fall of the newspaper industry in this country.

Introduction

1. Vanden Heuvel, Jon. *Untapped Sources: America's Newspaper Archives and Histories.*
    Gannett Foundation Media Center. 1991. 23.
2. Gaeddert, Raymond G. *First Newspapers in Kansas Counties*, Part 1 of 4.
    Kansas Historical Society. Vol. 10, No. 1. February 1941. 3-33.
3. Gaeddert, *First Newspapers*. 3-33.
4. Gaeddert, *First Newspapers*. 3-33.
5. Gaeddert, *First Newspapers*. 3-33.
6. Simons, W.C. "The First Newspaper in Lawrence."
    Lawrence Daily Journal. April 11, 1916. 8.
7. Kansapedia: *Sack of Lawrence.*
    Kansas Historical Society kshs.org
8. Cordley, Richard. *History of Douglas County, Kansas.*
    Lawrence Journal Press. 1895.

9. Simons, W.C. *A talk to a group of ladies.*
   W.C. Simons. Personal papers at The Cedars. Circa 1907. 3.
10. Mott, Frank L. *American Journalism: A History 1690 – 1960.*
    MacMillan, 1962.
11. "Sesquicentennial Point." 1891 - The Simons Family - City of Lawrence, Kansas
    https://lawrenceks.org/lprd/parks/sesquicentennialpoint/steps/1891simons/
12. Simons, W.C. *From the Landing of the Pilgrims in 1620. A Genealogy.*
    The World Company, 1950. 28.
13. Roberts, Senator Pat. *Dolph Simons Jr. Induction to Lawrence Business Hall of Fame.*
    Lawrence Business Hall of Fame, https://vimeo.com/76087706. 2013.

Chapter 1 Momentous Times

1. Simons, W.C. *Editorial.*
   Lawrence Journal-World, Lawrence, Kansas, December 14, 1948.
2. "Father and Son in Lawrence, Kansas, Operate Daily Journal-World."
   Editor & Publisher. April 4, 1936.
3. Simons, W.C. "Letter to Brady."
   Personal correspondence. Simons Collection. Spencer Library.
   The University of Kansas. December 15, 1923.
4. Simons, W.C. *Editorial.* "It was 40 years ago today..."
   Lawrence Journal-World, Lawrence, Kansas, December 14, 1931.
5. Simons, Dolph Jr. "A Century of Newspapering: The Simons of Lawrence."
   The Newcomen Society. December 12, 1991.
6. Oscar Eugene Learnard. https://en.wikipedia.org/wiki/Oscar_Eugene_Learnard
7. Simons, Dolph Jr. "A Century of Newspapering." 9.
8. "The World Company at Your Fingertips." Special Issue of the *Lawrence Journal-World*.
   Lawrence Journal-World, Lawrence, Kansas. January 2003.
9. VandenHeuvel, Jon. *Untapped Sources: America's Newspaper Archives and Stories.*
   Gannett Foundation Media Center. 1991. 11.
10. "About the City."
    www.lawrenceks.org
11. Simons, W.C. *A talk given to the Old Settlers Association of Lawrence, Kansas.*
    Kansas State Historical Society. September 15, 1924.
12. Teachinghistory.org
13. De Bres, Karen. "Come To The "Champagne Air" Changing Promotional
    Images Of The Kansa" by Karen De Bres (unl.edu)
    Great Plains Quarterly, University of Nebraska. Spring, 2003.
14. Simons, Dolph Jr. "A Century of Newspapering." 7.
15. Simons, W.C. "Letter to Brady." 1923.
16. VanderHeuvel. *Untapped Sources.* 11.
17. Simons, W.C. "Letter to Brady." 1923.
18. Simons, W.C. *A speech to the Kansas Historical Society.*
    W.C. Simons. Personal papers at The Cedars. 1924.

Chapter 2 Breaking Ground

1. Simons, W.C. *From the Landing of the Pilgrims*. 117.
2. Simons, Jennie B. *Personal Diaries 1851 to 1880*.
    Simons Collection. Spencer Library. The University of Kansas.
    Collection: Simons family papers | Kenneth Spencer Research Library
    Archival Collections (ku.edu)
3. John B. L. Soule - Wikipedia
4. Homestead Act - Definition, Dates & Significance - HISTORY
5. Simons, W.C. *From the Landing of the Pilgrims*. 43.
6. Simons, W.C. *From the Landing of the Pilgrims*. 43.
7. Simons, W.C. *From the Landing of the Pilgrims*. 43.
8. Simons, W.C. *A talk given to the Old Settlers Association of Lawrence, Kansas*.
    Kansas Historical Society. September 15, 1924.
9. Simons, W.C. *From the Landing of the Pilgrims*. 37.
10. Simons, W. C. "Billy the Irishman."
    W.C. Simons. Personal papers at The Cedars. Undated.
11. Simons, Jennie B. *Personal Diaries*.
    Simons Collection, Spencer Library, the University of Kansas. 1852.
12. Simons, W.C. *From the Landing of the Pilgrims*. 42.
13. U.S. Census. 1850.
14. Simons, Jennie B. *Personal Diaries*.
    Simons Collection, Spencer Library, the University of Kansas. 1852.
15. "Request to Increase Pension." Illinois State Marriage Records. Online index.
    Illinois State Public Record Offices. 1885.
16. Hoinville, Julia Simons. "Recollections."
    From the Landing of the Pilgrims. 20.
17. Hoinville, Julia Simons. "Recollections." 20.
18. U.S. Senate: The Civil War: The Senate's Story
19. Union Volunteers Fife & Drum Corps.
    www.unionvolunteersfifeanddrum.com
20. Hoinville, Julia Simons. "Recollections." 20.
21. 37th Illinois Infantry Regiment - Wikipedia
22. Thirty-Seventh Illinois Infantry Regiment – Fort Hill Cemetery
23. Hoinville, Julia Simons. "Recollections." 42-43.
24. Simons, W.C. *From the Landing of the Pilgrims*. 23.
25. Simons, W.C. *From the Landing of the Pilgrims*. 24.
26. Simons, W.C. *From the Landing of the Pilgrims*. 115.
27. Simons. Wilford Collins. "Application for *Who's Who*."
    W.C. Simons. Personal papers at The Cedars. Undated.
28. https://www.findagrave.com/memorial/117826069/john-leeford-brady
29. Simons, W.C. *History of Jennie B. Simons*.
    Unpublished draft, personal files at The Cedars. Undated.
30. *The Salina Republican*
    Salina, Kansas. July 29, 1888. 1.
31. *The Jetmore Republican*
    Jetmore, Kansas. December 27, 1893. 1.
32. Library of Congress
    https://www.loc.gov/resource/sn83040052/1890-07-07/ed-1

33. Simons, W.C. *From the Landing of the Pilgrims*. 44.
34. Kansas Notes. *Lawrence Journal-World*. May 15, 1952.

Chapter 3 Making News

1. 10 Things Pauline Maier Taught Us About Ratification and the Bill of Rights - Journal of the American Revolution (allthingsliberty.com)
2. Anderson, David A. *Celebrating the 200th Birthday of Our Nation's Bill of Rights*. The Newcomen Society. 1991. 22.
3. Anderson, David A. "Celebrating the 200th Birthday..." 22.
4. Jefferson, Thomas. *Letter to Judge John Tyler Washington*.
     To Judge John Tyler Washington, June 28, 1804 < The Letters of Thomas Jefferson 1743-1826 < Thomas Jefferson < Presidents < American History From Revolution To Reconstruction and beyond (rug.nl) June 28, 1804.
5. Doll, Jen. Noah Webster, Father of the American Dictionary, Was Unemployable - The Atlantic
     The Atlantic Monthly. October 16, 2012.
6. Stephens, Mitchell. *Beyond News: The Future of Journalism*. Columbia University Press. 2014.
7. Starr, Louis M. *James Gordon Bennett, Beneficent Rascal*.
     https://www.americanheritage.com/james-gordon-bennett-beneficent-rascal# 1955.
8. Stephens, Mitchell. *Beyond News*. 77.
9. Barley, Angela. *The Functions of a Newspaper*.
     https://bizfluent.com/info-8576575-functions-newspaper.html September 26, 2017.
10. https://americanpressassociation.com/principles-of-journalism/
11. History of American newspapers - Wikipedia
12. Kurtz, Jenifer. "Nineteenth Century Newspapers and Literature of Reform."
     American Literature I: An Anthology of Texts From Early America Through the Civil War. https://viva.pressbooks.pub/amlit1/chapter/introduction-to-nineteenth-century-literature-of-reform/
13. Kurtz, Jenifer. "Nineteenth Century Newspapers and Literature of Reform."
14. *Kansas Notes* in the *Lawrence Journal-World*.
     Lawrence, Kansas. May 15, 1952.
15. *Kansas Notes*. May 15, 1952.
16. *Kansas Notes*. May 15, 1952.
17. Marvin, Burton W. "Announcement of the Election of W.C. Simons to the Kansas Newspaper Hall of Fame."
     Simons, W.C. | Kansas Press Association (kspress.com). 1952.
18. Yellow Journalism: The "Fake News" of the 19th Century – The Public Domain Review
19. *Lawrence Daily Journal*. "Things that Happen."
     Lawrence, Kansas. September 29, 1892.
20. Simons. W.C. *From the Landing of the Pilgrims*. 115.
21. Simons W.C. *"Reflections on early Kansas."*
     W.C. Simons. Personal Papers at The Cedars. Undated.

22. Myer, John L. "*Lawrence Daily Journal-World Learned Well the Art of Swim-or-Sink.*"
    National Printer Journalist. September 1925. 16-20.
23. *Lawrence Daily Journal-World*
    Lawrence, Kansas, Wednesday, September 5, 1917. 1.
    https://www.newspapers.com/clip/102131873/lawrence-daily-journal-world/
24. Simons, W.C. "The morning of my 67th birthday was beautiful."
    W.C. Simons. Personal files at The Cedars. July 8, 1938.
25. Simons, W.C. *Our Little Mother.*
    Lawrence Daily Journal-World. November 23, 1921. 4.
26. "The World Company at Your Fingertips." v.2.
    Special Issue of the *Lawrence Journal-World.* January 2003.
27. Kansas State Historical Society, Annals.
    Kansas Historical Society (kshs.org).1924. 523.
28. Myer, John L. "*Lawrence Daily Journal-World Learned Well the Art of Swim-or-Sink.*"
    National Printer Journalist, September 1925. 16-20.
29. Myer, John L. "*Lawrence Daily Journal-World Learned Well the Art of Swim-or-Sink.*" 16-20.
30. Myer, John L. "*Lawrence Daily Journal-World Learned Well the Art of Swim-or-Sink.*" 16-20.
31. Simons, W.C. Editorial.
    Lawrence Daily Journal-World. February 4, 1927.
32. *Lawrence Daily Journal World,* December 6, 1938. 4.
33. Simons, W.C. *Curriculum Vitae.*
    W.C. Simons. Personal papers at The Cedars. Circa 1952.
34. Simons, W.C. *Curriculum Vitae.* 1952.
35. Simons W.C. *A talk given to the Old Settlers Association of Lawrence.*
    Lawrence, Kansas. September 15, 1924.
36. Simons, W.C. *Curriculum Vitae.* 1952.

Chapter 4 The Journalist

1. Simons, Dolph Sr. "Germany and Austria in May-June 1947."
   The World Company. Dolph Simons Sr. Personal papers at The Cedars. 1947.
2. Simons, Dolph Sr. "Germany and Austria in May-June 1947."
3. Stephens, Mitchell. "The History of Television."
   https://stephens.hosting.nyu.edu/History%20of%20Television%20page.html
4. Robins-Early, Nick. "How *The New York Times* reported the Liberation of Auschwitz in 1945."
   How The New York Times Reported The Liberation Of Auschwitz In 1945 | HuffPost The World Post. Jan. 27, 2015.
5. Simons, W.C. "The Story of Broncho."
   W.C. Simons. Personal papers at The Cedars. Undated.
6. Simons, Dolph Sr. *A speech,* "The Printed Word," *given to the W.A. White Foundation.*
   Dolph Simons Sr. Personal papers at The Cedars. February 10, 1959.

7.   *The Daily Gazette*
     https://www.newspapers.com/clip/100292213/the-daily-gazette/
     Lawrence, Kansas. Friday, January 19, 1917. 4.
8.   Patee, Clair M. "The Photoplay Age."
     The Daily Gazette. Lawrence, Kansas. March 1, 1916.
9.   Simons, Dolph Sr. *A talk to the Saturday Night Club.*
     Dolph Simons Sr. Personal Papers at The Cedars. January 23, 1943.
10. Simons, Dolph Sr. "Leopold-Loeb" paper.
     Dolph Simons Sr. Personal papers at The Cedars. July 16, 1925.
11. Simons, Dolph Sr. "Leopold-Loeb."
12. Simons, Dolph Sr. "Leopold-Loeb."
13. *Lawrence Journal-World*. July 1, 1925. 1.
14. Beth, E.F., and Dolph Simons Sr. "Script for KFKU LIVE Broadcast on
     Censorship, Freedom of the Press."
     Dolph Simons Sr. Personal papers at The Cedars. November 5, 1943.
15. Palmer, Cruise. "Letter to Dolph Simons."
     Simons Sr. Personal papers at The Cedars. October 23, 1976.
16. King, Major Walter. PID War Department. "Letter to D. Simons."
     Dolph Simons Sr. Personal papers at The Cedars. July 18, 1947.
17. Stephens, Mitchell. *Beyond News*. xviii.
18. *Belleville Telescope*. June 8, 1950.
19. Lathrop, William. "Letter to D. Simons."
     Dolph Simons Sr. Personal papers at The Cedars. May 6, 1949.
20. Kiraghi, Captain Zahid. "Letter to D. Simons."
     Dolph Simons Sr. Personal papers at The Cedars. July 14, 1949.
21. MacPherson, J. vice president of Arabian American Oil Company. Dhahran,
     Saudi Arabia. "Letter to Simons."
     Dolph Simons Sr. Personal papers at The Cedars. June 8, 1949.
22. Willoughby, Major J.D. "Letter to Dolph Simons Sr."
     Dolph Simons Sr. Personal papers at The Cedars. June 19, 1947
23. Simons, Dolph Sr. "The History of the AP."
     Dolph Simons Sr. Personal papers at The Cedars. Circa late 1950s.
24. Simons, Dolph Sr. *Talks.*
     Dolph Simons Sr. Personal papers at The Cedars. Circa 1950.
25. Simons, Dolph Sr. "The Associated Press Today."
     Dolph Simons Sr. Personal papers at The Cedars. November 15, 1954.
26. Simons, Dolph Sr. *A speech*, "The Printed Word." February 10, 1959.
27. Simons, Dolph Sr. *A clipping* "Whose Freedom?" *of his article photocopied from
     unidentified magazine.*
     Dolph Simons Sr. Personal papers at The Cedars. Undated.
28. Simons, Dolph Sr. *Speech on Hallmark Company given to Lawrence Chamber of
     Commerce.*
     Dolph Simons Sr. Personal papers at The Cedars. November 4, 1957.
29. Simons, Dolph Sr. *Talks.*
     Dolph Simons Sr. Personal papers at The Cedars. Circa 1933. 3-4.
30. Simons, Dolph Sr. *Draft of an editorial.*
     Dolph Simons Sr. Personal papers at The Cedars. Circa 1950s-'60s.
31. Simons, Dolph Sr. "On the Landon Campaign Train."
     Dolph Simons Sr. Personal papers at The Cedars. November 1936.

32. Simons, Dolph Sr. *Editorial.*
    Lawrence Journal-World. June 4, 1952.
33. Simons, Dolph Sr. "Letter to Philip Young."
    The American Assembly at Columbia University. May 10, 1952.
34. Seaton, Richard. "A Name to Reckon With."
    The Manhattan Mercury. January 7, 1954. 10.
35. Simons, Dolph Sr. *A speech to KU journalism school graduates.*
    Dolph Simons Sr. Personal papers at The Cedars. May 1955.
36. Simons, Dolph Sr. "Socializing the Wager." *Part III in* "Talks."
    Dolph Simons Sr. Personal papers at The Cedars. Circa 1933. 6-8.
37. Myer, John L. "*Lawrence Daily Journal-World Learned Well the Art of Swim-or-Sink.*" 16-20.
38. "All Out Junk Hunt Coming Up."
    The Hutchinson News. September 14, 1942.
39. Simons, Dolph Sr. "Letter to Philip Young."
    Dolph Simons Sr. Personal papers at The Cedars. May 10, 1952.
40. Spears, Rose. "Letter to the Editor."
    Lawrence Journal-World. Tuesday, October 16, 1956. 4.
41. Simons, Dolph Sr. *Editorial.*
    Lawrence Journal-World. Wednesday, October 17, 1956. 4.
42. Simons, Dolph Sr. *A talk,* "The Trouble with Money."
    Dolph Simons Sr. Personal papers at The Cedars. Circa 1960s.
43. Simons, Dolph Sr. *Commencement Address at Haskell Institute.*
    Dolph Simons Sr. Personal papers at The Cedars. May 23, 1945.
44. Simons, Dolph Sr. *A talk given to the Saturday Night Club.*
    Dolph Simons Sr. Personal papers at The Cedars. January 23, 1943. 5.
45. Simons, Dolph. *A talk given to the Saturday Night Club.*
    Dolph Simons Sr. Personal papers at The Cedars. January 23, 1943.
46. Simons, Dolph Sr. *The University of Kansas commencement dinner speech.*
    Dolph Simons Sr. Personal papers at The Cedars. May 18, 1975.
47. "Dedication of the Dolph Simons Biosciences Research Laboratories."
    Event program. University of Kansas Office of University Relations. May 6, 1996.
48. Simons, Dolph Sr. *A speech given to an unnamed club of which he was a new member.*
    Dolph Simons Sr. Personal papers at The Cedars. Undated.
49. Simons, Dolph Sr. *A talk given to the Saturday Night Club.*
    Dolph Simons Sr. Personal papers at The Cedars. January 23, 1943. 13.
50. Simons, Dolph Sr. *Editorial.*
    Lawrence Journal-World. June 23, 1967.
51. Simons, Dolph Sr. "A Globe Circler's Diary." 1949.
52. Simons, Dolph Sr. *A speech to the Hawk Watch Society.*
    Dolph Simons Sr. Personal papers at The Cedars. November 7, 1949.
53. Monhollan, Rusty L. "This is America: The Sixties in Lawrence, Kansas."
    https://link.springer.com/book/10.1057/9781403982407 2002. 13.
54. "Simons' Opinions on World Affairs."
    Council Grove Republican. June 1, 1949. 1.
55. Simons, Dolph Sr. *Editorial.*
    Lawrence Journal-World. August 22, 1969.

56. Simons, Dolph Sr. *A speech to advertising and sales executives in Kansas City.*
    Dolph Simons Sr. Personal papers at The Cedars. November 13, 1950.
57. Simons, Dolph Sr. *A talk,* "The Disturbed Condition of the World Today," *given to the Saturday Night Club.*
    Dolph Simons Sr. Personal papers at The Cedars. December 12, 1944.
58. Simons, Dolph Sr. *Many talks given to the Saturday Night Club and others.*
    Dolph Simons Sr. Personal papers at The Cedars. Circa 1930s–'50s.
59. Simons, Dolph Sr. *A speech to the KU journalism school.*
    Dolph Simons Sr. Personal papers at The Cedars. March 11, 1952.
60. Simons, Dolph Sr. "A Globe-Circler's Diary" *and talks given about that trip.*
    Dolph Simons Sr. Personal papers at The Cedars. 1949–'50.
61. Simons, Dolph Sr. as quoted in *The New Orleans Times Picayune.*
    Dolph Simons Sr. Personal papers at The Cedars. June 5, 1959. 6.
62. White, W.L. "Dolph Simons of Kansas."
    Editor's Roll Call. ANSE Bulletin. Undated.
63. Simons, Dolph Sr. "The Printed Word." February 10, 1959.
64. Simons, Dolph Sr. *A talk given to the Saturday Night Club.*
    Dolph Simons Sr. Personal papers at The Cedars. January 23, 1943.
65. Simons, Dolph Sr. "The Printed Word." February 10, 1959.

Chapter 5 Ink in His Veins

1. Historic Resources - City of Lawrence, Kansas (lawrenceks.org) Application for recognition. HRC Packet Information 04-20-2017. Item No. 4: L-17-00061. 1
2. Simons, John. *Interview with Leeanne Seaver.* July 8, 2022.
3. Cronkite: In His Own Words - Bing video
4. Simons, Marie. *Clippings from the Kansas City Star,* the *Omaha World-Herald, Along the Jayhawker Trail,* the *Daily Kansan,* and *Collier's magazine.*
    Scrapbook on Dolph Jr. at The Cedars. Circa 1950s.
5. de Menocal, Linda Simons. *Interview with Leeanne Seaver.* May 2023.
6. Malott, Chancellor Deane W. "Letter of Recommendation to the Marines."
    Dolph Simons Jr. Personal papers at The Cedars. May 28, 1951.
7. Collection: Personal papers of Oswald P. Backus III | Kenneth Spencer Research Library Archival Collections
8. Simons, Dolph Jr. "The History of the Class of 1951."
    Dolph Simons Jr. Personal papers at The Cedars. 1951.
9. Simons, W.C. "Letter to Dr. and Mrs. Virgil Counseller."
    Dolph Simons Jr. Personal papers at The Cedars. January 22, 1952.
10. Blakemore, Erin. "Why the Korean War Never Technically Ended."
    https://www.nationalgeographic.com/history/article/why-korean-war-never-technically-ended. *National Geographic Magazine.* June 2020.

Chapter 6 The Catalyst

1. Bowson, Indiana Congressman Charles B.
    Attribution. The Big Apple: "Never argue with a man who buys ink by the barrel" (barrypopik.com)
2. https://newspaperarchive.com/lawrence-journal-world-mar-24-1956-p-2/

3. Wright, Marshall, special assistant, U.S. State Department. "Letter to Dolph Simons Jr."
    Dolph Simons Jr. Personal papers at The Cedars. July 9, 1964.
4. "Vietnam War Protest · 1970: The Year that Rocked KU · KU Libraries Exhibits
5. Moyers, Bill. "Listening to America."
    Harper's Magazine. December 1970. 57.
6. Brown Foundation | For Educational Equity, Excellence and Research (brownvboard.org)
7. Report shows how KC schools have maintained segregation through geographic, economic means | The University of Kansas (ku.edu)
8. 1970: Racial unrest sparked deadly violence | News, Sports, Jobs - Lawrence Journal-World: news, information, headlines and events in Lawrence, Kansas (ljworld.com) 2010.
9. "Kansas Highway Patrol Intelligence Report."
    Lawrence Journal-World. December 11, 1970.
10. "This is a communication from the Weatherman Underground." A letter to the *Lawrence Journal-World.*
    Dolph Simons Jr. Personal papers at The Cedars. October 22, 1970.
11. "Kansas Highway Patrol Intelligence Report." *Lawrence Journal-World.* 1970.
12. News Release promoting "Listening to America."
    Harper's Magazine. November 16, 1970.
13. Nelson, Bryce, staff writer. "Kansas Town's Trouble May Lead to Vigilantes."
    Los Angeles Times. December 25, 1970.
14. Moyers, Bill. "Listening to America."
    Harpers Magazine. December 1970. 58.
15. Lovejoy 1972 Fellow - Dolph C. Simons, Jr - Goldfarb Center (colby.edu)
16. Gage, Ralph. *Unpublished writings about Dolph Simons Jr. 2011.*
    Ralph Gage files shared with Leeanne Seaver. May 2021.
17. Menninger Foundation – Wikipedia
18. Goff, Marsha Henry. *History of the Lawrence Chamber of Commerce, 1878 – 2000.*
    Booklet documents evolution of chamber of commerce | News, Sports, Jobs - Lawrence Journal-World: news, information, headlines and events in Lawrence, Kansas (ljworld.com)
19. Scott, Charles Jr. *Interview with Leeanne Seaver.* November and December 2022.
20. Heron, David W. "Letter to Dolph Simons Jr."
    Dolph Simons Jr. Personal papers at The Cedars. December 10, 1970.
21. Lawhorn, Chad. *Interview with Leeanne Seaver.* January 12, 2023.
22. Moyers, Bill. "Listening to America." *Harper's Magazine.* 56.
23. O'Brien, Tim. "The Newspaper of the Future."
    The New York Times. June 26, 2005.
    https://www.nytimes.com/2005/06/26/business/yourmoney/the-newspaper-of-the-future.html
24. Simons, W.C. *Editorial.*
    Lawrence Journal-World. December 14, 1948.
25. Gardner, Ann. *Interview with Leeanne Seaver.* September 9, 2021.
26. https://www.kcconfidential.com/2014/03/03/hearne-small-town-journalism-bain-of-sleepy-lawrence-kansas/
27. DOLPH SIMONS JR DEMO on Vimeo

28. Altevogt, John. "Public Comment Response." Hearne: Small Town 'Journalism' Bane of Sleepy Lawrence, Kansas | KC Confidential. March 2014.

29. "Excerpts KCConfidential.com."
   Hearne: End of an Era @ Lawrence Journal World | KC Confidential March 3, 2014 and August 8, 2016.

30. Porter, Dr. Charles. *Interview with Leeanne Seaver*. January 12, 2023.

31. Cartter, Paul. "In the summer of 1970."
   Paul Cartter essay. January 29, 2023.

32. Seaver, Rob. *Interview with Leeanne Seaver*. December 15, 2022.

33. Gage, Ralph. *Interview with Leeanne Seaver*. May 27, 2021.

34. Moos, Dr. Felix. *Interview with Leeanne Seaver*. January 28, 2023.

35. Gage, Ralph. *Quoting Chancellor Gene Budig* in "Unpublished retrospective about Dolph Simons Jr." June 17, 2011.
   Ralph Gage files shared with Leeanne Seaver. May 2021.

36. Curley, Tom. "Notes on Dolph Simons Jr." May 8, 2007.
   Ralph Gage files shared with Leeanne Seaver. May 2021.

Chapter 7 The Full Court Press

1. Graham, Katharine. "Freedom Forum interview with former-Newseum President Peter Pritchard." The late Katharine Graham on the 25th anniversary of the Watergate scandal - YouTube June 2, 1997.

2. The late Katharine Graham on the 25th anniversary of the Watergate scandal - YouTube

3. Boccardi, Louis. *Interview with Leeanne Seaver*. December 7, 2022.

4. Simons, Dolph Sr. "Letter to Keith Fuller, Associated Press."
   Dolph Simons Sr. Personal papers at The Cedars. August 6, 1976.

5. Boccardi, Louis. *Interview with Leeanne Seaver*. September 9, 2022.

6. Boccardi interview with Seaver. September 2022.

7. Inland Daily Press Association, Chicago, Illinois, 15 October 1957 (Robert F. Kennedy speech) | JFK Library

8. Mulligan, Hugh. "Keith Fuller, former AP President, dies at 79."
   ThePlainview.com. June 6, 2002.

9. Curley, Tom. "Notes on Dolph Simons Jr." May 8, 2007.
   Ralph Gage files shared with Leeanne Seaver. May 2021.

10. Boccardi, Lou. *Phone call with Dolph Simons Jr.* December 9, 2022.

11. Thomson, James C. Jr. *Nieman Reports*.
   Published by the Nieman Foundation, Harvard University. December 1972; March 1973.

12. Louis, Arthur. "Independents are an endangered species."
   Fortune Magazine. June 19, 1978.

13. https://www.columbiamissourian.com/news/local/update-robert-m-white-ii-renowned-journalist-dies/article_532e6b00-f394-5379-aa11-a64206770035.html

14. https://www.freedomforum.org/about-freedom-forum/what-we-do/

15. Quinn, John C. "The Long-Rage Planning Report."
   Gannett Foundation. 1990. 12-13.

16. Freedom Forum on-line. www.freedomforum.org
   Graham interview: https://www.youtube.com/watch?v=kAJf8Sx4c0M

17. Moos, Dr. Felix. *Interview with Leeanne Seaver*. January 28, 2023.

18. Thomson, James C. Jr. *Nieman Reports.*
     Published by the Nieman Foundation, Harvard University. December 1972; March 1973.
19. Roberts, Senator Pat. *Dolph Simons Jr. Induction to Lawrence Business Hall of Fame.*
     Lawrence Business Hall of Fame, https://vimeo.com/76087706. 2013.

Chapter 8 Above the Fold

1.   'It's just a tough environment': Kansas sales highlight the challenges for family-owned papers - Columbia Journalism Review (cjr.org) June 24, 2016.
2.   Galas, Judith. *Interview with Leeanne Seaver.* February 1, 2023.
3.   Simons, Marie. *Clippings from the Kansas City Star and unidentified newspapers.*
     Scrapbook on Dolph Jr. at The Cedars. Circa 1950s.
4.   https://www.ancestry.com/family-tree/tree/175871191/family/pedigree?cfpid=132283985241
5.   Simons, W.C. *A talk given to the Saturday Night Club.*
     Simons Collection. Spencer Library. University of Kansas. Circa early 1930s.
6.   Hoinville, Julia Simons Brady. "Letter to W.C. Simons."
     Simons Collection. Spencer Library. University of Kansas. December 25, 1926.
7.   Dennis Domer. *Embattled Lawrence, Kansas. Volume 2: The Enduring Struggle for Freedom.*
     Douglas County Historical Society and the Watkins Museum of History, June 2023.
8.   *The Kansas City Weekly Gazette Globe*
     https://www.newspapers.com/clip/992086/the-weekly-gazette-globe/
     December 31, 1914. 1.
9.   Domer. *Embattled Lawrence.* 444.
10. Domer. *Embattled Lawrence.* 444.
11. Domer. *Embattled Lawrence.* 444.
12. Domer. *Embattled Lawrence.* 445.
13. Domer. *Embattled Lawrence.* 445.
14. Domer. *Embattled Lawrence.* 445.
15. Domer. *Embattled Lawrence.* 447.
16. Domer. *Embattled Lawrence.* 448.
17. "A Resolution by the Board of Directors of The World Company."
     W.C. Simons. Personal papers at The Cedars. May 14, 1947.
18. Simons, W.C. "Letter to Julia Simons Brady Hoinville."
     Simons Collection. Spencer Library. University of Kansas. December 29, 1926.
19. Simons, W.C. *A talk given to the Saturday Night Club.*
     The Simons Collection. Spencer Library. University of Kansas. Circa early 1930s.
20. Simons, Mary Gertrude. *Notes on the Remodel.*
     Simons Collection. Spencer Library. University of Kansas. 1917.
21. https://newspaperarchive.com/lawrence-journal-world-may-20-1920-p-1/
22. Trapp, Bob. *Interview with Leeanne Seaver.* August 28, 2021.

Chapter 9 Convergence

1. Simons, W.C. *A talk to the Saturday Night Club.*
W.C. Simons. Personal papers at The Cedars. Undated.
2. Simons, Dolph Sr. *Talks*. Undated.
3. O'Brien. Tim. "Newspaper of the Future."
https://www.nytimes.com/2005/06/26/business/yourmoney/the-newspaper-of-the-future.html
4. Chima, Aneel and Ron Gutman. "What It Takes to Lead Through an Era of Exponential Change."
Harvard Business Review. https://hbr.org/2020/10/what-it-takes-to-lead-through-an-era-of-exponential-change October 2020.
5. Gage, Ralph. *Interview with Leeanne Seaver.* May 2021.
6. Boccardi, Lou. *Interview with Seaver.* September 9, 2022.
7. Runett, Rob. "Face to Face with World Company Leaders." www.poynter.org.
https://www.poynter.org/reporting-editing/2003/face-to-face-with-world-co-leaders/ August 14, 2003.
8. Eisenmann, Ph.D., Thomas R. Cable TV: From Community Antennas to Wired Cities - HBS Working Knowledge
Harvard Business School. July 10, 2000.
9. Bogdon, Thomas. *Kansas City Star.* May 1972.
10. https://www.cablefax.com/archives/2009-top-ops-awards-independent-technology-award-mdash-sunflower-broadband
11. Simons, Dolph Jr. *Interviews with Leeanne Seaver and blogposts*:
https://www.lawrenceopinions.com/proud-history-of-sunflower-broadband/
12. Bogdon, Thomas. *Kansas City Star.* May 1972.
13. List of Retro Cable lineups in the United States – TVCL – TV Channel Lists
CableCenter.org. 16-17.
14. List of Retro Cable lineups. CableCenter.org. 16-17.
15. https://www.cablecenter.org/images/files/pdf/CableHistory/CableTimelineFall2015.pdf p 16
16. Gage, Ralph. *Notes on Dolph Simons Jr.* Revised June 17, 2011.
17. Simons, Dan. *As quoted by Randy Craig in* "Faith in print product inspires Web, cable ventures."
The Inlander. April 4, 1997. 4.
18. Plotting A Route For Local Newspapers | 1A (the1a.org)
April 30, 2018.
19. "Plotting a Route." www.the1a.org. April 30, 2018.
20. Lawrence, Kansas: Convergence Capital USA : NPR
21. Gage, Ralph. "Navigating the Road to Convergence."
Nieman Reports. December 15, 2005.
22. Gage. *Nieman Reports.* December 2005.
23. Gage, Ralph. *Interview and files shared with Leeanne Seaver.* May 27, 2021.
24. Lawrence-born Django, which revolutionized website construction, celebrating its 10th anniversary | News, Sports, Jobs - Lawrence Journal-World: news, information, headlines and events in Lawrence, Kansas (ljworld.com)

25. "World Company announces management changes."
     https://www2.ljworld.com/news/2004/jan/25/world_company_announces/.
     January 25, 2004.
26. https://digitaljournalist.org/issue0308/ljw_intro.html
27. Gage. *Notes on Dolph Simons Jr.* Revised June 2011.
28. Shields, Mike. "Edgie Story including Cox."
     Email from Mike Shields to Ralph Gage. February 20, 2006.

Chapter 10 The World Company

1. Salierno, Rich. *Interview with Leeanne Seaver.* October 3, 2022.
2. https://en.wikipedia.org/wiki/List_of_family-owned_newspapers_in_the_
     United_States)
3. Lawrence, Kansas: Convergence Capital USA : NPR
4. Simons, Wilford Collins. *Application for Who's Who Autobiographical background.*
     W.C. Simons. Personal papers. Undated.
5. *Editorial.*
     Abilene Reflector. December 20, 1888.
6. Simons, W.C. *Editorial.* "It was 40 years ago today..."
     Lawrence Journal-World. December 14, 1931.
7. Learnard, C.E. *Editorial.*
     Lawrence Daily Journal. March 2, 1892.
8. Simons, Dolph Jr. "A Century of Newspapering: The Simons of Lawrence."
     December 1991. 8.
9. *The Kansas City Weekly Gazette Globe.*
     December 31, 1914. 1.
10. Myer, John L. "*Lawrence Daily Journal-World* Learned Well the Art of Swim-or-
     Sink."
     National Printer Journalist. September 1925. 18.
11. Snead, Bill. "Windows on Lawrence 1855-1961."
     Lawrence Journal-World. Special edition. 1961.
12. *Editor & Publisher* Magazine. April 4, 1936.
13. Love, Ruth. "A Sixtieth Anniversary."
     Lawrence Journal-World. 1951.
14. A pamphlet. "Working at the Journal-World."
     The World Company. August 1, 1953.
15. "We're a Century Old, too." Special Centennial Parade Edition
     Lawrence Journal-World. September 25, 1954.
16. A pamphlet. "Facts about the Journal-World."
     The World Company. March 17, 1955.
17. Bill Snead - Warren McElwain Mortuary
18. https://news.google.com/
     newspapers?id=JP4xAAAAIBAJ&sjid=IOUFAAAAIBAJ&pg=5520%2C5592625
19. Simons, Dolph Jr. *Interview with Leeanne Seaver.* Dec. 3, 2021.
20. 1968 Democratic National Convention - Wikipedia
21. Kenneth Spencer Research Library Blog » Smoke and Fire: Political and Civil
     Unrest at the University (ku.edu)
22. "Publisher is elected."
     Lawrence Journal-World. April 10, 1975. 3.

23. *Lawrence Journal-World Tour Guide information sheet.* Circa 1970s.
24. "J-W to introduce Sunday edition."
        University Daily Kansan. November 10, 1978. 12.
25. Gardner, Ann. *Interview with Leeanne Seaver.* September 10, 2021.
26. Bonfield, Tim. "Officials back latest proposal for downtown."
        Lawrence Journal-World. February 10, 1988. 1.
27. Gage, Ralph. *Interview with Leeanne Seaver.* May 27, 2021.
28. Gage interview with Seaver. May 2021.
29. www.freedomforum.org.
30. Underwood, Kathy. *Email to Leeanne Seaver.*
        March 21-22, 2023.
31. "Face to Face with World Company Leaders."
        https://www.poynter.org/reporting-editing/2003/face-to-face-with-world-
        co-leaders/
32. *Promotional DVD:* "The World Company."
        6 Productions. Lawrence, Kansas. 2003.
33. "News Center Wins Recognition for State Preservation."
        https://www2.ljworld.com/news/2004/apr/10/news_center_wins/
34. O'Brien, Tim. "The Newspaper of the Future."
        https://www.nytimes.com/2005/06/26/business/yourmoney/the-newspaper-
        of-the-future.html
35. Folkenflik, David. Lawrence, Kansas: Convergence Capital USA : NPR
        National Public Radio. April 12, 2005.
36. *Promotional DVD:* "The World Company."
        Free State Communications. 2006-07.
37. Gage, Ralph. *Interview and shared files with Leeanne Seaver.* May 2021.
38. Lawrence Journal-World 05-02-11 by Lawrence Journal-World - Issuu
39. Abernathy, Penny. "The State of Local News."
        The State of Local News | Local News Initiative (northwestern.edu) June
        29, 2022.
40. *National media monitoring analytics report.*
        www.Meltwater.com March 31-May 18, 2020.
41. https://twitter.com/ljw_guild/status/1310630191832739840?s=20
42. "*Lawrence Journal-World Votes to Join United Media Guild*".
        The United Media Guild. Retrieved December 28, 2020.

Chapter 11 The End of News as We Know It

1. Simons, Dolph Jr. "Newspapers in the Future."
        Midcontinent Perspectives. Midwest Research Institute. 2001. 11.
2. "Woman's Body Found in Home; Probe Begins."
        Lawrence Journal-World. November 8, 1977. 1.
3. Simons, Dolph Sr. "Letter to Michael J. Malone, Douglas County Attorney."
        Dolph Simons Sr. Personal papers at The Cedars. November 15, 1977.
4. *Subcommittee on Communications, Technology, and the Internet.* "The Future of
    Journalism."
        Published by the United States Senate. 2011.

5. Fioroni, Sarah. "Local News Most Trusted in Keeping Americans Informed About Their Communities." https://knightfoundation.org/articles/local-news-most-trusted-in-keeping-americans-informed-about-their-communities/ May 19, 2022.

6. Johnson, Tom. *Interview with Leeanne Seaver*. March 22, 2023.

7. Simons, Dolph Jr. "Newspapers in the Year 2001." April 12, 1977. 5.

8. Trends and Facts on Newspapers | State of the News Media | Pew Research Center

9. https://www.pewresearch.org/journalism/fact-sheet/newspapers/

10. Number of daily newspapers in the U.S. 2018 | Statista

11. How we know journalism is good for democracy | by Josh Stearns | Office of Citizen | Medium

12. Gibbs, Ian. "'Trust in News' study shows more trust for print publications than digital." 'Trust in News' study shows more trust for print publications than digital | International Journalists' Network (ijnet.org) October 2018.

13. Bhuller, Manudeep, et al. "How the internet changed the market for print media." https://www.nber.org/papers/w30939 February 2023.

14. Bhuller. February 2023.

15. Fioroni, Sarah. "Local news most trusted in keeping Americans informed about their communities."* https://knightfoundation.org/articles/local-news-most-trusted-in-keeping-americans-informed-about-their-communities/ May 19, 2022. *Used with permission of the Knight Foundation.

16. Pickard, Victor. Journalism's Market Failure Is a Crisis for Democracy (hbr.org) March 12, 2020.

17. Simons, Dolph Jr. *Excerpts from an interview for* "Who Needs Newspapers." http://www.whoneedsnewspapers.org/np_interviews.php?npId=ksljw&ivId=ksljwo1 2015.

18. Dallos, Robert E. and John F. Lawrence. "*Life* and *Look* in Desperate Battle to Stay Alive." *The Los Angeles Times*. December 21, 1970. 1.

19. Rogers, Tony. "Are Newspapers Dead or Adapting in the Age of Digital News?" Newspapers vs. Digital News: Who Will Win? (thoughtco.com) 2019

20. Who Owns Your News? The Top 100 Digital News Outlets and Their Ownership | TitleMax

21. English, Kathy. "David Carr, High Priest of Journalism's Existential Angst." *The Toronto Star*. September 21, 2012 https://www.thestar.com/opinion/public_editor/2012/09/21/david_carr_high_priest_of_journalisms_existential_angst.html

22. Phares, Doug. *Interview with Leeanne Seaver*. August 17, 2022.

23. (https://localnewsinitiative.northwestern.edu/posts/2021/12/17/medill-adenauer-report/index.html)

24. Holder, Sarah. https://www.bloomberg.com/news/articles/2019-04-11/as-local-newspapers-shrink-so-do-voters-choices April 11, 2019.

25. Local Newspaper Closures Come With Hefty Price Tag For Residents : NPR 2018

26. Lawless, Dr. Jennifer. *As quoted in* "Local Journalism: Shrinking Resources, Growing Challenges A report on how the crisis in local news is affecting coverage of the major issues of this era."
        https://localnewsinitiative.northwestern.edu/assets/medill-kas-report-2021. pdf Northwestern University. November-December 2021.
27. Krishtalka, Leonard. *Interview with Leeanne Seaver.* April 20, 2022.
28. Domer, Dennis. *Interview with Leeanne Seaver.* April 19, 2022.
29. Gannett and the Death of Local Newspapers - The Atlantic
30. Simons, Dolph Jr. *Draft of speech to employees.* August 2016.

Chapter 12 Op-Ed on Life

1. Simons, W.C. "Letter to Gertie and children."
        W.C. Simons. Personal papers at The Cedars. February 20, 1936.
2. Simons, W.C. "Recollections of Wilford Collins Simons."
        From the Landing of the Pilgrims. 111.

The Simons Timeline

1. Simons, W.C. *From the Landing of the Pilgrims.* 23.
2. https://www.newspapers.com/clip/100974192/the-salina-semi-weekly-journal/
3. *Salina Daily Republican.* Friday, April 5, 1888. 2. https://www.newspapers.com/clip/100974845/salina-daily-republican/
4. *Salina Daily Republican.*"Masthead"
        The Salina Printing Company. July 2, 1888.
5. *Lawrence Daily World and Evening Gazette.* October 24, 1895.
6. Simons, W.C. *Curriculum Vitae.*
        W.C. Simons. Personal papers at The Cedars. Circa 1952.
7. https://www.kshs.org/kansapedia/simons-family/17696
8. https://www.dollartimes.com/inflation/inflation.php?amount=1000&year=1950
9. *The Manhattan Republic.* May 24, 1950.
10. Simons, Dolph C. Jr. | Kansas Press Association (kspress.com)
11. Richard Clarkson | Kansas Press Association (kspress.com)
12. Brill, Ann, Dean of KU School of Journalism. November 2, 2022.
13. Original Certificate.
        Dolph Simons Sr. Personal papers at The Cedars.
14. *Lawrence Journal-World.* October 17, 1966. 2.
15. Simons, Dolph Jr. *Interview with Leeanne Seaver.* July 19, 2022.
16. *Lawrence Journal-World.* May 16, 1973. 2.
17. Goff, Marsha Henry. Lawrence Chamber of Commerce History.
18. Ellsworth Award Winners.
        https://kualumni.org/programs/other-programs/awards/ellsworth-former-recipients-alphabetical/
19. Ellsworth. https://kualumni.org/programs/other-programs/awards/ellsworth-former-recipients-alphabetical/

The Family Lineage of Dolph Simons Jr.

The Simons trace their origins in America back to Plymouth Rock as described in W.C. Simons' exhaustive genealogy, "From the Landing of the Pilgrims in 1620." Governor William Bradford of Plymouth Colony is Dolph Simons Jr.'s ninth great-grandfather.

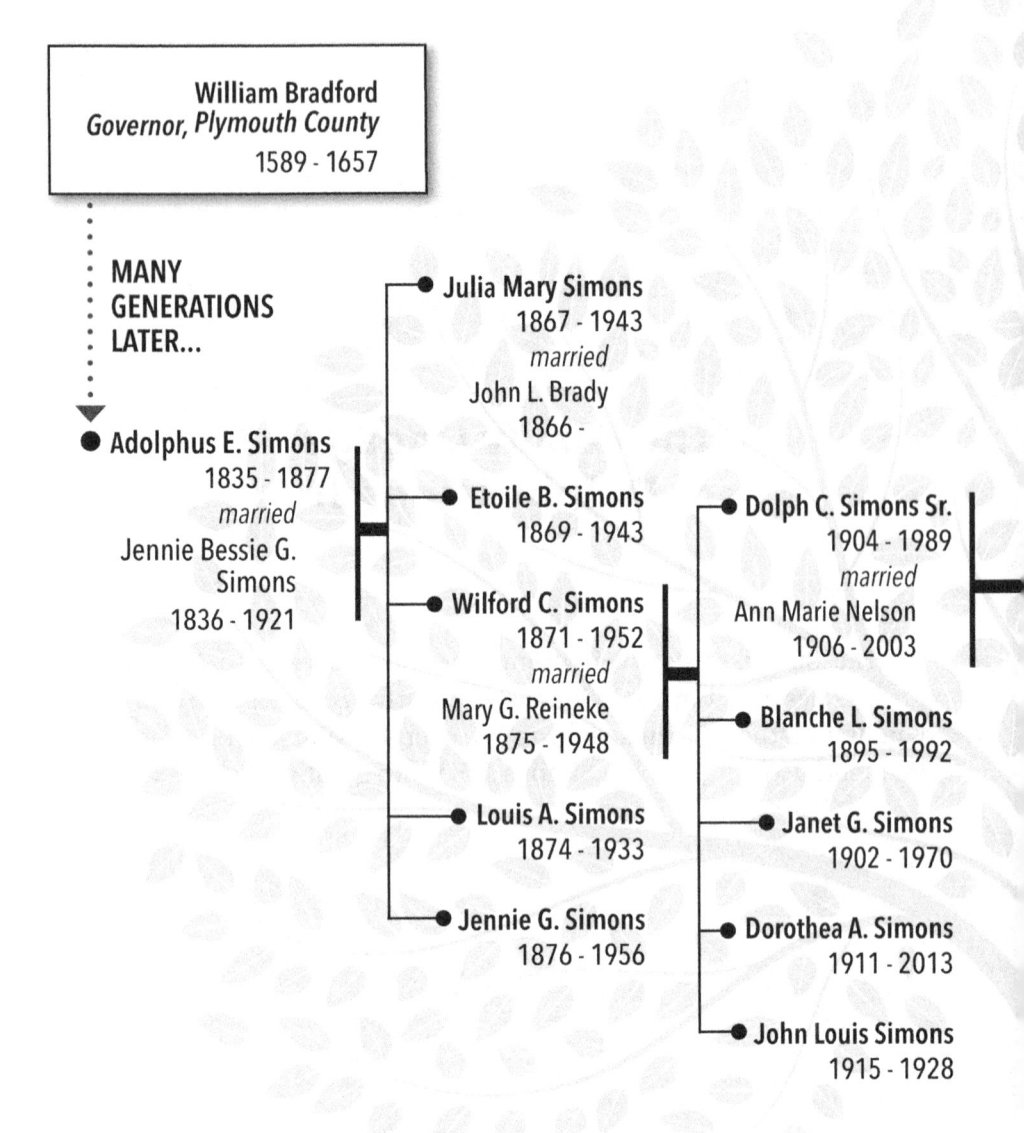

William Bradford
Governor, Plymouth County
1589 - 1657

**MANY
GENERATIONS
LATER...**

● **Adolphus E. Simons**
1835 - 1877
married
Jennie Bessie G.
Simons
1836 - 1921

● **Julia Mary Simons**
1867 - 1943
married
John L. Brady
1866 -

● **Etoile B. Simons**
1869 - 1943

● **Wilford C. Simons**
1871 - 1952
married
Mary G. Reineke
1875 - 1948

● **Louis A. Simons**
1874 - 1933

● **Jennie G. Simons**
1876 - 1956

● **Dolph C. Simons Sr.**
1904 - 1989
married
Ann Marie Nelson
1906 - 2003

● **Blanche L. Simons**
1895 - 1992

● **Janet G. Simons**
1902 - 1970

● **Dorothea A. Simons**
1911 - 2013

● **John Louis Simons**
1915 - 1928

Dolph Simons

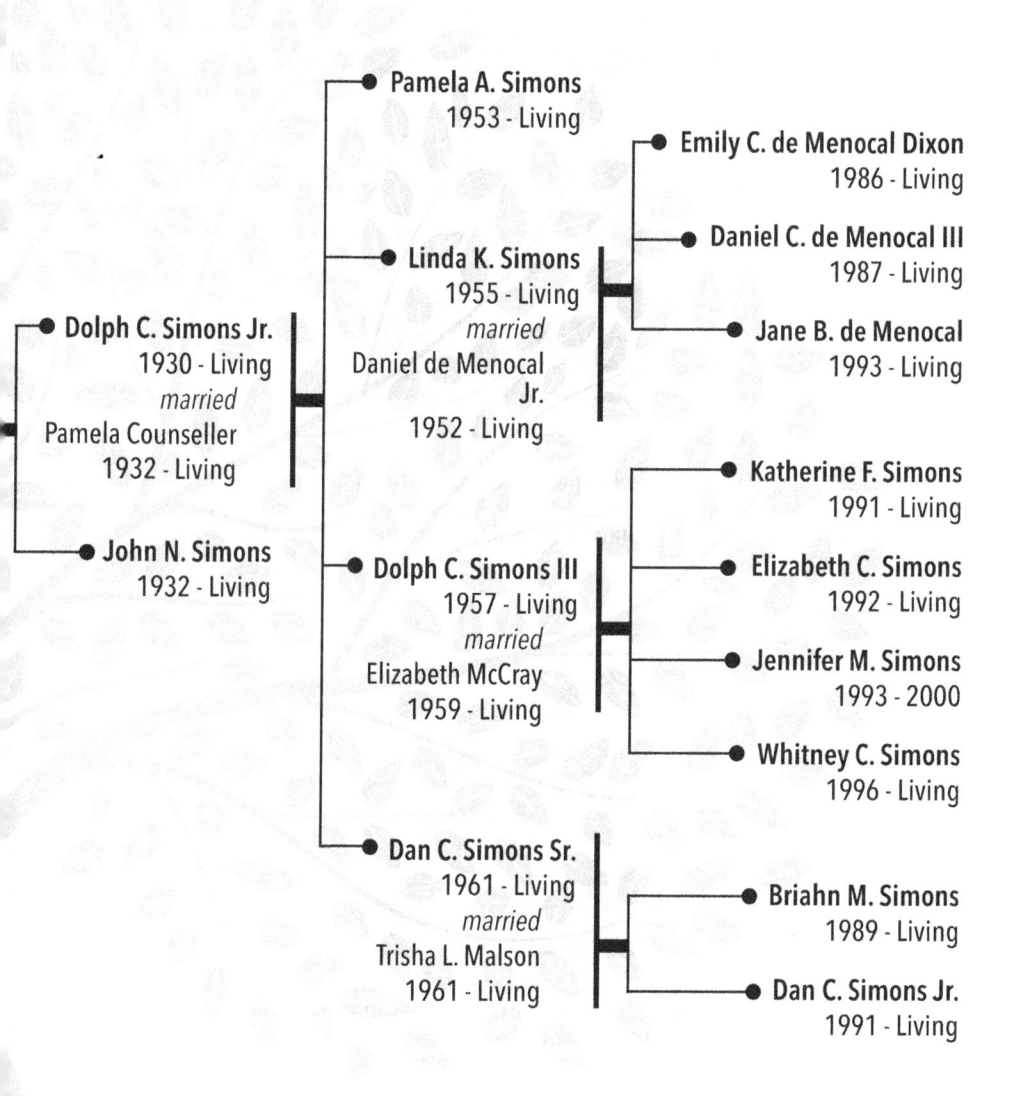

Pamela A. Simons
1953 - Living

Emily C. de Menocal Dixon
1986 - Living

Daniel C. de Menocal III
1987 - Living

Linda K. Simons
1955 - Living
married
Daniel de Menocal
Jr.
1952 - Living

Jane B. de Menocal
1993 - Living

Dolph C. Simons Jr.
1930 - Living
married
Pamela Counseller
1932 - Living

Katherine F. Simons
1991 - Living

Elizabeth C. Simons
1992 - Living

Dolph C. Simons III
1957 - Living
married
Elizabeth McCray
1959 - Living

Jennifer M. Simons
1993 - 2000

Whitney C. Simons
1996 - Living

John N. Simons
1932 - Living

Dan C. Simons Sr.
1961 - Living
married
Trisha L. Malson
1961 - Living

Briahn M. Simons
1989 - Living

Dan C. Simons Jr.
1991 - Living

Jr. Family Tree
2023

At age 93, author
Dolph C. Simons Jr. is still
writing and blogging from
Lawrence, Kansas.
lawrenceopinions.com

Co-author Leeanne Seaver,
a cross-genre writer and member
of the Authors Guild, writes from
Michigan and Colorado.
seavercreative.com

Made in the USA
Las Vegas, NV
02 October 2023

78486058R00230